The Ambassadors' Secret

Holbein and the World of the Renaissance

JOHN NORTH

Hambledon and London
New York

A Hambledon and London Paperback

First published in Great Britain in 2002
by Hambledon and London
This paperback edition published in the USA 2004
by Hambledon and London
175 Fifth Avenue
New York, NY 10010
USA

Revised edition

A CIP catalogue record for this book
is available from the British Library.

ISBN 1 85285 447 2

Typeset at The Spartan Press Ltd,
Lymington, Hants

Printed and bound in Great Britain by
Clays Ltd, St Ives plc

'N… rage; but Joh… ok of art his… ne of the wo… liar than it c…

'A… magical, ed… ore that, wh… not, is a spl… Th…

'A… n Renais-sa… *Review*

'A… of "The Ar… fords due se…

Greg Walker, *English Historical Review*

John North's books include *The Measure of the Universe* and *Stonehenge.* He is Emeritus Professor of the History of Philosophy and the Exact Sciences at the University of Groningen, the Netherlands.

By John North

The Ambassadors' Secret
Storia della scienza dell'Istituto della Enciclopedia Italiana, vol. 4 (*ed.*)
Stonehenge
Fontana History of Astronomy and Cosmology
Chaucer's Universe
The Universal Frame
Stars, Minds and Fate
Horoscopes and History
Richard of Wallingford (*3 vols*)
The Measure of the Universe

CONTENTS

II. THE PAINTING

III. THE MEANING

ILLUSTRATIONS

PLATES

TEXT ILLUSTRATIONS

PREFACE

This book is an attempt to discover what lies behind Hans Holbein's most famous and most enigmatic painting. *The Ambassadors* has a tantalising quality. Why has Holbein beguiled us with his portrait of two youthful ambassadors standing to the side of a still life with many unfamiliar artefacts, and why did he place the distorted image of a human skull in the foreground? It clearly belongs to a world with a different set of values from our own. That it has an allegorical content is plain enough, although when I began to write I was sceptical of the idea that its allegory ran very deep. Gradually, however, I began to appreciate the extraordinary precision with which *The Ambassadors* had been planned. It was this that forced me to admit that the allegory was of a much more highly contrived form than had previously been recognised. There is no shortage of Renaissance paintings making use of symbolic forms, many of them still imperfectly understood, which nevertheless give the impression that the artist could have whispered the secret in our ear in a few simple sentences. This is certainly not so in the case of *The Ambassadors*, which is not only a convoluted labyrinth but has many threads running through it. What is its secret? Where do the threads meet?

Allegory is rather like a haunted house: the greatest danger is in one's own imagination. Visual images from the past can deceive us twice over. They may do so in the way an artist intended, but they will also deceive us when we are out of tune with the thought of the period in which the image was created. The same holds true of the written word, but since we drink in images much more quickly than words we are more likely to think that we can understand them, and to forget the importance of the historical context. Even taking art to be no more than a means of stimulating feeling, it should be obvious that we are not stirred in the same way by a painting as were those to whom it was first shown. There were in the age of Holbein many beliefs about mankind, the world, the heavens and God which were commonplaces among the educated classes. They would have required no commentary then but do require it now. In this book I have offered a brief introduction to a number of ordinary and extraordinary beliefs which I hope may help the ordinary reader to look with a fresh eye not only at *The Ambassadors* but at other paintings of the period.

Where does this all lead? It soon becomes clear that, whatever else its purpose, this painting by Holbein has a religious theme. That is easily said and should not be surprising, since religion was at the very core of sixteenth-century European systems of thought and behaviour. Even a painting embodying symbols of political power can be expected to have had a religious dimension, in view of the fact that all rulers, like those they ruled, were set in a hierarchy with God at the highest level. Holbein's brilliant naturalism, together with what appears at first sight to be a secular theme, help to hide this from us. When Robert Browning made his Prior say to the painter Fra Lippo Lippi, 'Paint the soul, never mind the legs and arms!', he was expressing a prejudice of his own time, the view that naturalism in art betrays a lack of interest in the spiritual dimension of life. This is entirely false, but there are more pernicious prejudices that stem from it. One of them is that science in a painting is a sign of soulless materialism – just legs and arms. I hope to show by this study of *The Ambassadors* that the opinion is mistaken. There is even more naturalism in the painting than has previously been recognised, but it does not betoken worldliness, in the sense of an indifference either to life beyond the grave or to the aesthetic potential of the sciences. It is a naturalism that is witness to a love of science and of mystery – often it seems for its own sake – and of God.

While the religious theme of *The Ambassadors* was a commonplace in Holbein's day, his treatment of it was far from conventional, invoking as he did astronomy and geometry, optics and various occult arts. The idea that religious art could have had an astrological component without shocking its public is seemingly hard to accept by those unaware of the degree to which astrology had penetrated almost all branches of learning in the middle ages and Renaissance. Even before this barrier to sympathy with the past has been crossed, however, the secret of the painting begins to unfold. It rests in the first instance not on astrology but on a simple astronomical fact, concerning the elevation of the Sun. How Holbein would have explained his allegory I cannot say, but I strongly suspect that he would have taken us into his labyrinth through the most conspicuous of all the painting's mysteries, the distorted skull. That was my own starting point, but I was entirely unprepared for the many threads that came together there. Of course that was only a beginning. The true secret of the painting is found only when we discover where the threads finally meet.

This book came into existence almost by chance. I had made a passing acquaintance with *The Ambassadors*, which depicts instruments made by Holbein's friend, the astronomer Nicolaus Kratzer, when I was writing on Kratzer in the late 1960s. In January 1998 I visited the exhibition mounted at the National Gallery, showing the newly restored painting in all its splendour, but I was far from convinced by the interpretations that were being offered in the commentary on it, or by others in the press at that time. I expressed my reservations in lectures later in the same year, and while there was enthusiasm on the part of many who claimed to know nothing much about art history, most of those who would have described themselves differently greeted my various conclusions with thunderous silence. Clearly more was needed if I was to win them over.

My debts are many, and they begin with that to my wife, who without realising what she was doing set the book in motion. When it threatened to become perpetual motion, her forbearance was exemplary. Needless to say, I have relied heavily on the researches of others. My greatest single debt is to Mary Hervey, who wrote more than a century ago: I wish I could have met her. I must thank the host of friends who have helped me more materially, and in particular Rachel North and Daniel Scott, whose understanding of art history is matched only by their understanding of art historians. As for publishers, none could have been more considerate than Martin Sheppard and Tony Morris. Those who thought that editing was a lost art are evidently unfamiliar with Hambledon and London.

August 2001 Oxford

PREFACE TO THE PAPERBACK EDITION

The present edition, apart from a few minor adjustments, includes several significant additions which confirm suggestions I made previously. Some of them relate to the anamorphosis. Having examined the back of the frame of the anamorphosed portrait of Prince Edward by Willem Scrots, I can now mention evidence for its once having held a hinged rule and vane with the dimensions I proposed earlier. I had also previously failed to notice that the viewing position I had derived for *The Ambassadors* is one from which Dinteville may be imagined fingering the strings of the lute; and that all three major lines of sight, on my reconstruction of the overall plan, pass through the middle of a hexagram. Equally remarkable, as I now see more clearly, is the part played by the 'umbra versa' triangle, in both its dimensions and its position.

Like most moderns, I am happier with lines of sight than with the cabala, so it is reassuring to find support for a conjecture I made in the second category, but could not previously justify. The Petreius edition of the famous cabalistical work by Pico della Mirandola was issued in the year before the painting was done. It contains several passages which seem to throw light on the plan of the painting. I here show how, in particular, it seems to confirm the idea that we face a cross in the middle of the painting.

I earlier explained the symbolism of the Swan on the celestial sphere, but did not take the trouble to superimpose my Schickard sketch on the globe. I find that doing so yields yet another instance of one of the painting's key symbols. To appreciate it fully requires a discussion of the perspective representation of the celestial globe. Since this needs to be rather elaborate, it is here put into a new appendix. Some of Holbein's venial mistakes are also noted there. They are mistakes which can help us to understand his extraordinary technique in handling what must have been one of the most difficult parts of the painting.

Finally, I have rephrased a sentence which gave one reviewer the impression that I was criticising the recent restoration of the painting. Nothing could have been further from the truth. Holbein himself would have approved the National Gallery's extraordinary achievement, and I can only hope that he would have felt the same about my restoration of his meaning.

J.N.
November 2003

For
William · Miriam · Alexander
Gabriel · Samuel · Benjamin

ACKNOWLEDGEMENTS

The author and publisher wish to thank the following institutions for their kind permission to reproduce illustrative material:

The Bodleian Library, Oxford, Fig. 58; President and Fellows of Corpus Christi College, Oxford, Fig. 16; The Museum of the History of Science, Oxford, Fig. 72, upper section; The Trustees of the National Gallery, London, Plate 1 (*The Ambassadors*) and all plates and figures derived from it; The Trustees of the National Portrait Gallery, London, Plate 5, Figs 23, 25; The Trustees of the Wallace Collection, London, Plate 2; The Governors of the Wellcome Trust, Fig. 73.

PART ONE

The Painter and His World

You will meet many English nobles and men of learning. They will be infinitely kind to you, but be careful not to presume upon it. When they condescend, be modest. Great men do not always mean what their faces promise, so treat them reverently, as if they were gods. They are generous and will offer you presents, but recollect the proverb, 'Not everything everywhere and from everyone' . . . Smile on as many as you please, but trust only those you know, and be especially careful to find no fault with English things or customs. They are proud of their country, as well they may be.

Erasmus to Nicholas Cann, 17 May 1527

ONE
PORTRAYAL

> I turned into the National Gallery yesterday where I saw for the first time the new acquisition, Holbein's *Ambassadors*, a damned ugly picture I assure you.
>
> Aubrey Beardsley, letter to G. F. Scotson-Clark, 9 August 1891

> I am beginning to feel somewhat ashamed of what I said about Holbein's *Ambassadors*. I have seen it several times since . . .
>
> Aubrey Beardsley, letter to G. F. Scotson-Clark, some time in September 1891[1]

Hans Holbein's painting of the diplomats Jean de Dinteville and his friend, Georges de Selve, the bishop of Lavaur, done in 1533 and now going under the title *The Ambassadors*, is one of the finest examples of Renaissance portraiture and one of the best known. Its appeal is not always immediate, but Aubrey Beardsley was not easily shamed, and whatever his initial feelings he would surely not have denied that Holbein's painting is a masterpiece of technical brilliance, from the portrayal of the two men's faces to that of the luxurious fabrics – the sable lining of the clerical gown, the fur, slashed satin and velvet of the more worldly figure, even the turkey rug on the stand between the two men, with its strong tactile quality. This painting has been well described as the most spectacular *tour de force* of Holbein's career, and no one who has seen it in its newly restored state is likely to disagree.[2] Holbein's technique still has the power to astonish that it had in his own day. He had been well schooled in the art of accurate representation, having learned long before from his father how to make careful drawings from life and paint from them, but by 1533 he had outgrown mere accuracy. He had learned to give to his colours greater richness and subtlety, and to make his portraiture generally more intimate. These qualities are all conspicuous in *The Ambassadors*.

The painting is much more than a portrait, but even judged

as that, nothing surviving by Holbein is more ambitious or more successful. It is testimony to a close friendship between the two sitters, which the artist persuades us that he has understood well, as he relates and reconciles their seemingly very different characters. Holbein had painted another double portrait – now lost – of Desiderius Erasmus and his publisher and friend Johannes Froben some years earlier, so in this respect the London painting was not breaking new ground.[3]

It is often said that what marks the transition from the middle ages to the fifteenth-century Renaissance in art was a new emphasis on the values and personalities of individuals. Their characters, it is said, are now to be read in their faces, rather than in a story underlying some scene – typically religious – in which they were conceived to play what was usually only a subservient part. They move with a new freedom of body and spirit. Holbein did much to reinforce that new tradition in northern art. It would hardly have been possible without the subtlety of new painting techniques and artifice that could give depth to the image – such as where Holbein has one of the ambassadors bring his foot forward, so creating a sense of real space inhabited by real people. All this was a symptom of a loosening of the old social hierarchies. Painted when the artist was in his mid-thirties and at the height of his powers, *The Ambassadors* well illustrates the break between the old order and the new.

The two men in the painting were ambassadors, and to that extent the modern title is an accurate one. There are some who object to it in much the way that aficionados of Mozart object to the use of worded titles to identify his compositions. No one expects a title to reveal everything about a painting, but it should not mislead. To describe Holbein's monumental painting simply as *The Ambassadors* is to present it first and foremost as a portrait, and so to beg a number of questions that have never been properly addressed, for it is many other things besides. That it seems to offer scope for endless commentary and interpretation has less to do with the demeanour and biographies of the sitters than with the fact that the centre ground is occupied not by them, but by various objects on the table between them, not to mention a grossly distorted skull painted slantwise right across the foreground. Those tokens of the world of learning and human mortality are no doubt meant to throw light on the personalities, circumstances and aspirations of the sitters, and yet for reasons that are not at all obvious Holbein seems to have given pride of place to them.

Most earlier interpretations of those qualities have been given in very general terms. Some have seized on the melancholia of one or even both ambassadors, and have presented the whole thing as a *memento mori,* an elaborate statement of the omnipresence and inevitability of death. Others have been content to rest their case after a brief appeal to the contrast between the worldly and the spiritual, the vanity of the arts and sciences contrasted with the deeper truths of religion. The complexity of the still life at the centre of the painting is without parallel in Holbein's work. Some have seen it as hinting at the glories of sixteenth-century learning and discovery, but have rarely been more specific. Those who have looked deeper into the potential symbolism of the painting have done so chiefly with reference to Reformation history and the political and religious unrest of the time. We are typically encouraged to read the sitters' thoughts, and in particular their concern over the religious crises facing Christendom, in which they were implicated by their ambassadorial function and their other offices. A Lutheran text on the lower shelf is seen as an indication of their broadly liberal religious sympathies, as an appeal to the Holy Spirit for guidance at that critical moment in history, or even as a plea for complete tolerance of the Protestant cause, to which they did not themselves subscribe. Whether or not that approach can yield an acceptable reading of the painting, there is at least general agreement that *The Ambassadors* conceals more than a study of its technical and aesthetic merits alone can explain. It is certainly much more than a portrait, in the narrowest sense of the word. It conceals hidden qualities, and the aim of this book is to discover and explain them.

PROVENANCE AND DATE

The Ambassadors is the largest and most complex of all of Holbein's surviving works. The only painting by him likely to have been of comparable quality and on a larger scale was done at a later date. High on the wall of the king's privy chamber in Whitehall Palace, it showed Henry VIII and his third queen, Jane Seymour, with his parents Henry VII and Elizabeth of York above and behind them. That vast royal wall painting perished in a fire in 1698 and is now known only through part of a preparatory cartoon for it, and later copies of the whole.[4] Both of these two great paintings are outwardly complex, but they cannot really be compared. *The Ambassadors* has an extraordinary inner complexity. It was never intended as an item of public spectacle, but was meant for private display at its owner's home in France. It carries a message more important than the men portrayed in it.

That we now tend to regard it as belonging to the trappings of state is partly due to its modern title, partly because it was painted in the orbit of the royal court by a man who became the king's painter, and perhaps also because it has hung in the National Gallery in London for more than a century. Its provenance is reasonably well known. It is presumed to have left London with its owner, Jean de Dinteville, when he returned to France in 1533. It was moved to Paris from the Dinteville château in 1653 by François de Cazillac, a descendant of the sitter, at a remove of three generations. Sold at auction in Paris by a later descendant in 1787, it was bought by the art historian and dealer J.-B. Lebrun, who exported it to England. The earl of Radnor bought it in 1808, and it was acquired for the nation from the fifth earl in 1890.[5] Intense scholarly and public interest in the painting was aroused at that time. It had earlier been argued that the sitters were the poet Sir Thomas Wyatt and the antiquary and chaplain to Henry VIII, John Leland.[6] In 1900 the historian Mary F. S. Hervey was in a position to devote a complete book to it, in which she presented convincing arguments for the identity of the sitters. She had been fortunate enough to trace and purchase a seventeenth-century manuscript that gave the identity of both. The subject on the right was apparently Georges de Selve, the bishop of Lavaur. Jean de Dinteville on the left had already been correctly identified by Sidney Colvin in 1890 on the basis of the naming of Polisy – the Dinteville château – on the terrestrial globe, and this was confirmed by the new evidence.[7] Rival speculation did not stop at once and is still not entirely dead. W. F. Dickes was reluctant to abandon his earlier conclusions, and in 1903 offered a book of his own to the trustees and director of the National Gallery, dissatisfied as he said he was with the statement on the 'suppositious parchment label' – by which he presumably meant the 1653 fragment of parchment inventory presented to the National Gallery by Hervey, which contained the names of the sitters. He argued instead for Otto Henry and Phillip, counts Palatine, as the sitters, and for the Treaty of Nürnberg (1532) as the occasion.[8]

Riccardo Famiglietti recently found what is at present the earliest known written source claiming to identify the sitters. Dating from 1589, it makes them out to be Jean de Dinteville and his brother François, bishop of Auxerre.[9] This was a natural enough supposition to be made by a person with limited local knowledge, since the two brothers lived on the family estates together at the ends of their lives, but it is almost certainly mistaken. The bishop of Auxerre was at the French court on the date commemorated in the double portrait, having just returned from service in Rome. On 28 March he despatched a letter to his brother in London, asking him to tell the English king that he wished Henry could be at the forthcoming interview that he, François, would be having with the pope. There is no hint in the letter of any plan to visit London.

Hervey's view has prevailed, and almost all subsequent work on the painting has rested heavily on her outstanding study of it.[10] The dual portrait is explicitly signed and dated 1533,[11] in which year Dinteville was in London, on his second diplomatic visit, to protect the interests of the French king, François I, at the court of Henry VIII. The bishop leans on a book, an inscription on the edge of which puts him in his twenty-fifth year, while Dinteville carries a dagger with an embossed inscription on the sheath putting him in his twenty-ninth year. A cylinder sundial on the upper shelf of the table on which the two men lean has a setting that is superficially ambiguous as between two specific dates, one in mid-April and one in mid-August.[12] Despite a number of uncertainties about the precise timing of the bishop's visit to London – he arrived between February and Easter, and left before the end of May, although he might conceivably have returned – the general coherence of the evidence assembled by Hervey and others is very satisfying.

A HIDDEN MEANING?

Holbein's usual way with his sitters was to paint them from the waist up, to include appropriate commonplaces as symbols of their characters or occupations, and to spell out their names and ages explicitly. *The Ambassadors* is not the only portrait of his in which he dispenses with those conventions, but it is the most enigmatic. What is the meaning of the scholarly still life that dominates the centre of the painting? Most of those who have looked for subtleties in the details of the instruments depicted there have claimed to find technical errors in them – sighting holes in the wrong place, shadows that curve wrongly, a design that would have been useless anywhere north of Africa, and so forth. Are those supposed errors any more than one should expect in the work of a scientifically unschooled painter? Are they indeed mistakes? And if so, can it be that Holbein was making them *deliberately*? In this case, are we to suppose that he was making conscious allusion to historical events, great or small? Or might he have been making some more general, aphoristic, point? Of the making of aphorisms there is no end. One of the sundials shows different times on two of its faces, and one commentator on a recent National Gallery exhibition took this to mean 'It is later than you think'. No doubt in time others will come to prefer 'It is earlier than you think'. By what ineffable token is the art historian to judge such claims, or even to know where a natural representation ends and an allegorical one begins? It is usually wise to prefer the simple explanation to one requiring abstruse calculation, but how is simplicity to be judged in an age unable to use a sixteenth-century sundial, let alone appreciate the tricks that Holbein might have played with one? On balance, he has been more renowned for his realism than for his feeling, more for his technique than for his scheming, but he was not entirely above riddles. In one painting, a portrait of Georg Gisze dated 1532, he put a slip of paper covered in writing in the background and closed it with sealing wax. In *The Ambassadors,* he splashed the distorted skull across the foreground so prominently that some of those who have seen the work in the National Gallery in London will confess that they can remember little else about it. That skull can hardly be described as a playful gesture, but was it really meant as nothing more than a reminder of human mortality, as many now seem to believe? Or even as an ostentatious Holbein signature, relying on a German pun – '*hohles Bein*', namely 'hollow bone'?

Whatever the answer, the distorted skull does at least show that the painting is not to be understood by reference to immediate appearances alone. The biographical circumstances of the painter and his sitters are of obvious importance, but there are other certainties that should not be overlooked. The composition generally, and the geometrical properties of the painting in particular, have a measure of objectivity and prove to be no less important. Its pattern is surprisingly complex – in fact there seem to be at least three distinct geometrical patterns to be found in the composition, each of them with a basis in the learned world of the time. If this is no illusion, what are we to make of it all? Sealing wax and hollow bones do not make Holbein a Renaissance mystagogue. He was a superb craftsman but he seems to have been a relatively impassive human being, and we must respect the consensus among his biographers that he was not the kind of man to devise geometrical patterns for anything approaching an occult or cabalistic use. Like his father and his brother before him,[13] Hans Holbein was quite capable of making respectable use of the new-found arts of perspective representation, but he was prepared to admit inconsistencies in his work and did not flaunt that particular skill in the way so many of his contemporaries did. (He was not as obsessed as

Uccello, for instance, whose wife – if we are to believe Giorgio Vasari – reported that she could not get him to bed at nights, so in love was he with perspective.) His experiments with perspective drawing may have persuaded him to try his hand at other simple geometrical schemes, but few will wish to claim more than that. Holbein was the supreme technician in paint, but he seems to have been an unlikely maker of geometrical riddles, despite the distorted skull. Here is one of the many hurdles to be crossed by anyone who claims to have found meaningful patterns in the double portrait. But an even greater hurdle is the biography of the ordinary modern reader, who is usually only dimly aware of the mental and spiritual baggage carried by the ordinary educated person of the sixteenth century.

Whatever Holbein's character, he did not work in intellectual isolation, and he moved in the vicinity of people who had an excessive fondness for enigmas, especially literary enigmas. As the composer of music at the English court John Taverner said a few years later of Erasmus, the greatest humanist scholar of them all, 'He pronounced also many enigmata or symboles'. Somehow we do not expect this of a class of scholars – the *umanista,* as they were known in Italy – who concentrated primarily on the grammar, rhetoric, history, poetry, morality and civic values of Greek and Roman antiquity. Even their obsession with textual purity seems at odds with the half-mystical use of symbolic expressions, until we recall how many of the classical art forms had exploited them earlier. Christianity, with its invisible worlds, had done so, and had conquered Rome, and the new humanists were almost without exception brought up in the Faith. 'Pronouncing many enigmas or symbols' was a foible that reached down from the highest humanist scholar to the lowest, and the more of Plato they had in their curriculum, the more it told. This book will be very largely concerned with sixteenth-century humanism of an intellectual and artistic character, but it is as well to remember that there was another powerful movement sponsored by the same class of scholars, with a very different aim, namely to encourage the individual to take an active part in civic affairs.

Here again Plato was an important influence, but now Roman models seemed nearer to home. The two ambassadors in Holbein's painting were no strangers to that type of civic humanism.

Nor can they have been total strangers to the practicalities of the artist's studio. At regular intervals over the century since Hervey's book was published, interest has been shown in one or another aspect of the painting. Its restoration, and the special exhibition to celebrate the event and Holbein's five hundredth anniversary, provided the occasion for another well-documented study, by Susan Foister, Ashok Roy and Martin Wyld.[14] The restoration report by Wyld is especially important, offering as it does numerous insights into the evolution – and later deterioration – of the painting. Among other things it reveals the enormous care Holbein took over small details. His treatment of Dinteville's dagger case, for instance, beginning with a chestnut-coloured paint for the overall design, followed by a greyish-yellow oil mordant over that, to highlight the detail, then by the application of gold leaf. As if that were not enough, the minutest detail was then added with a brush in shell gold, leaving us with the feeling that it would have cost Holbein less trouble to have created the real thing.[15] The occasional losses of such fine brushwork are of course regrettable, but so too are the distortions of the planned image, relative and absolute, that have occurred over the centuries. The painting was done on a series of ten vertical planks of oak, of various widths, originally joined by dowels, carvel fashion, but later fitted with a cradle for support. They were well seasoned: by tree-ring dating the planks are known to be from 1515 or before. They have been subject to concave warping across the grain, and various corrective trimming has been undertaken in the past, that of 1891 being the most drastic. The recent report discusses such matters in detail – misalignment of the seventh and eighth planks, for instance – and while such degeneration is mildly depressing, it is not as serious as it might have been, since the resulting displacements are visible from the painted objects which they affect. In the last analysis, however, we are in the hands of the restorers.

TWO

HANS HOLBEIN

[IL]LE EGO IOANNES HOLBEIN NON FACILE [VLL]VS [TAM MICHI] MIMUS ERIT QUAM MICHI [MOMUS ERI]T

I am Hans Holbein, whom men will find it easier to criticise than to imitate.

Inscription (after Apollodorus) provided by Erasmus
for a Holbein portrait of him (1523)

In age, if not in style, Hans Holbein the Younger was a generation later than the three great German painters Albrecht Dürer, Matthias Grünewald and Lucas Cranach. He was born in Augsburg in 1497 or 1498 – we know only from a portrait of him by his father that he was in his fourteenth year in 1511. His was a family of artists. A grandfather had been a goldsmith, just as his own sons were later to become; and an uncle, Sigmund Holbein, was a painter. His father, now usually distinguished as Hans Holbein the Elder, when in his prime was Augsburg's leading painter, a fine draughtsman and colourist working within a tradition that looked more to its Gothic past than to the revolutionary achievements of contemporary artists in Italy. Augsburg, however, was no backwater. A city of the Holy Roman Empire, it was an important commercial and artistic centre that from the 1490s had been enjoying a period of rebuilding and refurbishing, supported by a newly buoyant prosperity. Its artists were beginning to pay heed to developments south of the Alps, first in architecture and then in portraiture. The Holbein family was touched lightly by those influences before Hans left home. He and his brother Ambrosius had worked with their uncle Sigmund and with their father before the father moved to Isenheim (Alsace) in 1515. Ambrosius left Augsburg to become a journeyman painter at much the same time, and later Hans joined him. Before the end of 1515 the two brothers apprenticed themselves to Hans Herbst, the leading painter in Basel.

Basel was the city that had helped Dürer to fame as a young journeyman many years before.[16] It was home to a relatively new university, and partly for that reason had become an important publishing centre. Basel was more or less loyal to the empire, despite the fact that it had been a member of the independent Swiss Federation since 1501. It was a place of promised opportunity, and a natural centre for the brothers to gravitate towards. Fragments of biographical information from this period of the younger Hans Holbein's life show that he was already held in some esteem. He painted a double portrait of the burgomaster Jacob Meyer and his second wife, for example, in 1516, but more important than his civic connections, in the long run, were his links with the world of European learning. At the end of 1515 and the beginning of 1516 he spent ten days illustrating (with a few contributions from his brother) the margins of a copy of the second edition of Erasmus's enormously successful *Praise of Folly*, an ironical view of the sorry state of church and scholarship. There is no question here of close friendship – the great scholar was many years his senior and on a very different intellectual plane – but, whether he knew it or not, Holbein was laying down a useful network of social connections. His success had more to do with his skills than with his social bearing, which left something to be desired if we are to judge by the fact that he was fined once for brawling – with a goldsmith called Caspar, who was fined too – and once for involvement in a fight with knives.

From 1517 to 1519 Hans worked in Luzern, where he joined up with his father again to collaborate with him in decorating the residence of the chief magistrate of the town, Jacob von Hertenstein. He joined the painters' brotherhood of St Luke in Luzern, and we learn of his activities there as a painter on glass. Preparing designs for the painting of glass was until about 1531 a way by which he supplemented his income, but his real ambitions lay elsewhere. It has been suggested that he made a visit to northern Italy around 1517, perhaps whilst he was still working for Hans Herbst. His first biographer, Carel van

Mander, writing in 1604, insisted that he had never been to Italy. Van Mander's aim was to prove that northern artists had no need of Italian schooling, and that they visited Italy not to drink at the fountain of modern art but for the sake of classical antiquities. He was able to quote the Italian painter Federico Zucchero to the effect that some of Holbein's work outshone anything by Raphael.[17] Oskar Bätschmann, on the other hand, has argued – on the strength of a much later contract (one dated 1538) drawn up between Holbein and the city of Basel – that he had worked in the duchy of Milan previously to that date. The contract in question allowed him to sell his works in France, England, Milan or the Netherlands, three out of the four of which he had certainly visited by that time, making it likely that he had also visited the fourth.[18] In fact when Holbein made a journey through France and the Netherlands, in 1523–24, it was in an unsuccessful search for patronage and employment.

This extended excursion seems to have visibly affected his treatment of portraiture and religious themes, which as a result became less stark than older German taste had dictated. In his 'Noli me tangere' painting of the resurrected Christ, which dates from this period and is now in Hampton Court, Mary Magdalene is dressed in the French fashion. It is thought that in his later style of portraiture in chalk Holbein was following the work of the leading French court artist Jean Clouet, work that he probably saw at this time. And if, as is still often claimed, the influence of Leonardo, Mantegna and Andrea del Sarto is to be detected in Holbein's later paintings, this too presumably stemmed from his experiences in this early period of his life.

MASTER PAINTER

When he returned from Luzern to Basel in 1519, Holbein was received into the artists' guild *Zum Himmel* as master painter, and this entitled him to set up independently. His brother Ambrosius disappears from the records after this time, and it seems more plausible to assume that he died in 1519 or 1520 than that he abandoned his trade for something completely different. Hans now married. His wife, Elsbeth Schmid (née Binzenstock), was the widow of a tanner who had been killed in battle, and she brought with her a son by her first marriage. In 1520 Holbein was elected chamber master of the painters' guild, and by purchase he became a burgher of the city of Basel. Even during his apprenticeship he had achieved a reputation for fine book illustration, and for much of his life he continued this lucrative work. His most famous drawings for publishers at this time were those of his 'Dance of Death' series and his illustrations to the Old Testament – notably the title page to Luther's Bible (1522). The former was a series of forty-one scenes illustrating a typical medieval allegory, and is thought to have been influenced by similar scenes from a Dominican convent in Basel and by a play of 1523 by Niklaus Manuel. The designs were his, but the blocks were cut by another artist (Hans Lützelburger) at an unknown date – although certainly before 1526, when the block-cutter died. The series was not published until 1538, five years after *The Ambassadors* was painted, but it then became enormously popular. Its simple homespun message, conveyed with forceful economy, is that Death visits all categories of persons without distinction. Its superficial relations to the great double portrait are easily exaggerated. That they have been compared is chiefly due to the simple fact that both use a skull motif to great effect.

Between 1520 and 1524, during this second Basel period, Holbein was commissioned to paint house façades and murals in the council chamber of the city hall, excellent public advertisement which brought him a measure of commercial success. There are those who have sought to read his mind on the basis of the scenes he painted, but it would be foolish to assume that it was he who decided on what they should be, or on the shade of reformist theology, for example, at which they seem to hint. Those who pay the piper generally call the tune. While Holbein was now reckoned the leading painter in the city, his social position was little different from that of the many other good artisan-artists there. As far as one can tell, his education had been modest. It was certainly very different from that of the Basel publishers and their humanist authors with whom he began to rub shoulders as he took more and more commissions for their portraits. Even so, he made many close friends among them. One of Holbein's Basel friends, Bonifacius Amerbach – himself the son of a publisher – was a member of a circle of humanist scholars into whose company Holbein entered, to his great advantage. A fine Holbein portrait of Amerbach (dated 1519) was probably done at the request of Erasmus, the greatest of all northern humanists and a close friend of Amerbach.[19]

When he had first moved to Basel as a young man in 1515, Holbein had taken lessons for a time from the humanist theologian Oswald Geisshüsler, alias Myconius, and it was in this way that he had made his first acquaintance with Erasmus, at the end of the same year. When, as mentioned earlier, he illustrated Erasmus's *Praise of Folly (*ΜΩΡΙΑΣ ΕΓΚΩΜΙΟΝ, *id est Stultitiae Laus),* it was already in its second edition and was one of the books that Myconius used for teaching purposes. It was in the margins of a copy of the book that the young artist did his sketches, over a period of ten days. A few Latin words written under them in a good hand suggest that he was already reasonably literate, but there is surprisingly little evidence of his writing from a later period. The book's influence on the young painter is impossible to judge, but its satirical edge, especially in its attacks on corruption within the church, cannot have left him entirely unaffected. One of the marginal sketches is of a not-so-young but ever self-conscious Erasmus, whose comment on seeing it (according to a marginal note) was that if he still really looked like that he could certainly take a wife.[20] (He never did.)

Theirs was no more than a fleeting acquaintance at this time, but the artist got to know Erasmus well in Basel after 1521, when the scholar again stayed there with his publisher Froben. Later still, Holbein painted what has become the best-known of all portraits of Erasmus (1523), one of two oil paintings that the scholar sent to friends in England. One of them went to the closest of his English friends, Archbishop Warham of Canterbury, who as matters turned out was to be painted by Holbein in exactly the same unusual standing position three years later.

The formula of the scholar in his study had been used by the Flemish painter Quinten Metsys for a portrait of Erasmus in 1517, so it seems probable that the sitter rather than the artist chose it for the Holbein portrait.

These were stormy times in ecclesiastical history, in the city republic of Basel in particular. Lutheran Protestantism was introduced there in 1522, after which it quickly gained ground, turning allegiance to the empire on its head. Erasmus was to remain in Basel until 1529 – a record stay for that wandering scholar – when events forced him to leave for Freiburg. He had begun in Basel by preaching tolerance and reconciliation between Protestant and Catholic. From the beginning, he had regarded Martin Luther with great apprehension. The man who to Protestant tradition has always been the regenerator of Christendom was at first to Erasmus no more than an imprudent monk who constituted a distinct threat to the general peace and to his own safety. Their names were all too often coupled, and there was also the small matter of Erasmus's own lapsed vows as an Augustinian monk of seventeen, from which the bishop of Cambrai had obtained for him only temporary dispensation. His stance had been consistent, however: Luther should be answered, and not suppressed unheard. But now Erasmus was growing steadily more exasperated with the Lutherans, and his numerous letters refer to the ever wilder talk of heresy and orthodoxy and Antichrist. Strict censorship of the press and the mindless destruction of religious art were taking increasingly unpleasant forms.

Erasmus's disagreements with Luther were questions of principle rather than of the practice of his unruly followers. Through the publication of his writings on the theology of free will (1524 and 1526), Erasmus broke openly with Luther, and lived for some time in the fear that the revolutionary party might hold him by force. He sensed that war was coming, and he knew that revolutions were not made with rose-water. As for the city of Basel, through the preaching of Johannes Oecolampadius after Easter 1529, the views of the Swiss reformer Huldrych Zwingli were widely adopted there. The core of Zwingli's teaching was that the mass was only in *remembrance* of Christ's sacrifice on the cross, and was not a re-enactment of it. While this was heretical in the eyes of orthodox Catholics, it did not offer a direct threat to the political fabric. Oecolampadius touched on more politically sensitive matters, however, when he opposed the dominance of local government in church affairs and advocated that pastors and lay elders should share in church government. This added a new dimension to an already inflammatory situation.

There was bigotry enough on the other side of the religious divide, and Erasmus suffered a personal blow when a distinguished young French scholar and friend, Louis Berquin, was burned at the stake by the church authorities in Paris for his opinions. The violence that frightened Erasmus most was nearer home, however, and so it was that in 1529 he left Basel. By October 1531, Zwingli was dead, killed at the second battle of Kappel – following an attack on his city of Zürich by enemies from the forest cantons. His Basel disciple Oecolampadius died a broken man soon afterwards.

These were events of European significance but they had effects on his adopted city that disturbed Holbein deeply. During the later episodes, however, he was at a safe distance, albeit without his family. His nerve had given way much sooner than that of his learned patron. It does not have to be assumed that, as a painter, he was necessarily without sympathy for those who were rejecting religious images. Many painters and artisans who were familiar to him were siding with the new ideas, even though these owed more to Zwingli and other Swiss reformers than to Luther, who was not especially hostile to devotional imagery. Holbein's unease at the turn of events must have had much in common with that of Erasmus, but there was one obvious difference. No artist could remain entirely indifferent to the idea of having his work physically destroyed, but this was the age of the printed book, and the new situation could not put an end to the written word as such – quite the contrary. It did more or less put an end to the demand for devotional art of the sort that had so far provided Holbein with his main livelihood. His energies and his ambitions too were a spur to a shift of scene. By 1526 he had decided to leave the city to seek his fortune elsewhere, and it was with a letter of introduction from Erasmus that he went in that year first to the southern Netherlands – he visited Quinten Metsys in Antwerp – and from there to England. Erasmus's letter, addressed to his Antwerp friend Pieter Gillis (Petrus Aegidius), says quite explicitly that Holbein's aim was to earn money (angels) in England, since the arts in his own part of the world were freezing.[21] Before long, some of the arts in Basel were on the contrary burning, but by then Holbein had left the city.

HOLBEIN'S FIRST VISIT TO ENGLAND

In England a recommendation from Erasmus to his friend the chancellor, Sir Thomas More, and of course Holbein's evident genius as a portraitist, seem to have helped him to a comfortable existence and the opportunity to develop his skills still further. His portrait of More is almost as well known as that of Erasmus, and it is clear that the artist put exceptional care into both. It is not necessary to suppose that he was under More's protection or that he was 'More's man' in a strong sense, but the connection served the artist well.

It was almost certainly in More's household at this time that Holbein first met Nicolaus Kratzer, who among other things taught astronomy to More's daughters – three daughters by his first wife and one stepdaughter.[22] Thomas More himself seems to have had more than a passing interest in mathematics and astronomy, if we are to judge by an account given by William Roper, his son-in-law, of how he gave lessons to the king. There was a new cult of intellectual debate among the laity of the upper classes, and no doubt the king was anxious not to be left out. We are told that on holy days, after making his devotions, the king would summon More to his private room where he would take instruction in astronomy, geometry, divinity and other subjects. This would have been a year or two before or after 1520. On some nights they would go up on the roof together to consider 'the diversities, courses, motions, and operations of the stars and planets'.[23] Already in his *Utopia* (1516), More had shown his admiration for the subject, although he professed himself repelled by astrology, 'the cheat of divining by the stars'. Whatever the depth of his knowledge, he was at least a man able to judge the quality of the tutor he later employed for his family. And astronomy was no game for a dilettante, but a subject at the very core of the traditional educational process.

It was in More's household in 1527 that Holbein completed a life-size group portrait of More's family, commissioned on the occasion of More's fiftieth birthday. The work is lost, although the preparatory design and seven studies of heads for it still survive, as well as variant copies of the entire painting. It is generally accepted that the work was influenced by Andrea Mantegna's group portrait of Lodovico Gonzaga and his court, which Holbein is often presumed to have copied on a visit to the palace in Mantua during his tour of Lombardy. An original Holbein pen sketch of the English family group was sent by More to Erasmus in Basel, as a way of keeping his friend in touch with the family.[24] It has the names and ages of the sitters added in Kratzer's hand, perhaps at Erasmus's request. Erasmus had described the More household as a Christian version of Plato's Academy. He could hardly have invented a more lavish compliment, or one that the portrait of the More group better illustrates. As is often pointed out, it breaks new ground in northern European art: it is not of a passive and pious family at prayer but of people at ease in their own environment, with thoughts and worries of their own. Holbein had learned how to accord to his sitters the individuality so prized by the new humanists.[25] The need to do so was a commercial as well as a spiritual imperative.

Whether or not it was through More that Holbein was introduced to the court of Henry VIII is not known, but his first royal appointments were humble enough. He was employed as a painter on the large scale needed by the master of the revels, Sir Henry Guildford. He would no doubt have given satisfaction had he worked to the standard of the humdrum painting of the exteriors of houses in Basel, but he was clearly determined to impress with his growing skill in detailed work. With the help of assistants, and directed in technical matters by

Nicolaus Kratzer, he painted what was evidently a fine cosmographic display on a false canvas ceiling for a room at Greenwich. In it masques were enacted as part of the spectacular festivities which began on 5 May 1527 to celebrate the betrothal of Princess Mary. It was there that Anne Boleyn appeared in public with the king for the first time.

The ceiling in question touches obliquely on the theme of *The Ambassadors.* It was described in tantalisingly vague terms by the chronicler Edward Hall as showing 'the whole Earth environed with the sea, like a very map or cart'. It was described by the Venetian ambassador as a *mappamondo* in which the names of the chief provinces could be read – which in itself tells us something of its scale, since it was high on a ceiling. The globe of the Earth and its seas, however, were evidently shown surrounded by a zodiac, on which were placed the stars as well as the planets in their correct houses.[26]

What sort of map of the Earth could it have displayed? There are three or four excellent candidates for a prototype. Martin Waldseemüller's splendid – but elongated – world map of 1507 had spawned others, including one that has been claimed as Sebastian Münster's work, the block for which was supposedly by Holbein and published in 1532. On the other hand, Dürer and Stabius produced a world map in 1515 that had a circular boundary, thus lending itself to being placed at the centre of a rotating sky; and from a letter that Kratzer wrote to Dürer in 1524 we conclude that he is likely to have been familiar with this.[27] Peter Apian published a heart-shaped world map in 1530 which would have served as well, and which by its shape might have amused the onlookers more. In fact in 1524 Apian had published a work of cosmography which seems as though it might reflect on *The Ambassadors* in two or three respects, and which adapts the principle of the astrolabe to a map of the Earth in a very curious and unusual way. The north pole of the Earth is now at the centre of the disc as we see it, and America is drawn, of necessity rather crudely, with both east and west coasts. It is impossible to choose between these four possibilities, but all had a serious mathematical background while lending themselves to display.[28] My own money is on the last of the four, which would have been the most unusual, although the other three would have been nearer the cutting edge of cosmography.

The idea of a zodiac around the Earth presents us with a problem. The fact that the stars go round the Earth, and that the entire celestial scene turns with daily motion with respect to the terrestrial, prompts us to ask – and this is a question which can be asked of *The Ambassadors* – whether the Greenwich ceiling was painted to represent the situation on a fixed date and at a fixed time. How could the ceiling, depicting moving stars and planets, have been otherwise? The answer is implicit in Hall's description of those circles around the Earth. They were clearly superimposed on the background but separate from it. The Earth and its seas were 'on the ground of the roof', in other words they were fixed, but the encircling 'girdles' were realised by 'a connyng makyng of another cloth'. This is clearly an allusion to painted muslin, or something of the sort, serving as a semi-transparent overlay in the manner of the plastic overlay of a modern planisphere (the simple device still sold by stationers, by which one may see what part of the night sky is visible at a particular time and season). In sixteenth-century terms, the ceiling would very probably have had the character of the instrument known as an astrolabe – which was indeed the prototype of modern planispheres – but with the addition of the figure of the Earth in the middle. (The pole of the instrument would have been centred on that, which rather tends to favour the fourth option of the last paragraph, illustrated for other reasons in Fig. 58 of a later chapter.)

Alas, the Greenwich display was just as ephemeral as its great circular successor, the Millennium Dome. If a fuller description of the Greenwich ceiling ever comes to light, it would not be surprising to discover that the overlay was meant to be rotated by degrees as the occasion required, or even that the representations of the Sun, Moon and planets were so arranged as to be movable separately. There were medieval precedents for such a planetarium, although it is unlikely that most of the onlookers at Greenwich knew of them.[29]

From this commission, begun on 6 February and ready for

inspection by the king on 11 March 1527, Holbein turned his talents to painting a large arch that divided the newly built banqueting house from the theatre, depicting the siege of Thérouanne and the Battle of the Spurs, which had taken place in 1513. This scene of a French military embarrassment was ready to be brought down river by boat on 4 April of the same year, and was the king's bluff way of greeting French diplomats in May, to celebrate the new peace between the two countries. The work was evidently done in minute detail, of a quality that may be conjectured on the basis of Holbein's other paintings from the period. The detail earned admiration, but what mattered more to him, no doubt, was the fact that with Kratzer's help he was being called upon to help create a royal illusion, in which Henry was at once Renaissance cosmographer and flower of chivalry.

RETURN TO BASEL

Under a contractual obligation to the council of the city of Basel to do so, after two years in England Holbein returned and rejoined his family. He had become moderately wealthy from his English tour, enabling him to sport clothes of silk and velvet and to buy a sizeable house, together eventually with a smaller adjacent property. (He left some of that rich apparel with his wife in Basel, as we know from an inventory of her possessions at her death in 1549.) Helped by the prestige accorded him in England, he was also able to negotiate with the city council for an annual retaining fee of 50 florins. He was admitted, albeit with some delay, to the Lutheran faith. The reason for the delay may be gauged from the circumspect answer he gave to a McCarthy-style committee set up by the reform party to enquire into citizens' religious orthodoxy. From the 'Registers of the Christian Recruitment' we learn that 'Master Hans Holbein the painter says that he needs a better explanation of Holy Communion before he will go'. Presumably he got it, since we later find his name among those 'who do not object but want to conform to other Christians'.[30] He knew that Europe extended beyond the limits of Basel, and may well have suspected that even there the pendulum might soon swing back in the other direction.

The religious side of his painting had always been ambiguous, and so it remained. Some of his early religious works were impressively stark, but critics have more often than not failed to find in them any deep Christian spirituality. It has often been said that he was the supreme representative of German Reformation art, and that, for example, two of his designs for woodcuts done a few years before 1526 show Lutheran sympathies. One of them is directed against the Catholic Church's sale of indulgences, the other against the philosophy of the university schools. The second, entitled *Christus vera lux* (Christ the True Light), makes interesting use of a metaphor of light. The light of a candle in a holder decorated with images of the four evangelists is presented by Christ to a group of true believers, but is spurned by a group of blind Catholic scholastics, who are enticed by the doctrines of Aristotle and Plato, and are shown falling into an abyss with Plato's name at its edge. Whether or not Fritz Saxl was right to see in these works a 'vision of a new humanity', a pit with Plato's name on it is hardly a symbol of the new humanism, in which Plato figured as something of a patron saint.[31] Another woodcut of perhaps three years earlier – and rediscovered in the twentieth century – shares the crudity of these pro-Lutheran images. It shows Luther as 'Hercules Germanicus', the German Hercules, club in hand, lambasting his enemy the monk and inquisitor Hoogstraten, surrounded by a vanquished Aristotle and numerous medieval clerics and scholastics who have suffered the same fate. When it was first issued, this particular woodcut was thought by some to have been commissioned by Erasmus or a sympathiser who could see in Luther only his belligerence, and who failed to value him for his faith. To use this as evidence that Holbein was somehow close to Erasmus is to do a disservice to the subtlety of Erasmus's view of the Lutheran movement. On the other hand, when we ask where Holbein stood, we can surely agree with Saxl that he was temperamentally closer to Erasmus than to Luther, in whom both saw 'only his fearsomeness, his *atrocitas* and not his vigorous faith'.[32]

The Reformation was far from being a simple unified movement. Protestant clerics have been traditionally regarded as bound together tightly by the doctrine of 'justification by faith alone'. For a time this was also a mark of Erasmian Christianity in general, but it was not until the Council of Trent (1545–63) that it was treated by the Catholics as a distinguishing badge of Protestantism. In practice, even self-acknowledged Protestants could disagree strongly on most theological questions – even on the nature of the eucharist, the consecrated bread and wine in the sacrament of the Lord's Supper. Attitudes to the Reformation varied considerably from one social group to another. Most showed a strong self-interest – for example, the knights and nobility in acquiring church lands, professional people in the improvement of their social condition, and the lesser townspeople in the stability of their local communities. The need for order was in the end largely responsible for shifting power from the original church reformers to the authorities in the larger towns.

There were so many conflicting interests at stake, over and above the central religious issues, that Holbein must often have longed for the days when life for a painter was simple, and when one knew the direction from which patronage could be expected and the taste of the patron. He belonged neither to the fervent and pious early following of Luther, nor to the cold, analytical theology of the universities, but occupied some middle ground. He was phlegmatic, deliberate, but not indifferent. By the early 1530s the attention he was giving to religious themes was dwindling, and for good reason. Some of his religious paintings were among those destroyed by the mob in a notorious outburst of iconoclasm in Basel on Shrove Tuesday, 1529. In a separate incident, iconoclasts destroyed his father's altarpiece in the church of St Moritz in Augsburg. The uncertainties of the political future must have persuaded him to avoid subjects that might be misinterpreted and held against him, but even outside Basel at a later date he apparently found no strong religious patronage. Perhaps he sought none, or perhaps it was merely that those who in England commissioned fine religious art tended to have a taste for the products of the

Low Countries. A deeper cause was without doubt the changed nature of piety and devotion in Protestant circles in general. There was still a need for the simple story-telling woodcut or painting, for those who could not easily read the word of the biblical story, but the theologians had sterner ideas. When it was created out of paint or wood or stone, even the greatest of all symbols of Christian religious mystery, the crucifixion, was for many of the reformers no more necessary to personal faith than was a mediating priesthood. The worldly-wise artist needed to change direction quickly. Perhaps the example of his collaborator Kratzer helped to persuade him that he had a future within the orbit of the court of Henry VIII.

Holbein remained in Basel from 1528 to 1532. Even though the council of the city offered him a pension, he was not persuaded to stay. He left his unhappy wife and her children yet again, and most of the remaining eleven years of his life were spent back in England. A portrait of his wife and two of the children (Philip and Catherine) had probably been painted in 1528 at the beginning of his stay. She sold that painting before he died, and it is often supposed that she did so to make ends meet, but her reasons may have had more to do with her anger at his having deserted her. It is widely accepted that he had already been unfaithful to her with Magdalena Offenburg, the subject of three of his paintings dating from around 1526,[33] and he certainly fathered children by a woman in London after he left Basel. It is hard to pass judgement on Holbein in the absence of more evidence, but the look of resignation on his wife's face goes far towards providing it (Fig. 1).

LONDON AGAIN

The London he had left in 1528 was very different from that he found when he returned in 1532. Having fled the Reformation in Basel he arrived in a country on the verge of a break with Rome. Matters would soon be brought to a head by Henry VIII 's wish to divorce Catherine of Aragon and marry Anne Boleyn, a question which touched Holbein's career. He is so often referred to as the king's painter – to which office he is usually

1. Holbein's wife with their children, Philip and Catherine, Basel 1528. Öffentliche Kunstsammlung, Basel.

thought to have come through Cromwell's influence – that we are inclined to overlook the possibility that it was Anne Boleyn who gave him more useful patronage at first. Holbein drew her portrait around the time of her triumph over Catherine in May 1533. He designed the 'Parnassus' tableau for her state entry to London, a work commissioned by the merchants of the mainly German Steelyard. When Henry showered her with gifts of jewelry, Holbein was commissioned to design it. He was entering into a useful network of personal acquaintance and patronage that touched lightly on the new scholarship and religion. Anne's father, Sir Thomas Boleyn, was a scholar of some repute, a friend of Erasmus and one who helped to promote Erasmus's attitude to religion at the English court. He is thought to have commissioned the anonymous English translation of the Dutch scholar's *Explanatio symboli* of 1533, which appeared as the *Playne and Godly Exposytion of the Commune Crede* in 1537. Jewels and theology were perhaps closer than we generally imagine.

The divorce question must have had serious repercussions on the artist's network of friendships. Almost every one of his earlier patrons sooner or later became caught up in the resulting civil and religious conflict. To be on the safe side, it was expedient to seek out new patrons. When he had first visited London he had found only the weakest of traditions in portraiture. It comes as no surprise to find Thomas More expressing his view – in a letter written at that time to Erasmus – that Holbein would be unlikely to find the city rewarding. Holbein had himself done much to create a demand for portraiture during his first stay, and his absence seems to have created something of a vacuum in more than one set of wealthy patrons. The new series of portraits he now began to paint in London was for members of the Norfolk gentry and for Hanseatic merchants, members of the Steelyard. Soon he began to acquire a clientele in court circles. *The Ambassadors,* a product of 1533, must have represented a magnificent advertisement for his talents in and around court, but when he painted it he was still not in an official capacity at court. It is not known precisely when he was officially engaged as the king's painter. In 1536 a letter by the French poet Nicolas Bourbon refers to him as the king's painter, and the first recorded royal payments are from that same year, although it has been suggested that the royal accounts may contain gaps in places where payments to him were recorded earlier.

We can only guess at Holbein's feelings when he saw his earlier patron Sir Thomas More first resign from the chancellorship (16 May 1532), later refuse to attend Anne Boleyn's coronation (Whit Sunday, 1 June 1533), and finally (6 July 1535) suffer execution for refusing to take the oath required by the Act of Supremacy. More could have brought himself to accept the king's divorce, but he could not accept the idea of Henry as supreme head of the church of England, God's representative on earth and the custodian of the souls and consciences of all English men and women. Erasmus's response to news of More's death was to express a view that he had conveyed to the man himself in his lifetime: the chancellor should have left theology to priests. Throughout Europe, Protestants and Catholics alike were shocked by the event, but it should serve to remind us that Erasmian humanism was a very broad church, and that More was on the conservative wing which henceforth had to adopt a low profile in England if it was to survive there. More had been no ordinary patron of Holbein's, but the artist could not afford to become too bound up with the affairs of those who paid him. We can only guess at his thoughts when in 1534 he painted Thomas Cromwell, who shortly afterwards became secretary to King Henry VIII, and who bore much of the responsibility for More's fate – a fate that Holbein lived to see him share in 1540. The evangelical and ruthless Cromwell was effectively the director of Henry's propaganda machine in the 1530s, and Holbein had slowly been drawn into his circle. It must have been with Cromwell's acquiescence that he painted the bishop of Rochester, John Fisher, in the Tower, not long before Fisher was executed (22 June 1535). Not only did he paint Cromwell, he portrayed Sir Richard Southwell, who had helped materially to bring More down. The cool detachment of the subject in this portrait surely reflects a little on that of the man who painted it.

It was probably through Cromwell that Holbein eventually entered fully the king's service. Given a workshop in a tower of the palace of Whitehall, Holbein painted portraits of the king himself as well as of successive wives and members of the royal family. It is hardly an exaggeration to say that his portraits of the king, which were in large part a propaganda exercise orchestrated by Cromwell, quickly became the standard image of Henry and his monarchy. They have been interpreted by some as symbolising the grandeur of the Tudor court, rather than that of a mere person. Even so, Holbein's candid eye has penetrated the pomp – as Charles Dickens well perceived when, tongue in cheek, he used Holbein's portraits of the king as evidence that Henry was 'one of the most detestable villains that ever drew breath'.[34] The king was not dissatisfied with his portraits, and had enough confidence in his painter to attach him to delegations abroad, prospecting for suitable brides – in which capacity Holbein's skill in portraiture was at a premium. Christina of Denmark managed to slip through the net, having left to history a remark every bit as perceptive as Holbein's excellent portrait of her. (Had she possessed two heads, she said, she would willingly have put one at the disposal of the king of England.) The plainness of Anne of Cleves presented Holbein with greater problems. His portrait of her was an exercise in making the truth palatable, and he overshot the mark. The reality turned out to be more than Henry could bear, but this second Anne was allowed to part from him with her head where Holbein had painted it.

Holbein painted unremittingly, producing portraits in all formats, from the largest to the smallest. He is often said to have learned the art of the portrait miniature from another painter in the king's service, Lucas Hornebout. In fact the story stems from Holbein's first biographer Van Mander, who said that Hornebout taught Holbein the art of manuscript illumination. Whatever the truth of the tradition, it tells us something of court taste that this Flemish artist, the son of a manuscript illuminator from Ghent, received a slightly higher salary than Holbein's. Holbein, however, was able to spread his net more widely.

A volume of drawings preserved in the Royal Library at Windsor Castle contains eighty-five portraits by Holbein. Most of them are unconnected with surviving paintings.[35] Together the drawings present us with one of the most vivid records of a royal court ever assembled. While requiring different techniques from the paintings, and certainly techniques very different from those demanded by *The Ambassadors,* they are of comparable artistry. They bring to life – to take just three examples – the obdurate saintliness of Sir Thomas More, the dispassionate treachery of Sir Richard Southwell, Cromwell's unscrupulous henchman, and the resolute modesty of Jane Seymour, Henry's 'entirely beloved' queen. What makes the drawings truly remarkable, however, is that most of the sitters were of no great weight in the political scale. Many are unidentified, but they are as real as the people we pass in the street every day.

Holbein did much besides painting and drawing: he made designs for buttons and buckles, tableware, gold and jewelry, bookbindings and title pages, painting for theatrical events, ceiling paintings, state robes, and even ladies' court dress. Tedious though some might have found that kind of work, it was his métier, and one that yielded artistic dividends. It gave him an unparalleled feel for the textures of materials of all kinds, and it also gave him the habit of relating physical accessories to face and personality in his portraiture. It is as though he was consciously striving to show the inner person only indirectly – indeed, his determination to reveal emotion only obliquely may be seen as a strong source of his appeal to the English. And since in so many of his portraits he chose to hint at the inner life of the sitters through light but skilful touches of the real world surrounding them, we are encouraged to suppose that he did something similar in his double portrait of the two French ambassadors. As we shall discover, however, the problem here is one of determining where the characters of his sitters end and external forces and circumstances take over.

DEATH AND REPUTATION

Hans Holbein died in 1543, as did the great astronomer Nicholas Copernicus, whose work *De revolutionibus* (itself published in 1543) marks a watershed between the old and the new understanding of the cosmic order. In as much as the painter was ever caught up in such intellectual affairs, he belongs emphatically with the old order. He died in the parish of St Andrew Undershaft in London in October, very probably a victim of the plague epidemic of that year. He is buried either in the parish church of St Andrew (in Cornhill) or in the church of St Katharine Cree (in Leadenhall Street). Both churches still survive. His will, dated 8 October, made no mention of his family in Basel but set aside money for two illegitimate London children who were still 'at nurse'. The identity of their mother is unknown. In 1538 Basel city council had agreed to pay some of his standing salary to his wife. This arrangement is unlikely to have lasted long, but she was not destitute. When Hans Holbein's uncle Sigmund died in 1540, Hans was represented for his inheritance by his wife and her guardian, brother to her first husband.

In his own will, Holbein discharged debts to Mr Anthony of Greenwich, the king's servant (perhaps Anthony Denny), and to Mr John (Hans) of Antwerp, goldsmith.[36] That it was witnessed by the latter and by Olrycke Obynger, merchant, and Harry Maynert, painter, tells us something about the social milieu of the greatest portrait painter of the age. But it is not the whole story. When in 1536 Nicolas Bourbon dedicated a book to Thomas Soulemant, the English king's French secretary, he asked him to pass on greetings to Holbein and Kratzer, whom he named in the company of Archbishop Thomas Cranmer, Thomas Cromwell, Dr William Butts the royal physician, Cornelius Heyss (Hayes) the king's goldsmith, and Sir Francis Bryan.[37] There was evidently nothing incongruous in the idea of placing Holbein in the company of men of such standing. It was his virtuosity that had first allowed him to rub shoulders with that group, all of a radical and reformist disposition holding allegiance to Anne Boleyn. On balance, it seems likely that he was more to them than a mere artisan, and more sympathetic to their ideals than to those propagated by Thomas More, the patron he had once served no less loyally.

Conjecture on his religious position is difficult, in view of the fact that there is hardly a scrap of continuous prose by him. Surrounded though he often was by humanist scholars, no letters in his hand survive, and even the main annotations on his drawing of the More family are by Kratzer. Most of his artistic output is ambiguous, since it was largely designed to meet the wishes of his clients. We seize on the least ambiguous fragments of evidence we can find, but they amount to very little. Apart from those instances already mentioned, there is the elaborate woodcut provided by Holbein for Miles Coverdale's English Bible of 1535. Its iconography not only shows Henry VIII as supreme head of the church but attempts to put across the new doctrine of justification by faith. The title page was printed with the Bible in Cologne, and the printing had to be orchestrated in near secrecy. It has often been suggested that Cromwell was connected with the operation, and certainly the message of the woodcut fitted well with his political plans. In that case, Holbein had put more than his skill in portraiture at the disposal of Cromwell and his faction, and had done so while More was still alive.

Far less is known of Holbein's life than of his painting technique – for which the studies most relevant to *The Ambassadors* are the two books published in connection with its most recent restoration.[38] This is no place to go into that much studied subject, except perhaps to draw attention to something that is often treated as a weakness in a great artist, namely his known use of geometrical instruments (compasses, ruler and set-square) in his preparatory drawings. To single out this aspect of his practice is not to suggest that it loomed large in the view he took of his own art, but it does speak for a certain matter of factness, not to say a punctilious approach to design, that has a marked relevance to the character of *The Ambassadors.* His modern critics speak of his truth and honesty, but by this they usually mean no more than that he could read the mind's construction in the face, and reproduce it so that we can read it. Outside his studio Holbein may have merited a very different description.

The social and scholarly distinction of his patrons did much to advance Holbein's reputation in the world at large. His fame has always depended to some degree on the wide appeal of his subjects. In England he has always been the cameraman of Tudor history. In nineteenth-century Germany in particular he assumed the mantle of artist of the Reformation. Throughout Europe he is remembered as portrayer of the face of humanism. The first of his portraits to reach a wide audience was one of Erasmus, which was eventually reproduced in print in 1550 in a cosmographical work by Sebastian Münster. At the English court Holbein's circle was probably small, and it was sixty years before a few of the circumstances of his life were systematically committed to print. Even in a book by Matthew Parker, archbishop of Canterbury under Elizabeth but formerly chaplain to Anne Boleyn and later to Henry VIII in Holbein's lifetime, under a reproduction of his portrait of Archbishop Warham, the artist is simply named as 'Hans Holby Flandrensis', Hans Holby the Fleming. The Elizabethan artist Nicholas Hilliard acknowledged a debt to Holbein's technique, but he was born after Holbein's death and his few biographical asides are empty self-advertisement. Carel van Mander's was the first attempt at biography. As we have already seen, he too had a deeper purpose, to sing the praises of northern artists, this in answer to Giorgio Vasari's *Lives.* First appearing in 1550 as a series of biographies of 'the most eminent Italian architects, painters and sculptors', Vasari had moved the painters up to first place in the title by the time he published a much enlarged second edition (1568). There he tells of the Tuscan renaissance of classical art after its medieval eclipse, a renaissance initiated by Giotto and culminating in the works of Michelangelo. Van Mander's answer to this was his *Schilder-Boeck (Painter-Book),* first published in 1604, in which he adapted some of Vasari's rhetorical devices to make counter-claims on behalf of northern art.[39]

Van Mander, a painter himself, wished to explain genius in entirely personal terms, relating neither to place nor to birth. He was nettled by Vasari's idea that places such as Florence were blessed by God as the natural homes of great achievement. He presented Holbein as a man born he knew not where – not in Augsburg, he believes – who matured in Basel, an artistic desert. (His jaundiced view of that city was not improved by a request for payment he had received in answer to a letter he had written to a descendant of Amerbach, asking for information about Holbein.) His short biography, penned as it was with this thinly concealed agenda, does at least seem to have been based on methodically gathered information, however richly embroidered it may have been by the writer. Even assuming that it was based on hearsay at second or third hand, it is unlikely to have been pure invention. That Holbein left Basel because of a nagging wife, for example, is not so much an untruth as a crude abstract of a half-known tradition. What of the story that he was in Thomas More's household for three years when More put on an exhibition of his work for the king, to whom he offered it in its entirety? The details may be wrong, but it does have the ring of an often-told tale, and it ends perfectly. Henry preferred to take the artist.

That Van Mander added colour to his account by insisting on the irrelevance of social rank is one of the reasons why modern biographers are hesitant to repeat it. They doubt the story of the quick-tempered Holbein throwing an English noble down stairs when he persisted in trying to visit the artist. They doubt it because the general point that Van Mander is illustrating is one that he makes again in connection with Dürer and the Emperor Maximilian. That in itself hardly reflects on the incidents that supposedly gave rise to either. True or false, the Holbein story is that, frightened at what he had done, he climbed out of the window and hastened to confess his crime to the king, who asked him to wait in a side room. The bandaged noble was duly carried in, and was so enraged by the king's reluctance to punish his painter that he threatened to punish the man himself. At this the king is said to have responded angrily: 'If it pleased me to make seven dukes of seven peasants I could do so, but I could not make out of seven earls one Hans Holbein, or any other artist as eminent as he.' The frightened noble backed down and promised restraint, and Van Mander the painter could make his egalitarian point.

Bearing in mind how many people Holbein knew in prominent positions on the European historical stage, it is surprising that so little is known of him from others. Erasmus recommended him, as we have already noted, but on another occasion made an aside that suggests mild irritation. Material ambition doubtless explains away much of Holbein's behaviour, and it is quite possible that Erasmus – a cosmopolitan of a very different sort – disapproved of his having twice deserted his family. Yet again we can only speculate. For want of biographical detail it is tempting to be dismissive of what we have, and to say that Holbein's painting was his life. It was not, but it does take up the lion's share of what is known of him.

2. Modified version of a woodcut portrait of Erasmus of Rotterdam ('ER. ROT.') by Veit Specklin, drawn by Holbein around 1538, for an edition of the scholar's collected works. The original was not ready by the time of printing (1540), so it was sold as a separate print. The classical Terminus statue was a device adopted by Erasmus. The prosaic lines in the cartouche, added only in later editions, translate 'Pallas, recently admiring this Apellean picture, says that the library must keep it for ever. Holbein shows his Daedalus-like art to the Muses, while the great Erasmus shows a wealth of the highest intellect' (Pallas Apellæam nuper mirata tabellam, / Hanc ait, æternum Bibliotheca colat. / Dædaleam monstrat Musis HOLBEINNIUS artem / Et summi Ingenii Magnus ERASMUS opes).

THREE
THE TWO AMBASSADORS

Oh that Peter had recovered his senses at the crowing of the Cock!

Pierre Danès, 1542 [40]

In the Holbein portrait of the two young diplomats, Jean de Dinteville and his friend Georges de Selve, the celestial globe at Dinteville's elbow has often been thought to give pride of place to the cock as a symbol of France. Whether or not this was the intention, it is as well to remember that the two men were in London to promote the interests of France, of Catholicism, and of the see of St Peter. The world of diplomacy into which the two had been drawn was changing fast. In France, diplomacy was close to the crown. Both men belonged to families concerned with affairs of state. Of the two, Jean de Dinteville, the older, was ostensibly much the closer to its royal centre, but churchmen-diplomats had a special position in France, and it would be a mistake to think of Georges de Selve as no more than a casual visitor to the English court.

THE WORLD OF DIPLOMACY

Many of the diplomatic conventions we now take for granted evolved from long practice in the Venetian republic, but the system of diplomacy based on permanent missions, with a diplomatic class acting as an international force, was still relatively new in the early sixteenth century. It had matured in the Italian states, not because rivalries were absent there – quite the contrary – but because feudal hierarchy was less important there than in the rest of Europe. The chief aim of the system was to maintain commercial and political advantage while preserving a peaceful status quo. Continuous monitoring of the other party made both things easier. Humanist writers also played their part, through their pleas for peaceful coexistence.

We hear Erasmus, for example, deeming a loss of face to be preferable to a bloodbath. More influential, however, were those at the other extreme of morality, who wrote as though diplomacy was nothing more than an exercise in game theory. The classic work underlying Italian aspirations and practice was written by the Florentine political writer and dramatist Niccolò Machiavelli, and the most memorable part of the message he set down in his little treatise *Il principe (The Prince)* of 1513 has a ring of cynicism that has turned his name quite unfairly into a synonym for duplicity. It is that the present must learn from the past, and that history teaches us that the best courses of a ruler's action cannot be judged by the morality of the individual. The idea is one which François I called when – under circumstances to be explained shortly – he broke solemn oaths he had sworn earlier in an imperial prison. As he said afterwards, echoing Machiavelli, oaths taken by a man deprived of his freedom count for nothing. Holbein's two young ambassadors, less well schooled in the ways of the world, might have been offended by Machiavelli's idea that the world of political success should be carefully distinguished from that in which the goal of every man and woman should be salvation through Christ. Had they been able to challenge him – he had died in 1527 – he might have said that he was describing the world as it was, rather than as it ought to be. But of course he was also describing ways in which it might be changed to what the state wanted it to be. One of the most often quoted definitions of an ambassador catches the Machiavellian spirit of the diplomatic world well. Written in jest (in Latin) by the poet and diplomat Sir Henry Wotton in 1604, in a friend's album, he described an ambassador as an honest man sent abroad to lie for the good of his country. Wotton had served as ambassador to Venice, where the rules had not changed much in three centuries. His definition no doubt fitted Dinteville's office well, but it certainly does not seem to have matched either his character or that of his friend.

As Garrett Mattingly observed long ago, the full triumph of Italian permanent diplomacy 'coincided with the full triumph of the new humanism and the new arts, and under the same patrons, Cosimo de' Medici, Francesco Sforza and Pope Nicholas V'.[41] Italian diplomatic style and protocol entered European political life in earnest after the onset of the Italian wars in 1494, and spread quickly to the European powers implicated in them. Milan was then already represented in Paris by a permanent ambassador. Florence was speedily represented there, and also at the imperial court. Soon Venice was employing ambassadors at the London court of Henry VII. Henry, who valued safety more than foreign territory, at first made use of Italian envoys. Spain had been permanently represented in London since 1487. In the next century England was represented at the imperial court intermittently, until in 1520 the mutual appointment of ambassadors was made a condition of the treaty between the Holy Roman Emperor Charles V and Henry. Charles V's inability to speak for many of his vassals, the German princes, led to a reluctance on his part to establish imperial embassies at European courts, but he was effectively represented in his role as king of Spain and archduke of Austria. For sixteen years, beginning in 1529, he was expertly represented in London by Eustache Chapuys, one of the most professional of all the ambassadors of the age, although one who faced an almost impossible task. He was meant to ensure an English alliance, or at least English neutrality, in the empire's contest with France. The divorce question put paid to that. He did at least manage to distract the French while Charles V coped with the Lutheran princes, which was no mean achievement. As for the English, they might not have had such a dedicated ambassador, but since the 1520s they had promoted a diplomatic service of some note, created by Henry VIII's chancellor, Cardinal Wolsey. At the period that most interests us, however, Wolsey was dead and François I was working hard to create an organised diplomatic organisation that would outplay all others north or south of the Alps.

The broad principles of effective diplomatic behaviour that governed the world of Dinteville and de Selve were by this time widely recognised. Foreign missions must keep up a pretence of morality. Diplomats' private lives must be seen to be above reproach. Wives were to be left at home – although such hostages to indiscretion were not a problem in the case of the two men Holbein was painting. The discussion of foreign affairs with other embassies was generally forbidden, as was the ownership of fixed property in the foreign state. Ambassadors tended to be supplied with regular letters from the powers at home, bearing news of European affairs, often encoded. They were expected to be good linguists – Latin was still the *lingua franca* of diplomats, but falling from favour. Of the three sovereigns, Henry, François and Charles, only Henry was comfortable in it. When being cross-examined by Cardinal Campeggio over the divorce question, Queen Catherine – who could have coped with his Latin, not to mention his Italian, or French – insisted that he speak English so that her women could understand. As for Italian, it was used by diplomats throughout Europe, usually in the dialect of Rome rather than those of Tuscany or Venice. This was simply due to the old ecclesiastical connection, and was not a reflection on Venice's commercial and political power, which was great. (One result of this fact was that Venice greatly influenced English taste in art over a long period of time.) For many purposes the French language was all that was needed at the English court, especially in its higher reaches. When it came to assessing the public mood in England, the two Frenchmen would have been at a disadvantage, even in a worse situation than that of the wily imperial ambassador Chapuys. He was renowned for his poor English, but he insisted that his secretaries learn the language, and he took one of them around with him to pick up the gossip of those who thought him deaf to their language. He was adept at espionage, and when that failed he could spin a tale that he knew would go down well with his master Charles V.

Ambassadors were to mask any feeling of triumphalism to which circumstances might give rise. They must keep a good table, be men of taste and erudition, and cultivate the society of scholars and artists. In this particular branch of the diplomatic game of quiet one-upmanship, the fact that Dinteville had recruited the talents of Holbein, painter to the king, must have scored well. In a word, ambassadors were to create an image of relaxed affability that would assist them in the arts of making useful alliances, sowing the seeds of useful confusion, and procrastinating – and here the behaviour of the papal curia was the perfect model.

Ambassadors were in some respects successors to the medieval herald, inheritors of the code of chivalry, and they were often obsessed with the old forms of outward display. Occasionally they tried to impress with their entourage, as when the French ambassador negotiating the purchase of Tournai from Henry VIII in 1510 travelled with a party of eight hundred horse. There were less costly ways. The Dinteville of the pink satin blouse must have cut a suitably dashing and fashionable figure, well fitted to the courtly representation of France. Display was not without its purpose, however, and artistic display was rarely designed to give aesthetic satisfaction for itself alone. When Italian princes showered gifts of art on the all-powerful secretary of Charles V, Francisco de los Cobos, it was to buy influence in the ongoing struggle with the French. A bribe is best given in a currency appreciated by the recipient. When in 1501 the Florentines were trying to get French support for the reconquest of Pisa, they went to some lengths to ascertain the wishes of a powerful French councillor, and set about gratifying them, commissioning a bronze copy by Michelangelo of his *David* from the artist himself. When the councillor fell from grace, the gift was not delivered.[12] This was certainly not art for art's sake.

Ambassadors were usually well born, but not of necessity noble, except in the case of Venice. With outward display went a desire for precedence. France had more or less recovered its old position as first in size and wealth among the territorial states of Europe, but Spain had no intention of taking second place to France in diplomatic circles. As the fortunes of states fluctuated, so often did the ranking of their representatives. The division between Catholic and Protestant states eventually complicated matters, especially as regards papal representation. (There was also the thorny question of religious freedom within embassy walls, but that was mainly for the future.)

De Selve presents a very different figure from Dinteville. It was not that a man of the cloth would have been considered more trustworthy, but that he would have been thought more likely than the layman Dinteville to have access to Rome and the pope at this critical moment in English history. Scholars and churchmen were often chosen as diplomats, partly for their moral exteriors and their knowledge of Latin, but partly because the wealth of the church made them less of a drain on the state's resources. One of the chief councillors of King François I, Jean du Bellay, was bishop of Bayonne before being sent on five embassies to the English court between 1527 and 1534. During this period – in fact in 1532 – he was made bishop of Paris. In 1534 this future cardinal, who had become intimate with Henry and Anne Boleyn, was sent to Rome, ostensibly to argue Henry's case for divorce. (No matter that his mission ended in failure.) But the French king was not merely making use of men already in high church office, he appointed them to that office in order to make use of their services. After defeating papal forces at Marignano in 1515 he was received by the pope at Bologna and there negotiated a concordat that returned to Rome benefices lost earlier, while giving to the king the right to nominate prelates. François had the patronage of all sees and monasteries in France: he nominated in his lifetime ten archbishops, 182 bishops and 527 mitred abbots, not to mention numerous priors. The financial yield was enormous, and he used his patronage shamelessly, in part to recruit and pay diplomats and in part to bribe foreigners. Even then it was often not enough, and there began a practice of sending ambassadors of second class to lesser states, and even to states of comparable rank, as a means of saving expense. Much diplomatic correspondence – and Dinteville has left us specimens – reveals an obsession with the need to remain solvent while dutifully keeping up appearances in the sovereign's interest.

JEAN DE DINTEVILLE

Jean de Dinteville was not one of the great ambassadors of history, but almost every one of the points of diplomatic principle mentioned here is manifest in his biography. Born on

20 or 21 September 1504, he was the third son of Gaucher de Dinteville, seigneur of Polisy, and his wife Anne du Plessis.[43] Troyes is about 170 kilometres south east of Paris and Polisy is a further 40 kilometres beyond Troyes. The city is at the meeting of the rivers Laignes and Seine, and was in Burgundian territory, but on a spur of land cutting into Champagne – from which his mother's family came. This region had changed hands often in previous centuries, but now Burgundy was united with France. Gaucher, as the chief justiciary (bailly) of Troyes, was often at the French court, and had held important offices at home and abroad before settling at the château of Polisy, which he did shortly before Jean's birth. Jean was one of seven children surviving to maturity. He had two elder brothers: François became bishop of Auxerre, Louis a knight of St John. They both apparently studied at the college of Troyes, and since François went on to study at the university of Paris it is conceivable that Jean did so too. His involvement in court affairs from the age of fifteen or sixteen does not rule this out, but makes it unlikely that he ever took the bachelor's degree. Their father held office in the service of the dauphin and had responsibility for the three royal children, with the result that each of them was eventually placed in the immediate care of one of his own sons – Jean, Guillaume and Gaucher.

The family was well connected not only at this intimate royal level but through the fact that the most powerful man in France after the king, namely Anne, duke of Montmorency, was a cousin who aided the Dintevilles materially.[44] Another person who played an important part in Jean's life was Mme de Montreuil, sometime governess to the royal children. It was apparently she who ensured that Charles, duke of Angoulême, the youngest of the king's three sons, was put under the charge of Jean de Dinteville, whom 'she loved and trusted as her own son'.[45]

In 1525 French political life was suddenly thrown into turmoil following the heavy defeat of the country's forces by those of the Emperor Charles V. François I had realised for some years that he was under threat from hostile forces all around him: those of England and the Italian states could not be discounted, but they were not to be compared with those of the hereditary lands ruled by Charles v. No European ruler would again control such extensive territories until the time of Napoleon. By inheritance, Charles held much of the Low Countries, the whole of Spain and its Italian possessions and American dominions, and the Habsburg domains of Germany and Austria, added to which he had a claim to Burgundy and close ties through his brother with Bohemia and Hungary. And then, at the age of nineteen – he was as old as the century – he bribed his way to the elective title of Holy Roman Emperor, with its constellation of 'free' cities and lively principalities. François had every excuse not only for anxiety but for intense jealousy. Guided by his capable but scheming mother, Louise de Savoie, of whom he stood in great awe, he made a series of decisions that were less than wise but that need to be seen in the light of the events of ten years earlier. It was then, at the bloody battle of Marignano (1515), that the recently crowned François had led an army that defeated the supposedly invincible Swiss mercenaries of Duke Massimiliano Sforza and Pope Leo x. French claims to the duchy went back to the end of the fourteenth century, when François's great-grandmother, Valentina Visconti, married a Valois duke. Milan was his, and his determination to retain it at all costs was a question of misplaced honour that led to most of the political misfortunes that dogged him in later life. Charles v congratulated him, but knew that Milan was an important bridge between his own eastern and western lands. In the event, the French occupation lasted barely six years. After François declared war on Charles v in 1521, Milan was attacked by the imperial forces under Prospero Colonna, with the result that the French governor was forced to withdraw from the city and another Sforza was appointed duke. This was taken as a personal affront by the French king, who embarked on a plan to retake the duchy. He was soon faced with the treacherous defection of his vassal Charles, duke of Bourbon, the 'constable of Bourbon', who had hitherto been one of his finest military aides. Emboldened by his earlier success at Marignano, however, and aided by Montmorency, who recruited large numbers of Swiss mercenaries, the king pressed on with his plans. In due course he engaged the enemy at Pavia on 24 February 1525, in one of the bloodiest of all the battles fought between these two great European powers. The result was an unmitigated disaster for France. François I lost the cream of his army, including many of his closest friends, and was himself wounded and captured, together with Montmorency. Montmorency benefited from an exchange of prisoners. It was his loyalty at Pavia that brought him later to his high position. As for the unfortunate king, he was taken from prison to prison, ending up in Madrid. The headstrong knightly ruler now had ample opportunity for political reflection, a relatively new experience for him.

Charles V was in no hurry to release his royal prisoner, and in due course forced many concessions from him, although not as many as a more experienced ruler might have done. After protracted negotiations, the king was allowed to return to France, but at the cost of sending his two eldest sons – the dauphin François was eight years old and Henri was only seven – to a very unwholesome prison as hostages. The emperor announced that he would award the duchy of Milan to the duke of Bourbon, to whom the French king must also pay a pension of 20,000 livres, and here was another extremely bitter pill to swallow. François did at least refuse point blank when he was asked to accord suzerainty of Bourbon territory to its duke, who had helped to bring about his downfall. After the humiliation of the defeat at Pavia, the loss of various territories and rights, especially in the Low Countries, and the massive ransom of two million gold écus (crowns) that was eventually exacted by the emperor after François I had finally made clear his intention of holding on to Burgundy, France's leading statesmen became obsessed with revenge. The one outcome of the Madrid treaty that the king did not live to regret was his agreement to marry the emperor's sister Eleanor, widow of the Portuguese king Emmanuel. (Claude of France, François I's first queen, had died in childbed in 1524.) King and emperor were thus eventually brothers-in-law, but when they expressed themselves 'brothers and good friends', as they occasionally did when they were negotiating, their words were hollow and their mutual hostility never diminished. Not all brothers-in-law come as close as they did to fighting a duel.

For some years before the defeat of the French army at Pavia, England had taken the imperial side, supplying money and even an army, but after Pavia the situation changed. Cardinal Wolsey had seen the advantages of making peace with France and had tried to reverse alliances. Negotiating in secret with an agent of Louise de Savoie – who was acting as regent in her son's absence – Thomas More and the bishop of Ely arranged a truce. In August 1525 a treaty was signed (the Treaty of the More, in Hertfordshire), making France England's ally. An unfortunate result of this was that the Netherlands, as part of the empire, immediately took reprisals against the English cloth trade, greatly injuring the English economy. This, needless to say, helped to cement the new alliance.

French diplomatic missions were being despatched not only to England but to potential allies in a ring around the empire – to Poland, to the Protestant princes of Germany, to Venice, to Milan, and even to the Turks. One of the material consequences of all this was a treaty signed in May 1526 at Cognac between the French, the Venetians and the Milanese. This treaty, which set up the League of Cognac, effectively tore up an agreement that François had made, whilst a prisoner, to cede Burgundy to Charles v. Had it been ceded, Jean de Dinteville's estates at Polisy would have become a fief of Charles. In other words, when he was eventually sent on diplomatic business to London the young Frenchman went not as an ordinary diplomat, seeking to advance his career, but as a man whose person and family had much to lose if matters did not go France's way. Already by 1527 we hear of him as bailly of Troyes, in succession to his father, mostly at court in Paris but also having to raise money in Troyes towards the king's ransom. (He is often referred to simply as 'the bailly', and he signed himself 'Le Bailly' even in letters to his brother.) This was a period when ever more splendid diplomatic exchanges with England were taking place, to make common cause against Charles v. Montmorency had visited England in person to bring the country into the League of Cognac against the emperor.[46] Cardinal

Wolsey visited France as Henry's emissary, and honours were carried in both directions. One such honour, the order of St Michael, played a small part in the scheme behind Holbein's double portrait.

Religious questions were at the very heart of the new political divide, and strains were forming within the church along various subtly different lines of potential fracture, doctrinal as well as political. Even in France, Protestantism was a growing force, and it touched Dinteville, however obliquely. Martin Luther had focused attention not only on the personal iniquities of churchmen everywhere but on key points of doctrine, one of the most critical revolving around the question of personal responsibility in the matter of salvation. St Paul had posed the question, when he explained how the human individual is justified before God. It is not, Paul said, by works, or even by obeying the commandments, but is something depending entirely on God's grace. Luther demanded a reappraisal of that doctrine of justification. Whatever the outcome, it was inevitable that other sensitive points of doctrine would be dragged into the debate. For example, personal responsibility meant a personal understanding of the scriptures. And that in turn meant that they should be available in the vernacular, the language of the common people.

The movement to translate the Bible had begun to gather momentum before the upsurge of humanism, but it was fostered almost accidentally by this new brand of scholarship, as a by-product of the urge to plumb the meaning of the Greek text of the New Testament. Most of those involved at first had no intention whatsoever of separating from the Catholic Church, and many eventually did so only as a result of the church's response to their liberal actions. To most of the senior theologians in the Sorbonne, deviation from its traditional teachings was heresy, and Christian humanism was judged by them to be almost as dangerous as full-blown Lutheranism. In France, no less a person than the tutor to the royal children, the cleric Jacques Lefèvre d'Etaples, seemed to many to be a fellow-traveller. This scholar was no lightweight, but a renowned Parisian writer on Aristotelian philosophy and physics, as well as on mystical arithmetic and geometry. He had long been preaching the primacy of the Gospel over dogmas of the church that were man-made and undertook the translation of the Bible into French. Some of his ideas antedate Luther's more famous theses, although they were perceived as dangerous only after the Lutheran movement spurred the Sorbonne into action. Lefèvre d'Etaples opposed Lutheran methods and pressed for reform by the church and with the church, but still he twice had to flee Paris – in 1525 and 1531 – under threat from the church's conservative wing, to which Montmorency belonged. On both occasions Lefèvre was protected by his royal connections, notably by the king's sister Marguerite de Navarre, the most influential royal patron of Erasmianism in France. That he had given the king himself food for thought is evident from the conversations François held with his captor at Pavia, the Fleming Charles de Lannoy, viceroy of Naples.

Lefèvre d'Etaples enjoyed Jean de Dinteville's patronage, a fact which may offer a clue to Dinteville's religious sentiments. Were his beliefs ever a point of friction between him and Montmorency? Resistance to the reformers was stiffening by 1533, and the king himself was beginning to deplore what on one occasion he called 'the accursed heresy'. The imprisonment and execution of reformers, many of them well-educated men, had begun in earnest within a year of the painting of *The Ambassadors.* In November 1534 the printer Antoine Augereau was executed for printing a heretical book. It was written by none other than Marguerite de Navarre. That many intellectuals were drifting in a liberal direction was a plain consequence of the reaction against medieval scholasticism that humanist scholarship had set in motion. As James McConica has observed, the 'emphasis on good Latin was itself an expression of laicism, since it automatically repudiated the specialised theological language of the schools and emphasised clarity of discourse between educated laymen sharing the cultural heritage of the classics'.[47] Even the greatest of all French humanist scholars, Guillaume Budé – learned in Greek, the translator of many classic works, master of the king's library and the man who persuaded François to found the Collège Royal – eventually adopted Protestantism. Dinteville, who was well acquainted with him, was fully aware of the strains within the church in France; and, from a first mission to England in 1531, he knew of an even more serious situation there, where doctrinal disagreement was more intense because complicated by those political and personal problems that surrounded the sovereign himself.

THE FIRST LONDON EMBASSY AND THE KING'S DIVORCE

The English king needed an alliance with France for other reasons than the balance of power. Long before, in 1510 and soon after his accession, Henry had made Catherine of Aragon his queen in the hope that an alliance with her father, Ferdinand of Aragon, would keep France in check. Now he blamed her for failing to produce a male heir. Simultaneously with his aversion to her came his infatuation with Anne Boleyn, the sister of one of his earlier mistresses. Anne had long served Henry's sister Mary, queen of Louis XII, at the French court. She was no great beauty, but her chic French ways and her familiarity with French fashion and French manners served to enhance her attractions at a time when the younger members of the English court were doing their utmost to imitate all things French. Anne was forceful and ambitious and in her prime – she was as old as the century – whereas Catherine was yesterday's queen. From 1527 Henry pursued his divorce single-mindedly, having convinced himself that his first marriage had been against divine law – more precisely, against the biblical injunction forbidding marriage to a brother's widow. (Catherine had been brought from Spain as the bride of his elder brother Arthur, prince of Wales, but she maintained that the union had never been consummated, something that Henry had no wish to hear at this juncture.) Henry's appeals to Rome for an annulment, and the political and religious consequences of their refusal, are well known. In 1527–28 Pope Clement VII was the emperor's prisoner, following the Sack of Rome in May 1527, and yet here was Henry asking him to find against a woman who was the emperor's aunt. The pope is said to have repeatedly told the bishop of Tarbes that he wished for the new marriage, provided he was not held responsible. He wept and wished he were dead, but chose to procrastinate – in the hallowed Vatican manner.

Liberal Catholics in France were broadly in favour of Henry's divorce, and Montmorency's antagonism towards Spain and the empire after the defeat at Pavia is easy enough to understand; but still he wanted to hold the church together, and he would not tolerate the Lutherans. François and all of France, on the other hand, were much beholden to Henry for money that had helped secure the release of the two sons who had been forced to stand proxy for him in Spanish captivity. He saw that the best hope of separating the interests of his enemy Charles V and Henry VIII was to support the English king in his pursuit of a divorce. It must have been on a mission somehow connected with this general strategy that Jean de Dinteville was sent to London for the first time in the autumn of 1531. His father had died earlier in the same year, and Jean had become head of his house. He had other family reasons to be melancholy: his brother Louis, a knight of St John, died in Malta very soon after the death of their father, and in the spring of 1531 their brother, the bishop of Auxerre, was disgraced. The bishop was charged with what the king himself declared an 'execrable crime', which apparently involved punishing one of his gamekeepers for dishonesty by having him fastened to a post with a nail through his hands. The bishop, who had effectively broken the injunction that a priest should not shed blood, was saved from rougher justice through the offices of Anne de Montmorency, who persuaded the king to send him to the papal court as ambassador. Embassies had more uses than one. He was not allowed to return to France until early in 1533, the year of the Holbein painting.[48]

For all Jean de Dinteville's family troubles, he was well favoured at the French court. At about this time he succeeded to the knighthood of the order of St Michael, vacated by his father but in the royal gift. His journey to London in the autumn of 1531 was not without honour, even though it was brief and even though he was not of the rank of resident French ambassador in London. The resident ambassador was Gilles de la Pommeraye – a friend of Montmorency and of Dinteville's brother the bishop – who was lodged in the king's palace at Bridewell.

Once he was back in Paris, Jean returned to the service of the king's son, the duke of Angoulême, but he seems to have moved around the country a great deal, visiting Polisy only briefly. Then, in October 1532, an important meeting took place between the English and French kings in the neighbourhood of Calais, still an English possession. Henry completed the gift to the princes of his contribution towards the ransom on their father – and the Dinteville brothers who had the princes in their charge were presumably present. Royal orders of merit were exchanged, the dukes of Norfolk and Suffolk being admitted to the order of St Michael, and Henry reciprocating with the order of the Garter to Montmorency and Brion. There were diplomatic machinations in plenty; but, from the point of view of common gossip, the most memorable event was that Henry took with him not his queen but Anne Boleyn. The two brought back with them to London a new ambassador, Montpesat, who was not favoured with residence in Bridewell palace, perhaps because he showed himself less anxious for the king's divorce than his predecessor had been. His choice as ambassador was clearly not in the interests of entente, and by the beginning of February in the following year, 1533, he too was replaced, this time by Jean de Dinteville. He at least knew the nature of his posting.

THE SECOND VISIT TO LONDON

Dinteville had good news to carry to London, although the year had started badly enough. Pope Clement, who had threatened Henry with excommunication the previous November, had in January 1533 received the emperor with great honour in Bologna, and the emperor had with much humility kissed the pope's foot. ('Happy hit was in no nother place', wrote one English diplomat.) This was seen as a setback, but then the pope agreed to meet François, which was thought to be a hopeful sign in the divorce proceedings. Clement's reward was the secret cession of certain Italian territories and the marriage of his distant niece, Catherine de' Medici, to the French king's second son, the future Henri II. (Popes Leo X and Clement VII were both members of the Medici family, a fact that had done nothing to diminish the growing cynicism with which the Catholic church was regarded outside Italy.) François I, for his part, hoped to exploit the weakness of Rome and to draw Clement away from the emperor's camp without openly breaking any of his promises to the emperor. Henry was here the fly in the ointment. Dinteville – whose own brother the bishop was the French king's papal ambassador and informant – was meant to use sweet words to constrain the English king's wilder impulses. He was to pass on from the French king 'certain things which the perfect friendship between them requires to be declared',[49] but no degree of French diplomacy could keep Henry under control any longer. His loyal servant Wolsey had previously incurred his wrath for the papal insult he had suffered; but, with Wolsey disgraced and dead, and papal authority virtually non-existent, the king was looking for his own solution. He pinned his hopes for a separation from Catherine on the so-called 'Reformation' Parliament, which first met at the end of 1529. The next step was to intimidate the church in England, extracting large sums of money from it and cutting off papal revenues. All this had happened by December 1532, before it became clear that Anne Boleyn was pregnant. On or around 25 January 1533, when Dinteville was still in France, she was married to Henry in the presence of a few trusted courtiers who were sworn to secrecy. If the king was to avoid bigamy – in the eyes of men, at least – and if his child was to be legitimate, he had perhaps seven months in which to divorce Catherine.

When Dinteville arrived in London the English church had no primate, the conservative archbishop, William Warham of Canterbury, having died in the previous August. By March 1533 the pope had reluctantly accepted Thomas Cranmer, whom he knew personally, as Warham's replacement. Cranmer's lobbying on the king's behalf in Cambridge had earlier earned him a place in the household of Anne Boleyn's father, the earl of Wiltshire, on the king's recommendation. In 1530 Cranmer accompanied his patron on an embassy to the papal court, where they argued the king's case in vain. By 1533 it was plain that the easiest way of obtaining Henry's divorce from Catherine was to sever links with the papacy, and the most important steps to this end were taken around the very time that Holbein's portrait of Dinteville and de Selve was being painted. One cannot be precise about the time of the *act* of painting, but it will soon be shown that everything in the picture that points to a date points to one date only, 11 April 1533. By then, events had moved fast and far. Pope Clement's gift of the traditional pallium that allowed Cranmer to be consecrated archbishop of Canterbury had arrived, and he was installed on 30 March. He presided at once over a subservient convocation, and on 9 April a deputation to Queen Catherine broke the news of the king's marriage to Anne. Catherine, in other words, was no longer queen. She probably already knew that Anne was pregnant, since she was close to Chapuys, who had known in February. On 10 April Chapuys, encouraged by Bishop Fisher, wrote to his master Charles V urging him to make war. ('This cursed Anne has her foot in the stirrup . . .' On other occasions she was 'the king's wench', or 'the English concubine'.) In the event Charles had other things on his mind, notably the threat from the Turks. On 11 April Cranmer wrote to the king asking that he be allowed 'to determine his great cause of matrimony', as something belonging to his office. There could be no doubt about his findings, for his own rise to power had been dependent on his advocacy of the king's right to divorce.

The following day Anne was waited on in greater state than Catherine had ever been, with sixty ladies in waiting and preceded by trumpeters as she went to pray at the chapel royal, and indeed to be prayed for as queen. The Act of Restraint of Appeals declared England an empire, and on 23 May Cranmer heard the divorce case formally. Five days later he decreed the marriage to Catherine null and void. On Whitsunday, 1 June 1533, Anne was crowned queen, and on 7 September her child was born. Henry had staked his dynasty's survival and, as he and many others thought, had put his very soul in jeopardy. For what? All for a girl child, Elizabeth. In the meantime the pope had declared Cranmer's judgement null and void, and had said that any child would be illegitimate. Another complication therefore was the succession: should it go to Catherine's daughter, Mary, or to Anne's daughter, Elizabeth? That thorny problem was for the future, and in due course the decision was postponed, because in the end Henry had a male heir, Edward. For the present, the break with Rome was a reality, and all this before Dinteville returned to France from his second mission to London.

GEORGES DE SELVE

Some weeks before matters came to a head, for reasons that are now unknown, Jean de Dinteville was joined in London by his intimate friend Georges de Selve, bishop of Lavaur. He arrived during February 1533, or at the very beginning of March. In the words of Jean de Dinteville, writing to his brother the bishop of Auxerre about three months later (23 May 1533),

> M. [the bishop] de Lavaur did me the honour of coming to see me, which was no small pleasure to me. There is no need for the *grand maître* to hear anything of it.[50]

The *grand maître,* Montmorency, need not be told – not necessarily an absolute injunction to secrecy, as is sometimes suggested. It is possible that the young bishop was sent on the orders of the king, bypassing Montmorency, although Dinteville's words might equally hint at the senior statesman's disapproval of the friendship. Before the end of May in that same year the young bishop returned to France. If the portrait of the two men was painted when both were simultaneously on hand to sit for Holbein, it must have been painted in that narrow interval of time. On the other hand, Holbein's method of working was such that much of it could well have been done after de Selve's departure.

Georges de Selve was the third son of Cécile de Buxi and her husband Jean de Selve, a distinguished lawyer and much admired president of the parlement of Paris. Georges was born in 1509 – probably in the first three months of the year, in our reckoning, since Holbein's portrait indicates that he is in his twenty-fifth year.[51] His physical appearance is such that we are not surprised to learn that a forebear of his father had come to France from Milan. His father was made vice-governor of the duchy of Milan after its conquest by the youthful François I through the battle of Marignano (1515). For the time being, Milan seemed secure, and the de Selve family stayed there until the French were forced to abandon the city at the approach of imperial forces in 1521, when Georges was nearly twelve. His linguistic abilities would inevitably have been stretched by his experiences in that period of six years, but it is not necessary to speculate about his erudition, for we know that he was thoroughly versed in Greek and Latin by Pierre Danès and remained a lifelong friend of this excellent humanist scholar – a man who was later nominated one of the first professors at the Collège Royal in Paris. Georges de Selve received royal patronage through his father's influence. A translation of eight of Plutarch's 'Lives' which he published in French in 1548 'by order of the king' also brought him credit. This Greek work had been written in the first place to exemplify virtue and vice through the biographies of great men, Greeks and Romans.[52] By the time he published his selection, de Selve knew a great deal about the reality behind the veil of greatness.

Georges de Selve's career might be described as meteoric, except that it shot heavenwards. It was launched in the wake of his father's distinguished role in negotiating the treaty of Madrid, by which the French king was extricated from the bitter situation following his capture by the emperor's forces at Pavia in 1525. Imprisoned in Madrid, François I was under constant pressure to make a long list of concessions to Charles V, most notably to cede Burgundy to the empire. This he eventually agreed many times over to do, on his honour as a Christian knight, as a gentleman, and on the Gospel, but seemingly without any serious intention of keeping his promise.

The advice given to Charles v by his chancellor, the Italian Mercurino Gattinara, was not to release François before occupying Burgundy ('Sire, he would have promised you all of France if you had asked for it!'), and in view of this, not to say the emperor's own doubts, the treaty brought to the king by Jean de Selve must be judged a masterpiece of diplomacy. It did not solve the Burgundy question immediately, but by allowing for the exchange of the king with his two eldest sons until its other conditions were satisfied, it played for time. Jean de Selve was duly rewarded for his diplomacy, and among other privileges received what was to all intents and purposes a royal gift to his son. When the bishopric of Lavaur fell vacant in October 1526 on the death of Pierre de Buxi – a relative of Georges de Selve's mother – Georges was translated to it. This was an unusual appointment, even by the conventions of the time. (The scandalous appointments of a bishop of Lodève at the age of four and of an abbot of Mont-Saint-Michel at barely sixteen months were still in the future.) By church law, de Selve could not be consecrated bishop until he was twenty-five, but his administrative duties began in principle immediately, and he could enjoy many of the worldly advantages of his high position at once. The king's choice did not go unchallenged by French churchmen, but local opposition eventually died away, doubtless aided by the bishop's prolonged absences from his diocese.

It seems likely that the appointment was part of the king's strategy for using the church to bolster his diplomatic service, for within two years we find him making use of de Selve on embassies to Charles v and to the republic of Venice. Mary Hervey found much significance in his visit to the emperor in 1529, and thought it probable that he attended the Diet of Speyer (in English Spires or Spiers) in that year, 'a mission which assorts well with the presence of the Lutheran hymn-book placed near to him in Holbein's picture'.[53] A diet was a general assembly of the Holy Roman Empire. One such diet, held three years previous to that at Speyer, had decided on the notorious principle that each prince of the empire should be free to determine the religion of all within his own territory.

The Diet of 1529 was packed with churchmen bent on reversing that decision. Protestantism clearly existed in a sense long before this time, but still it lacked a name or a rallying cry. So heavily defeated was the minority at the new assembly that they drew up a formal 'Protestation', to the effect that 'in matters relating to God's honour and salvation and the eternal life of our souls, everyone must stand and give account before God for himself'. It was this act of defiance that gave rise to the generic term Protestant.

The text we have of Georges de Selve's plea for pacification, assuming it to have been meant for the Diet of 1529, is couched in extremely vague and almost apologetic terms, reflecting the fact that he was deeply conscious of his own youth. How comfortable he would have been four years later with the Lutheran hymnal placed near him on the lower shelf in the painting is something about which we can only speculate. Of course, if Holbein completed the picture after de Selve's departure for France, the bishop may not have discovered this Lutheran touch until long afterwards. It is impossible to say. Hervey adds references to de Selve's later addresses to the Germans, recalling them to the obedience of the church. It would be rash to rule out absolutely the idea that such an address, made in 1540 in response to a request from Charles v, might throw light on a painting of 1533, but circumstances do alter cases, and the most we can say with certainty is that the young bishop saw religious harmony in terms of Catholic supremacy rather than Catholic compromise.

Georges de Selve had lost both of his parents by the time of his visit to London in 1533.[54] The visit he paid to his friend was, as we have seen, a fleeting one. A few months after returning to France he was appointed ambassador to Venice for the second time. The court was then at Lyon, and de Selve met Dinteville again there before departing for Venice with his erstwhile tutor Pierre Danès, who was an avid tourist in search of antiquities. Among other scholars of the first rank whose acquaintance de Selve made in Venice were the Italian Cardinal Pietro Bembo and the future Cardinal Reginald Pole – a thorn in the flesh of his cousin Henry viii to the point of opposing the latter's claim to supremacy in the English church and even trying to raise a rebellion in England. In 1549 Pole almost became pope. He was destined to become archbishop of Canterbury after the accession of Mary Tudor, and to receive England back into the Catholic faith in 1554. This was far in the future, but one cannot help wondering whether de Selve's intimacy with the young scholar Pole – who was only nine years his senior – gives a fair indication of where in the spectrum of Catholicism his own sentiments lay in the 1530s. Looked at in this way, it is hard to think of a Lutheran hymnal as giving him much pleasure.

AFTER CRANMER'S JUDGEMENT

The tactics of the two young ambassors to London do not suggest anything out of the ordinary, French ambitions being what they were. Dinteville wanted Henry to keep secret his intention of having Archbishop Cranmer pass judgement on his case, but the king was impatient and wanted to combine Whitsuntide with the pomp and circumstance of Anne's coronation – something that would make up for the indignity of the secret marriage. A letter from Dinteville to his brother, the bishop of Auxerre, is dated the very day of Cranmer's judgement. The fact that he asked only in a postscript that the *grand maître* (Montmorency) obtain coronation expenses for him from the king suggests that he had heard the news just before sending the letter. François acceded to the request, and at the end of the year the ambassador was granted five hundred crowns.

The coronation was on Whit Sunday. On 29 May, the preceding Friday, the lord mayor and aldermen of London accompanied Anne's barge from Greenwich to the Tower. Guns were fired in salute as she was rowed upstream. Eighteen knights of the Bath were dubbed, in the first such ceremony since Henry's own coronation, twenty-four years earlier, but all this paled into insignificance by comparison with the events of Saturday. As Hervey pointed out, in view of his office it seems more than likely that Dinteville was responsible for one of the most vivid of all surviving descriptions of the festivities on that day.[55] Written for Montmorency, it tells of how Queen Anne, at five in the afternoon, wearing royal robes in much the same fashion as those of France, mounted a litter that was covered inside and out with white satin. Above her was a canopy of cloth of gold, carried – and we may interleave the French ambassador's account with other authorities – by four knights. The litter was drawn by palfreys similarly decked in white. Twelve ladies on horseback followed, with trappings of gold, and another twelve with crimson velvet. There followed a carriage decked in cloth of gold with Anne's mother and the duchess of Norfolk, and behind it other carriages and horsewomen with horses draped in black. Dinteville rode in the same carriage as Archbishop Cranmer, which many must have considered a symbol of French acquiescence in the new status quo. And so it went on, the procession numbering two or three hundred in all. At its head, it seems, were twelve of the French ambassador's own men in blue and yellow velvet, with horses similarly apparelled. Dinteville's five hundred crowns were well earned. The queen's destination was Westminster Hall, and later Whitehall, where she joined Henry. The pageantry as a whole had been orchestrated by John Leland, the king's antiquary. He ensured that the queen's badge, the white falcon, was on high in every street through which they passed on their way to the abbey; he ensured that there was music in plenty; but what he could not ensure was popular rejoicing. As a substitute of sorts, Nicholas Udall, headmaster of Eton, declaimed Latin verses at various set halts, praising the queen's beauty and – more to the point – expressing the hope that she would bear a son. To emphasise the reality of the new situation for any who may have doubted it, the entire proceedings were later published by Wynkyn de Worde in a state pamphlet. These were the circumstances for which Holbein had designed his set-piece, the triumphal arch commissioned by the merchants of the Steelyard, depicting – as we know from the drawing for it – Apollo on Mount Parnassus, Calliope below him, and some decidedly sixteenth-century Muses playing musical instruments.

On Whit Sunday a procession formed again in Westminster Hall and moved across to the abbey. Those eyes that were not on the queen's girth were on the costly string of pearls she wore. And finally she had what she wanted, St Edward's crown on her head, placed there in front of the high altar by Archbishop Cranmer. (It was quickly replaced by a lighter substitute.) Henry was present neither at this ceremony nor at the following banquet, but the less symbolic festivities were only just beginning. The royal couple moved on to Greenwich, for a tournament and dance, in neither of which Dinteville is known to have taken any interest.

In his letter to his brother the bishop, who at this time seemed likely to be despatched on a second embassy to the papal court, Jean de Dinteville recommended that if this should come to pass he soften the blow of Henry's actions by representing his marriage to Anne as something the pope had himself advised to the French ambassador in Rome. The letter in question is no less interesting from a personal point of view. In it Jean declines his brother's offer of yew branches (for bows) and of falcons, declaring himself a poor archer and saying that there is no shortage of either commodity in England. He asks instead for what he calls 'le porctrait du compas auvale', of which the bishop had spoken and which he could not understand. This is the briefest of remarks, but one that we would like to understand. The Latin words in use at this time that resemble our word 'compass' (notably *compassa)* were commonly used to denote a portable quadrant, but the so-called 'old quadrant' rather than the type in the painting that we shall have occasion to discuss at a later stage. This was an age in which astronomers were beginning to seek out amusing new shapes for sundials and similar instruments, shapes that were often suggested by the lines engraved on them. It has been noted that the German word *Kompasz* had already been used for half a century and more to refer to a portable sundial containing a magnetic compass (by which it could be set in position), and since there were oval-shaped examples it is quite possible that this was intended. The modern French word *compas* shares something of the ambiguities of the English, but all senses have been recorded in English at one time or another. We are at least no longer forced to conclude that Holbein wanted a 'compass for drawing ovals'. Whatever the answer, this passing remark does seem to indicate that Dinteville had an interest in a question of current scientific concern. It is an interest that he may have shared with Kratzer and Holbein too, and Kratzer may even have asked him to probe for more information, although it is hard to believe that an 'oval compass', in the sense of an 'egg dial' with a built-in magnetic compass, would have astonished him greatly.[56]

On the political front he told his brother of hopes for a truce between England and Scotland, and commended the duke of Norfolk to him. Dinteville seems to have invested much energy in the Scottish question, but the imperial ambassador outflanked him when he invested the Scottish king with the order of the Golden Fleece, 'so that the Scots are no longer inclined to France'.[57] Nations might not have been bought with baubles, but they certainly helped. Chapuys, writing to the emperor, was always deeply suspicious of underhand French diplomacy, but his antennae were even more sensitive to reformist theologians, in particular Martin Luther's stalwart supporter Phillip Melanchthon, who was reported as having visited Henry in secret. Chapuys could pin very little on the French ambassador. Dinteville's thoughts, however, were on the English climate as much as on Lutheranism. He had suffered a tertian fever, he told his brother, but it had passed. From this aside it is impossible to give a diagnosis, since the expression was often used loosely. His illness may have been malarial, brought from France. It is unlikely to have been a form of the 'sweating sickness', which was often quickly fatal, but the exact nature of which is a matter of disagreement even today. He is known to have had the advice of the king's physician, Dr William Butts, a man perhaps best known to history by virtue of the fact that a remorseful king had sent him to attend Wolsey at the end of his days. Butts was close to the king. He had strong Protestant leanings and – as we shall see shortly – his name was loosely coupled with Dinteville's on a later occasion.[58]

Above all else, the message conveyed by Dinteville's letter is that he is exceedingly bored. He cannot wait for the expiry of his term of service, due to end on 22 July, and he prays to God that the *grand maître* will keep his word and release him then, for he is 'the most melancholy, weary and wearisome ambassador that ever was seen'. His spirits seem to have been lifted a little by the splendours of the coronation ceremony, on which he reported at length to Montmorency, paying much attention to fashions and their similarity to those prevailing in Paris.[59] Shortly afterwards, however, we find him writing to France to report Henry's VIII's anger at hearing of François's persecution of French Lutherans, as this made forging alliances with the German princes more difficult. And then again he writes, pleading to be brought back to France. He has known not more than a week of good health in England, he tells Jean du Bellay. Either Holbein's glowing portrait caught him during that week, or his ill health was a malady of spirit rather than body.

Sources of personal information about Jean de Dinteville are not so numerous that we can pass over another trifle. It comes from a scholar, of more or less the same age, who was long known to him. Nicolas Bourbon was born in 1503, the son of an ironmaster of Vandoeuvre in Champagne. By 1533 he was a poet and teacher of Latin of minor reputation in Paris, when he was arrested following the publication of his first work, a collection entitled *Nugae (Trifles)*. He stood accused before the parlement of Paris of attacking the church, but was released from prison in March of the following year, on the personal order of François I. It is clear from his verses that his release was in response to a request from Henry VIII, prompted by Anne Boleyn, whose reputation still stood high at the French court. Indeed, the evangelical sympathies that she owed to her time in France were still not a great hindrance there.

Once freed, in the spring of 1534, Bourbon crossed to England and was lodged with the king's goldsmith, Cornelius Hayes, whom we have already met as an executor to Holbein's will. Bourbon rewarded the queen with verses, as he did many others at court, Henry not excepted.[60] He hints at having received help in London from two people in particular, one of them Dr Butts, the king's physician, the other Jean de Dinteville, who had studied at the college of Troyes at the same time as Bourbon, who was two years his senior. Dinteville had very probably interceded with the queen on the poet's behalf. He later received a teasing poem about his mistress from Bourbon. Mistress he may have had, but her identity is not known and he never married. Another of Bourbon's poems describes his own reaction to Holbein's image of a sleeping Cupid – one painted on ivory, no longer extant:

> In that image love slept . . . As I approached more closely, nothing was dearer to me in my heart; soon I was on fire with fierce flames. I began to shower it with kisses. I ceased to exist.

Anne Boleyn, in her wisdom, made use of this ardent poet to teach Latin to boys, children from her circle of supporters. Bourbon left England before her execution, but in his writings he always remained loyal to her memory.[61]

FURTHER EMBASSIES AND FINAL RETREAT

Unfortunately for Jean de Dinteville, the equilibrium of European diplomacy was disturbed in the summer of 1533 by the duplicity of Francesco Sforza, duke of Milan, albeit in response to the duplicity of the French. The murder by the Milanese of a man called Maraviglia (or in French Merveilles), whom France had used as a sort of double agent, resulted in the break-up of the League of Cognac. Dinteville was told that he must stay longer in London. He stayed beyond the birth of Elizabeth – at Greenwich palace – and beyond the time of a truce between England and Scotland that he helped to broker, and on until the much-delayed arrival of a letter releasing him. On 11 November 1533 a grant was recorded of permission to him to pass 'beyond the sea, with his servants, baggage, etc., and to convey out of the realm horses, mules and mulettes, to the number of twenty-six'. An ambassador's leave-taking was a serious affair, requiring all the formality and courtesies of arrival, and even more if there were clouds on the horizon. In the event it was a week before he left, on 18 November, and when he did leave it is likely that as part of his baggage he took with him that very large and very precious wooden panel on which were Holbein's portraits of him and his friend Georges de Selve, bishop of Lavaur.

This was not Dinteville's last visit to England. He was there again in the autumn of 1535 on diplomatic business, and on this occasion he needed even greater diplomatic tact than before, in view of papal and French horror over the execution of Bishop John Fisher and Sir Thomas More. And yet again Dinteville was sent to England, arriving this time immediately before the execution of his friend Sir Francis Weston, one of four men arraigned on trumped-up charges of conspiracy and adultery with Queen Anne. Two days later, Anne Boleyn herself was executed (19 May 1536). Whether or not Dinteville ever thought of Holbein's painting as an allegory of time, he might have been forgiven for thinking that time moved more rapidly in London than in Paris. On this occasion he pressed the case of the duke of Angoulême, his erstwhile royal charge, for the hand of the Princess Mary. Henry seems to have suspected that this was Dinteville's own idea, but in truth Dinteville's chief aim was to discover English political intentions with regard to France's struggle with the empire.

After returning to France on this last occasion, Jean de Dinteville disappears from history for a time, only to reappear when we hear of the disgrace of two separate members of his family. The Dintevilles did not do things by halves. His brother Guillaume was accused of involvement in an alleged poisoning of the dauphin, François, in 1536. (François died in that year and it was his younger brother, Henri, who eventually acceded to the throne in 1547.) Guillaume was fortunate to be cleared of the charge by his hapless accuser, Sebastiano da Montecuculli, who was executed in October of the same year for the crime of which he had accused Guillaume. More serious for the Dinteville family was the storm that blew up after their brother Gaucher, lord of Vanlay, was in 1538 accused of sodomy by his maternal cousin Jean du Plessis. To make matters worse,

Gaucher and eight companions immediately forced entry to du Plessis' house and forced him at sword point to sign a retraction. The king's wrath was aroused repeatedly in this connection, and eventually the unfortunate brother, François de Dinteville, bishop of Auxerre, was dragged into the mire. For a second time, therefore, he was disgraced. He lost his bishopric for a while in all but name. The pope refused to remove him, but Pierre de Mareuil took over the running of the see of Auxerre, and plundered it ruthlessly.[62]

The three Dinteville brothers fled to various places in Italy, where they were continually hounded by agents of the French king. That the French king's own affairs were now in a precarious state is unlikely to have alleviated Jean de Dinteville's depression or alarm at his family's predicament. It was probably at about this time that he relinquished his membership of the order of St Michael and the collar which he had worn so proudly in Holbein's dual portrait. Not until 1553, six years into the reign of Henri II, did the family's affairs return to something approaching an even keel.

DIPLOMATIC CATHOLICS

Georges de Selve, bishop of Lavaur, was in the end a much more successful career diplomat than his erstwhile companion Jean de Dinteville, and that fact helped to keep them apart. In 1537, jointly with Cardinal Mâcon, the bishop was appointed ambassador to the Holy See, where much of their energy was expended on neutralising the activities of Cardinal Carpi. The pope's confidant, Carpi was a churchman with an ambassadorial function in France. Diplomatic intrigue in Rome reached such a pitch that de Selve was ordered home to report. Plans were laid for him to be sent, in response to a request from the Emperor Charles himself, to represent France at a new imperial Diet. In the event he did not go, but the draft of a speech he intended to make there is what led Mary Hervey to interpret the Holbein painting as an allegory of the desired healing of the split in the church. She read between the lines of his draft to find there the idea that 'the chief responsibility for the divisions of the Church rested upon the shoulders of the Roman priesthood'.[63] It is true that he there hinted at the avarice and greed of churchmen; but he also insisted on papal supremacy and called for the Germans to conform to it.

A measure of his growing diplomatic stature is that in 1539 he travelled with the imperial party in a show of solidarity between France and the empire, which entailed king and emperor crossing France together. (It so happens that the English courtier and poet Sir Thomas Wyatt, a man fluent in Italian, was in the same party.) They headed in a triumphal progress in the direction of the Netherlands, hinting broadly at promises that were doomed never to materialise, the chief points at issue being over Milan and Burgundy. De Selve, in his capacity as ambassador, went on with the emperor to the rebellious town of Ghent. The messages he sent back to Montmorency in Paris were unacceptable to France, and relations with Charles cooled very rapidly. A discourse on the 'true and only means' to peace that he penned at this time has a faint ring of Erasmian humanism. It speaks more of the idealism befitting a bishop than the political realism expected of an ambassador. He went on with the emperor to The Hague, but he was tiring of his duties, and in letters to Paris expressed a wish to return to his diocese. In The Hague he became seriously ill with what was described as tertian fever.[64] Returning to France, he died at Lavaur within a few months – on 12 April 1541, almost eight years to the day from that which is symbolised in Holbein's double portrait. The youngest of the four men most directly concerned with the painting was therefore survived by the other three.

With Georges de Selve dead, it must have been a grievous moment for Jean de Dinteville when Pierre de Mareuil, the bitter rival to his brother François, was appointed as his old friend's successor. Jean himself was nevertheless nominally reinstated as court chamberlain at about the same time, in the household of the king's son Charles, although during his later years he lived mostly at Polisy in a state of ill health. He was afflicted by some sort of lasting paralysis after 1546, and spent much of his time resisting his brother Guillaume, who was

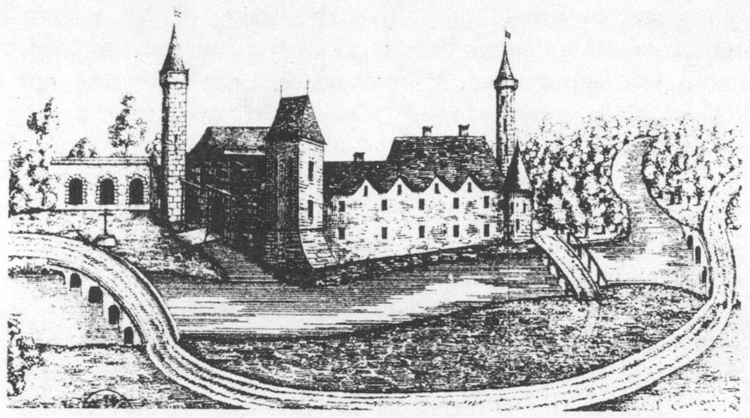

3. The château of Polisy, from a lost early seventeenth-century drawing, reproduced by Mary Hervey from the *Almanach de Bar-sur-Seine.*

trying to recover property from him. Jean gradually rebuilt and decorated his château with the help of Italian artists. His brother François also played a part in this enterprise, erecting a house in the neighbourhood which made copious use of the family arms and a motto that must have comforted rather than convinced – *Virtuti fortuna comes* (Fortune is a companion to merit).[65] Much of the remainder of the two brothers' lives was given over to the complex game of recovering royal favour, in which Jean was the more successful. A younger relative, Jean de Mergey, brought up in the château from 1547, left a short memoir in which he tells of the fame of cousin Jean, bailly of Troyes – 'governor of the duke of Orléans and ambassador to England' – and of his being unable to continue at court by reason of illness. Diplomatic skills evidently ran in the Dinteville blood.

Jean never married – his heir was his brother Guillaume, who made a brilliant military and diplomatic career for himself. The line finally became extinct in 1619. Holbein's was not his only portrait: at least three others are said to be of him. One of them with his brothers is an Old Testament allegory with a strong Roman flavour, a genre then in vogue. (Compare Henry VIII, for example, and his fondness for having himself represented as King David.) It is an allegory of the exile and sufferings of family members, and is based on a scene of Moses and Aaron before Pharaoh. François, the erstwhile bishop who had probably commissioned it, is depicted as Aaron, casting down his rod which becomes a snake. The chestnut-bearded Jean is portrayed as Moses, with the traditional golden-rayed horns issuing from his head![66]

He left no writings of an original scholarly character, but the memoir by his cousin does give us a faint hint of some academic training. 'He would take the trouble', wrote his young kinsman, 'to instruct me himself in all the sciences of which my youth was capable.' This is no more than a fragment, but it does hold open the possibility that some of the scheming that went into the Holbein portrait was done, if not with Dinteville's help, at least with his understanding. He died at Polisy in his fifty-first year, in the early months of 1555. *The Ambassadors* continued to hang in the upper great hall at Polisy for almost a hundred years thereafter. And as already explained, with the passage of time it was wrongly considered to be a portrait of the two brothers who had invested so much energy in the estate, François the bishop and Jean the ambassador.

FOUR

NICOLAUS KRATZER

> A dial is the visible Map of Time, till whose invention, the Sun seem'd to committ follie to play with a shadow . . . Heaven itself is but a general dial, and a Dial heaven in a lesser volume.
>
> Robert Hegge on Kratzer's dial at Corpus Christi College

Judged only by position, the most important part of the painting is the still life at its centre. Looking at it in this impersonal way, calling the painting 'The Ambassadors' is rather like calling a Christmas nativity 'Joseph and Mary'. Even if the centre panel is to take second place to the two human subjects, that it is somehow highly significant can hardly be doubted. When it was first produced it would have seemed intriguing and new, like Holbein's style of painting, straying beyond native English traditions. To the educated eye there would have been something familiar about its array of symbols of learning and belief, but its debts to new intellectual movements in the German-speaking world would have been plain enough. To whom do we owe it? We have already seen that Holbein collaborated with the astronomer Nicolaus Kratzer on the astronomical allegory painted on the ceiling at Greenwich in 1527. When they first met in London, they would have discovered that they had several acquaintances in common, including not only Erasmus but the scholar-poet Heinrich Glareanus. We should not forget, however, that Kratzer was the older man by ten years and already had a certain social standing in England. As late as 1533, when *The Ambassadors* was painted and when Kratzer had been in the king's employ for fifteen years, Holbein had still to appear in the royal accounts as the king's painter. Even so, they are likely to have been thrown together often. What John Rowlands has described as in many ways Holbein's 'most accomplished portrait' was the one he painted of Kratzer in 1528 (Plate 5). The astronomer sits at a table, surrounded by instruments and some of the tools for making them. It is easy to accept the judgement that, 'while it had many worthy and sometimes masterly successors, in none is the balance of interest struck so well, rightly tipping it in favour of the sitter rather than his setting'.[67] To agree with Rowlands that Holbein captures the astronomer's character, however, we first need to know what that character was.

There is much of scientific interest to be gleaned from the Kratzer portrait, and when, in a later chapter, we come to examine more closely the individual items on show in the central display of *The Ambassadors,* we shall find that they have instruments in common. This is not as surprising as the fact that there are such items present at all in the double portrait. To explain why they are there is more difficult than deciding on the likeliest person responsible, namely Kratzer, but the two questions are inevitably intertwined. It is not simply that he was available at court at the time the painting was done, or that he was a collaborator on whom Holbein would naturally have called, speaking as they did the same language. The strongest argument is that Kratzer was an expert astronomer with an unusual interest and skill in precisely the types of calculation that were necessary to the planning of the painting. Had he been no more than an artisan, working to a pattern-book designed by others, he would have merited no great attention, but he was much more than that. He was one of those wandering spirits who manage to disseminate learning, subtly changing the attitudes of those around them without necessarily breaking any new ground whatsoever. The ideas he brought to the More household, to Oxford and to the court were not new in the way that the Copernican system of the world was new, but Kratzer's contacts with the Low Countries and Vienna, and his familiarity with the latest writings of scholars in his native Bavaria, gave his activities a freshness that English scientific learning was in danger of losing. His life can tell us something of the scientific temper of the age, but also it can tell us something of the painting.

ASTRONOMY AND THE LIBERAL ARTS

Two centuries earlier, the leading centres of European astronomy – a subject that was then far and away the most advanced of the exact sciences – had been the universities of Paris and Oxford. By the early sixteenth century, they had rivals in many other parts of Europe, largely as a result of the rapid growth of the European university system and the invention of printing. Already in the mid-fifteenth century, to take a notable illustration of both of these forces for change, Georg Peurbach of the university of Vienna and his more famous pupil Regiomontanus (Johann Müller) had begun to commit to print some of the best of medieval astronomy. To the extent that they shared an ambition to recover Greek classics in astronomy and mathematics in their purest state, both men may be deemed honorary humanists. In 1472 Regiomontanus issued a prospectus with an impressive list of specific titles he planned to print at his newly established Nürnberg press, but he died before he could achieve his ambition. The importance the two men attached to texts does not mean that they ignored the practical side of astronomy, although for all too long its place in the lecture room had caused many to forget that it had empirical origins. Instrument-making was by this time beginning to help materially with its rescue, especially in the Low Countries and in such southern German cities as Nürnberg and Augsburg. New types of instruments were both a symptom and a secondary cause of vigorous new initiatives in astronomy, which would in the long run prove to be of crucial importance to the growth of western science in general. It is one of the ironies of history that astrology provided much of the motivation for those new developments.

To concentrate on astronomy in isolation would be to miss one of the most important properties of medieval and Renaissance learning, that is, its holistic character. While it is usual to describe Kratzer as an astronomer, or even more specifically as an instrument maker, like all men educated in the European university tradition his true home was the liberal arts. The seven liberal arts were the *trivium* of grammar, dialectic and rhetoric, and the more advanced *quadrivium* of the sciences, namely arithmetic, music, geometry and astronomy. To treat them as we should do today, merely as subjects into which it was convenient to divide the curriculum, would be to undervalue them seriously. Throughout the middle ages they had provided a framework that many seem to have treated as a reality mirroring that of the universe itself. They were regarded with respect and affection: it is hard to imagine a modern student of sociology or nuclear physics writing as did Dante of the liberal arts, saying of rhetoric, for example, that 'it resembled Venus in being loveliest of all the sciences'. Astronomy was the highest hurdle for the young bachelor in arts, but none could qualify without having shown competence in all seven subjects, something we should remember whenever we are tempted to dismiss a particular astronomical allegory as being too complicated for the audience of the time. It is true that the architecture of the Ptolemaic universe as understood by the ordinary student of arts was a pale shadow of what it had been in Ptolemy's monumental work, the *Almagest*, but the details of that were well known at least in the higher reaches of the universities. They had of course been steadily improved upon in the course of the fourteen centuries between his time and Kratzer's, especially in the Muslim world, but intensively also in the later middle ages in Europe.

This is not the place to write a history of European astronomy, but it is important to bear in mind a distinction between five different streams of intellectual activity connected with the subject which are easily confused. First there were those rare astronomers of genius who could create mathematical theories on the basis of observation. After them there came those capable of using astronomical theory to make accurate predictions of planetary positions and to perform a host of other calculations that for some were an end in themselves. Astronomers needed to be something less ethereal than pure mathematicians, however, if they were to be true to their subject. They needed instruments with which to make observations, measurements of the heavens; and they were grateful too for other instruments which – while not being absolutely necessary

– could ease the subsequent burden of calculation. The need for accurate instruments eventually gave rise to a separate class of artisan-astronomers, but very often the theoretical and practical sides of astronomy were the province of a single scholar, and this was so in Kratzer's case. Parasitic on the instrument makers were those who owned their work. Instruments were a useful tool for impressing colleagues or patrons or a wider public, as in the case of monumental dials and astronomical clocks in wealthier churches; but here we are leaving astronomy as such.

A fourth stream of activity might best be called cosmological. University astronomers trained in the liberal arts, and in the higher faculties of natural and metaphysical philosophy, often felt a more basic need, to explain the whys and wherefores of celestial motions. What causes the stars and planets to move as they do? Here the answers that were given usually rested heavily on the teaching of Aristotle, who had explained how motions are transmitted inwards through a succession of stellar and planetary spheres, starting with the First Mover, the *Primum Mobile,* beyond which there was nothing – neither space nor void nor time. Whether we describe this type of explanation as astronomy or physics or metaphysics will depend on our place in history, but what mattered to most Christian scholars – and we recall that almost all of them were clerics – was that it was easily adapted to a Judaeo-Christian world view. The Nothing that was outside heaven soon became the very heaven itself, in which was the abode of God and his spheres of angels. All worldly movement could therefore be very easily ascribed to the action of God, so that a certain brand of theology, the theology of the Empyreum, spilled over into astronomy.

This is one of several points at which the high academic justification of astrology crept in. It is not that astrology was new – on the contrary, it had roots that were two millennia old and more – but that Aristotelian physics, with its various types of causation, could be readily transformed into a doctrine of astrological influence. The practical details of astrology were an entirely separate question. We might think of it as astronomy's 'fifth column', for while it was intensively studied in universities it was never given great prominence in the formal curriculum. Scholars satisfied themselves that the subject was physically plausible and then were usually content to put their trust in the standard authorities, that is, in mostly Arabic astrological lore, founded on ancient principles which in many instances seem to have been plucked out of thin air. More profound spirits raised objections to the politically and theologically dangerous practices of the astrologer. Some objected to the apparent restrictions that astrology seemed to place on the freedom of the will, and hence on human responsibility. Some at times even had to warn against practices verging on pagan worship of the planetary gods. The historical record, however, proves that the temptations were all too often more powerful than the counter-arguments. There was a widespread feeling that astrology had a scientific core. Not for another century did academic astrology go into decline, and for the time being scholars cleared their consciences with the age-old escape clause: 'the stars incline but do not compel'.

WANDERING SCHOLAR

Nicolaus Kratzer was certainly familiar with our five modes of astronomical thought, although he does not seem to have been a theoretical astronomer of note. Whatever his philosophical or theological breadth and education, he was a man with a career to make and he chose a more mundane path. He moved among the wordsmiths, the contemporary humanists who now catch so much of the limelight, but he was cast in a very different mould from theirs. Born the son of a Munich sawsmith in 1487, Kratzer may have learned something of metal-working from his father, but it was not his family's intention that he should follow his father's trade.[68] He left Munich for the university of Cologne in 1506, graduating as bachelor in 1509. As it happens, he was an almost exact contemporary there of the notorious writer on alchemy and occult philosophy, Heinrich Cornelius Agrippa. From Cologne, Kratzer went to the new university at Wittenberg, some years before Luther managed to bring that insignificant provincial town in Saxony to the notice of Europe generally. The old and familiar story – invented long afterwards, but as much a part of human history as Newton and the apple – is that Luther nailed his famous Ninety-Five Theses to the wooden doors of Wittenberg castle church on 31 October 1517, 'from which moment the Reformation began'. The posting of theses for academic disputation was a standard practice – the dean of the theology faculty at Wittenberg had posted fifty-one theses earlier in the same year, and Luther's action was not in itself as intolerably defiant as it is often represented – but, true or false, Kratzer had by that time been safely away from Wittenberg for at least two years.

He was in the Carthusian monastery of Maurbach near Vienna by 1515 at the latest, and a manuscript he penned there still survives in Oxford.[69] We learn of his whereabouts in January 1517 from a letter written by Pieter Gillis, town clerk of Antwerp, informing his old teacher Erasmus that the skilled mathematician Kratzer is on his way with astrolabes and spheres and a Greek book. And then, in the following November, we have Erasmus writing from Louvain – perhaps not his first reply – in these mysterious terms:

> Admonish Nicolaus, first of all, to keep the thing secret, and to tell no one whom he is to visit in England, or who summoned him. He is to invent an excuse as far from the truth as possible. You will understand the problem from the Secretary's letter and from the spoken explanation of my [courier] James.

Erasmus added that he would go to Antwerp if it were necessary to do something 'in the affair of Nicolaus'. We can only guess at the meaning of all this.[70] Both Gillis and Erasmus were close to Thomas More, and in regular correspondence with him, so that More may have been the mysterious Englishman whom Kratzer was to visit. (Gillis was More's host in *Utopia*.) The idea is strengthened by the knowledge that Kratzer was later in his service. Erasmus had spent several years in England, largely in Cambridge (1509–14), and had been an outspoken critic of dissolute clerics, but he was always a sincere believer in the unity of the church. Those who wish to apply a label to him are often driven to see him as a pusillanimous scholar who sat on the fence, but that is partly because he recoiled from religious persecution, which he saw practised on both sides of the religious divide. He was for the time being in Brabant, where he had friends at the Habsburg court of the Netherlands. Through its chancellor, Jean Sauvage, he advised the future Emperor Charles V, and wrote works for the young man that were thinly disguised pleas for peace with France. At about the time of his letter to Gillis from Louvain, Erasmus joined the theology faculty there. He was perhaps using Kratzer to carry intelligence concerning papal initiatives in southern Germany, which might have been of value to those who wanted to cement the imperial alliance with England; or perhaps he was merely using him to carry imperial messages.

In his progress from Austria by way of the Low Countries to London, Kratzer arrived in the English capital possibly early in 1518. We soon find Henry VIII using him as he used many of the German merchants in London, to learn the intentions of the German princes. In a letter of 12 October 1520 we hear the conservative theologian Cuthbert Tunstall, writing to Henry from Liège, saying that he had met Kratzer, 'deviser of the king's horologes', in Antwerp. Kratzer, he says, had told him that he had been given leave of absence, something that seems to hint at the astronomer's dual role at the English court, for he was certainly used to carry books and papers and so presumably to gather intelligence. (Ten days after Tunstall's letter, Charles was crowned emperor at Aix-la-Chapelle.) This visit by Kratzer to the southern Netherlands was the occasion for Dürer to do a portrait of him in silver point, but it is no longer extant.

As we have already seen, Erasmus chose to leave Brabant for Basel at the end of 1521, in large part to avoid having to write a book against Luther. Four or five years later he actually published two such books, but there remained a certain ambiguity in his stance that some found irritating. Kratzer's case is to us no less ambiguous, although here the texts at our disposal are few and far between. In 1520, in a note at the front of the manuscript he penned mainly at Maurbach, Kratzer describes himself as the king's servant and as teaching at Oxford. It was in 1521 that the king summoned theologians from both Oxford and Cambridge to report on the Lutheran schism. Cardinal Wolsey commissioned certain Oxford scholars to write a defence of Catholic orthodoxy, and under pressure from him, the university of Oxford eventually condemned Luther in 1523. It was given to Kratzer to fasten the university's verdict on the sundial he had designed for the university, and Luther's books were at the same time burned publicly, in both Oxford and Cambridge. Only a year later, however, a letter that Kratzer wrote to Albrecht Dürer is couched in terms that, taken in isolation, might be construed as sympathetic to the Lutherans. Dürer had met Luther in Augsburg in 1518 and had become a devoted follower. Kratzer now alluded to this fact, adding simply 'May God send you grace so that you may be steadfast to the end, for while the opposition is strong, God is still stronger'.[71] The most we can say on this subject is that Kratzer managed to remain in the English king's service, perhaps to the end of his life. He kept his head low, but he was not of sufficient political importance for it ever to have been in much danger.

THOMAS MORE AND OXFORD

Soon after his return to England, perhaps early in 1521, Kratzer entered the service of Sir Thomas More and acted as tutor to a group that included some of More's children. His writing on the Holbein sketch of the More family, done perhaps in 1527, shows that he was still then loosely connected with the More household, although he was also drawing a regular salary of £5 per quarter from the royal purse. (This was the same salary as was given to Vincent Voulp the court painter, but it is instructive to compare it with £10 for the master of the king's hawks, £10 for the king's second physician, and £25 for the first physician.) Not only that, by 1527 Kratzer was trading in Toulouse woad and Gascon wine; and from a document of 1529 it emerges that he was prospecting for metal ores in Cornwall. Throughout the century, German expertise in the assaying, mining and smelting of ores was exploited by the Crown and by some of the great English landowners. Kratzer's was a royal commission, and he was assisted by Hugh Boyvell and Hans Bour, a compatriot. There was a less pragmatic side to Kratzer's character, however, for he played some sort of role in Cardinal Wolsey's scheme for the establishment of a new collegiate foundation at Oxford, and the circumstances tell us much about the dissemination of the kind of knowledge that Kratzer had, and that later found its way into *The Ambassadors*.

Wolsey had long entertained ambitions of this sort. Early in the sixteenth century there was a movement to institute 'public' lectures open to all members of the arts faculty, regardless of college or hall, and in 1518 Wolsey announced that he would create lectureships to this end. Some such posts seem to have been attached in his name to the newly founded Corpus Christi College – they were held by Thomas Lupset and Juan Luis Vives in humanities, by the astronomer and physician Thomas Mosgroff, and by Thomas Brinknell in theology. It was very probably in the same capacity that Kratzer, 'servant of the king', gave lectures in astronomy in 1523. Wolsey himself took astrological advice on occasion. Perhaps Kratzer was recommended by Thomas More, who was regularly in touch with Oxford University, where he was given an important judicial appointment (high steward) the following year. We recall that, after the condemnation of Luther in Oxford, Kratzer designed a pillar sundial to be placed in front of the university church and on it wrote the university's condemnation. The fact that Vives wrote elegant Latin verses for the same dial tells us something of the esteem in which an object of that kind might then be held. Different though they were in size, the university dial had much the same intellectual status as the instruments illustrated in *The Ambassadors*. They were not toys, but tokens of a highly regarded science.

It is difficult to decide on the length of time Kratzer spent in Oxford. In 1524 Wolsey was empowered by the pope to dissolve St Frideswide's priory and twenty other religious houses to provide finance and a site for a splendid new college to be called Cardinal College. In 1528 the cardinal suppressed something

4. A polyhedral dial with the arms of Cardinal Wolsey, very probably made by Nicolaus Kratzer. *(Museum of the History of Science, Oxford)*

approaching a Lutheran heresy among the ranks of his new recruits, but a year later came his fall from power, before the buildings were complete or the posts within it properly established.

By 1530 it was the king's turn to begin to whip the university into line, over the divorce question. Wolsey's institution was replaced by Henry VIII College, but on a more modest scale. Its rescue owed most to Stephen Gardiner, secretary of state, supported by Thomas More, but there is no reason for subscribing to the pious tradition that links Kratzer to it. Even the commonly accepted story that he was a fellow of Corpus Christi College may have been a later invention, although the fact that he set up a fine dial in the garden there seems to argue for some sort of connection with that new foundation. It seems likely that this college was seen only as a temporary home for Wolsey's scholars whilst Cardinal College was being built. There are remains of a crude garden dial, now in Bristol, that may well have been connected with Kratzer, but there is only one extant instrument of any complexity that is likely to have been designed and perhaps made by him, and that is a polyhedral dial ostensibly destined for none other than his patron

Wolsey (Fig. 4). It is of gilt brass and has a cardinal's hat on each of the sloping sides of the base. On the other sides are the arms of Wolsey and the arms of the cathedral church of York, Wolsey's archdiocese. The cardinal died a broken man in 1530, and this instrument was probably made at some time in the mid-1520s. It is of a general type illustrated several times over in Kratzer's Maurbach papers, a type that lent itself to portable or monumental use – whether as a garden ornament or in a more public place.

KRATZER AND THE CONTINENT

The Hansa merchants of the Steelyard in London must have played as important a part in Kratzer's life as they did in Holbein's, who before 1537 was chiefly dependent on private commissions from that source.[72] The Steelyard was a fortified complex of dwellings, offices and warehouses, a little way upstream from London Bridge on the north bank. The Baltic origins of the oak panels on which *The Ambassadors* is painted suggests that they were obtained from Hansa merchants – although not necessarily in London, for Holbein is known to have bought oak panels when passing through Antwerp in 1532.[73] In the Steelyard the two men could speak their own language, and there they are likely to have entered into a discussion of political and religious affairs abroad, and perhaps also of intellectual movements.

It is highly probable that Kratzer kept up a steady correspondence with continental scholars, but if so it is almost all lost. In the letter he wrote to Dürer in 1524, mentioned earlier as hinting at a certain sympathy with the Lutheran cause, he showed that he wished to keep in touch with friends and astronomical affairs in Germany. He was plainly on intimate terms with two men with a certain reputation in the history of astronomy, mathematics and geography, namely Johannes Werner, who had died in 1522, and Johannes Stabius, an imperial historian and cosmographer. Kratzer's short letter provides us with an insight into the variety of his activities in England. He hopes shortly to make a map of England, 'a large country unknown to Ptolemy'. Newly discovered Byzantine manuscripts of that great second-century Alexandrian astronomer's work on geography were providing the main source of inspiration for sophisticated styles in cartography. It influenced the Bavarian astronomer Peter Apian, for example, whose writings Kratzer almost certainly knew.

From Dürer's reply it appears that Kratzer had once said that he would translate Euclid's *Elements of Geometry* into German. Dürer's interests had taken a mathematical turn after travelling in Italy – some of his later statements on perspective are taken word for word from Piero della Francesca. He asked Kratzer whether he had done what he promised. The answer was fairly obviously that he had not, but this raises the question of whether Kratzer knew any Greek. This seems unlikely, unless he had been persuaded by such acquaintances as More and Vives to learn the language. He would probably have used a Latin translation of Euclid, of which there were several to be had, the best known being an old version by Campanus of Novara that was already in print (Venice, 1482). The first printed edition of the Greek eventually appeared from the press of the Basel printer Simon Grynaeus in 1533, the year of the painting. The exchange of letters with Dürer is of interest for another reason, however. The great German artist was not only an adept at the simple geometry of perspective, he had also ventured into cartography and the geometrical procedures required for global mapping when in 1515 he produced – for their mutual friend Johannes Stabius – a good perspective map of the northern and southern hemispheres.[74] The various perspective techniques, rooted in optics, geometry and astronomy, were gradually becoming not only an essential drafting tool but a modish accessory.

Kratzer of course had a larger continental acquaintance than that of most English scholars of his day, especially in the German states, and his restless spirit no doubt made him a useful courier for intelligence of value to the English crown, if only on a small scale. The shadowy details we have of his life leave us with the impression that he preferred to look down the Thames valley rather than up, and that he was as much at home in the Low Countries as in London. He is known to have visited that predominantly Catholic part of the empire on several occasions, and Vives is one of those likely to have provided him with useful insights into intellectual and political affairs there. (Movement back and forth may have been by Hansa vessels through Antwerp or even through the English town of Calais.) Vives has a high reputation today for his classical learning, his enlightened views on psychology, on the organisation of provision for the poor, on education, and especially on the education of women. He was a natural ally for his compatriot, Queen Catherine, and to please her wrote a treatise for the Princess Mary. He occupied an important place in the select network of northern Renaissance humanists, and reminds us that not all were of a reformist disposition. Moving first from Valencia to Paris, then to Bruges, he later shuttled restlessly back and forth between those cities and Oxford and London. From a material point of view, Bruges was a richer society than Oxford – indeed in 1525 Erasmus went so far as to compare the genius of the Brugeois with that of the Athenians. In the case of Vives it was also the home of his bride, the daughter of a Bruges merchant who like Vives himself was of Jewish descent. When the question of the royal divorce came to a head in the 1530s, Henry VIII found much support within the universities of Oxford and Cambridge, and yet the most distinguished of the English humanists took the other side – More and Fisher, Polydore Vergil, and Tyndale. Vives was in dangerous company. How close he was to his Bavarian colleague would have depended to some extent on where Kratzer's religious sympathies lay.

Whatever the answer, the expatriate status of the two scholars would doubtless have encouraged them to exchange views about other types of belief and institution. Vives had no real prospects of an academic chair or a princely patron, but he had built up an influential following in Louvain and his example helps us to dismiss the common idea that the type of scholarship Kratzer pursued was necessarily remote from the humanist vision. Vives's humanism did not rule out an interest in astrology. His was perhaps more the interest of a man of letters and historian than that of a total sympathiser, but he nevertheless addressed astrological, astronomical and cosmographical questions seriously, and helped to bring scholars together whose astrological tastes were less fastidious than his own. In Louvain he had befriended a young prodigy from the coastal town of Nieuwpoort, Cornelius Scepper, who was yet another scholar with tastes and interests he could share with Kratzer, with whom he had almost certainly become acquainted by October 1524 at the latest.[75] It was then that Scepper came to London as secretary-astrologer in the train of the deposed King Christian II of Denmark – a diplomat who had risen from the ranks, in his case.

That Scepper admired Kratzer is something he tells us himself. He was planning a treatise on the planetary conjunctions of 1524 that were the talk of the age – they were deemed to be astrologically relevant to the momentous religious changes that were then taking place in Europe, and were thought to signal a new Flood, although it failed to materialise. Scepper tells us of a dream he had about Kratzer that came to him after a dinner-party among friends in Antwerp, at which the astronomer had been discussed. We can only speculate about the identity of his host at dinner. Erasmus's old student Pieter Gillis knew Kratzer, and he seems a distinct possibility. While wondering whether he should dedicate his book to Kratzer, Scepper fell into a deep sleep in which he dreamed of flying on winged horses with a handsome young man. (Did Gillis describe Kratzer so, or had Scepper met him previously?) Together, in time-honoured fashion, they flew over many lands, among them Thomas More's Utopia. They eventually found themselves witnessing a battle, an allegory of the battle between astrology and religion. There was a Fortress of Faith, which armies led by Henry VIII and Charles V were trying to enter by military and literary means. (Note the political alliance being postulated.) Scepper himself gained entrance through a combination of humanistic and Christian virtues.

The point he was making most forcibly was that even Christian astrologers are generally unreliable, especially when they try to show that the manner of Christ's death was to be foretold from His birth horoscope. No doubt Scepper was implicitly recommending himself as a true Christian astrologer, worthy of a better court position than that he already had. We are reminded that a court astrologer without a second string to his bow was in a vulnerable position. In Kratzer's case it was horology and teaching, while many a court astrologer was primarily a physician. In Scepper's case the second string was diplomacy. He was sent off to Madrid soon afterwards, and for many years lived the existence of a relatively insignificant diplomat, moving back and forth between there, London and the Low Countries. In Madrid, Scepper was able to discuss questions of astrology and religion with the Polish ambassador and astronomer, Johannes Dantiscus. We may assume that Kratzer would have had much to discuss with him in London. One of the assets of the expert astrologer was that he could deal in materials that were of interest at the highest political level. When Scepper's astrology touched on politics he was criticised by Phillip Melanchthon, but only to have some of his imperial horoscopes appropriated by his critic. We have no documentary evidence that Kratzer dabbled extensively in such waters, but it is important to recognise that had he done so he would have been entirely typical of his age. We do know that he copied out snippets of astrological material into his notebooks.

Kratzer's astronomical knowledge was not only, or even chiefly, derived from his contemporaries. It was well and truly bedded in the past, if we are to judge by the few fragments and three modest manuscripts which survive from his pen. The most interesting of the manuscripts is the one that he copied – as his opening inscription in it tells us – from texts he found in his Carthusian monastery at Maurbach, 'two miles from Vienna'. The items the volume contains do not all date from that period of his life, but probably span the period from around 1515 to 1523. They include fifteen or more medieval Latin astronomical texts, mostly having to do with instruments, together with a few fragments, some in German. There are a few astrological notes interspersed, while another text deals with the arithmetic of fractions, a subject of some relevance to *The Ambassadors*.[76] What is surprising is that, out of about a dozen instruments discussed at length in the bound volume, only two are of a sort even roughly approximating to those illustrated in either that painting or Holbein's portrait of Kratzer – one of them being a torquetum and the other a ten-faced polyhedral sundial. (Their purposes will be discussed more fully in the following chapter.) One interesting aspect of the manuscript is that, while most of the paper bears watermarks that are known from books printed in Innsbruck and Augsburg, some of the paper seems to have originated in Italy – Vicenza and Venice being the most likely sources. It is therefore not inconceivable that Kratzer followed the road to Italy at some stage, just as Holbein seems to have done.

KRATZER AT COURT

Both of the other two surviving Kratzer manuscripts of any substance describe an instrument that he called his *horoptrum*. The finer of the two manuscripts was intended as a New Year's present for the king himself, and was copied out by John Colet's Brabantine scribe and letter carrier, the one-eyed Peter Meghen. It opens with an elaborate decorated initial by Holbein, and dates from 1528 – the year of the Kratzer portrait – so that it must be counted as one of our earliest pieces of firm evidence for the collaboration of Holbein and Kratzer.[77] (The earliest is the evidence for their collaboration on the painted zodiac ceiling in the early part of 1527, already described.) There is no illustration of the *horoptrum*, but we can picture it well enough. It was on a rectangular card, possibly mounted on wood, in the middle of which was a circular calculating device that drew heavily on the principles of the astrolabe. Astrolabes were the most widely dispersed astronomical instruments of any complexity available between classical times and the seventeenth century. They could be used for observation of the heavens as well as for many types of calculation, and there were several listed in the inventory of Henry VIII's possessions compiled at his death. The *horoptrum* was a much simpler affair, abstracting only what was needed to calculate the daily movements of the Sun across the sky, rather than those of the heavenly bodies generally. (Perhaps one of the insufferably vague descriptions of instruments in the inventory was of just such a device.)[78] Flanking it were various charts giving auxiliary information, such as the fixed feasts of the church year (according to the Sarum calendar, as commonly used in England), the means of determining the movable feasts of the Christian year (the so-called 'Sunday letters', and so forth), and the changing daily positions of the Sun. This was in truth a rather inaccurate device, working only to degrees and not fractions of degrees, and the king's knowledge would not have been very seriously taxed by it, bearing in mind that he had taken some instruction in astronomy from Thomas More.

While it does not concern Kratzer directly, Holbein's earlier involvement in illustrating yet another astronomical work is of some interest, if only to show that the painter himself was not entirely foreign to this kind of subject-matter. Anonymous woodcuts designed by Holbein were used to illustrate a work by Sebastian Münster, a Franciscan astrologer and geographer who had turned to Protestantism when he went to Basel in 1529. The book deals with an instrument known as a *luminarium,* one by

CANONES SVPER
NOVVM INSTRVMENTVM LVMINARIVM, DOcentes quo pacto per illud inueniantur Solis & Lunæ medij & ueri motus, lunationes, coniunctiones, oppoſitiones, caput draconis, eclipſes, horæ inæquales, & nocturnæ æquales, ortus ſolis & occaſus, aſcendens cœli, interuallum, aureus numerus, &c. Per Sebaſt. Munſterum.

5. Title page to Sebastian Münster, *Canones super novum instrumentum luminarium* (Basel, 1534), after a design by Holbein.

which the principal types of astronomical calculation concerning Sun and Moon could be fairly easily carried out. The work was widely circulated in Latin in a Basel edition of 1534 (see Fig. 5), but an earlier version printed in German with Holbein's illustration pre-dated *The Ambassadors*.[79]

There is further evidence of close collaboration between the two satellites at the English court, this time from the very end of Holbein's life. Kratzer annotated a design by Holbein for a 'clocksalt' that was commissioned by the king's chamberlain, Anthony Denny, and that was presented to the king as a New Year's gift in 1544. It was an elaborate sand-glass, topped by a double sundial with putti holding rods as gnomons. The dials, and Kratzer's annotations, strongly suggest that he was concerned with the overall design. Since his notes refer to the presentation in the past tense, they must have been added after Holbein's death.[80]

Long before, in 1531, Kratzer had been paid 40 shillings for mending a clock. This was a considerable sum of money, and seems to indicate that an elaborate mechanism was involved, but it should not tempt us to read Tunstall's 1520 reference to him – 'deviser of the king's horologes' – as an allusion primarily to mechanical clocks, or even to them at all. At the time *The Ambassadors* was painted, Kratzer was surely much the same person as when Holbein painted him in 1528. In that portrait he is caught in the act of assembling a polyhedral sundial, a 'horologe' of a mechanically simpler but intellectually more taxing sort, with the tools of a maker of such devices close at hand (Plate 4). Apart from the finer tools on the table, there are others hanging on the wall which would have been useful only for large-scale work in either carpentry or masonry, possibly for monumental dials. Presumably they too were his. There is no reason to think of Kratzer, son of a humble sawsmith, as a craftsman in the same league as some of the king's French artisans. That was not his chosen métier, but to repair is not to make. Perhaps there is more to that word 'deviser' than meets the eye. The design of trains of wheels for clocks with astronomical dials was something he could well have undertaken. There were more than seventy mechanical timepieces distributed around Henry VIII's various palaces at the time of his death, as the 1547 inventory shows, and several of them are likely to have had a much coveted astronomical display.

THE MIND'S CONSTRUCTION

One story told of Kratzer has become so distorted over the years that he is occasionally described as having known no English. The story originated with a Dutch visitor, who tells us that in answer to the king's question as to why he could not speak *better* English, Kratzer replied 'Forgive me, your majesty, but how much English can one learn in only thirty years?' The language in which that story was told was Dutch, and the visitor could not even say whether Kratzer himself was German or Dutch. Even through such a linguistic veil – and even for those unfortunate enough to have had no personal experience of the situation – it should not be difficult to appreciate the point of the story. It was obviously a standing joke, and was in keeping with Kratzer's reputation, judging by the dedicatory letter to the book of 1536 by Nicolas Bourbon. The letter carries greetings to friends, including Kratzer, 'the wanton, facetious and witty king's astronomer'. Those who had read Kratzer's verse, written for the university dial, would have known one side of his humour. On it he boasted of his capacity, and that of the stonecutter William East, for drinking beer in the German manner. This was not a common scholarly convention. Certainly his erstwhile colleague Vives had very different sensibilities, regarding strong drink as an iniquity almost as culpable as scholastic philosophy. But Vives was of an unbending nature – a fact that led to a period of imprisonment for his resistance to Henry's divorce of Catherine of Aragon. Kratzer was made of a more malleable metal.

Are we entitled to read Kratzer's character from his face in Holbein's portrait of him? Oscar Bätschmann and Pascal Griener give away their own attitudes to the mathematical sciences when they try to do so. In the picture, they say,

> science is celebrated through the depiction of a close friend; but the cold, absent, gaze of the sitter, his immobility, the

> colour of his face, so similar to that of the wood he is shown carving, everything turns him into the *Typus geometriae.*

That last allusion is to a woodcut included in Gregorius Reisch's popular scientific encyclopaedia of 1505, in which a geometer sits at a table surrounded by geometrical figures while others perform geometrical tasks. Such things are plainly not to everyone's taste. But then the latter-day vision of the cold absent gaze of a friend leads on to a conclusion that concerns not just Kratzer but *The Ambassadors.* While they say that the portrait of the astronomer 'may be read as a celebration of science', they add that in the later painting the space of the *theatrum mundi,* the theatre of the world, 'in the light of that same science, is denounced as a pale illusion soon destined to be ravaged by Death'.[81] This cheerless judgement will perhaps strike a chord in the hearts of many of their readers, but I can only say that I think that Kratzer, and even Holbein, would have been horrified. It is not that the portrait of Kratzer conveys the impression of a vivacious individual – far from it – but that creating *The Ambassadors* must have meant more to the two friends than solemn moralising about the bloodless body of science. While it can never be proved conclusively that Kratzer collaborated with Holbein on the painting, we shall eventually be forced to conclude that a scholar with precisely Kratzer's talents was needed for its design, and that he remains far and away the most likely candidate.

If Kratzer was truly thirty years in England then he lived beyond 1548. Two documents by him dated 1546, which surfaced in the library of Otto Henry, prince of the Palatinate, may indicate a return to Germany, or merely further travels at the end of his days. Nicolaus Prugner, a Tübingen professor of astronomy, mentions him in the preface of a book published in Basel in 1550, and it seems that he may still have been alive then.[82] A London letter, now badly burnt, which he wrote to Thomas Cromwell in 1538, shows that he married when he was about fifty and had at least one child. There was something to be said for Protestantism after all. One can only hope that he was kinder to his family than was Holbein to his wife and children in Basel – but then, Holbein had children in London too.

PART TWO

The Painting

The piece is esteemed the richest and best wrought to be found in all of France.

Memorandum of 1653 on the de Selve family[83]

FIVE
STRANGE DEVICES

To describe . . . how usuall howers may be (by the Sunnes shadow) truly determined, will be found no sleight Painters worke.

John Dee, Preface to H. Billingsley's translation of Euclid's *Elements* (London, 1570), p. 37

Holbein's *The Ambassadors* can in many respects speak for itself. It lends itself to being broken up into its constituent parts – some have even said to advantage. Either of the superb portraits of Dinteville and de Selve could stand alone, half-length or full, and a dozen still-life studies could be taken out of the centre of the panel, each worthy of regard in its own right. On our left stands Dinteville, with a slashed pink satin shirt over a fine white undershirt: the latter is pulled through the slashings to produce the blistered effect that was then so fashionable. His doublet is of knee length, and has a rich black velvet skirt. Over that he wears a jerkin of black satin trimmed with velvet and lynx fur – lucern, as it was usually called in English at the time. (The fur is surprisingly free from the typical mottling of lynx except at its lower ends, where its markings show plainly that it is not ermine. The hair of ermine is in any case shorter.) The lynx fur was incidentally a mark of rank, for like black genet and sable its use was restricted to the upper nobility both in England and France by various strict sumptuary laws. The jerkin's short cut was sported by younger men of fashion in Paris and London at this time, and the shoulders are fashionably well padded and broad. The doublet is open below the waist, and reveals the merest hint of a codpiece, to which the recent restoration did not try to do justice. Belts had by the 1530s given way to cords or sashes such as Dinteville wears. His secures his sword, of which we can see the guard to the right of the medallion and the point directed to the lute case on the floor behind him. His stockings seem to be of heavy silk, and two garters are visible round his left knee. His shoes are bun-toed, as worn by most people of wealth or position, old or young, at the time. Dinteville's hat has a mildly French character, although it differs only trivially from that worn by some of Holbein's young English sitters. If the ambassador's aristocratic status is not evident from his dress, his gold accoutrements put it beyond all doubt: the dagger handle and case, the gold wire in the tassel, the hat badge, the fibulas in his puffed sleeves, and above all else his chain with the medallion of the order of St Michael.

On our right is the bishop of Lavaur, in a long, purplish brown, double-breasted robe of brocaded velvet. Lined most probably with sable, it is of a richer quality than anything a member of the lesser clergy is likely to have worn, and its brocade patterning is very striking. De Selve's shoes are of a more restrained design than his friend's. He has a neck-cloth – hardly an amice – and carries gloves, of which more in due course. He is not dressed for the celebration of mass: his is seemingly a bishop's court dress, although it could also have been worn for services other than mass. His square black cap is of a kind worn by many clergy of the time when preaching, walking abroad, or at 'choir services' generally. It does not have the ear flaps worn by many clerics, both in England and on the Continent, but it is in a style that has not yet evolved into the stiff biretta of later centuries.

Such things might seem obvious – although the details of my description would probably not have satisfied a master of the wardrobe – but the overall design of the painting is quite certainly not so, and will be found only if we are prepared to take a few steps into the Renaissance world of learning. Holbein's collaboration with Kratzer during his first visit to England, and their continuing friendship, should at least make us question the idea that the astronomical, musical, and other instruments and books were scattered around the scene merely 'to establish an academic context', or 'to raise the painting's learned tone'. Like its devotional content – such as the Lutheran hymnal on the lower shelf and the crucifix half-concealed by the green brocaded curtain behind – these objects will prove to have been introduced in ways that were highly contrived. For that simple reason, it must be supposed that they were meant to point to a deeper meaning than any conveyed at first sight.

There is nothing else in Holbein's oeuvre with which the overall composition of the work can be compared. It will eventually prove possible to relate the notorious distorted skull to the astronomical instruments, to the calendar, to the theology of the time, to astrology, and perhaps in a distant sense even to magic. Through these various subjects Holbein touched on a unifying theme about which medieval and Renaissance academic writers seem never to have tired of writing, the half-pagan, half-Christian, theme of cosmic harmony. But his painting makes a statement that for those around him was of far greater moment than this. In ways to be explained, it was also an affirmation of a Christian's faith in God's saving grace. This reading need not detract from the now conventional idea that Holbein's work was hinting at the growing discord within church and state, a discord that his ambassadorial sitters hoped to put to rights. That sentiment might well have given the work some of its resonance, but it would have taken second place to what in Holbein's day was a truth of far greater importance to Christians of all persuasions, but in the painting concealed many times over.

LINES AND METHOD

Our analysis of the plan underlying *The Ambassadors* will in many respects be out of key with current fashion. Art historians are rightly suspicious of those who superimpose lines on paintings, unless the lines are drawn to support an idea for which they believe they have clear textual evidence. That is a wonderful escape clause, since – with a few notable exceptions, such as Leonardo da Vinci and Albrecht Dürer – great painters are not usually writers. Worded commentary for which there are no historical words in support is for some strange reason acceptable but, with a few honorable exceptions, geometrical lines are anathema. (The exceptions have mostly to do with perspective constructions, which are fairly easily put to the test, especially when they go with chequered pavements or rectangular buildings.) The reasons usually offered for this state of mind are of various sorts, ranging from a half-learned lesson in philosophical scepticism – which could at least have some merit – to an argument that has virtually none, namely that since absolute precision in measuring a painting is impossible, one can never establish a painter's intentions from paint alone. An even worse argument is that since it is possible to superimpose composition-lines on a painting in many different ways none can be acceptable.

Merely uttering the name of Piero della Francesca is often used as a substitute for all argument, as though it were a magic spell. The reason is that much recent discussion of the general problem has centred on analyses of Piero's work, and in particular on his *The Baptism of Christ.* It may seem odd to begin an account of Holbein's work with reference to a painting done in Italy more than eighty years earlier, but the debate that has turned around it does have a bearing on our reading of *The Ambassadors.* Not only does it offer us an object lesson in how not to proceed, it may be used to illustrate briefly and easily two very different approaches to the general problem of unravelling a painter's formal intentions, approaches that will need to be very clearly distinguished at a later stage. It also underlines the importance of biography and mathematical taste.

Piero della Francesca (1415/20–1492) lived most of his life in the town of Sansepolcro in the Florentine Republic. The son of a prosperous artisan, he was moderately well educated in literary and mathematical studies, and later in life had intellectual connections with Renaissance scholars in Ferrara and Rimini. It is important to notice that he was a good mathematician, not perhaps the genius he is often made out to be, but a man unusually well versed in the best of classical geometry (that of Archimedes, as well as Euclid's, which was then far better known), in arithmetic, and in some out-of-the-way medieval contributions to mathematics. Late in life he wrote two substantial and commendable mathematical text books. One was on the five regular geometrical solids known as the Platonic solids – the cube, tetrahedron, octahedron, icosahedron and dodecahedron. The other was on the abacus – a calculating table or frame. The second also contained much practical geometry, including items on the Platonic solids and on how to calculate their properties.[84] He is often credited with the first description of an instrument for producing perspective drawings. Under these circumstances, it would not be at all surprising to find evidence that he painted according to carefully calculated geometrical patterns, and this despite the fact that his various writings make no clear reference to the use of mathematical forms or symbolism in painting. Evidence that he did so is notoriously difficult to appraise. Kenneth Clark, in his important study of Piero, calls *The Baptism of Christ* 'the least rigidly mathematical' of all his paintings, but still does not hesitate to add that in it 'we are at once conscious of a geometric framework', and that a 'a few seconds' analysis shows us that it is divided into thirds horizontally and into quarters vertically'. Attempts to extend or to refute the conclusions of those few seconds of analysis have provided Clark's professional colleagues with many hours, indeed in some cases years, of employment. His words prompted B. A. R. Carter to publish a more intricate analysis of the *Baptism* in 1981.[85]

Piero's painting is ostensibly much simpler than Holbein's, in that it seems to embody a complex geometrical plan but no astronomy. For this very reason it lends itself more readily to an illustration of certain general principles. Consider the problem from the point of view of the painter. It is undeniable that it is possible to draw a geometrical figure – a triangle, a circle, or whatever – and then to superimpose on it human figures, trees, buildings, landscapes, or whatsoever the artist chooses. Perhaps relatively few great painters have ever worked in this rigidly controlled way, but the technique is certainly a workable one. The *form* of the original geometrical figure may in such a case have been prompted by one of at least two motives. The artist may simply have found the form aesthetically pleasing; or it might have symbolised for him something deeper – as when a triangle was used to represent the Holy Trinity, for example.

Even granting that there is a scheme present in a painting, uncovering it is bound to be difficult unless we are able to decide somehow between those two motives. In both cases, to uncover the plan it will also be necessary to have a good idea of the sorts of *objects* that the painter would have wanted to place in significant positions on it to mark out its form. In the second case, it will be necessary to know something more. We shall need to be aware of the most important *symbolic forms* that the artist might be expected to have used – a triangle might have been used for the Holy Trinity, perhaps, but not in the sixteenth century for an area in the neighbourhood of Bermuda, to take an exaggerated illustration of the importance of biography and historical context.

Most criticism of attempts to determine the geometrical plan that a painter may have used starts from the very obvious fact that joining up conspicuous items in a painting is a doubly dangerous activity, since those items can rarely be identified with precise points, and since there may be very many objects that catch the attention, and many seemingly plausible alternative schemes in which they are joined together. There is hardly an object, hardly a splash of paint, that cannot be found a meaning, a reason for supposing that it might have been deliberately placed in line with others. A tree? Ancestry! A bird? Freedom! A river? Time! An eye? Knowledge! If such readings of a particular painting do not fit with your preconceived ideas about the painter's intentions – so the sceptic's argument goes – then you are likely to change them until they do fit. How can I trust you not to force the evidence until it fits, say with the help of nothing more than Roget's *Thesaurus,* or some text more appropriate to the historical period. A tree? The Tree of Knowledge! A bird? The Dove of the Holy Spirit! A river? The Washing Away of Sins! An eye? The Eye of God! Faced with almost endless opportunities for wishful thinking, where are we to turn? The easiest way out of the difficulty is to stick to technique, to biography, to social context, to patronage, to history generally – in short, to worded commentary – and to leave drawing lines on paintings to those lacking in sensibility.

Those who are not so easily frightened should remember that

there is a two-way process that puts them in a rather similar position to that of the experimental scientist, who knows that data do not always come in neat packages in advance of theory. Thus to take a make-believe illustration: one art historian might have decided on the basis of wider evidence that Renaissance artists who painted on square panels tended to divide them into four equal horizontal strips, that is, that they tended to follow a geometrical *rule*. That scholar may discover only at a late stage that the angels' eyes in Piero's painting (five eyes are to be seen) are on a horizontal line quartering the rectangular area of the painting, so apparently *confirming* the rule. Another person, however, might have begun from the idea that *eyes* are commonly found on the list of what I have called 'conspicuous items'. The line of five eyes might then draw that person's attention to the *possibility* that there was a rule of quartering being adopted in this painting. (Indeed, since the eyes of Jesus and John the Baptist are on a parallel line that comes close to a *fifth* of the way down the main square, the rule might be thought worth extending – or even rejecting. Such complications do not affect the distinction we are drawing.) There are advantages and disadvantages in both approaches. It is probably true to say that most of those analysts who join up 'significant points' have a rough idea at the outset of what it is they hope to find. Like those who set up an *ad hoc* scientific theory, even as a hypothesis, they are likely to be accused of prejudging the issue, and of making self-fulfilling prophecies. This in itself is no sin. There is much uninformed criticism of such procedures, especially in the art-historical world. The chief sin is in drafting the prophecy so loosely that it is bound to be fulfilled. Almost as serious is the sin of ignoring unpalatable evidence, which in the art-historical case means ignoring contemporary practice and belief. In fact the main difference between this and the scientific case is the added complication of the artist's intentions, which invariably means adding not only a psychological but a historical dimension.

No attempt to discover the hidden forms that may lie beneath a painting is likely to pass entirely beyond the realm of conjecture unless written testimony, X-ray evidence of the painting, or something of the sort, can be found proving the existence of an overpainted geometrical figure. That is not a reason for abandoning hope. Like its twin 'speculation', 'conjecture' is a word that is often regarded as pointing to a worthless activity, but most knowledge, not only scientific knowledge, progresses by conjecture and tentative solutions. Conjecture and speculation may turn out to be unjustified or even unjustifiable, but if kept under control by criticism their resistance to refutation gives us a rough measure of their worth. What lies at the end of the road is not certainty but – given good fortune – a strong moral conviction. I have no doubt whatsoever that Holbein laid out his painting with the help of a handful of lines that were worked out for him by Kratzer, but even a resolute sceptic ought to agree that, whether or not it leads to conviction, presentation of the evidence may be worthwhile for any insights it yields along the way. There is, for example, quite certainly one (half-visible) star-hexagram in Holbein's painting that needs to be explained, but I have given reasons for thinking that there is another, wholly concealed within its plan. Reject the one and you still have the problem of explaining the other. Does either of them hint at alchemy, astrology, theology, or some other subject, esoteric or otherwise? While favouring one answer over the rest, I have thought it necessary to explore the others, however lightly. It is not enough to base ourselves on Holbein's supposed character and habit alone, without reference to external influence.

In deciding whether a tentative hypothesis deserves to be taken seriously, a knowledge of past mentalities is indispensable. Was the painter a Protestant or a Catholic, an alchemist or an astrologer, a mathematician or a farmer? There are historians who become obsessed with intellectual affairs simply because they are reasonably accessible. That obviously cannot of itself guarantee them relevance. Suppose that someone formulates the theory that when a Renaissance painter touches on a theme related to heaven he is likely to have made use of a plan involving a circle, the sphere being the universally accepted form of the heavens. Perhaps the idea was inspired by leafing through that famous Book of Hours known as the *Très riches heures,* painted by the Limburg brothers for the duke of Berri, in which every scene has a semicircular top representing a part of the zodiac. We look at Piero's *Baptism of Christ* and find something similar. But no, the sceptic replies, the semicircular top means only that the painting was done for the central section of an altarpiece (in the chapel of St John the Baptist, Borgo Sansepolcro). To this the proud maker of the hypothesis answers that there is no absolute necessity to paint altarpiece panels with tops that are round rather than square. But was there not perhaps a common *tradition* of round-topped panels in polyptychs in Italy? The evidence is reviewed in the hope of finding out. And so the debate may continue, without hope of an absolutely demonstrable conclusion, in the absence of a statement of intent (possibly in the form of an underdrawing) on the part of the artist, but hopefully with a relative strengthening of one hypothesis or another along the way. This is a common enough situation in the humanities, where weighing the evidence requires more than blind scepticism and the bald assertion that one is not convinced. It requires intelligent and constructive scepticism, and with good fortune a hypothesis may point to unforeseen consequences that can themselves be put to the test.

The most basic hypothesis is not that this or that geometrical scheme was chosen, but that that there is a hidden scheme there at all. The obvious symmetries of Piero's painting encourage the assumption in his case, even if they do not prove it. Of course, what is to count as obvious is no straightforward matter. Once we feel reasonably sure that the exercise is worth pursuing, we explore as many historically plausible possibilities as we can find, and rank them as best we can, again with reference to historical circumstance. I have elsewhere suggested an alternative explanation of the plan of Piero's painting, differing slightly from Carter's.* In a book about Holbein its details are less important than the handful of general truths that the case of Piero illustrates, one of the most important of which concerns a question of aesthetics.

* See Appendix 1.

Assume that the idea that a particular artist worked to some or other geometrical plan seems inescapable, but that – as in Piero's case – there are alternatives to consider. In selecting from among them, aesthetic qualities will be called into the reckoning that require an appreciation of *mathematical* relationships. The qualities in question are those of the suggested schemes underlying the painting, and not of what is to be more immediately perceived in it. They are the qualities that mathematicians have in mind when they speak of elegance in a proof, and they depend to some extent on simplicity and economy. There is nothing new in this, but it is a truth that is better experienced by those who have struggled with particular mathematical examples than by those who are content to parrot the much-quoted sayings of Pythagoras or Plato on this point. And once the point is admitted, it will be a rash person indeed who insists that Piero della Francesca, an excellent mathematician who delighted in geometrical construction and calculation, is unlikely to have based any of his paintings on a carefully contrived mathematical plan – and I do not mean a trivial division of his panels into thirds, fourths and fifths. Appreciating the point does not of itself prove that he played such games, but if – as seems likely – he did so, then deciding between proposed mathematical schemes will clearly demand some first-hand sense of what mathematicians find, or might have found, appealing. And where a love of mathematics cannot provide a likely motive, we shall need to search other branches of Renaissance learning on which the artist might have drawn. In the case of *The Ambassadors*, there is an overwhelming sense that we are in the province not of geometry pure and simple but of cosmography, the representation of the entire universe. There, in addition to a strong sense of harmony and scientific propriety, scholars believed there to be profound links with human destiny. Whether or not there was any consciousness of them in Holbein's painting, they will certainly not be detected by those who have never been introduced to them.

ON DETECTING ANOMALY

Passing beyond the supposed truths of the sciences of the day, there is also the possibility that the artist has introduced an element of paradox. Many of those who have looked closely at the scientific 'still life' at the centre of Holbein's painting have claimed to detect anomalies in it. How are we to decide on what is artificial or anomalous? Unless it is oddly positioned, an utter commonplace cannot be an effective symbol, since by definition it cannot draw attention to itself. (Even a seeming commonplace that is being used to shock requires an inappropriate setting.) Take the name 'Polisy', which is marked near the central meridian of the terrestrial globe. It is no accident that the name of Dinteville's château is marked on a globe that is not shown in enough detail even to display the name of London, where it was painted. That piece of symbolism, at least, seems plain enough, but it leaves unanswered questions of reality and illusion. Does Holbein's having painted the name of Polisy on the globe mean that it is an imaginary globe, only painted to flatter the Seigneur de Polisy? Or was it a real globe, made or modified in this way, one that might in principle turn up tomorrow? The answer may turn out to be central to the understanding of some contrived scheme that is not immediately obvious, and there are many other aspects of the painting that may be thought to depict quite unreal situations about which the same might be said. What of them?

Deliberate distortion must have some purpose, as Susan Foister tacitly acknowledges:

> It is difficult to avoid the conclusion that either the instruments are no more than an elaborate backdrop suggesting the passing of time, for which accuracy of depiction seems to have been unnecessary, or that they are deliberately intended to be read as mis-depicted and mis-set, to suggest that the times are somehow 'out of joint'.[86]

This conclusion seems to have become an accepted part of the modern folklore of *The Ambassadors*, and it is utterly mistaken, but not because it is unprincipled. It is simply based on misinformation, not on instinct, but that does not make it any the less dangerous. For some of those who are mesmerised by the painting's complexity, instinct has a habit of taking over. Since positional astronomy and geometry try modern patience, we seem to hear the subconscious refrain 'Let it not be too complex'. This tends to lead on to a high-handed dismissal of the 'scientific props', the items in it that are no longer of interest – 'the table is strewn with astronomical paraphernalia', and so on. Other commentators are prepared to acknowledge the 'props' as broadly symbolic of the liberal arts, but nothing more. Such analyses are merely superficial. To read deep meaning into supposedly deliberate error is not trivial, but it does require us to be sure that the error is there and is deliberate.

Taste is often the enemy of understanding. It can make us so certain that we know the gist of the painting that we are content to ignore what does not fit with our views. There have been commentaries that have failed to mention the crucifix in the upper left corner, for example, and that have been accompanied by reproductions of the painting with the crucifix trimmed off. This habit can be traced back to a period when the crucifix, like the curtain, was overpainted in a 'dark heavy green', until the overpainting was removed in the first National Gallery restoration by William Morrill and William Dyer in 1891.[87] Whether or not, conversely, understanding is the enemy of taste, it will be necessary to begin by studying closely the scientific instruments in the painting as a means to gauging its intellectual depth. Only then can we move on to its possible meaning. After the next two chapters, when our guide to the instruments is out of the way, we shall come to the perspective of the skull, which truly marks the beginning of the path to the chief of the painting's hidden qualities. All this will require a relatively straightforward application of astronomy and geometry, which will not be to everyone's taste, but is something on which it is not unreasonable to expect a consensus among informed critics. These chapters are not based on a scrying of symbols. Writing about an artist's geometrical or astronomical plans is in some respects much easier than writing, say, about his use of pigment and colour, of light or of texture. Those who say that three points are in a line or that four are on a circle, or that a column is vertical, or that the Sun is too large in relation to the Moon, can be charged with inducing boredom but not with making entirely unverifiable utterances. And they can at least check their own consciences. There are others who will insist, for example, that an artist delights in shadows for their own sakes, that he creates a poignant atmosphere from his frugal use of expensive pigments, or that he shapes the world out of the clay of Greek philosophies that sit uneasily together. Such critics inhabit a higher critical world, in which they should expect to be judged by very different criteria. The two worlds may be very different, but neither has access to certain conclusions, and both suffer from critics who think it enough to issue the bald and unqualified assertion 'I simply cannot agree'. Most people would much sooner read the great art critics – sages, satirists and prophets such as John Ruskin and Kenneth Clark – than a treatise on celestial geometry or perspective, but circumstances alter cases. Just as a ruler is useless for measuring the emotions, so a poem is not much of a tool for drawing a line, and if the artist is suspected of having played with a ruler and compasses when he was at work, then it is irresponsible to leave the question of why he did so unexplored.

SIX
INSTRUMENTS FOR THE HEAVENS

Not every kind of knowledge is called an art, but only that which becomes a rule for doing something. Those things that happen at random or by chance are not done by art – as, for example, the picture of a horse foaming at the mouth, which was the result of the painter's having thrown a sponge at the picture in a fit of anger.

Juan Luis Vives, *De disciplinis* (Antwerp, 1531), i, ch. 2, alluding to Pliny, *Natural History,* xxxv

It can hardly have been by accident that the instruments standing on the upper shelf of the table at the heart of the painting were all designed to reflect on the state of the heavens, while those on the lower level were concerned with the affairs of the world below. The distinction would not have been the simple modern one between 'above' and 'below', however, for when Aristotle ruled in the universities there were thought to be fundamental differences between the two regions, between the laws, for example, that operate above and below the sphere of the Moon. It may be asking too much to bear these distinctions in mind as we review the various artefacts on display: it will be more rewarding in the first instance to scrutinise them individually – not as an exercise in the history of instrumentation, but because interpreting the painting will depend to a surprising degree on small points of detail in them which have previously been overlooked, or dismissed as signs of ignorance or carelessness on Holbein's part. It will be necessary to show that such criticism has entirely missed the point. The painting has many interlocking layers of meaning which are heavily dependent on a grand geometrical plan, and in that plan each of the objects on the table has its part to play.

With a few exceptions, the descriptions that follow will be stripped of speculation as to any symbolic role the items in the still life may have played. The panel went to Polisy, presumably within a few months of its execution. Jean de Dinteville was plainly its intended owner, so that any deliberately concealed meaning is likely to have conformed to his general outlook, even if the painting was commissioned by Georges de Selve as a gift for him. This is to say very little, since what we know about his mentality is very slight. It would be a great mistake to try at the outset to project what is known of his biography and political aspirations on the painting, or those of de Selve, even though it is a portrait of them. To do so would be to reduce all life to public show. No doubt they were privy to Holbein's design, but in the end we shall find nothing in the main theme of the painting that would have been unacceptable to any ordinary educated Christian scholar of the time. The underlying truth was a religious commonplace, but that is not to say that it would have been apparent without a guide. And an act of concealment can itself have meaning.

THE CELESTIAL GLOBE AND HOLBEIN'S VIEWPOINTS

Of all the astronomical objects on the table, it seems that the most aesthetically appealing has always been the conspicuously placed celestial globe at Dinteville's elbow (Plate 6). On such a globe the brightest stars in the heavens are represented, grouped into constellations that are depicted in fairly conventional ways by suitable figures. Apart from the bird now usually known as Cygnus, the Swan, we can see much of Cepheus, for example, and parts of his daughter Andromeda. (It is her inelegant leg that points upwards from the horizon ring at the right-hand side.) The winged horse, often called Pegasus, is largely visible on the globe, but below the horizon. (Did Kratzer have an attachment to flying horses, as Scepper's dream might suggest?) There are many more constellations that one can make out with some difficulty, using such a map of the heavens as Albrecht Dürer's (Fig. 7).

The idea behind such a globe is that the sphere of the stars, at the centre of which we conceive ourselves to be, turns roughly

6. The celestial globe. For more detail see Plate 6.

once a day around the polar axis, and that what is in principle visible above our horizon at a given moment will correspond to what can be seen on the hemisphere of the globe that lies above its horizon ring. (One may see no stars at night, but the globe would have allowed an astrologer, for example, to take them into account.) The sky is also divided by the ring passing through the poles and containing the meridian circle. The north pole of the globe is towards the viewer of the painting, and a small graduated dial is centred on it, with a pointer. This can be used for calculations requiring a knowledge of the rotation of the globe, such as a calculation of the time of day. (The rotation, the 'hour angle', is conventionally measured in hours and minutes rather than in degrees, but it is to be considered an angle, even so. The small scale is accordingly graduated in hours and fractions of an hour.) The globe in the painting is mounted in a brass armillary stand, with rams' heads as supporters for the horizon ring. Rams' heads were a not uncommon architectural device of the period. A woodcut of a terrestrial globe in a popular work by Peter Apian, for example, shows supporters in the form of nondescript animal heads, with rings in their mouths, and Holbein himself included something similar in his design for the woodcut portrait

#71 06-05-2007 3:38PM
Item(s) checked out to EDWARDS LINDA.

TITLE: God is not great : how religion p
BARCODE: 1440000534742
DUE DATE: 06-19-07

TITLE: The Ambassadors' secret : Holbein
BARCODE: 1440000401886
DUE DATE: 06-19-07

TITLE: Picasso : creator and destroyer /
BARCODE: 1440000206776
DUE DATE: 06-19-07

TITLE: The glass menagerie [sound record
BARCODE: 1440000302430
DUE DATE: 06-19-07

TITLE: Loving Picasso : the private jour
BARCODE: 1440000310378
DUE DATE: 06-19-07

TITLE: Margaret Bourke-White : her pictu
BARCODE: 1440000261821
DUE DATE: 06-19-07

Basalt Regional Library
927-4311 www.basaltrld.org

7. A chart of the constellations of the northern heavens (Nürnberg, 1515) produced jointly by Albrecht Dürer (artist), Conrad Heinvogel (who positioned the stars) and Johannes Stabius (who directed the enterprise). Woodcut, 43 x 43 cm. Note Aries, the Ram, at the top. Dürer's figures were much copied by others after him, but they were directly based on medieval western examples, which in turn owed much to Muslim artists. The astronomers in the corners are Aratus, Ptolemy, Manilius and al-Sufi, all of whom had been responsible for star catalogues. An accompanying chart of what was known of the southern hemisphere was published in the same year.

of Erasmus (Fig. 2).[88] Here, as will be explained, it is almost certain that the rams' heads had a deep symbolical purpose, and that they were being associated with the Ram (Aries) in the heavens – the *constellation* rather than the zodiacal *sign* of Aries.

The inventory of Henry VIII's possessions at his death lists several globes, but all in ways too vague for us to even begin to speculate on whether one of them was the celestial sphere in the painting. (We find a sphere with a globe of copper and gilt, for instance, and even 'three globes made of paste', as well as 'a globe of paper', from which we can deduce almost nothing.) Hervey did not identify the source of the gores, the paper segments covering the globe, on which the constellations were mapped before they were glued on. It has since been shown that they were modelled closely on gores which were being printed by Johannes Schöner from around 1515. Johannes Schöner was a priest who taught astronomy and mathematics in Nürnberg. He had great expertise of a sort that can hardly be conveyed by so mathematically simple an object as a celestial globe. His publications were not yet well known in England, although some of his best work makes extensive use of the theoretical writings of the fourteenth-century English astronomer Richard of Wallingford. Schöner helped to raise the general level of education in his subject – not to say money – by his work as a printer. He converted to Lutheranism, like so many others of the cloth, in the mid-1520s, and was a friend of Melanchthon.

Two incomplete sets of unmounted Schöner gores are known, and two globes with a full complement of gores survive, on stands dated 1534 and 1535. The former is now in the Duchess Anna Amalia Library in Weimar, while the latter, owned by the Royal Astronomical Society, is at present on loan to the London Science Museum.[89] Ten constellation figures are shown on the globe in *The Ambassadors,* all of them partly hidden and most of them hard to recognise, although nine are named. It is a peculiarity of the constellation figure of Perseus in the painting, as in Schöner's woodcut, that the hero's outstretched hand is empty, rather than holding his sword. In the other he holds the head of the Gorgon as usual. It has to be said that the sword is absent in some medieval drawings of star maps, but Holbein paints so skilfully that he leaves us in little doubt that his globe gores are based on woodcut originals. The Holbein and Schöner images of Cassiopeia are similar and unusual. Elly Dekker and Kristen Lippincott, noting other resemblances, find it surprising that the artist should have used upper case lettering where Schöner used lower case, and therefore toy with the idea of a Parisian original by Oronce Fine – who uses upper case lettering rather like Holbein's. Having decided that Fine's gores too derive from Schöner's, however, they conclude that Holbein's image was probably rendered on the basis of a lost printing of Schöner gores, postdating those of 1515.[90] Did the painter not perhaps modify what he saw, and use upper case letters because he valued legibility more than authenticity? It is impossible to say.

THE GLOBE AND THE PAINTING'S PERSPECTIVE

The earlier of the two surviving Schöner globes, that in Weimar, is about 28 cm in diameter. If this was the size of the globe Holbein was painting, then he reproduced it at almost exactly full scale. The implications of this state of affairs are not easy to state briefly, for it is almost as though he has deliberately obscured key lines on his panel that would have helped us to establish his perspective – for instance on the pavement and stand – in order to veil his inconsistencies. From even a cursory analysis it soon becomes clear that while the perspective of separate parts of the work may be excellent, there are several viewpoints in use. This is not at all surprising. The distance at which the painter needed to stand to survey the overall scene was very much greater than the distance he needed to be from the smaller objects, if each was to be painted with precision. Some parts were seemingly painted from a sitting position at relatively close quarters – from a distance of five or six feet from the stand, perhaps (say 160 cm). The various objects on the shelves would have been done from a smaller distance for their detail but from a more remote standing position when it came to placing them in the final composition. For this, the vanishing point that we derive from the pavement turns out to be generally very reliable. In principle it also gives us the level of Holbein's eye, opposite the left of the centre of the painting and on or close to the horizon ring of the celestial globe. This in itself is an extremely interesting result, as we shall see shortly.

There are conclusions we might like to draw from the perspective of the painting, for instance about the physical heights of the two ambassadors, but the use of multiple perspective centres complicates matters. The sitters would have been painted on separate occasions, but was this with the final composition in mind? Were they done life-size, as is so often said to be the case? If, like the globe, they were life-size, then since they are nearer at hand we are faced with a very obvious inconsistency – but only to those who worry about such things. The artistic effect hardly depends on accuracy of scale. If the ambassadors were indeed done life-size, then they were not tall, but not impossibly short. Dinteville would have been only about 156 cm (5 ft 2 ins) and de Selve very slightly shorter. At the other extreme, if truly drawn in perspective with the pavement, Dinteville would have been as much as 191 cm tall (6 ft 3 ins) and de Selve nearly as tall. That they should both have been so tall seems extremely unlikely.

We are on somewhat safer ground if we try to derive Holbein's height from the height of the vanishing point. This would suggest that Holbein's eye was about 155 cm from the ground for the distant view, making him about 165 cm tall (5 ft 6 ins). To make him taller we might say that he had some perspective device that required him to stoop slightly, or that the painting was raised above his floor level slightly – but obviously not by very much.

Another measurement that we should like to obtain is that of the pavement. Here the problem is easier. It is tempting to suppose that the pavement is full scale at its near edge. This would make the side of the square of the pavement (inclusive of the outer strip) close to 9 ft 9 ins (297 cm). The idea is simply not borne out by the overall perspective, which suggests a measurement within an inch or two of 8 ft 8 ins (264 cm). This is not only intrinsically more likely to be correct, it is supported by other evidence that we shall introduce at a later stage.[91] Making the painting larger than life at the near edge allowed Holbein to make objects and people further back true to life – although as already noted, not the globe and Dinteville simultaneously. One might qualify these observations at greater length, but the main conclusion is unavoidable: the various elements in the painting were prepared on different occasions and from different viewpoints, and they were assembled at a later stage to fit a preconceived design. This is an impression we shall get on many other occasions, and the point is not trivial, as we shall see when we consider how Holbein set about planning certain details of the globe.

THE SETTING OF THE CELESTIAL GLOBE

The way the globe is set in *The Ambassadors* has been much discussed. Holbein's extraordinary technique has had the effect of persuading many that the painting is capable of yielding exact and coherent results, in the way a photograph might do. Abstracting the globe from the painting, this optimism will turn out to be justified, although past disagreements might lead one to think otherwise. From the point of view of its symbolic value it has generally been assumed that the constellation image of Cygnus was meant to be the focus of attention. Whether or not this is true, its stars are certainly well placed for analysis. A celestial globe needs to be set in its stand with its axis at an angle that is appropriate to the place at which it is meant to be used, or for which a calculation is being performed. A few moments' consideration with pencil and paper will show that the angle between the polar axis and the horizon must be made equal to the geographical latitude of the place. Following an early analysis by F. A. Stebbins, it has been repeatedly claimed that the globe is wrongly set for London, but this is not so. The meridian ring and pole are surprisingly accurately drawn for a London latitude, a fact of some importance when we come to analyse other astronomical properties of the painting.[92] This, however, says nothing of the accuracy with which the stars are placed. Speaking generally, the visible area has a remarkably large number of those stars that it was customary to place on constellation maps at the time. The coordinates they were assigned at this period of history are all well known. Following standard practice, stars were all, or almost all, placed on the globe on the basis of Ptolemy's star catalogue of 1022 stars, dating from the second century AD. This needed to be duly updated for the slow drift of the equinoxes, which by Schöner's time had increased all their longitudes by approximately 20° over their values at Ptolemy's epoch.

With the help of this knowledge, at least some of Holbein's intentions can be clearly made out. Matters are simplified by the fact that the observer's eye is only slightly below the level of the horizon ring. (We are speaking here of how the globe was painted at close quarters, and not of the vanishing point of the painting as a whole, although it is gratifying to find that both agree so well.) Added to this, there are two or three bright and easily identifiable stars in key positions. Mankar, for example, the brightest star in Pegasus and the fourth on Ptolemy's list for that constellation, is adjacent to the northern section of the meridian ring. The eighth star on Ptolemy's list for Cepheus is likewise; and the eleventh star on Ptolemy's list for Cygnus appears to be just above the horizon. (Even this needs correction for perspective, for which see the fuller account below.)* It will gradually become clear that the globe was set in a very carefully contrived manner, and not at all in the way that is usually supposed. Here are the chief possible ways of handling the evidence:

(1) Assuming that the hour-angle scale has been set to show the time of day, which amounts to saying that the pointer is directed towards the Sun in the zodiac (that is, to its place on the ecliptic), one may derive a rough value for the ecliptic position and hence for the day of the year.

(2) Assuming the time of day, supposedly known independently, one may derive a date on which the stars will have the positions as painted. (This disregards the hour-angle scale, but that is of no consequence. The pointer is only semi-rigidly fixed to the globe and its position may even have had a separate significance.)

(3) Assuming the day of the year, and the star positions, one may derive the time of day (again disregarding the hour-angle scale).

* See p. 200 below.

(4) Any one of the previous conclusions may be drawn in combination with an assumption as to (for example) the numerological or geometrical structuring of the design.

(5) It is conceivable that the globe is placed without any regard for a strict astronomical interpretation. It may still have had some sort of concealed structural meaning.

Dekker and Lippincott could apparently see only the first option, from which they derived a date of 12 July – it is not clear how precise they meant that date to be – for a time of 2h 40m; and from this date they drew various strong negative conclusions.[93] It is certainly tempting to see the globe as yet another time indicator, like the various dials to the side of it, but a celestial globe has many other purposes. It will eventually emerge that the globe is not being used as a time-telling instrument at all. In all strictness, not a single one of the time-telling instruments is set up as though it were in use. For the moment it must suffice if we make a few simple points in preparation for our own preference for the fourth option, selected here because it makes excellent sense of the symbolism of the painting many times over. In the following section it will be shown that the date was 11 April 1533. The Sun was then judged to have entered the second degree of the sign of Taurus, but (because of the drift of the equinoxes mentioned earlier) the constellation of Aries, the Ram, was mainly situated in the sign of Taurus. In fact, assuming that date, we can ask where the Sun would have been marked on the globe. The Ram is not visible in the painting, but had it been added in the conventional way the Sun *would have been just below the head of the Ram.* Using standard catalogues we can be even more specific. The Sun was at the time in question almost precisely in line with, and adjacent to, the two stars in the Ram's muzzle, as described by Ptolemy. (The iconography of such diagrams is of course restricted by the positions of named stars for the epoch in question.)

This was almost certainly a part of the reason for using the rams' heads as supporters for the horizon ring. No known example of a globe mounted with Schöner gores has those heads. They may well have existed, although it seems more likely that they were meant to serve only their present symbolic purpose, underscoring the Sun's position. Whether or not this is true, the time set by the Sun and globe together would be about nine in the evening, in our familiar equal-hours reckoning. On the interpretation that will be offered at a later stage, while this may have a symbolic meaning, the main point at issue is the Sun's position on the globe as it relates to the painting as a whole. (It has another property of the same general kind which we shall only be able to explain later.) The constellation image for Aries cannot be made out, since it is immersed in shadow below the horizon ring on the right hand side of the globe. There would in any case have been drastic foreshortening of its image, since it is at the very edge of the visible hemisphere. To all intents and purposes the Sun itself can be taken as opposite the breast of the adjacent ram that acts as a supporter of the horizon ring, and close to the continuation of the arc passing through Andromeda's leg.[94]

A more detailed discussion will be given in due course, for the Sun's position on the globe as painted is a matter of great consequence. Since interpreting its role in the symbolism of the painting leaves various questions unanswered, however, it will be as well to bear in mind that the statements made at the present stage are in principle more or less exact. The assumptions on which they rest have been spelt out, and are not based on a particular allegorical reading of the painting. They are compatible with many a conjecture made in the past on quite different grounds, for instance with Mary Hervey's idea that the cock-like constellation of Cygnus was given prominence because it was a gallic symbol that honoured Jean de Dinteville and his country. That idea is not at all implausible. The image of the adjacent constellation of *Lyra*, the Lyre, is given its common alternative name on the globe – it is *Vultur Cadens*, the Falling Vulture – but Cygnus has been left unlabelled.[95] In general style, the Cygnus figure is not unusual. It is close not only to Schöner's representation of the bird but also to most medieval western (Alfonsine) prototypes and their Arab sources, except in its neck, which resembles that of a cock rather than a swan. In the middle ages Cygnus was often known by various names for 'hen', such as the Latin word *Gallina*, and was then drawn appropriately. Schöner calls the constellation by that name, but gives the bird a smooth neck. Dekker and Lippincott refer to Holbein's bird as a hen. Here its head is obscured by Dinteville's white fur, perhaps to save appearances, but the ruff on the visible part of its neck suggests a cock rather than a hen. Is that why it was not labelled *Gallina*? In rare cases, the constellation was actually named as a cock.[96] In short, Hervey, unaware of how close Holbein's was to many a conventional representation of Cygnus, could well have been right to interpret the bird as symbolising 'the onslaught of France upon her foes, and their ultimate downfall and flight'.[97] That we believe the globe to have had other and more important purposes does not rule out the possibility that she was right, and that it was turned to show a symbol of France to advantage.

There is one further detail that might be used in support of Hervey's idea. In the centre of the lower half of the globe, above Dinteville's left elbow and to the left of the knees of Pegasus, there is part of the constellation of the Dolphin to be seen, with part of its Latin name *Delphinus*. This word is the source of the name for the eldest son of the king of France. The region known as the Dauphiné took its name from the fish, and when it was ceded to France in 1349 it was on condition that the eldest son of the king be given the title dauphin. Jean de Dinteville's father had responsibilities to the dauphin, at that time the king's son François, and Jean's brother Guillaume was the dauphin's equerry. In 1532 Jean sent his own brother François (then in Rome in disgrace) a cast of the dauphin's face, presumably so that a royal portrait could be painted there. A dolphin on the globe under a cock would not have been out of place, especially as the dauphin was well known to many of those who are likely to have viewed Holbein's freshly painted masterpiece, starting with Henry VIII himself. Only a few months earlier, at the time of the Field of the Cloth of Gold, Henry had met the boy privately by arrangement at Calais, treating him with great kindness and even playing tennis there with him and his brothers.[98]

Even for the Dolphin there is another explanation, as we shall see at a later stage. That we may 'read' the globe in more ways than one would have been regarded as a virtuoso achievement on the part of whoever planned it. If it is possible to derive latitudes for Polisy (about 48° latitude north) and Rome (about 42°) from the meridian scale with its dual numbering, while they do not fit with the setting of the rings and the globe as painted (which is for London), that fact would have been no burden on the conscience of anyone who wished to cram as much symbolism into the painting as possible. It seems preferable when dealing with the surface detail of the globe, however, to attempt to find an interpretation that is astronomically coherent.

THE CYLINDER DIAL

A fine celestial globe is unlikely to have been found in the possession of any but men of means. Next to the globe on the upper shelf, however, is an instrument (Plate 6) that any poor scholar might have fashioned for himself. It is cylinder sundial of turned wood, of a sort that on a more modest scale was probably not rare in the sixteenth century, while at the other social extreme the king himself owned examples in precious metals. The instrument is often simply known in medieval English texts as a 'cylinder' (or 'chilyndre', Latin *chilindrum),* while a pocketable example could be called a 'wayfarer's dial' (Latin *horologium viatorum).* In sixteenth-century England the name 'pillar dial' was not uncommon. Another, larger, specimen stands in the recess in the wall behind Kratzer in Holbein's portrait of him (Plate 4), and there is one drawn by Kratzer, copied from a medieval text, among his extant manuscripts. He there adopts the spelling *kilindrum.*[99]

Set on a level surface, or suspended so that it hangs perfectly vertically, if well balanced, the dial when in use has a perfectly horizontal gnomon. This is directed so that it heads in the direction of the Sun in such a way that its shadow falls vertically. The tip of the shadow cast on the body of the cylinder then gives the time, as judged by the grid of hour lines

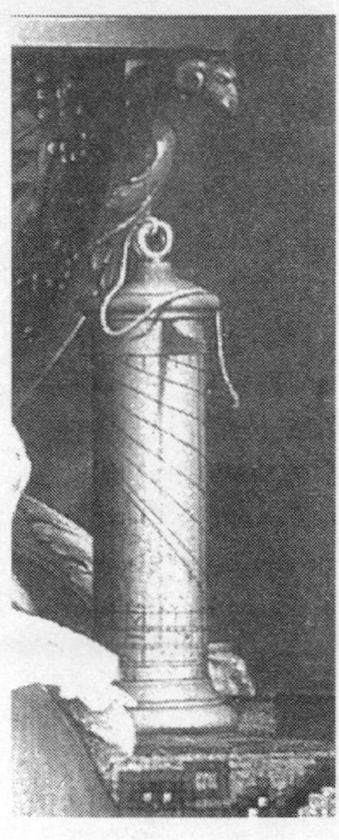

8. The cylinder sundial. For more detail see Plate 6.

engraved on it.[100] Before the dial is used, the gnomon must be set correctly for the time of year. It protrudes from a knob on the top of the dial. The knob is twisted round until the gnomon is opposite the correct date on a graduated band wrapped round the cylinder (either round the rim or, as in this case, the bottom). The band is graduated with the signs (and hopefully the degrees) of the zodiac, and with the months (and hopefully the days of the month). Part of this band is shown schematically in Fig. 9. How much detail is possible will depend on the size of the instrument. The graduation is not universally valid, but is appropriate to a particular geographical latitude. It seems that the dial illustrated is for latitudes around that of London, judging by the 5 a.m. / 7 p.m. line that terminates directly under the gnomon. This might seem obvious, but after all, Kratzer could have made Dinteville a dial for the latitude of Polisy. Such a dial would have been very similar to that in the painting, even though the evidence is weighted very slightly in London's favour. We can at least say that it is not a dial meant for such southern latitudes as those of Bavaria or Rome.

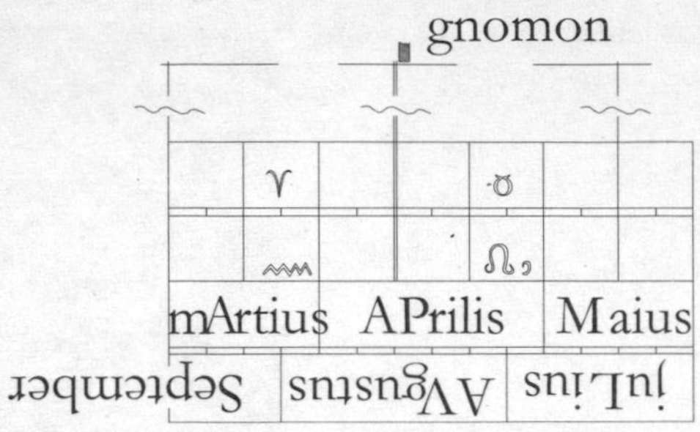

9. The critical part of the scale of the cylinder dial, mostly visible. The scale is here opened out flat and drawn in an idealised form, as a guide to what are likely to have been the painter's intentions. The body of the dial is omitted, but the position of the lower edge of the gnomon is marked. Each symbol for a sign of the zodiac is in the middle range of the sign's 30° span. Top row: the sign for Aries is correct; Libra was at some stage wrongly overpainted on Taurus or a blank division (the latest restoration leaves a blank). Second row: the zig-zag was surely never meant as Aquarius (a double zig-zag) but as Virgo (conventionally ♍, but written in a more open way); the sign of Leo (as here supplied) survives only in part, barely recognisable. The dial very probably had only two-letter abbreviations for the names of months, some of them out of sight to the painter. Upper case letters are used in the present figure to show those letters that can be seen on the painting.

There has been paint loss in this area. If there was ever a symbol for Taurus, it had been transmuted into that for Libra (now rightly removed). Virgo still looks more like half of the Aquarius symbol, giving rise to some misunderstanding. There is no reason for thinking that Holbein meant Libra or Aquarius, and we can mentally restore the strip unambiguously. The position of the gnomon in relation to the signs is of crucial importance to us for two reasons:

First, it reveals that the date was almost certainly meant to be 11 April 1533.[101] There are alternatives to be considered, but the date of 11 April is supported many times over. It falls within the period of Bishop Lavaur's known stay in England. In 1533 it was a very special day, namely Good Friday, the day on which Christ's crucifixion is commemorated. It fits with the setting of the globe in a way that the alternative date in August would not. And it will later be confirmed in a remarkable way by the torquetum and by a shadow on the pavement. The last reason is in turn supported by the next consideration.

The time that would be deduced from a naive reading of the shadow on the instrument is about 8:15 a.m. or 3:45 p.m. (to an accuracy of say five minutes). The tiny magnetic compass in the polyhedral dial seems to point to south as being roughly in the direction of the bishop's elbow, but this is entirely irrelevant, since the compass box was less than an inch across and was tipped into such a position that the needle would in any case not have swung freely. If sunlight is causing the shadow on the floor then not only can we see that the gnomon is heading *almost* into the Sun – so that its shadow is not purely symbolic – but we get an unexpected and invaluable insight into the meticulous planning that went into the painting. The symmetry of the geometrical pattern on the pavement allows us to say rather precisely that the direction of the Sun is about 74° from the fore-edge of the table, over the viewer's right shoulder. It is almost as though those responsible wanted us to have a means of making the calculation. Even the line to the Sun from the corner of the table leg passes through an easily remembered point, the sharp corner of the pattern at the lower middle of the painting. The analysis to be offered shortly will allow us to calculate the direction (azimuth) of the Sun with some precision. It turns out to be close to 15.5° south of west. There is a very strong presumption, therefore, that *the table edge runs precisely north-south*. When we view *The Ambassadors* from the front in the normal way we should be conscious of the fact that we are facing due east. This is all incompatible with a morning Sun, for that would imply that the table was around thirty degrees east of north, a thoroughly nondescript option. (Of course there are those who will feel compelled to add that it is a perfectly possible one. It will eventually be ruled out categorically.)

As depicted, the cylinder dial has all the appearance of just another instrument casually placed on the table. The carelessness of the arrangement seems to be emphasised by the very fact that the gnomon does not quite head for the source of light.

Not that Holbein himself can be called careless here, for observe how he has given the shadow line on the dial a slight curvature, of just the sort that an oblique shadow would have made on a cylindrical surface. This is an extraordinarily perceptive touch that would have escaped a lesser observer of the natural world. Had the gnomon been set in its ideal position the shadow would have shown a time very close to 8 a.m. or 4 p.m.[102] The altitude of the Sun (the angle of elevation between the Sun and the horizontal) would have been very close to 27°. This angle will prove to be as crucial in its way to an understanding of the painting as is the Good Friday connection. Of course, the assumption being made is that the dial presents a situation true to life, with a shadow cast by the Sun rather than some other source of light. Dekker and Lippincott hold to the contrary that 'it would be impossible to argue with any conviction that this sundial is recording the natural phenomena of a particular time of day'. That is plainly false – witness the subtlety of the curved shadow before doubting Holbein's skill in such matters. They add that 'If Holbein meant to indicate a specific time, he has done so only by undermining an essential principle of how dials work'. But Holbein – or his guide – was not aiming at anything so obvious as a portrayal of the laws of sundials. He has flirted with them but he has given us instead an example of how to show the time, the true time, in an amusingly devious way. And it will not be his last exercise in apparent ambiguity.

How these ideas fall into place will be evident only when we come to consider the role of the crucifix in the painting. For the time being, it is worth noting how the cylinder dial is placed directly below the right-hand ram that acts as a supporter of the horizon ring of the globe. In this context the ram marks the place of the Sun on the globe, and is in a sense a symbol for the Sun, so it would not be at all inappropriate if it were meant to be loosely associated with the shadow on the cylinder dial. (This is not to suggest that we are to think of the globe as having a point source of light on it, casting the shadow that is painted. In that case my remarks about the general orientation of the scene might lose their relevance.) Are we in a courtyard, open to the sky, or in a room with large windows, or is every shadow meant to be interpreted allegorically? The cylinder dial seems to indicate the true time, in a slightly oblique way, but more or less according to its ordinary way of functioning. Accepting this, the globe seems to be positioned to make an elegant statement about the Sun for the same day of the year without any reference to shadows. It is not a shadow instrument, but it lends support to the matter-of-fact reading of the cylinder dial that is.

THE COMPOUND SOLAR INSTRUMENT

Next on the upper shelf comes an unusual adjustable instrument, for which we can suggest three or four different modes of operation (Plate 7). It is conceivable that this is the instrument after which Kratzer enquired in his letter of 1524 to Dürer, who in his reply tells Kratzer that its owner, Willibald Pirkheimer, has promised to have it copied and despatched to England. It is not one of the standard medieval instruments that are described in the surviving Kratzer papers. If he designed it himself then he was probably very proud of it, although it is hard to believe that the best astronomers of his time would have esteemed it

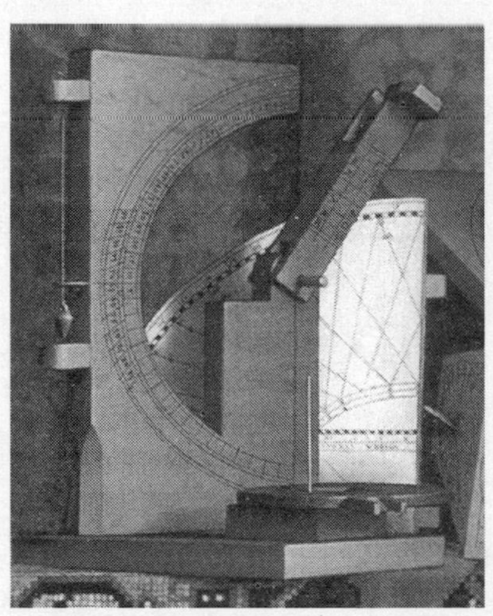

10. The solar instrument and the quadrant behind it. For more detail see Plate 7.

very highly.[103] It seems to be the same example as that included in Holbein's 1528 portrait of him (Plate 5), where we see its other side. With the paintings to hand, a general description of the instrument is more or less superfluous. It has a pivoted arm and hollow semicircle carrying graduated scales, although in neither painting is the ensemble shown as it would have been arranged when actually in use. It could have been used in two different ways as a sundial. (Technically an 'equinoctial dial', since it refers the Sun's position to the equinoctial circle, the celestial equator.) In both cases the main frame had to be set in the plane of the meridian. There might have been a magnetic compass in the base, although that would have been neither essential nor accurate. One can more or less reconstruct its maker's intentions on the basis of an accessory disc, lying open to view on the table in the Kratzer portrait, and it is not without certain mechanical disadvantages. Even without the accessory disc it could have been used as a device for measuring the Sun's altitude. Note the plumbline fitted to ensure that the instrument is correctly set vertical. Made of wood, and hardly more than 20 cm high, this is not an instrument of precision, but most of the criticisms that have been made of the paintings of it and its accessory disc are not called for. There is no generally accepted term for this instrument, and since no early text or example is known, its possible uses are further explored in Appendix 11. They seem to have little bearing on the scheme behind the painting, which will later be shown to use the instrument in an almost jesting way, in conjunction with the quadrant behind it and and partially concealed by it.

Another suggestion as to why it is shown in a disassembled state is given by Dekker and Lippincott, who hold that this may be 'to show it being employed in the laying out of the other dials, such as the pillar dial and the horary quadrant'. They do not say how this was to be done. The methods used to lay out those instruments were in any case simple and well known. They might have made better use of the idea that it was for graduating another instrument had they considered the polyhedral dial (see below): the solar instrument might in principle have been used to hold that block in different positions. They have been beguiled by what they see as a resemblance between this instrument and one that Kratzer describes in a notebook that was meant to assist the dial maker when he was placing the hour-lines on sundials. The two have very little in common, however, beyond a connection with time-telling by the Sun.[104]

THE QUADRANT

The white quadrant, partly obscured by the solar instrument (Plate 7), would in real life have been of about 16.5 cm radius (6.5 ins) – not large but not uncommonly small. Astronomical quadrants are of many types, some of them highly complex, but it would be as pointless to treat quadrants as a group, merely on account of their shape, as it would be to put all circular instruments under one head.[105] This is a horary (time-telling) quadrant, the chief purpose of which was to provide the time in equal hours – our own hours of the clock, as opposed to the unequal hours that by the sixteenth century were fast passing out of use. (With unequal or seasonal hours one divides up daylight into twelve parts, and night also. Only when day and night are equal – that is, at the equinoxes – will day hours and night hours be equal. Equal hours are for this reason often called equinoctial hours.) Older horary quadrants have curved hour lines, whereas these are straight, following a system described in print by Johannes Stöffler (1452–1531) and Oronce Fine (1494–1555) shortly before the time of the painting. They were not the inventors of the device with straight lines, however, and indeed Kratzer's Maurbach manuscript contains instructions on how to make such an instrument, copied from an earlier treatise. Most surviving examples of horary quadrants are of brass, but wooden quadrants must once have been much more common, and the specimen shown in the painting was seemingly of painted wood or just possibly paper on wood.

The quadrant contributes a great deal to a proper understanding of the strategy being followed by Holbein and his collaborators. It has been the subject of many extravagant claims that are best passed over in silence, most of them starting from the premiss that since it is not in use it cannot reveal the time. In fact it does show the time, and that in an extremely ingenious way. (It might even be said to be shown 'in use', but that would be stretching a point.) In order to explain how it does so, a short explanation of its general character and position is called for. Since much of the quadrant in the painting is hidden from view, the drawing of Fig. 11 is provided to supplement the painting.

The first stage in using the instrument with the Sun is to find the Sun's altitude, not by direct observation through pin holes in vanes (as one would do in observing a star) but by the less dangerous expedient of allowing the pinhole image of the Sun from one vane to fall on the pinhole on the other (see the bottom right corner of the figure). The plumbline then falls over the scale at the altitude of the Sun, marked *a* in the figure. One unnecessary criticism of the painting is that there are pinnules (pierced sighting vanes) visible on the right-hand side, whereas we should expect them to be hidden. What can be seen, however, might not be vanes at all, but the ends of battens that were added to prevent warping. They may even have been pierced as sighting tubes, or have carried vanes that are entirely out of sight. There are so many possible arrangements of a legitimate sort that it would be foolish to criticise the painting on the strength of such feeble evidence.[106]

Having found the altitude, we need to know the place of the Sun in the zodiac for the date in question, using some independent source, such as a calendar. Using the instrument in its calculating mode, the thread of the plumbline is drawn out along the zodiac scale at the bottom, and a small bead (usually a seed pearl) is slid along it to mark the Sun's place in the zodiac (better known as its ecliptic longitude). This is just a case of getting the bead at the right distance from the point of suspension of the thread. The thread is then swung round and drawn out over its place on the altitude scale. The bead will then mark the hour on the appropriate set of hour lines. There are two sets of hour lines, slanting in different directions, and it is important to take readings from the right set. Each of the straight hour lines apart from that for noon is for two hours of the day, morning and afternoon (for example for 1 p.m. and 11 a.m.) but

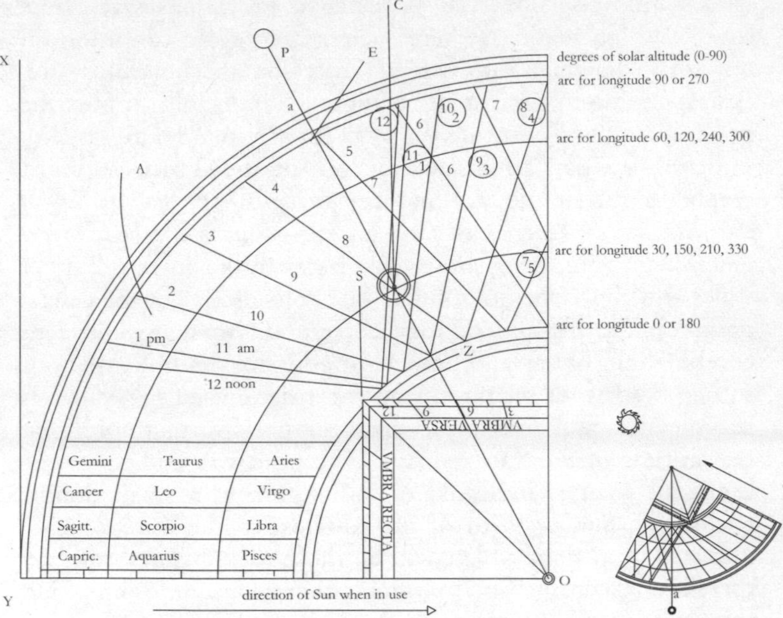

11. A conjectured outline of the quadrant that Holbein painted, with hour lines here drawn as close as possible to his, while yet being correctly computed, as briefly explained in our text. The orientation of the quadrant when in use is shown at the lower right, where the angle *a* is the Sun's altitude. Two intermediate arcs are drawn here (as was usual, but was not strictly necessary, and not on Holbein's quadrant) to help the eye locate the places where the Sun passes from one sign of the zodiac to the next. There are additional lines on this drawing that have nothing to do with the quadrant as such, but relate to its place in the painting. *XY* is the line of the plumbline of the adjacent solar instrument. The slanting line from *E* marks the upper edge of its movable arm, allowing us to read the scale beyond the 27-degree division. The arc from *A* marks the edge of the solar instrument that blocks the view again beyond the 54-degree division. The vertical from *C* is the line of the right-hand edge of the solar instrument. The line through its pivot, also defining the end of its semicircular scale, is the vertical through *S*. *OP* is the plumbline of the quadrant, with bob at P. The hour numbers are usually (and in the painting, but not here) shown on the innermost scale. The painting has no such numbers at *Z*.

one set of lines is needed when the Sun is north of the equator (between spring and autumn equinoxes) and another set when it is south. The lines can be labelled in various ways. The southern hour marks are here encircled, to avoid confusion on our small drawing. The two sets meet on the innermost arc, corresponding to time at the equinoxes, and Holbein puts the hour labels there, omitting the label for 4 p.m. / 8 a.m.

Before we pass to his artistic use of the device we must emphasise the simple fact that *any daylight hour on any day of the year may be represented by a unique point on the body of the quadrant*, a point lying somewhere between the outer and inner scales and above the noon line. (The converse is not the case: a point on the instrument may correspond to many different combinations of day and hour.) Suppose, for example, that our sliding bead is set on the thread for a date when the Sun was leaving Aries and entering Taurus. Suppose, furthermore, that the altitude of the Sun was 27°. The bead will end up at the centre of what is indicated on our figure as a small double circle. The Sun is north of the equator, so the lines slanting upwards from right to left will be those to use. The bead will therefore fall on the line marking either 4 p.m. or 8 a.m. Had the day been one on which the Sun was passing from Aquarius to Pisces, the other set of hour lines would have been needed, and the hour would have been about 11 a.m. or 1 p.m. It is not necessary to enter here into the question of how to interpolate, when the bead falls between hour lines. In practice it was done intuitively. In the case considered, at least, the time is more or less precisely on the hour.

Having set out the way of calculating with the instrument, we can now explain how Holbein has made use of it, in conjunction with the compound solar instrument that partially conceals it. *He has used it to reiterate the statement of time and date made with the help of the cylinder dial*, namely 4 p.m. on 11 April 1533. The arguments given against a morning hour, and against a date later in the year, will not be repeated here, but those who favour a date roughly six months later will need to use the other hour lines.

How he reaffirms this hour, if we are not mistaken, is by means of revealing the solar altitude as 27° and then blocking the intended hour line at the appropriate point on it. He reveals the 27 mark using the wooden arm of the solar instrument (see *E* in the figure) and he marks the correct point on the hour line by means of the wooden vertical of that same instrument (see the line down from *C* in the figure). The hour line is *the only one in principle visible that he does not label.* It is marked in our figure as *Z*. He needed no thread and no bead to indicate the hour in this way.

Note that the light conveniently illuminates the scale around both the 27 and the 54 marks. Was there any deeper purpose in blocking the scale again beyond the 54-degree mark? Was the effect an inevitable and trivial consequence of the size of the aperture in the foreground instrument? Or was it perhaps a numerological point, the number being the double of 27? Or should we look further afield, noting for example that 54° was the approximate noon altitude of the Sun at Polisy on the day in question? A simpler explanation will be offered at a later stage,* but the ground must first be prepared for it.

As for the 27-degree reading, is it again nothing more than an extraordinary coincidence that the two instruments fit together to produce an agreement with the hour indicated by the cylinder dial? Those who believe it to be a chance alignment will need to explain why Holbein seems to have gone to such pains to relate the two instruments through their positions. As shown in the figure, the plumbline on the solar instrument is exactly tangential to the quadrant (see *XY* in the figure), while the line through its pin is exactly in line with the tangent scale (see *S* and the standard 'umbra recta' scale that has to be as reconstructed here). This did not happen by the artist throwing a Plinian sponge at the painting.

What I have said up to this point is as much as is needed for an understanding of the plan of this part of *The Ambassadors,* but there are many qualifications that need to be made for those who are more concerned with the instrument itself and its qualities. Such a quadrant is designed for a specific geographical latitude, and it should be possible to deduce the latitude from its hour lines. It takes a Holbein to draw a six-inch version of

* See p. 192 below.

our Fig. 11 with a brush rather than a pen, but Holbein could have done better, for some of the lines are a couple of degrees askew for any latitude. Has there been any bad repainting? It seems hard on him to subject his figure to such analysis, but we are inclined to do so by the fact that his *scale* is surprisingly accurate. He offers us more than a dozen points at which to test his hour lines, and when we do so, calculating the errors for a wide range of latitudes, we find that the errors are minimised for approximately latitude 49.3°.[107] The penned figure of the similar quadrant in the Kratzer manuscript shows significant but lesser errors; and yet they too are minimised at a closely similar latitude.[108] The reconstruction offered in our own drawing of the quadrant is based not on a London latitude but on that which fits best the instrument shown in the painting. It does not at first sight appear to be a Polisy instrument or one for a more southerly place, for which it would have given appreciably worse results. For the crucial hour line (not for the extreme lines) a London instrument would have given much the same result as ours. One way or another it seems likely that when the use to be made of the quadrant was worked out, Kratzer provided an instrument that he had made using data for another place.

How much importance should we attach to the fact that he did not provide a London instrument? It is hard to believe that he had never made himself such a thing, although the calculation required would not have been considered trivial. There is one argument which could be offered for an instrument he had made specially for Polisy. That place is marked on the terrestrial globe *due east of Paris.* In reality it is appreciably further south (latitude 48.08° rather than 48.83°). If the quadrant was made on the strength of Dinteville's belief that east was the true direction, then Kratzer would have been happy to take over data from a Parisian source, such as Oronce Fine. One consequence of this shaky argument is that Dinteville had never made serious astronomical observations at his home, for latitude was one of the easiest things for an astronomer to measure.

The quadrant in the painting is drawn as a mirror image of

that in Kratzer's manuscript. It is quite possible that he provided Holbein not with an instrument but with a drawing, with instructions as to how it was to be placed. There was no perspective skill required for the quadrant in the painting, which is square to the line of sight. Some weight is lent to the idea of a manuscript or printed quadrant by the fact that the scale of *umbra versa* is wrongly painted. Its diagonal at 45° is very clearly indicated on the painting, and the scale should end on it, out of sight. It finishes in quite the wrong place, and open to view. This last point is of some importance since, as we shall see later. It is almost certain that a part of the plan was to draw attention to a property of the angle (near to 27°) that has 0.5 as its tangent, 1 in 2. This is of course the modern language of trigonometry. As it would have been expressed when the painting was done, the angle's *umbra versa* is 6 parts in 12. There is no thread drawn across at this crucial angle in the picture, of course. To have included it would have been to destroy a part of the painting's mystique. Had it been drawn in, as it is in Fig. 11, the mistake in the scale of *umbra versa* would have become glaringly obvious.

One last remark about the design of this type of quadrant: it rests on an assumption that the hours determined in the way explained (12 noon, 11 a.m., 10 a.m., and so on) for any given solar longitude lie on arcs of circles. This is not strictly true but is not a serious source of error. And even if it were, it would not alter the use found for the instrument in the painting, which is to indicate the time. And to indicate it correctly albeit deviously.

THE POLYHEDRAL DIAL

The polyhedral dial, placed to the right of the quadrant and at the front of the table (Plate 8), poses questions far more difficult to answer than any of the other instruments. How was it to be used? Is it set up correctly? Do the dials not show different times? Could a properly made dial show the times that this does? Does it reveal incompetence on its maker's part? Or in Holbein's perspective representation of it? Why was it included in the painting in a way that arouses so much controversy? As far as I am aware, not one of these questions has ever been provided with a satisfactory answer. For those who lack the will to enter into the three-dimensional world of polyhedral dials of this kind, the short answer is that Holbein and Kratzer were presenting the viewer with riddles more difficult by far than that of the skull stretched across the foreground of the painting, but they were riddles with moderately simple answers, and the dial will eventually prove to have been painted exactly as it would have appeared. The representation of it will furthermore be shown to make tacit allusion to the number 27.

Polyhedral dials were dear to Kratzer, and the example in wood depicted in *The Ambassadors* is very similar to the unfinished example he is holding in Holbein's portrait of him. (The two depictions are not of the same instrument, as we shall see.) The geometrical form of this type of polyhedron can be variously described, but perhaps the easiest way of regarding it is as a pair of identical truncated square pyramids, set base to base. Any pair of diametrically opposed faces will lie in parallel planes, so that, for example, when one face is on a level surface the opposite face will also be level. There are ten faces in all, and it is quite likely that each of the ten had a dial of some sort inscribed on it, each capable of having a suitable gnomon plugged into it. The gnomon has to be carefully chosen, since the positioning of the lines on any component dial depends on the angle between the gnomon and the face, as well as on the method of use. In the Kratzer portrait there are three different brass gnomons on the table, and they were doubtless easily removed and replaced, correctly or incorrectly.

This type of dial was not an instrument for serious scientific observation. It was a timepiece, but not a particularly reliable one, even by the standards of portable instruments in general. It required workmanship and positioning of the utmost precision to give the time to much better than a quarter of an hour, or even an hour at certain times of day. It was probably more often considered to be a showpiece, an astronomical conceit, and this with good reason. Not only is the example illustrated

12. The polyhedral dial, with the torquetum behind it. For more detail see Plate 8.

well constructed, it is painted by Holbein with consummate skill, something that can be put to the test astronomically many times over.

It is fortunate that the proportions of the wooden polyhedral block in *The Ambassadors* can be estimated fairly accurately and verified with the help of the circular scales on three of its faces. To an arbitrary unit, the lengths of the three different edges turn out to be about 1.9 units for the sides of the small square, 4 units for the sides of the large central square section of the block, and 3.3 units for the sloping (connecting) edges – all probably true to within a tenth of a unit. It is hard to deduce a precise value for the length of that unit, that is, on the size of the original dial, but the base measurement was chosen here as 4 in order to make the unit approximately one inch. The actual size will not affect our general conclusions. The block that Kratzer holds in Holbein's 1528 portrait of him seems to be roughly as wide as his hand at its widest, which will not be far removed from 4 inches, and that earlier block seems to have been scaled only slightly differently (1.9 to to 4 to 3.0). It might be thought that Holbein was taking less care with his perspective in that painting, or that perhaps Kratzer had not yet arrived at the 1533 design, which has a highly desirable property that the older instrument lacks. (In one of its potential uses it is well suited to latitudes in the neighbourhood of that of London.) I am inclined to reject both of these ideas, however, for the simple reason that the block in the Kratzer portrait has faces inclined (in section) at about 45°, which would have had certain advantages *in construction.* It would have been astronomically less remarkable, unless it was designed for his earlier career in southern places, but both would have had perfectly sound astronomical uses *at any latitude,* despite frequent recent claims to the contrary.

The dial cannot be discussed seriously – which is to say artistically – without an understanding of a few basic principles of its design. While we shall need to consider several different arrangements, all will share one property: when the dial is set up correctly for use, the working edge of the gnomon (or 'stylus') will lie parallel to the polar axis of the Earth. If several faces are used simultaneously, all of their gnomons will therefore be parallel, and will point to one of the poles, north or south.

How to engrave the hour lines on its various faces will depend on the use envisaged for it, which is to say on the angle of the gnomon and the manner in which the dial is supported. The easiest type of face to engrave is one at right angles to the polar axis. In London the polar axis is at about 51.5° to the horizontal, but no matter what the place of use, on a dial at right angles to the gnomon – such as the dial on the near end of the block – the twenty-four hour lines will be equally spaced. Even a dial on a level surface, a 'horizontal dial', such as the well-known (horizontal) garden sundial, will lack this property; but the art of splaying the hour lines correctly no matter what the tilt of the face, given a polar gnomon, was well enough known in antiquity, and would have presented Kratzer with no problems. For London latitudes, the resulting sheaf of lines for a horizontal dial is as case *B* in Fig. 13.

To discuss the polyhedral dial in *The Ambassadors* we must

consider more difficult cases. In the first place we must distinguish between dials on side faces (such as the large face nearest to the viewer of the painting) and dials on the remaining faces. For the sake of brevity they will here be called *side faces* and *outer faces.*[109] It is not necessary to know how exactly they are graduated, but there are a few vital principles that must be borne in mind if we are to avoid common misunderstandings:

First, taking a single face, without regard to the possibility of its being paired with any other face, the splaying of the graduations depends only on the angle between the working edge of the gnomon and the face. The graduations do not depend on the geographical latitude of the user (but see below). This is to assume that the gnomon edge is directed correctly towards the north or south pole. The inclination of this to the horizon does of course vary with latitude – in fact it is equal to it.

Second, the angular arrangement of the hour lines with respect to the line of the gnomon will be the same on side and outer faces, given that the gnomons make the same angles to their faces; but *the numbering of them will be different,* the gnomon being at a '12' mark for an outer dial and at a '6' mark for a side dial.

Third, a side dial and an outer dial may be used simultaneously, but only under certain conditions. Since both of their gnomons must point to the pole, the gnomons must still therefore be parallel to one another. (In all simple cases they will be also parallel to the rod gnomon visible on the near end face.) With a symmetrical block like that in the painting, this means that the gnomons (assuming that they are of dart shape, as in the painting) must be darts of equal angle.

If the polyhedron in the painting had been set up for use, the plane of the meridian would have passed through the '12' mark on the face with the rod gnomon, through that rod and the gnomon on the upper face, the '12' on the upper face, and the centre of the compass box. It could not possibly have been set up correctly as shown, resting on the table as it does, since the geometrical form of the block puts the gnomon edges at only about 20° to the horizontal. By tilting it upwards through

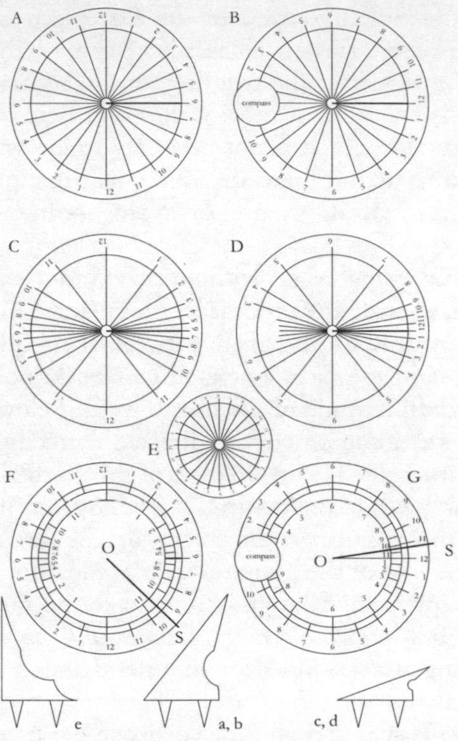

13. The hour lines and numbering of different types of face that might be found on a polyhedral dial of the sort depicted in *The Ambassadors*. *E* is the simplest, of the sort seen on its smaller end face, with a rod gnomon that would have been made to point to either the north or the south celestial pole. Its hour lines are evenly spaced. Gnomon *e* is like one visible in the Kratzer portrait. Its straight edge is the equivalent of a normal rod gnomon. *A* and *B* have the lines appropriate to faces of what I have called 'side' and 'outer' type, assuming that they carried gnomons angled at 51.5° (see *a, b*). On a horizontal dial, for example, such a gnomon could be straightforwardly directed to the London pole. *C* and *D* are respectively faces of 'side' and 'outer' type for use with gnomons of about 20° (see *c, d*), as explained in the text. The clustering of lines is in both clearly much more pronounced than in the other cases. (We recall that it is the angle between the gnomon and the face that decides the splay of lines on the dial.) The precise differences can be easily appreciated from *F* and *G*, where the inner scales are for 20° gnomons and the outer for 51.5° gnomons. The two lines *OS* are needed for a discussion of the ambiguous shadows seen on the instrument in the painting.

another 31.5° or so, to bring the gnomons into line with the polar axis, it could have worked perfectly with the gnomons depicted, *but only if each dial were suitably inscribed for a 20° inclination of face to polar axis.* This was emphatically not the case. Dials for this angle are shown at *C* and *D* in Fig. 13. To suppose that Kratzer miscalculated them or that Holbein misrepresented such strongly clustered lines is at odds with all the evidence we have about the competence of both men, evidence even from other aspects of the dial in question.

Most published discussions of the polyhedral dial have concentrated on its use with two or three faces simultaneously (the two sides and the top). It seems to be automatically assumed that polyhedral dials were only used in this 'simultaneous' mode, but that is wrong. No doubt simultaneous use was always regarded as the chief part of their charm: when the polyhedron is set correctly with its main axis in the meridian, at certain seasons there may be only one face that is not reached by the Sun at some time in the course of the day, namely that on which it stands. (Indeed, if it were to be cleverly suspended in a suitable way, *all* faces might catch the Sun at some time or other.) But we should not forget the designer who wanted a dial with a single reliable face. Ten faces offer great scope for variety, after all. Faces of 'side' type are extraordinarily difficult to use with any semblance of accuracy. Even the 'outer' (upper or lower) dials, when graduated for small inclinations like that of 20°, are largely unreliable. (Note the tight clustering of the hour lines on scales *C* and *D* in Fig. 13.)

It is another common – and mistaken – assumption that polyhedral dials must be used on a level surface. There are clear virtues in that arrangement, of course. A polyhedral block referred to the latitude of London, with much the same general appearance as the dials in the two paintings, is drawn in side view in various positions in the upper row of Fig. 14. The smallest face visible in the painting is a simple equinoctial dial, but it is clear that if the block sits naturally on a horizontal table the rod on the dial depicted will not reach the required altitude. The same is true of the outer edges of the dart gnomons. Whether the block were to have been tipped down or tipped

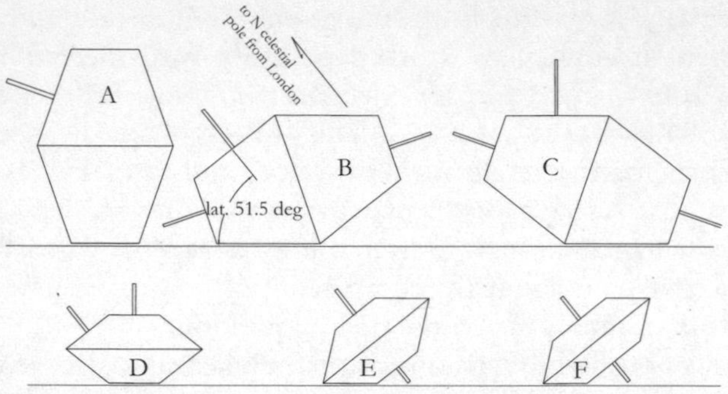

14. Sectional views of polyhedral dials, illustrating the angles achieved by rod gnomons when the block is placed on a level surface. (These are commonly but wrongly imagined to be the only correct ways of using such dials.) Shapes *A, B* and *C* share the character of that in the painting, but show how the rod gnomon does not reach to the inclination of the polar axis at London, as required. The other three blocks, of the same general shape, are included merely to show how the rod gnomon on the end of each could reach the required angle. Case *F* is geometrically acceptable but the block will topple if it has no support. *D* and *E* show mechanically stable arrangements with end faces of a reasonable size.

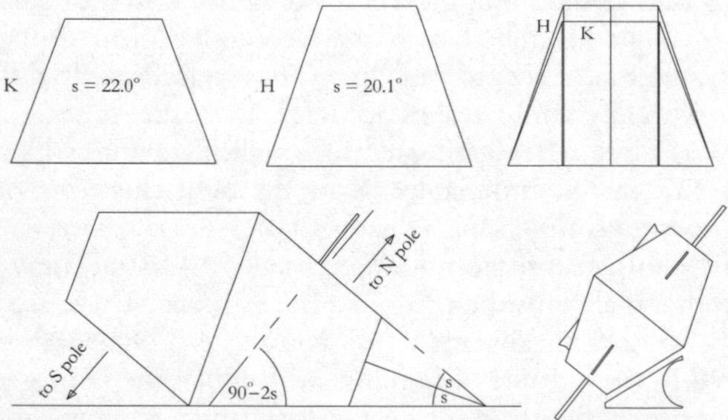

15. Cross-sections (not faces) of the polyhedral dials in *The Ambassadors* (*H*) and the Kratzer portrait (*K*). The two are superimposed at upper right. The dimensions are deduced from the paintings, and must be treated as approximate. With *H*, Kratzer was presumably aiming at a value of 19.25° for *s*, which gives what is needed for London – in the way shown at lower left, where 90°-2*s* must be 51.5°. At lower right, the block is supported in such a way as to make it usable in London with dart gnomons of 20°.

up on the table, the angle reached would in no case have been more than 38.5°, making it unsuitable for table use anywhere north of the toe of Italy. The large 'outer' faces of the dial in the painting, however, are admirably suited to at least two workable options, as will be seen from Figs 14 and 15. The face containing the compass, for example – which could have been used to orientate the block north-south, albeit very imprecisely – could have carried a *horizontal dial* of a type explained earlier (the gnomon dart then having angle 51.5°). Tipping the block forward, *a rod gnomon* (or its equivalent) could be substituted for the dart on that same face, and in this case the dimensions chosen for the block *would guarantee that it pointed to the pole.* (It is assumed that the required semi-angle of the block, 19.25°, was the true figure that we estimated at around 20°. The resulting hour lines are virtually indistinguishable.)

What then of the graduations that are actually there to be seen? They are not uniform, so the rod option was presumably implemented on another face. We can say this with reasonable confidence, for why else choose a block with these dimensions? Allowing for perspective, the actual graduations conform quite closely to a correct graduation for a dial with its plane inclined at 51.5° to the polar axis. In short, *the 20° dart gnomon has been plugged into the wrong face, deliberately or otherwise* – I believe deliberately.

And while we are dealing with the top face, what of the near side? Exactly the same conclusion is reached. This is a correctly graduated 'side' face for London, but *with the wrong gnomon.* We must on no account charge Kratzer or anyone else with incompetence. On the contrary, there is much subtlety in the arrangement, as will be seen when we seek an explanation for the 'times' indicated by the shadow lines on visible faces.

THE POLYHEDRAL DIAL: WHAT THE PAINTER SAW

We have now reached the stage of asking whether what we are shown in the painting is what Holbein could have seen. There is no need to go on apologising for the fact that the instruments in the painting are not set up in working positions. Of course they are not. It is not for us to say that they should have been. But how could a dial, even casually set on the table, have had shadows seemingly indicating a time of 9:30 on the large near face and 10:30 on the two others that are visible? (For the time being I follow conventional wisdom, although I shall shortly reject one of those readings.)

It is generally assumed that even with a dial that is not properly set up, if its gnomon edges are parallel, the shadows of the gnomons on all faces should give the same readings. The best argument I can provide goes like this:

> From our earlier principles we know that the latitude of place is irrelevant to agreement between readings on 'side' and 'outer' dials. The Sun is the Sun, a source of light, and while the dial may not 'know' the meridian, and so will not in general give a correct indication of the Sun's position relative to the meridian, as long as the dial is not twisted with reference to the horizon, all faces should agree.

This may seem plausible enough, but it embodies a mistake that lies at the root of many fallacious conclusions drawn from the representation of time in the painting. Foister, for example, states categorically that different times on the faces would have been impossible. (She adds for good measure that the instrument is in fact designed for a North African latitude, which is of course false. We have already explained how 20° gnomons, for example, can be used at any latitude.) Alexander Sturgis tacitly agrees. Insisting that there is no natural sunlight in the room, he finds it 'tempting . . . to see the shadows of the sundial as reflecting the passage of time during the painting's making, for although one of the faces clearly shows the time as 9.30, on the two others an hour has elapsed and it is 10.30'.[110] Dekker and Lippincott believe that 'like all the other instruments in *The Ambassadors,* the polyhedral dial, while revealing quite a bit of information, does not tell the time'. In reaching this more restrained conclusion they argue that the instrument's orientation is wrong. While that is true, if they mean 'wrong for use', they base themselves on the reading of the tiny compass, which is quite certainly jammed in a meaningless position, tipped forward as it is. More to the point, they insist that the side dials are wrongly engraved. They make the second criticism of the dial in the Kratzer portrait too.

Kratzer was no greenhorn in the matter of dialling, and Holbein was an unequalled technician in paint. The dials are sound enough, but a game is being played with them. It is extremely fortunate that we can check twice over our previous claim that the top dial has a 20° gnomon on 'side' and 'outer' faces for the latitude of London. It is not difficult to calculate the approximate positions of the shadows of the three gnomons, basing ourselves on the position of the Sun in direction and height as deduced earlier (azimuth about 15° south of west, altitude 27°, table north-south). They turn out to be about 10:30 (rod), 9:30 (near side) and 11:15 (top). To this it will be objected that the painting has a shadow on the top face at 10:30. It is true that there is a smudge of shadow there, but this has been misinterpreted. *It cannot have been meant to represent the straight shadow of the working edge of the gnomon*, which would have been completely hidden from the painter's view. (The light rays from the tips of the gnomons to the ends of their shadows must all be parallel. That from the tip of the upper gnomon disappears from view before reaching the dial surface.) In a sentence, Holbein painted what he saw, just conceivably hinting at a shadow to affirm that there was shadow behind the gnomon.

There is a second way of reaching the same conclusion, a way that makes use of the broad principles of dial design already laid down here. The block is not set up for use, but it is at least not 'twisted'. It lies with its planes correctly orientated with respect to the horizon and some *imaginary* polar axis. The gnomons are all correctly aligned towards that. Whatever hour the shadow of the rod indicates on the end dial (10:30) would therefore have registered as the same on a 20° side dial and also on a 20° outer dial. But the side and upper dials are fitted with hour lines appropriate not to 20° but to 51.5°. The shadows will therefore indicate other hours than 10:30. In Fig. 13, the two side dials are superimposed at *F* and the two outer dials at *G*. It will be seen that 10:30 on the imagined 20° side dial (the inner scale of *F*) corresponds to 9:30 on the Kratzer-Holbein side dial, while the indicated equivalent time of 10.30 on an imagined 20° outer dial (inner scale of *G*) will be in the neighbourhood of 11:15 in the painting. And that last shadow is bound to be hidden from our view.

Since much hangs from this somewhat convoluted conclusion, it is right to draw attention to a certain implication that some may find unpalatable. A side dial for 51.5° is a very awkward thing, needing a special way of holding the dial in place. It needs a good geometrical intuition, which undoubtedly Kratzer had, but perhaps he also made use of what I have called his compound solar instrument for holding the polyhedral dial. The equivalent upper dial offers no difficulties, and indeed is the most intuitively useful of all.

We come at last to the all-important question of the artistic use of the polyhedral dial, in a painting that seems to be growing ever more complex. Whether an instrument can only 'tell the time' when it has been set up correctly is a question of semantics. From the dial in the painting an astronomer can deduce the time, and can show that it conforms with the time whimsically shown on the cylinder dial; but that is not what is normally meant by 'telling the time'. Our analysis, even so, should serve as a warning to all who wish to prove that 'time is out of joint' in the painting, that 'it is later than you think', that Holbein was 'underscoring the arbitrariness of time', or whatever.

Such a negative finding as this matters far less in the long run than two or three rather simple by-products of the argument offered here. First, if Holbein and Kratzer wished to make some sort of symbolic use of the hours of 9:30 and 10:30, then they did so strictly within the bounds of a realistic representation – as is surely the case with most symbolic acts. Second, the observer is facing due east, the direction of Christian worship. And finally, the recurrence of the number 27 gives us a growing sense of its importance to the symbolism of the painting. The angle *in the painting* that Holbein gave to the 20° dart gnomon on the most conspicuous dial face, the face with the compass, seems to be 27° to as high a degree of accuracy as one can expect (I think to better than half a degree). There was no other obvious need for that choice of angle. It is gradually revealing itself as the chief key to understanding the painting.

THE TORQUETUM

No instrument in *The Ambassadors* offers more vivid testimony to the collaboration between Holbein and an astronomer – surely Kratzer – than the instrument at Bishop Lavaur's right elbow (the larger instrument of Plate 8). The settings of the scales have been chosen with very great care, and we can draw such a firm conclusion only because Holbein too has worked to extremely fine tolerances. The instrument is what in its early history was known as a *torquetum* – a spelling that in Kratzer's day was often replaced by *turketum* or *turquetum*, and that in some English texts became 'turket'. (The earliest name was conceivably related to the Latin *torquere*, to turn or twist. It

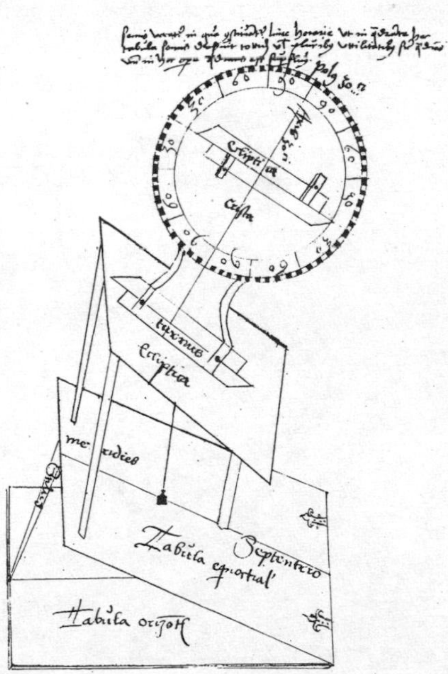

16. Kratzer's manuscript drawing of a rudimentary torquetum illustrating his copy of a treatise by Franco de Polonia (Oxford, Corpus Christi College, MS 152, fols 249–53, figure at 251v).

seems less likely that it points to a Turkish origin.) The example painted by Holbein must have been of the order of 40 cm high. Its upper parts, from the level alidade upwards, were of brass, while the rest was of wood. Finer examples survive from a later period which are entirely of brass, but Kratzer's instruments generally show a preference for wood, suggesting that his torquetum was a prized possession. It was certainly a great improvement on the version he drew to accompany his own manuscript copy of a medieval text describing the instrument (Fig. 16). This type of device is now best known from the published writings of Regiomontanus and Peter Apian, whose clear woodcut illustration of it, first published from his own Ingolstadt press in 1533, is often reproduced (Fig. 17). The instrument in the painting has many points in common with Apian's, which differs in several respects from that of Kratzer's earlier drawing, and it seems likely that he built the instrument in the painting with the Apian woodcut in hand.

The torquetum was already known in Europe at least as early as the thirteenth century.[111] It is not necessary to give a full

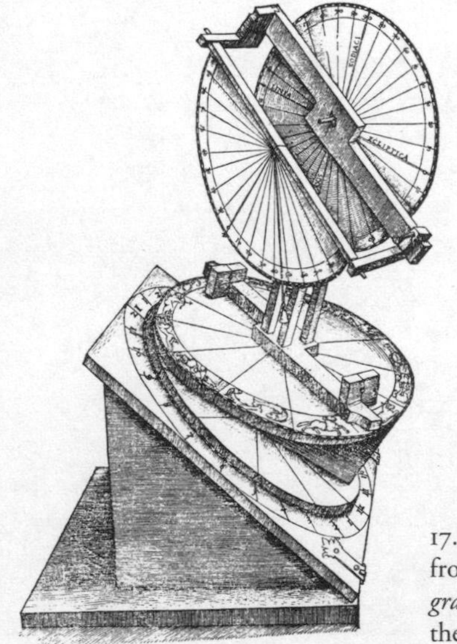

17. Woodcut illustration of a torquetum, from Petrus Apianus, *Introductio geographica* (Ingolstadt, 1533). Apian reused the cut in other works.

account of it here, but anyone who has pondered the problem of setting up a telescope that can pivot around a polar axis (to set the hour angle, or to follow a star with only a single rotary motion) and then around an axis at right angles to it (to allow for declination from the plane of the equator) should be able to see at once some of the merits of the design. In fact the torquetum actually uses this double-pivoting technique twice over, and it is useful to distinguish three fundamental planes: the level base plane, the inclined equatorial plane, and an ecliptic plane (in which lies the apparent path of the Sun). The ecliptic plane, through the middle of the band we call the zodiac, is inclined to the equator at an angle of about 23.5°. It can be imagined attached to the sphere of fixed stars, and to turn with them around the polar axis as a whole. Sitting on the ecliptic plane, and turning around an ecliptic axis (not the polar axis), there is what Kratzer in his manuscript notes calls the *ecliptica crista,* the 'ecliptic crest'.[112] As shown in the painting, it can be seen with some difficulty that the latter has been set so that the lower sighting rule (that on which stand four turned legs) comes very close to the line marking the head of the sign of Aries and the head of Libra – it seems to be a degree or two into Aries, and it will be the same into Libra. (On the near side we see clearly that the vane is near the division separating Pisces and Aries. The zodiacal sign of Pisces is visible, in shadow, on the painting.)

The torquetum, like so many other medieval astronomical instruments, had a double function: it was possible to use it for observation, giving the results in any of three chosen systems of coordinates, without undue calculation. There are several medieval records of its observational use. Alternatively it could be used for calculation alone, that is chiefly for switching between coordinate systems relatively painlessly. That it had this dual character we can see from the work of the fourteenth-century astronomer Richard of Wallingford, who presented the options when he produced an equivalent instrument built out of straight pivoted rods and with no circular scales. So anxious are Dekker and Lippincott to present the torquetum as an instrument of observation that – since the high reading on the ecliptic latitude scale rules out observations of Sun, Moon or planets – they toy with the idea that it might have been included in the painting as a record of the appearance of Halley's comet in 1531.[113] We do not need to ask ourselves how Kratzer used it in real life, or whether, indeed, he had acquired it as early as 1531. Certainly we can say that the base of the torquetum in the painting is not positioned correctly for ordinary observational use. In fact we now know enough about the arrangement of the table to say – from an analysis of its perspective – that the instrument's base makes an angle of approximately 45° with the table's edge. Its polar axis, instead of heading due north, therefore heads almost exactly south west. As in the case of the other instruments in this still life, there is no reason why it should necessarily have been set up for use. Does the torquetum in the painting then have some more devious purpose? Of course it does.

Having grasped the general plan of Holbein's configuration, we soon discover what must almost certainly have been at least a part of the reason behind it. *The instrument as a whole has been so positioned that the zodiacal place of the Sun on Good Friday 1533 is at the nearest point of the appropriate (ecliptic) disc to the viewer.* The precision with which the head of Taurus is placed in our line of view can be best appreciated by drawing a line through the AXIS ZODIACI, the line through the poles of the zodiac (the 90-degree marks) on the 'crest' disc. The line passes with great accuracy through the (unlabelled) dividing line between the end of Aries and the beginning of Taurus.

This exquisite indication of the date within the year – confirmatory rather than self-sufficient – persuades us to look for more, especially since one of the properties of a torquetum is that it has four or five different scales. Kratzer's manuscript drawing has fewer: it lacks the hanging scale with its plumbline on the right of the crest in the painting, but this is found in printed woodcuts, and it should be obvious from the painting how it allows altitudes above the horizon to be recorded easily, the line of sight being along the diameter of the pendant 'D'.[114] We must of course distinguish between ways of using the painting for our own purposes and trying to discern from it the messages that its makers meant to embody in it. It will be convenient to begin with the first. While the upper sights may give the impression of being steeply inclined, this is an illusion due to perspective, and the altitude set was in reality very slight. (The angle at which the diameter of the plate is painted – close to 45° – seems to have been aptly chosen for reasons to do with the overall plan of the painting, as we shall see in a later chapter.) We can read the altitude off the D-scale with the help of its plumbline as being close to 6°.[115] Against the scale of ecliptic latitude on the 'crest', the edge of the vane of the alidade registers a reading of 17.5° (two and a half divisions, where four make 10°). From these readings, and the fact that the first or second degree of the zodiacal sign of Aries is at 5 a.m., we can derive mathematically a value for the geographical latitude. *The instrument is set for a latitude within a degree of London's 51.5°*. Taking the problem in reverse: assuming the latitude of London, the reading on the altitude dial should have been just 6.5°, a figure that speaks volumes for the care invested in the painting, which is yet again clearly meant to mirror a London situation and not, for example, one for Polisy or Rome.

So much for our own use of the instrument. What of the use made of it by Holbein and company? As in the case of the compound solar instrument, *the torquetum records in a certain sense an angle of 27°*, although the reading is hidden from view. The angle would have been indicated to a person looking at the *upper* edge of the upper sighting alidade, the diametral rod at the end of which are vanes with sighting holes. (Only one of the vanes can be seen.) That the reading is on the wrong side of the vane would have been of no consequence if the reading had only a symbolic value. Since Kratzer and Holbein had complete freedom to turn the alidade to any reading they wished without modifying the remaining properties of their presentation – of which there are two more to come – and since 27 (invisible) and 17.5 (visible) are the only readings on the large disc, there is a strong presumption that here, yet again, we have a deliberate insertion of that special number.

There are at least two other items of potential symbolic

interest. One is *the choice of Libra*, towards the first or second degree of which the lower alidade is directed on the far side. We shall be able to make very good sense of this at a later stage. Again it has to be said that those responsible had much freedom of choice, and that this direction, for some reason, was what they meticulously *chose*.

The other intriguing fact about the painting of the torquetum is that it seems to include a mistake that would have been far too obvious to Kratzer for him to have left it uncorrected, if it was indeed a mistake. Near the right-hand corner of the polyhedral dial, on the edge of the lowest circular disc, there is an entirely erroneous symbol for one of the zodiacal signs, erroneous, that is, if it was the intention to paint an entirely authentic instrument. (The other marked sign, for Pisces, above the edge of the dial, is correct.) From the inclination of the zodiac plate above it, we can say that the sign that is so labelled can only have been Taurus. Perhaps here we have certain tokens of Dinteville and de Selve,* but there is another way of understanding the Sagittarius symbol. It fits so beautifully with everything we have learned about the esoteric settings of the instruments as a whole that its truth can scarcely be doubted.

It is as though Kratzer and Holbein have chosen that shady corner between the book, the dial and the torquetum, the very last place on the upper shelf that an astronomer would have perused in 'reading' the instruments from left to right, for their most brilliantly obscure allusion. Directly beneath the problematical symbol for Sagittarius (♐) is the number 2, an hour number on the equatorial disc, correctly placed. Having already noted how the place of the Sun on the equatorial disc lies on the axis of the 'crest', and comes directly towards the viewer, we cannot help noticing that the combination of Sagittarius and (hour) 2 has that same property, lower down the painting. And what those two tokens convey, in an astonishingly exact way, is *the position of the Moon at the moment recorded in the painting*.

To assess the exactness of the apparent reference, we need to

* A possibility considered again at p. 252 below.

consider two possibilities. Where would the Moon have been *observed* to be at around four in the afternoon of Good Friday 1533, and where would an astronomer of Kratzer's calibre have *calculated* it to be? In fact it was then unobservable, as is usually the case for the greater part of any Good Friday. (The rules for computing Easter mean that the Sun and Moon will not be more than a zodiacal sign or two from opposition, a time of full moon.) Since the astronomer could in principle have extrapolated from an earlier observation, however, and to remove any lingering doubt, we may as well consider both alternatives. In reality, the Moon was in longitude exactly 3.0° of Sagittarius at the hour in question, while a calculation done with the help of the Alfonsine tables, the most authoritative tables then in circulation, and within Kratzer's grasp, would have yielded a very similar answer, 3.9° of Sagittarius. If he had taken a figure from a simpler table of lunar positions, he might have used the rounded *noon* figure of 1° Sagittarius. And the Sun? Was it to be 1° or 1.2° Taurus? And as for the time, was it taken to be 4 o'clock exactly or ten minutes later, for example? We scarcely need to examine all combinations of these options, for all fit the painting well enough, and the most probable of them extremely well. The likelihood is that the Moon would have been regarded as at the 2 hour mark precisely, on the hour scale, or at least within one or two minutes of that mark.[116] When Holbein painted the seemingly erroneous '♐' symbol directly above the '2', he was drawing attention to that simple fact, 'to them that could it know'. In a sense, he was using the torquetum as a calculating instrument. But what is even more significant is that while every astronomical instrument on the upper shelf has made some sort of allusion to the Sun's position, here at last the Moon is being brought into the allegory, true to the traditional iconography of the crucifixion story. It will eventually point out to us another place where the Moon is hiding, namely on the globe.

This completes our survey of those instruments which have to do with celestial measurement, and that are placed on the upper shelf of the stand, on the turkey rug. Such a possession, to which most of us would now give little thought, was then a rare and expensive commodity. That of itself does not guarantee it an allegorical role, although it almost certainly had one. The rug is placed on the 'celestial' level of the stand, making us suspect that it had either an astronomical or spiritual meaning by association. (P. C. Claussen conjectured that the book on which Bishop de Selve's elbow rests was devoted to one or other of these subjects, for the same reason.)[117] There are independent reasons for suspecting that it had both. Its common English name, associating it with the Muslim world of Turkey, tends to obscure the fact that such rugs were often Christian in inspiration, as in the present case. They could be found an important place in English religious ritual at this period, as we know from the mention of a turkey rug on the communion table at London's St Paul's a few years later.[118] Turkey rugs and carpets are frequently encountered in French royal chronicles of the period, where they are often spoken of as hangings. Holbein included several oriental rugs in his paintings. There are examples in his Solothurn Madonna of 1522, his Meyer Madonna a few years later, his portraits of Archbishop William Warham (1527) and Georg Gisze (1532), and there are two different examples under the throne of Henry VIII in his portraits of the king with the barber surgeons (1540), one a painting and the other the cartoon for it. No two are exactly alike. (It is not surprising that collectors and traders still use Holbein's name to identify certain types, even though there are comparable examples in several earlier western paintings.) Only three of Holbein's rugs are in a religious setting, but we are not suggesting that all 'turkey carpets' are of such a character. From the royal inventory of 1547 we know that most were not.[119] As will be explained at a later stage, however, the rug in *The Ambassadors* can be securely placed in a Christian religious tradition that also had a cosmic component. There is also good reason for believing that its geometrical pattern was chosen in part to support a geometrical scheme underlying the design of the painting as a whole.

The accuracy of Holbein's draftsmanship is exceptional, and speaks for long and careful preparation. In view of the fact that

Kratzer made numerous drawings of instruments to illustrate his writings on them, it has been tentatively suggested in the past that Holbein might have used them, rather than real instruments, in preparation for his paintings.[120] This is highly improbable, with the exception of the quadrant, as discussed earlier. Kratzer's drawings are of a much poorer quality than Holbein's in every respect. There is no evidence that he had any special talent for making drawings in correct perspective, which may have been almost as hard for him to produce as the original instrument was to make. Even the fine woodcut in Apian's works is much inferior to Holbein's painted torquetum in the matter of perspective. It is inconceivable that the instruments in *The Ambassadors* were other than real, except in the small details suggested earlier. The help that the painter *must* have received – unless he led a secret life as scholar-astronomer – would have been verbal and computational rather than visual. On the other hand, to master the art of representing complex and finely graduated instruments in near perfect perspective, Holbein must surely have had the use of drawing aids, perspective frames through which Kratzer might first have looked to ensure the correct viewpoint and image. Subsidiary drawings would have been prepared and positioned for transfer at a later stage. This fits in with much of what is known of Holbein's techniques for tracing his working drawings, which he did with high precision.[121] The painting is not a photograph, and it would have occupied much time, in calculation alone, some of it perhaps long before the day being celebrated, and much of it after.

Holbein's eye may strike us as photographic, but that should not obscure the extent to which the painting was done through the mind's eye. Whose mind? Certainly someone using instruments best fitted to London, not Jerusalem nor Rome. Perhaps the quadrant was made for Polisy. So many are the astronomical conceits in the painting that Kratzer's deep involvement in it can hardly be doubted. This has often been denied on the strength of the supposed errors in the instruments, which is why it is so important to reiterate the general conclusion of this chapter. They reveal no serious errors whatsoever. Those that have been ascribed to them by art historians in the past have simply been the result of naive scientific expectations.

SEVEN

THE MUNDANE LEVEL

> The machine of the universe is divided into two, the ethereal region and the elementary region . . . For so God, the glorious and sublime, disposed.
>
> John of Sacrobosco, *On the Sphere*, ch. 1

When Sacrobosco penned what was to become one of the most widely used of all university texts before the seventeenth century, he was setting out a simple doctrine bequeathed by Aristotle and modified in only trifling ways to fit with Christian theology and the basic needs of students in arts. The four elements of the elementary region were assumed to take on a spherical form at the centre of the universe – earth surrounded by water, air and fire, the sphere of fire being just below the sphere of the Moon, with which the higher regions began. What chiefly distinguished the four elements from the immutable essences of the heavenly spheres was that they were subject to alteration, corruption and regeneration. This imperfect place was where mankind belonged. Here was an almost universally accepted truth that might easily have served as a starting point for any scholarly theologian who wished to expatiate on the wider meaning of the still life at the centre of Holbein's painting. As in the case of the upper shelf, however, it is the detail in the lower region that is our surest guide to any scheme that may have been behind it.

THE TERRESTRIAL GLOBE AND THE DIVIDERS

The globe of the Earth, at the left of the lower shelf, has been much discussed in the past. Not mounted in a stand, but meant to be hand-held, it is largely of interest because it records Polisy and part of the coastline of the Americas. Most of the place names are of countries or regions, especially of France. The spelling of 'Pritannia' (for Britanny) and 'Baris' (for Paris) obviously reflects German pronunciation. Not all German speakers interchanged 'p' and 'b' so readily, but we know from his letter to Dürer that Kratzer did so, and from the reply that Dürer did not.[122] The spelling on the globe tells us at the very least that the two Frenchmen were not breathing down Holbein's neck as he worked, although that does not mean that their wishes were not being heeded. Bayonne is recorded on the globe ('Baion'). Is this not in honour of Jean du Bellay, former bishop of Bayonne and now of Paris, the former ambassador to London to whom Dinteville was reporting? Rome is there, painted more or less precisely at the *geometrical centre* of the globe as it is presented to our view. This was surely no accident.

The form of the handle on the globe is said by its modern restorers to owe much to an old restoration of the painting, but there has always been some such handle, and the original globe was not in the same class as the fine mounted celestial globe above it.[123] Mary Hervey, following W. F. Dickes and C. H. Coote, related its twelve gores to those of a supposedly lost terrestrial globe, published in the 1880s in what was held to be a facsimile, by the bookseller Ludwig Rosenthal. It was said at the time that the original was published in 1523 by the astronomer and cartographer Johannes Schöner – the astronomer now thought to have been responsible for the celestial globe in the painting. Hervey did warn, however, that the expert A. E. Nordenskiöld thought otherwise. Others argued that Holbein was copying a lost globe by Maximilian Transsylvanus (described by Franciscus Monarchus in 1526), or one by the Antwerp scholar Gemma Frisius (1530). The most controversial of identifications was with a globe that was brought into the limelight by the expert collector Henry Stevens of Vermont in 1885, but that seems to be based on the Holbein painting. There is a unique set of 'Schöner' gores in the New York Public Library which do not correspond closely to the painted version; but since they turn out to have been printed from a later woodcut (between 1556 and 1560), their details can prove very little. The evidence for the most plausible identifications has been summarised by Elly Dekker and Kristen Lippincott, who note serious difficulties in connection with every one of them.[124] It seems probable that the globe in *The Ambassadors* may have been loosely based on an original with printed gores, and that either the original or the painting of it was modified by Holbein to flatter the sitter from Polisy. The man who could paint *The Ambassadors* could have modified and painted a material globe easily enough, especially with the help of an astronomer. As noted earlier, in connection with the quadrant, Polisy has been put on the painted globe incorrectly in relation to Paris – due east rather than south east – but this mistake may have been based on misinformation supplied by Dinteville himself. Rome, Venice and Genoa are on the globe, but not Milan. Nürnberg and Lyon are there, but nothing between – not Augsburg or Basel or any other Swiss town, for instance. The French court was often in Lyon at this period.

The royal inventory of 1547 lists several terrestrial globes in the usual abbreviated way. One that came from the king's study is described as 'great', another is on a wooden stand coloured green, and broken.[125] The terrestrial globe in the painting was a more modest affair than either of these, or than the magnificent celestial globe, but still it carried important messages of its own. A few place names, as we have seen, made a direct and simple reference to Dinteville's biography. One reason for placing Rome at its apparent centre will be explained at a later stage. As for the new found lands in the Americas, they are almost certainly depicted for reasons that have little to do with the great human achievements that we now tend to associate with them – their discovery, exploration and settlement in the four decades following the first voyage of Columbus. In the thoughts of French diplomats in the 1530s, the map of the Americas would have stirred the embers of resentment at the papal allocation of the New World to Spain and Portugal alone. The seeds of this resentment were sown shortly after Columbus's return. In 1493 the Spanish Pope Alexander VI issued a series of bulls giving Spain, among other privileges, exclusive rights to lands beyond a line stretching from pole to pole and passing through a point a hundred leagues west of the Azores and the Cape Verde islands. Unable to dissuade the pope, the Portuguese opened direct negotiations with Spain, and in 1494 the two countries agreed the treaty of Tordesillas, by which the boundary line was moved 270 leagues further west of the Azores. Portugal was given rights to all to the east of the line, Spain to all to the west of it, with the rider that both were to avoid territory already under other Christian rulers. The treaty – by which each thought the other to have been outwitted – was finally sanctioned by Pope Julius II in 1506. It effectively granted Portugal the true route to India, most of the southern Atlantic seabord of America, the imaginary land of Antilla and the vast real territory of Brazil.

Carving up the New World in this way brought material riches to the two countries concerned, but led to growing envy on the part of other Christian rulers. In view of his relations with Charles V, it came as no surprise when François I gave a mandate to the mariners of Dieppe not only to explore in forbidden waters but to attack Spanish vessels as well. The most famous of the Dieppe shipowners was Jean Anglo, who had an extensive fleet and who was happy to have state support for privateering.[126] His greatest triumph came in 1523, when one of his lieutenants intercepted three ships that had set out to carry the treasure of Montezuma II from Cortes to the emperor. A year later, Anglo's ships were making successful exploration of eastern North America, and by 1529 they had reached Sumatra. Spain and Portugal took counter action, and in 1530 François sanctioned raids on Portuguese shipping. An embassy from Portugal to François soon struck a compromise. In other words, Holbein's painted allusion to the treaty of Tordesillas would without question have turned the thoughts not only of Dinteville but of his English hosts to what had become a thorny political problem. The allusion is plain enough. The Holbein globe is divided into twelve segments by its black lines of longitude, and a thirteenth red line makes a very obvious reference to the Tordesillas agreement, as ratified by a former pope. Its precise position could of course not yet be accurately drawn. There is no such line on any of the great world maps that had followed the new discoveries – those of Giovanni Contarini (1506), Martin Waldseemüller (1507 and 1526), Francesco Roselli (1508) or Peter Apian (1530). The fact that the line is drawn on the 'facsimile' gores of the 1880s merely serves to reduce their plausibility.

Dividers of steel lie behind the terrestrial globe, to our right, and were possibly associated with it. They had so many other uses – for instance with celestial globes, in geometry, and as scribing instruments – that one cannot say with any confidence what they were meant to signify here. It is tempting to associate them with that commonplace image of God the Creator, who is so often depicted holding dividers in his role as God the Architect of the World. It may be worth noting that the point of one leg of the dividers (just emerging from behind and to the left of the lute keys) is on the line down the middle of the painting, a line of some importance; and it is not difficult to find images in which dividers seek a centre – interpreted, for example as virtue, equity or righteousness. When English uses the words 'compass' and 'compasses' for this instrument, it is following the French *compas,* and this is a word that occurs in the phrase *par compas* that could describe a regular or measured action. There is a Holbein design for a medallion that includes dividers and a motto in French making use of that phrase, but when Susan Foister tentatively associates it with Dinteville she omits a word from the motto that seems to speak against the connection.[127]

There is no likelihood that the question of an absolute symbolic value for the dividers, as opposed to the question of their use as an element in an overall design, will ever be convincingly settled. An established sixteenth-century tradition, represented by a fine anonymous Flemish painting now in Brussels is worth mentioning. Dating from around 1580, it quite explicitly portrays the seven liberal arts by means of a large terrestrial globe and dividers, both together portraying *geometry.*[128] This very fact draws attention to the difficult decision facing any painter who wished to include the newly fashionable science of cosmography in such a portrayal. It was a subject that made use of geometry and astronomy, but was fast acquiring its own identity. It was for a time the eighth of the liberal arts in all but name.

18. The terrestrial globe, the arithmetic book and the set square. For more detail see Plate 9.

THE ARITHMETIC BOOK AND SET-SQUARE

In front of the globe, a text-book of commercial arithmetic is held open by a set-square of unusual form.[129] The visible page allowed W. F. Dickes in 1892 to identify correctly the book with a treatise of 1527 written by Peter Apian (Fig. 19).[130] Two worked examples of long division with integral answers are given there, and a third with a fractional answer.

Since the angle of 27° will prove to have been so important to Holbein's general plan, it must be pointed out that the two integral results in the calculations illustrated on the given page come from the numbers 81648 and 1890000, both of them multiples of 27, the first twice over.[131] The examples open quite naturally with the German word *Dividirt.* This simple fact, taken together with the occurrence of a fraction (½) in the answer to the subsidiary worked example, has occasionally been taken as an indication of division and disharmony.

The second property is one that has appealed to those who wish to interpret the painting in terms of the Reformation of the church, seeing in the word a reference to the division of

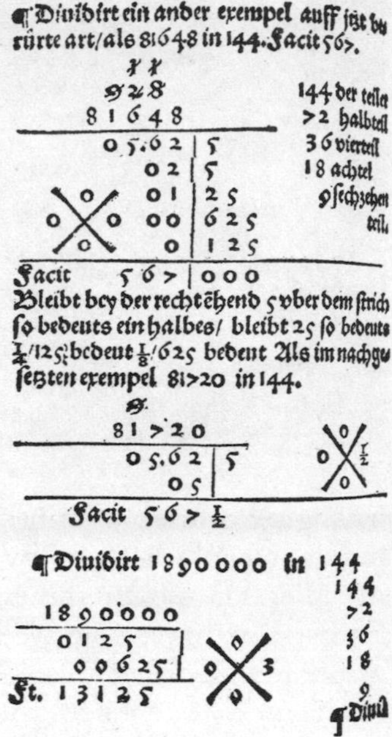

¶ Diuidirt ein ander exempel auff jtzt be-
rürte art/als 81648 in 144. Facit 567.

81648 — 144 der teiler
05.62 | 5 — 72 halbteil
02 | 5 — 36 vierteil
01 | 25 — 18 achtel
00 | 625 — 9 sechzehen teil.
0 | 125

Facit 567 | 000

Bleibt bey der rechtē hend 5 vber dem strich so bedeuts ein halbes/ bleibt 25 so bedeuts 1/4 /125 bedeut 1/8 /625 bedeut Als im nachgesetzten exempel 81720 in 144.

81720
05.62 | 5
05 |

Facit 567 1/2

¶ Diuidirt 1890000 in 144

144
72
1890000 — 36
0125 — 18
00625 — 9

Ft. 13125

19. The original of the page from Apian's arithmetic, just visible in the painting.

Christendom. This may of course have been intentional. It is difficult to know where to stop, in drawing attention to detail that may prove to be meaningful. Thus there are three occurences of a *cross* (in the St Andrew's form) used in setting out the arithmetical divisions. Were they meant to strike a chord in the minds of those contemplating the crucifix in the corner of the painting? I think not, but there is a sliding scale of potential relevance, and it is always possible that the fevered brow of the original schemer would have put to shame even that of his latter-day interpreter.

THE MUSICAL INSTRUMENTS

The eleven-stringed lute with one string broken, on the right of the lower shelf (Plate 10), is an accurate representation of an instrument that was played by many at court, professional musicians and courtiers. By the sixteenth century the principles of the classic lute were more or less fully developed, the instrument

20. The lute, dividers, hymnal and flutes. For more detail see Plate 10.

having six courses of strings (the top course a single string, the rest double) plucked now by the fingers rather than a plectrum as in earlier centuries. In this example the lower courses (the fourth, fifth and sixth) have octave stringing, and it is the octave string of the fourth course that is broken. Lute strings at this period lent themselves to a new system of musical notation ('tablature', with a staff reflecting the pattern of the strings). The pattern of the rose is typically complex, but difficult to make out. Complete six-course lutes from the sixteenth century are today extremely rare. Judging by its size, that painted by Holbein was perhaps an f′-sharp lute.

Long before Holbein's painting was executed, when Dürer wanted to illustrate a method of drawing in correct perspective, he took a lute as his model, yielding a result rather similar in form to Holbein's, and reminding us that, whatever technique he used, the perspective representation of the many objects he chose to include in his composition required not only skill but energy (see Figs 21 and 22.)

The English court was renowned throughout Europe for its music, and many fine musicians from the Continent were being enticed into the king's service. Henry himself composed motets which are still regularly sung, and he showed a strong interest in the technical problems associated with musical instrument making. The 1547 inventory of his former possessions includes numerous lutes and lute cases. The lute was a much loved

21. One of Albrecht Dürer's techniques for perspective representation, illustrated with the drawing of a lute. From his *Underweysung der Messung mit dem Zirkel und Richtscheyt* (Nürnberg, 1525).

instrument that could stand as a symbol for music itself, but the lute with a broken string, as in the present case, must have been something more. It is now often described as self-evidently a symbol of death or discord. Hervey and Dickes saw in it an allusion to an emblem included by Andrea Alciati in his enormously popular book of emblems, first published in Augsburg two years before the painting was done. This idea, which became a common dogma, will be discussed at a later stage.* There has been much debate in recent years about the purpose of such books of emblems – images with captions or mottos (which are usually placed above them) and epigrams or commentaries (usually placed below). Historically speaking, emblems seem to have their origin in texts, to which images were added, rather than the other way about. They were not at first meant to purvey hidden meanings but, on the contrary, to

* See p. 291 below.

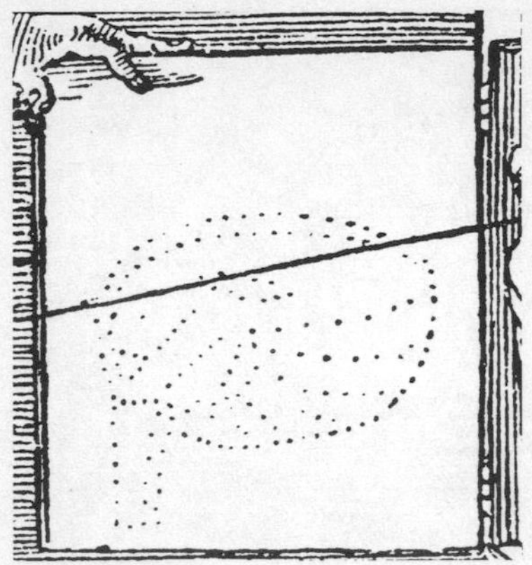

22. A detail of the previous figure.

clarify meaning. A painter might of course have made use of an emblem book as a sort of dictionary to assist in the visual encoding of textual meaning, in other words, to put across a broader message using a vocabulary which he might have expected those familiar with emblem books to understand. The problem with the broken lute string, as we shall see, is that diametrically opposite meanings can be found in it, even within the emblem tradition.

The lute case, inverted, is in shadow under the stand. The lute is not the only musical instrument in the painting. To the right of it on the same shelf there is a lockable leather case for five wooden flutes of different gauges, of which one is missing. Does their absence in some way parallel the broken string? The flutes have for some reason attracted less interest than the lute, and indeed, by a simple lapse one National Gallery catalogue refers only to 'a case of lutes'.[132]

THE HYMNAL

A Lutheran hymnal, the tenor partbook of the second edition of Johannes Walther's *Geystliche gesangk Buchleyn* (*Little Hymn-Book*, 1525), is opened at two of Martin Luther's own hymns.[133] That on the left, 'Kom Heiliger Geyst Herre Gott', is Luther's rendering of the solemn 'Veni Sancte Spiritus', one of the best-known hymns of all time. Holbein has for some reason omitted the final words on this page, a repeated 'Alleluia', but has instead repeated the last word of the hymn itself ('gesungen'). The hymn on the right, 'Mensch wiltu leben seliglich und bei Gott bliben e[wiglich] . . .', is Luther's introduction to his rendering of the ten commandments – 'Man, if thou wouldst live a good life and remain with God eternally . . .' It was noticed long ago – perhaps first by W. B. Squire in the 1890s – that the two hymns are separated in the source. It is possible that Holbein had in front of him a bound selection of hymns, but it seems more likely that the painted book was carefully contrived to harmonise with the general theme of the portrait. In the printed source the second hymn is numbered XIX, but here that number has been transferred to the first hymn. (In the source, the first is numbered XII.) The lure of number was perhaps enough to ensure that XIX was placed somewhere on these pages in veiled but deliberate allusion to the Easter period generally. If so, the reason would have been that – as every well-educated person then knew – the rules of Easter make use of a nineteen-year cycle, one that reconciles the periodic times of the Sun and Moon, the year and the month. Nineteen was simply Easter's number. This interpretation is compelling, in view of the fact that the 'Sun-Moon' line from the torquetum passes through the corner of that 'page XIX' of the hymnal. (The beginnings of this line were touched upon in connection with the torquetum.* It continues to the left eye of the skull, and a fuller explanation of it will be given below.)

Luther knew of the astrological use of the number 19. Hervey paid no attention to it, but saw in these hymns an expression of hope for the reunion of the Roman and Reformed churches. She also pointed out that the young bishop would soon be hearing the 'Veni Creator Spiritus' at his own consecration. (It is still used for this service in the Church of England, in the well-known English version 'Come, Holy Ghost, our souls inspire'.)[134] This is all true, but she has wrongly identified the hymn. It is therefore not very relevant to point out that the hymn she names has an important place

* See p. 149 above.

in the English coronation ceremony, although there will be occasion to mention the fact later, in connection with the design on the floor on which Dinteville and de Selve stand.*

While it is unlikely that Holbein would have placed a Lutheran hymnal in the painting without the permission of his two very Catholic sitters, it is unwise to make too much of the point, for both hymns, in one language or another, are in very general use in most of the older Christian sects. We can only speculate as to whose hymnal Holbein was painting. Copies of the printed versions were probably not then rare in London. Quite apart from Holbein and Kratzer, and one or two German artisans at court, Thomas Cranmer's German wife, Margaret, was niece of the reformer Andreas Osiander and is likely to have had her own circle of German-speaking acquaintances, not least from the community of the Steelyard.

To the same high degree of accuracy as in the case of the dart gnomon on the polyhedral dial, the angle between the visible edges of the hymnal's covers – here even easier to measure – is 27°. The corresponding angle between the covers of the arithmetic book is, by contrast, close to 45°, but the angle between the edges of the *pages* that are propped open by the set-square is yet again 27°.

So much for the artefacts on the upper and lower levels of the stand. Were they merely tokens of the four sciences, the quadrivium, as taught in the universities – astronomy, geometry, arithmetic and music? Two arguments speak against that simple explanation of their presence. They are not arranged systematically according to the standard scheme, and they are not the conventional representatives of the four subjects. Astronomy, for instance, was usually represented by the armillary sphere or astrolabe. It could be argued that Kratzer suggested the instruments we see in the painting as the most advanced in their respective classes. The best scholars of the time would have disagreed, but that sort of thing is an eternal occupational hazard. There is another point which might be made in con-

* See p. 270 below.

nection with the conventional statement that Holbein's aim was to portray the quadrivium: as already explained, in the circles in which he and Kratzer and Dinteville moved, cosmography had to all intents and purposes become a fifth science. Perhaps the terrestrial globe and dividers were meant to represent it. Whether that is true or false, there is certainly much more behind the still life at the centre than a conventional portrayal of the formal divisions of learning, old or new.

EIGHT
THE DISTORTED SKULL

[*The Stranger*] . . . there is a certain degree of deception; for were artists to give the true proportions of their fair works, the upper part, which is further off, would appear to be out of proportion in comparison with the lower, which is nearer; so they give up truth in their images and make only the proportions which appear to be beautiful, disregarding the real ones.

Plato, *Sophist*, 235–36

The most memorable aspect of Holbein's painting, for those who look at it in only a cursory fashion, is the skull in the foreground. Much attention has been paid to it in the hope of discovering, first, the intended viewing method, and then the technique used to produce it. Inspired by instances of deliberate distortion (anamorphosis) from a much later period, cylindrical mirrors and cylindrical lenses have been devised to rectify the image, but without success – something that can best be judged by physics and history taken together.[135] An old commonsense solution was to find a viewing position at the level of the ambassadors' heads somewhere to the right of the painting and not far from the plane of the painting's surface. There are historical precedents for this simple procedure, going back it seems to Leonardo da Vinci, and including portraits of Pope Paul III, Ferdinand I, Charles V and François I, all from the years between 1531 and 1534. They mark the beginning of a long-lasting obsession with anamorphosis, using various techniques that were well surveyed in a pioneering study by Jurgis Baltrusaitis. Most of his material relates to a later period and is scarcely relevant to Holbein, but he does have much to say about *The Ambassadors*, its meaning and what he imagined to be its dramatic purpose. He went so far as to imagine an elaborate situation, a 'drama in two acts', in which the viewer of the painting at Polisy, disappointed at failing to understand the distortion and leaving the room by a door on the right of the work, was forced back by sheer curiosity, only to find that all was revealed as the correct viewpoint was then enforced.[136] This ingenious reconstruction of the planning of the painting no longer has serious support: its basic requirement, the presence of a door to the right, is in any case unverifiable, since the château has been thoroughly restructured over the centuries. The assumption that nothing more than the human eye was needed to reconstitute the skull optically, and that it required no lenses or mirrors or other such paraphernalia, was supported by the general drift of Baltrusaitis's history, and is surely correct.

He had little of note to say about the precise position of the intended viewpoint, but a recent approach to that problem will be found in the work by Foister, Roy and Wyld. The National Gallery's restoration of the painting was complicated by the loss of paint in the region of the nose bone of the skull, but this does not affect the overall geometrical problem unduly.[137] They used computer assistance, but their solution is qualitatively equivalent to accepting the intuitive technique of looking at the skull at a low angle from a place on the right of the painting. It has something in common with the solution to be offered here, and yet there is a difference that is not a question of centimetres alone but of artistic meaning. Before explaining this, we must consider a few elementary geometrical properties of the anamorphosis. Here there is much to be learned from a painting of a very different style and quality, the portrait of Henry VIII's son Prince Edward, the future Edward VI, done by the Dutch painter Willem Scrots and now in the National Portrait Gallery (see Fig. 23). Scrots was court painter to Mary of Hungary, regent of the Netherlands, in 1537. By 1546 – three years after Holbein's death – he was in Henry VIII's service. It is not known whether he ever met Holbein.

THE SCROTS ANAMORPHIC PORTRAIT

There are many superficial differences between the anamorphs, notably in the angles and distances from which they were meant to be examined, but they share one common property:

when correctly reconstituted both present predominantly *circular* forms to the viewer. With the Holbein skull, the roughly circular arc is limited in extent to the back and top of it, but the curve is presentable enough. As is well known, viewing a circle obliquely presents an ellipse to the eye. Working in reverse, beginning with an ellipse and viewing that obliquely, will in general produce another ellipse, but it is possible to choose a viewpoint – indeed *an infinite number of viewpoints* – from which the ellipse presents itself to us as a circle. An artist who painted an elliptical shape with the intention of having it seen as a circle would usually have had only one of that infinite class of circles in mind, that is, a single circle with a specific angular size. As far as shape is concerned, all will be alike – a circle is a circle – but if the ellipse has any *contents,* they will not usually be presented as the artist intended from all viewpoints that yield a circular *outline*. With perseverance, the contents should in principle make it possible for us to select the unique intended viewpoint from what would otherwise have been a limitless set.

This can all be appreciated very easily with reference to the portrait of Prince Edward, where the contents include a second ellipse, reasonably complete. The two ellipses were clearly intended to appear as concentric circles, even though they are not themselves concentric in the painting. Consider the problem in reverse. Suppose, for example, that we take a

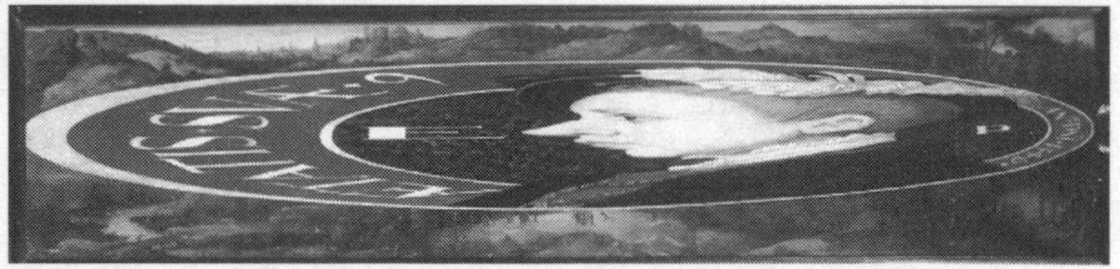

23. Scrots's anamorphosed portrait of Prince Edward in his ninth year, dated 1546. The landscape is a later addition. Oil on wood, in a frame 42.5 by 160 cm. National Portrait Gallery, London. Edward was born 12 October 1537 and reigned from 28 January 1547 to his death in 1553. Willem ('Guilhelmus') Scrots entered Henry's service in 1546. In 1713 the frame still had a signature 'Guilhelmus pingebat'.

photographic slide on which are two concentric circles and project it on an oblique screen using a bright point-source of light. The result will be non-concentric ellipses of just the sort we find round the edge of the Scrots painting. Taking them as our datum it should not be difficult to work the problem back and find the original centre of projection, that is, the point from which the curves appear as concentric circles.

It is easier to prove geometrically that there is such a point than it is to calculate its whereabouts. This is not the place to reproduce the details of either. There are uncertainties that result from the incompleteness of the inner ellipse, but in such situations as this we may hope for assistance from another quarter. It is reasonably certain that both Holbein and Scrots made use of standard linear measures in their work. In *The Ambassadors,* for example, the form of the painting will later be shown to be that of an 80 'inch' square, to which were added two narrow strips. Holbein's unit of length and the other conventions he followed will need to be demonstrated at some length. If we can determine the unit used in either painting, we might reasonably look for round numbers of units in the corresponding viewing arrangement – which is not to say that we shall necessarily find them – and so help ourselves out in the search for a viewpoint that should in principle be discoverable without such assistance. As matters turn out, it seems that Scrots worked so that the portrait could be correctly viewed from approximately two feet away from its end and six inches above its plane.

These are only approximate figures, and they can be improved upon. Assuming that the outlines of Willem Scrots's portrait of Prince Edward were drafted to a standard unit of length, one would draw the conclusion that he used an 'inch' of about 2.65 cm. (The modern 'imperial' inch is 2.54 cm.) This would make the larger of the ovals it contains (both are moderately good ellipses) 56 units long and 8 wide. The lesser ellipse is harder to measure, since part of it is hidden by the portrait, but to the outer edge of its rim it is 38 units long and perhaps 5.5 wide. The separation of the two ellipses so defined is at their leftmost extremes about 15.5 units. Now disregarding the fact that the portrait in the centre must emerge with acceptable proportions, the initial geometrical problem is, as explained, very simply that of finding a viewing position from which both ellipses will appear as concentric circles. Since the artist seems to have used round numbers of units up to this point, we try for a viewing position in a similarly memorable position. Working to half-units (half of the suggested Scrots 'inch') gives much better results than does the use of whole units. There are here two different and essentially independent criteria. A viewing position on the axis of the painting at a distance 25 units from the extreme right-hand end of the larger ellipse, and with the observer's eye 6.5 units above the painting's surface, gives an excellent compromise between circularity and concentricity (that is, it gives a good and uniform border). If whole units were used, 24 may have been the figure accepted for the horizontal distance, measuring from near the edge of the panel. At a later period the painting was enclosed in a box. A surviving cross-member at the back of the frame, however, and a slot in the back of its right-hand piece, were together clearly meant to accommodate a hinged rule and vane for viewing the painting, and the dimensions recommended here fit perfectly with that idea. In view of the need to make estimates of such things, we simply cannot pretend to an exact set of distances; but, judging by the final image (Fig. 24), we are probably as near as we are ever likely to get to Scrots's intentions. His ellipses are not perfect, but they are by no means as bad as is sometimes suggested.

24. The general appearance of Willem Scrots's portrait of Prince Edward as it would have been seen from the proposed viewing position.

25. Prince Edward in his sixth year. Detail, unsigned. *(National Portrait Gallery, London)*

Owned by the same gallery (but currently hanging in Montacute House, Somerset) there is a second portrait of Edward as prince (Fig. 25), closely related in turn to a third portrait that is now in the Metropolitan Museum in New York.[138] Both strongly resemble the Scrots portrait, correctly viewed, but it is more likely that the earlier – whatever that was – simply inspired the later, rather than that all are from Scrots's studio. The anamorphosed portrait of the older prince was not done in Holbein's lifetime, but it is quite possible that Scrots was aware of whatever technique for anamorphosis Holbein had used for *The Ambassadors,* since both artists worked within the orbit of the court. The New York portrait is circular and is quoted as 12¾ (imperial) inches across. If this was meant to be an exact number of units, then, as will be seen shortly, the unit did not match Holbein's inch. If its diameter was meant to be 12 units, the unit used (2.7 cm) was only one part in fifty larger than that deduced from the Scrots anamorphosis – a weak argument for their closeness.

SKULL AND SUN

What of the technique used for the anamorphosis in *The Ambassadors*? The painting as a whole is rather more than 80 inches square (81.5 by 82.5 imperial inches) and we can detect the use of a 40 'inch' unit within it.[139] It will emerge later why 80 of the appropriate sort of inches must be taken not as the overall height or width (which in any case differ) but as the height of the painting excluding the prominent white strip (seemingly of simulated marble) at its lower front edge. It will be convenient to refer to the dividing line between the two as 'the lower axis'. The oak boards on which the painting was done may have shrunk slightly over the centuries, even differentially, especially in view of some past dismemberment of the dowelled boards for restoration purposes. The fact remains that the ratio of height to width is still of the order of 1 per cent. When the rationale of the painting is understood, even that disparity will lose its relevance to the problem of shrinkage. If we define a unit as explained, then this turns out to be about 2.54 cm, or one modern imperial inch, and we can distinguish it with good historical warrant as a 'Tudor inch'. It is in any case clear that the English measure was in use, rather than a unit from the German world.[140] By quoting measurements in such units, we shall not find it necessary to refer to any other, old or modern. It gives measurements in round numbers that can be converted at will by those who prefer modernity to history.

The curve presented by the cranium of the Holbein skull is the only section with a reasonably simple geometrical form, so that finding a viewpoint is much more difficult than in the case of Scrots's ellipses. There is a very obvious axis to the distorted skull, however, and even by eye one may estimate its angle very accurately. Asked to regard the top-right section as part of an ellipse, an unprejudiced eye will put the axis of the ellipse within half a degree of 27°. That axis, when produced to the edges of the painting, cuts the right-hand edge almost exactly 30 Tudor inches from the bottom edge and the bottom edge itself just 60 of those units from its right-hand end. At last, the 27° begins to make sense: a line with a gradient of 1 in 2 (30 in 60) lies at an angle of 26.56°. All of our previous estimates of angles of 27° might therefore have been more correctly given as 'gradients of 1 in 2', although of course for most of them we are quite unable to measure the difference.

To decide next on the whereabouts of the end of the axis of the ellipse that we imagine as a frame to the skull, we begin by viewing the skull from sundry positions at the side, and soon realise that our imaginary framing circle comes to the very edge of the painting, or a shade beyond. This is to be expected, even if we suppose that the axis of its equivalent ellipse ends at the very edge of the painting, a fact that will be evident from the situation in the neighbourhood of *Z* in Fig. 26. The major axis of the ellipse will then be precisely 45 Tudor inches.

And the intended viewpoint? It has to be outside the painting, but, as already explained, there is an infinite number of ways of viewing an ellipse as a circle. There are various semi-geometrical approaches to this dilemma. For example, the orbits of the eyes of the skull must be more or less equalised – allowing for the fact that the skull as seen must still present an image in correct perspective. (Note this complication.) This condition leads us to place the viewpoint somewhere between thirty and forty inches from the upper end of the ellipse, along its '1 in 2' axis. Another desirable condition is that the *centre* of the circle that we imagine as a boundary for the skull – something that the position and eccentricity of the ellipse decides – be at or near the centre of the skull image. This condition is satisfied at similar distances.

But now a notable property of the painting comes to our aid. How was the viewer to know where to place the eye? It occurred to me that the rod gnomon of the polyhedral dial might have been meant as an aid in placing the eye correctly. The viewer might have been told to hold close to the wall and to place the left eye so that it was possible to look up along the line of that, or one of the other gnomons, and then down along the line of the skull, keeping the head in a more or less fixed position. This yields one mildly interesting result. One finds oneself looking directly at the 'INRI' inscription over Christ's head on the cross, but little else strikes a chord. Taking a very slightly lower angle, however, everything suddenly falls into place. Choosing the gnomon on the nearer 'side' face of the polyhedral dial, the eye is led through various potentially significant points until it reaches the head of the crucified Christ. The day is Good Friday. We are looking up at much the same angle as we look down at the skull. This is the broad

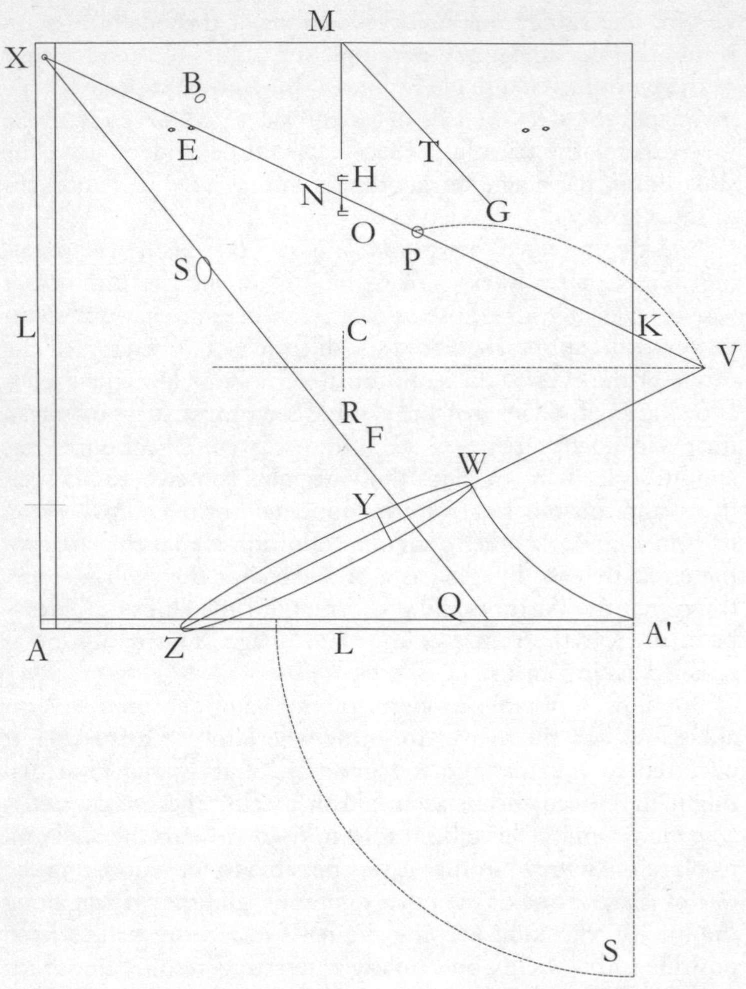

26. The two principal sighting lines from the viewpoint *V*, one through the line of the elongated skull (stylised as ellipse *WZ*) and the other the line *VKPEX*. Other lines are added to simplify a later discussion. The figure's proportions are not exact.

picture, and it was plainly deliberately contrived. From this point on, it is simply a question of settling the fine detail.

The situation is rather more complicated than we could have

wished, since slight variation in the positioning of the upper line of sight can produce different but still superficially plausible results. One of the several possibilities, however, is so much richer than the others that it was clearly what was intended. It has properties that cannot be instantly appreciated. We retain the idea that the observer's eye (*V* in the figure) was on the axis of the skull-ellipse at approximately 36 Tudor inches – a yard – from its tip (*W*). The strict assumption may be relaxed at a later stage, once the true line has been discovered. The line favoured is that from the viewing point *V* through the *nearest* face of the dial, which goes up to the head of Christ. To find three significant points on the line is a minimum requirement, but in the end we find perhaps as many as ten, making the probability of a chance alignment vanishingly small. The most obscure of them is the precise but unmarked place of the Sun on the celestial globe. Almost as elusive is the hour mark, which as explained earlier is cleverly indicated on the face of the white quadrant.

The line in question, from the observer's eye along the twelve o'clock line of the broad face of the polyhedral dial (the face nearest the ordinary viewer of the painting), next passes through the very origin of the quadrant scale and the tip of the nearby pin – that which seemed to draw our attention to the hour line on the quadrant. The fact that the triangle so created on the quadrant has a base of two inches and a vertical of one inch (see Fig. 28) suggests that it was very deliberately planned. The line continues through the zero of the scale of the compound solar instrument, through the invisible Sun on the celestial globe opposite the ram supporter,* and through the northern point (*N*) of the horizon circle of the globe. It is almost certain that we are meant to add to this list the brightest star (Deneb) in the constellation of Cygnus and the brightest star (Vega) in the head of the constellation that Ptolemy and we call the Lyre. The former constellation, it will be recalled, may have been meant as the gallic cock, although there is another meaning in store. The Lyre is a constellation represented here

* As explained at p. 115 above.

in a perfectly conventional way as a falling vulture or eagle, *Vultur Cadens*. From those two bright stars, the line continues upwards to the left eye of Dinteville; and finally reaches to the head of the crucified Christ. It is hard to say whether it was meant to pass through one of Christ's eyes rather than the other, for both are in deep shadow, but the left seems more likely. In any case, this situation should not be treated as a question of geometry or optics alone. Most of Holbein's educated contemporaries, versed in the New Testament and made conscious of the painter's use of the symbolism of light, might have considered the eye as a *source* of light, and Christ as the light of the world.[141] We shall have more to say shortly about the ambiguity in regard to the eyes of Christ.

This is such a rich collection of potentially meaningful material that it is worth now turning the question round, and asking for the optimum viewing position, given the above list of points. It turns out to be approximately 35.8 of our Tudor inches from the top edge of the skull – a good approximation to a yard. The alignment would not have been easy to turn into paint, and there is also the problem of panel shrinkage over the centuries. The angles to the horizontal of the lines radiating upwards (at about 26.0°) and down through the skull (at about 26.6°) are very close, and this is surely because both were meant to be at gradients of 1:2, or 26.56° rounded to 27°. We can almost see the measurer at work: the upper line crosses the right side of the painting at a certain distance below its nominal mid-point. The image of Christ is then lowered by a similar amount. But how are we to place our eye, to see everything correctly but easily? It seems likely that we should have been told to look first down the skull and then to put our eye on a level with the tips of Dinteville's fingers and the lute strings, as though he was touching them.

The two lines of sight, one up to (or down from) Christ and the other down from the viewer to the skull (or up from the skull to the viewer), are at the very heart of the painting's symbolic form, but, as pointed out earlier, there is yet another line with the same general character. It is that which passes through the axis of the 'crest' of the torquetum, and on through the key points that mark the places of the Sun and Moon on its different scales, the one conventionally, the other by sleight of hand. There can be little doubt about the great deliberation with which Holbein placed that Sun-Moon line on his panel, for it passes through the corner of 'page XIX' and through what we shall describe as the mid-point of the lower axis of the painting. That line too passes through the middle of the *left* eye of the skull.

RIGHT AND LEFT EYES

Geometry apart, what property is shared by what have been referred to here as 'lines of sight'? There is a great temptation to impose our own theology on the situation, for want of clearly appropriate texts. Throughout the history of the Christian church, the Sun had been considered a symbol of Christ. In the painting it is as though the visage of the crucified Christ is being presented as a Sun from another world, in temporary eclipse. The Sun on the globe is in shadow and below ground, reminding the contemplative viewer of the gloomy situation on the evening of Good Friday. The Sun of which we are obscurely informed by the line on the white quadrant and the shadows on the polyhedral dial is in a place that is correct for the *current* London time, after the end of the hour of Christ's death. (The same is true of the Sun of which the cylinder dial informs us, but we are for the moment concerned only with what is packed on to the upper line of sight.) In short there are three clear pieces of solar symbolism, apart from Christ himself, on that upper line. By contrast, the lower line is one of natural shadow, cast by the skull, a reminder of corruption and death. The line is in this case centred on the left eye of the skull, just as is the torquetum line. When considering that 'Sun-Moon line' upwards from the lifeless left eye of the skull, or indeed the line from the same eye to us, as we look down at it, we might invent our own script easily enough. It is no longer we who are contemplating death or salvation, but the dead who are recalling the glories of the created world – with thoughts that we could all of us put into words.

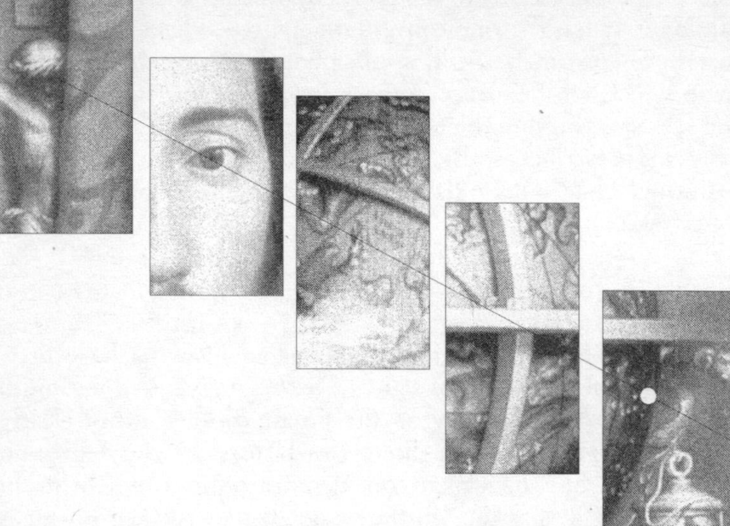

27. Details of the painting where the upward line of sight passes through significant points. From the left, the points are: the left eye of Christ, the left eye of Dinteville, the star Vega in Lyra, the star Deneb in Cygnus, the north point of the horizon, and the Sun on the globe (marked artificially here in white). The line continues in the next figure.

How likely is it that a devout Christian believer would have performed calculations in gnomonics, the astronomy of shadows, with that most revered of all symbols, Christ on the cross? If only to show that our own analysis of the painting's religious theme is not out of key with the mentality of all sixeenth-century theologians, we note that 1533 was the very year in which Charles de Bouelles (or Bouvelles, in Latin Bovillus), a polymath whom Dinteville had almost certainly met at the French court, published in Paris an intricate discourse requiring him to do precisely that. It is not that his work is particularly relevant to *The Ambassadors,* except to the extent that it blends theology and gnomonics. In it he goes to great lengths to decide on the direction in which Christ would have turned his eyes as he hung from the cross.[142] Half-heartedly deciding that Christ would have looked to the left, away from the glare of the Sun, de Bouelles in the end throws in the towel and leaves the final decision to the reader. At all events, such a combination of themes was plainly not out of bounds.

To return then to the painting: what of the choice of eye? The upper line passes through Dinteville's left eye; and through which of ours? It seems most natural to look down at the skull with our left, with our right cheek to the wall, although this is by no means necessary. Can the left eyes be no more than a mnemonic, to help us remember how to reconstitute the image of death? If not, what is the meaning of it all?

In view of the prejudices of a right-handed world, one might have expected to find that a metaphorical distinction between left and right eyes was as common in the past as that between right and left hands, dexter and sinister, but this seems not to have been so. It is not scriptural, for example, but it is not entirely unknown. It occurs in at least two places that could easily have come to the notice of Holbein, his sitters, or Kratzer. All of them would certainly have heard of a work that was on its way to becoming as influential as any in the history of Christian literature, apart from the Bible itself. *Of the Imitation of Christ (De Imitatione Christi),* ascribed to Thomas à Kempis, dates from the early fifteenth century. It was already well known in England when it was translated into English by Richard Whitford, an intimate friend of Erasmus and More, around the year 1531. In one passage the author notes that with the right eye we stand above the present and look upon the eternal and things heavenly, while with the left eye we behold things transitory.[143] This would make good sense of the painting, on the assumption that the viewer looking up to Christ did so with the right eye, but used the left to look down at the skull – the latter certainly requires the eye to be at a certain distance from the wall. This fits equally well with the idea that the skull's left eye, nominally looking up to the Sun and Moon (at the torquetum), or to you, the viewer, is regarding something less than eternal; and Dinteville's left eye is certainly not looking at the eternal. He too is looking at you.

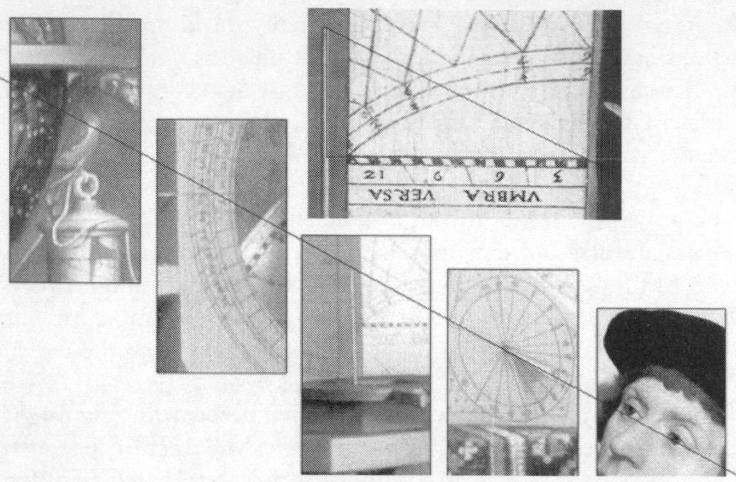

28. The line of sight through the Sun on the globe, the centre of the solar instrument scale, the tip of the pin for that instrument, the gnomon of the polyhedral dial, and an eye of the observer. The detail of the quadrant shows another remarkable property of the line. It passes through the very origin (zero) of the scale, while the triangle formed by the scale and the pin has a base of two inches and a vertical of one inch. The vertical was almost certainly designed to be 36 inches from the right hand edge of the painting. (It is now 35.7 inches.)

The other highly apposite text of the period comes from what is usually known as the *Theologia Germanica (The German Theology),* a much rarer fifteenth-century work, but one that was given much publicity after Martin Luther discovered and published it in 1516. He said of it that, next to the Bible and St Augustine, no book had ever come into his hands from which he had learned more 'of God and Christ and man and all the things that are'. The seventh chapter puts forward a very similar account to that in Thomas à Kempis, reminding us – but without mentioning a source – that 'it is written and said' that the soul of Christ had two eyes, the right eye belonging to the inner man and fixed upon eternity and the Godhead, the left eye belonging to the outer man, and standing with him 'in perfect suffering, in all tribulation, affliction and travail'.[144] *Even when Christ was on the cross*, we are told, the eyes of his soul were of two natures; and the created souls of ordinary men are the same, their right eyes with a power of seeing into eternity, their left of seeing into time and created things, and of relating to the life of the body. The writer goes on to point out that

> these two eyes of the soul of man cannot both perform their work at once; but if the soul shall see with the right eye into eternity, then the left eye must close itself and refrain from working, and be as though it were dead.

In short, 'You can't use both eyes at once'. This is as close as we are ever likely to come to a statement concerning the way to view, in every sense of the word, along the upper and lower lines. It is the left eye that looks down to the skull and the ravages of time on the created body, and the right that looks up, to Christ on the cross and the eternal verities, in the far corner of the painting. All this, as our text tells us, requires two separate acts.

TECHNIQUE

The arrangement for dual viewing, suggested in the first place only by the fact that it was compatible with one of a range of plausible points from which to reconstitute the distorted skull, carries with it a message so well fitted to Good Friday that we shall consider it proved. As explained, it seems that the distance of the viewpoint from the top of the skull (the distance projected on the plane of the painting) is very close indeed to a yard, Tudor or imperial. We recall our conclusion that Scrots chose a round number, in his case two feet. But it is still necessary to place the eye at the right distance from the wall.

This would be easier if the width of the token ellipse bounding the skull were accurately known. It seems to be in the region of 5 or 6 inches, but it may be a little more or less, and for every estimate of it we derive a different workable value for the distance of the eye to the plane of the painting. The following are our main findings, all in Tudor inches:

> With an ellipse of minor axis 5.8, the offset distance has to be 7. The visual results naturally differ somewhat, making for a longer cranium at the higher values. The most satisfying result seems to be when the offset distance is close to 6 and the ellipse's minor axis is 5. Since a distance of 6 pairs very well with the distance of 36, it will be accepted here as the most probable solution, all the more acceptable since it produces more convincing visual results than any other pairing tried in the range of offsets between 4 and 10. It is unexpected and noteworthy that the vertical distance of the viewpoint below the (nominal) mid-point of its right-hand side is also 6.

The highly satisfactory view of the skull from the 36 and 6 combination is shown in Fig. 29.

Deciding on Holbein's technique for *producing* the anamorphosis in his painting must remain a largely speculative matter, in the complete absence of documentation. It is true that we have a later explanation of a technique for producing anamorphosis. In 1559 Daniele Barbaro, the Patriarch of Aquileia and commentator on the Roman architect Vitruvius, published in Venice his *Pratica della perspettiva,* and set out a procedure for what he called a beautiful and secret part of perspective. The operation as he described it was to be in two phases. First the image was to be composed as it is normally seen; its outline on

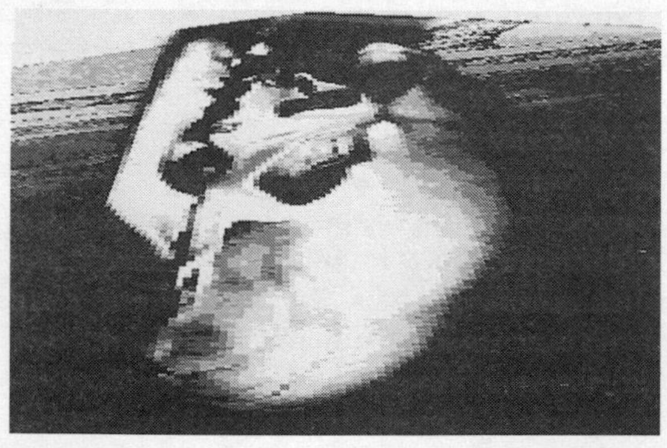

29. The skull as seen from the position explained.

30. A technique for painting from life directly on glass, from Albrecht Dürer, *Underweysung der Messung*, 1525. (Compare Fig. 21.)

the paper was then to be marked with perforations. Fixing the paper at right angles to the panel that was to receive the picture, the rays of the Sun or of a lantern were then to be projected through the holes, so tracing out the image. Barbaro also mentions a way of achieving the result without Sun, lantern or perforated paper, using instead geometrical constructions.[145]

It is possible that this was Holbein's way, but we must remember that Barbaro was a geometer through and through, and that he was really doing nothing more than turn Dürer inside out, so to speak. Clearly Holbein would have first produced the perspective view of the skull that he wished the viewer to see from the side, and then have transferred it to the panel by one of the techniques advocated by Dürer, but working in reverse. But by which? We might imagine his pencil at the place of the lute, in Fig. 21 above, so that the prepared perspective drawing would have been in the place of the Dürer drawing in progress. Such a method would have been tedious and very difficult indeed to apply. So narrow is the cone of light that the initial painting or drawing would have been very small – only 3 inches across, even if placed near *W* in Fig. 26. Barbaro's method with a lantern and paper would have been easier, although the small angle means that the paper would need to have been rigidly mounted – certainly not an impossible thing to do.

A modern procedure would be to use a transparency – the initial painting might be done on a rigid plate of glass, for example – in conjunction with an intense point-source of light, and no other sources of illumination. No lens is needed for such a technique, if the source is not large. Holbein was very familiar with the painting and staining of glass, having prepared designs in Basel for workers in that medium. His father had done much work of the same sort before him.[146] Dürer had previously described a device for painting or crayoning (with black chalk) the sitter's image on a sheet of glass (Fig. 30), after which the image was transferred to paper. The technique of working in that direction was used often in the sixteenth century – it was recommended for landscapes, for example, by Leonardo.[147] Even earlier, the humanist Leon Battista Alberti (1404–72), a pioneer in the technique of perspective representation, had spoken of the painter's ambition 'to represent the form of things seen on the plane as if it were of transparent glass'.[148] Every visitor to a church with sunlight shining through stained glass in the windows has seen distorted images on the floor, and no doubt every worker in stained glass had seen similar images from bright sources of light nearer at hand. Holbein could easily have been influenced from any or all of these quarters. But what of his source of light?

He would have had no very powerful point-source of light at his disposal – today we might think in terms of a small halogen bulb – to produce his distorted image of the perspective painting, or sketch, of the skull. Surprisingly enough, he would not have needed it. I have tried the method in a darkened room with a single candle, without even a reflector. Projecting a skull of the right dimensions from glass on to a white surface, I found it not only possible but positively easy to sketch the resulting image. Of course there are small practical problems to be solved, for example that of the changing position of the flame as the candle burns down. An oil lamp would not have presented the same problem, but in any case one does not know whether Holbein went directly into paint or whether he prepared an initial sketch, to be filled in subsequently in daylight. Painting in the gloom would not have been easy, but even that cannot be ruled out for a man with Holbein's skill and experience. The human eye adjusts fairly quickly to very low levels of lighting indeed. The eye needs to be dark-accommodated, especially where the illumination falls off rapidly (following an inverse square law of illumination) as one moves the pencil away from the flame, say beyond the middle of the elongated skull. We note that at distances where Holbein painted the *shadow* of the skull – a separate issue – the low level of illumination would have been troublesome.[149] These various considerations incline me to believe that Holbein proceeded in the way described, although Barbaro's method certainly cannot be ruled out. In the case of the much less subtle portrait by Scrots it is harder to choose.

ANOTHER ANAMORPH?

When first attempting to make sense of the polyhedral dial, and thinking that a flatter form would have been more suited to a London latitude, it occurred to me that Holbein might have distorted its image in much the way that he distorted the skull. If we imagine Dinteville stepping out of the painting, and standing still with his back to it at the level of what I called its lower axis (the line on the white strip), his eye would be 30 inches or so from the dial. Taking his eye to be half that distance above the plane of the painting, looking down to his left he would see – at a gradient of 1 in 2 twice over, as it happens – an image of a dial of flattened form that would have been usable if not perfect at a London latitude (Fig. 31). I do

31. Reconstruction (in perspective representation) of the polyhedral dial, treating it as a second instance of anamorphosis.

not, on balance, think that this was a part of Holbein's original plan. There is nothing more about the polyhedral dial that calls for an explanation; the idea is not needed to explain any of the problems addressed already; and there is no reason to think that Kratzer ever made a dial in flattened form. The figure is included here only as an exercise in anamorphosis, for those who crave more but have no wish to move into the anachronistic world of distorting mirrors and lenses, or complicated mathematical transformations.

NINE

FROM APELLES TO AN ABBEY PAVEMENT

And he made an hanging for the tabernacle door of blue, and purple, and scarlet, and fine twined linen, of needlework.

Exodus 36:37, on the rug covering the door of Solomon's temple

In addition to the line through the skull and that to the head of Christ, with their simple gradients of close on 1 in 2, and the Sun-Moon line from skull to torquetum, there are significant lines with other properties that are not far to seek, and at least three of them deserve mention.

THE APELLES LINE

The first is a vertical down the middle of the painting. More precisely: the 80-inch square (the area limited in ways explained earlier) is perfectly divided by the line of the plumbline of the compound solar instrument that stands on the upper shelf of the stand. That important line passes through the corner of the set-square (*F*) and less perfectly through one point of the dividers – both of them fiducial instruments. It seems to have been in use for the positioning of the Sun-Moon line. One may assign other geometrical properties to it, but they will not be spelled out here since they were perhaps attained only accidentally – as might of course be the case with the square and dividers. There is, on the other hand, good reason for suspecting that the central vertical was more to Holbein than a mere geometrical device, and that he intended it, if not as a signature, at least as an allusion to his own skill. To help explain the power of the image in his eyes we must look back to his early years in Basel, and to a woodcut he designed for use as a printer's plate then.

The cut in question was for Valentinus Curio's 1521

32. Holbein's design for a woodcut for Valentinus Curio's printer's device, as it appeared on Erasmus's *Enchiridion* (Basel, 1521). The hand drawing the central line makes allusion to the Apelles legend.

German-language edition of Erasmus's *Enchiridion* (Fig. 32). There is within it a panel flanked by two putti – it would be stretching irony too far to suggest that Dinteville and de Selve correspond to them – and there we find a central vertical line being drawn by a hand wreathed in cloud, an allusion to divinity in some sense or other. The motif, which Holbein used again in the border of the title page of the same book, alludes to the legendary contest between the ancient Greek painters Apelles and Protogenes, in which each tried to paint a finer line than the other. The story was well known at this time, from the version recounted by Pliny the Elder in his *Natural History*.[150] The very book by Erasmus that the young Holbein brothers had decorated with pen and ink sketches, the Latin version of *Praise of Folly*, referred to that account. Apelles, finding that Protogenes was away from home, left his signature, as it were, in the form of a fine line on a blank panel that had been prepared for painting. Protogenes returned, saw it, and superimposed a finer line down the middle of the first. Apelles, ashamed to be beaten, superimposed yet a third and finer line through the second. Pliny tells us that this painting, blank apart from its almost invisible lines, long afterwards became an object of wonderment in Caesar's palace on the Palatine. True to the legend, the hand in the 1521 woodcut draws a fine line down the middle of a previous line.

Was Holbein alluding to the Apelles story by placing a perfect plumbline in the central vertical when he was painting Dinteville and de Selve? He no doubt knew of several unseemly squabbles between Italian artists anxious to be known by Apelles' name and he was certainly aware that other northern painters had been honoured by a comparison with Apelles – notably Albrecht Dürer by the imperial poet Conrad Celtis in 1500. If we are to turn his median line into words they might have been in the spirit of 'I am a painter of Apellean quality' rather than 'I am Apelles'. In a letter to Pieter Gillis in Antwerp, Erasmus spoke of Holbein as an exceptional artist, but of Dürer as 'the Apelles of our time'. Oddly enough, in his *Praise of Folly*, Folly derides this habit scholars have of glorifying one another by awarding the names of great men from the past.[151] Erasmus was nevertheless prepared to do just that, years later, when he wrote a Latin inscription under Holbein's last portrait of him. It was intended for the Froben edition of a collection of the scholar's works that was published in 1540, but was too late for that and was issued separately later (see Fig. 2). There at last he more or less acknowledged the artist as Apelles.

There is no need to suppose that Holbein was covertly including a private signature in the printer's device of 1521, although it represented an accolade that he dearly wanted. The hand from the clouds is not his own, unless the block-cutter reversed his drawing, for it is a right hand, and Holbein painted only with his left. That the idea of a concealed signature was not alien to his practice is plain, however, from the notorious allusion to his own left-handedness in a wry signature that he had added to a design for stained glass, done before 1519. It took the form of the name of the Roman C. Mucius (Scaevola), written in mirror script – Mucius was renowned for having thrust his right hand in the fire as a proof to the Etruscans of his Roman indifference to the threat that he would be burned alive. Holbein portrayed that legendary event in the *midline* of his paintings on the façade of the Hertenstein house in Luzern during the same period of his life, and he included it in a design for a title page border used by the printers Froben in Basel (1515) and Pynson in London (1518).[152]

The Apelles idea surfaces yet again in connection with the portrait Holbein painted in 1526 entitled *Laïs of Corinth*. When it is assumed that it offers a clue to his intimate relationship with the sitter – thought to have been Magdalena Offenburg – this is chiefly on the grounds that Laïs was said to have been the mistress of Apelles.[153] There would be danger of a circular argument here were the evidence from elsewhere for his obsession with this comparison not so strong. Nicolas Bourbon, that master of facile flattery, made use of it often. In his *Nugae*, for instance:

> Whilst with a hand of outstanding skill, the godlike mind of Hans was portraying my features on the panel, my jaw dropped and I uttered this song: 'Hans painting me was greater than Apelles'.

Again, in his dedicatory letter of 1536 he qualified Holbein as 'the royal painter, the Apelles of our time'.* And then in a poem that prefaced a collection of Holbein's Old Testament woodcuts (1538–39), as Eric Ives remarks, he 'ran out of superlatives: the artist outclassed Apelles and Parrhasios and that third miracle of the ancient world, Xeuxis, all rolled into one!' The accolade soon became a platitude. When John Leland, antiquary to Henry VIII, composed two Latin poems on Holbein's painting of Edward, Prince of Wales, he drew an extravagant parallel between the occasion and that on which Apelles painted Alexander the Great. Literary conventions these numerous allusions may have been, but if Holbein did not positively help them into existence he would certainly not have disagreed with them.[154] In short, there is nothing intrinsically unlikely in the idea that he wanted to hint at his Apelles-like qualities by means of the plumbline that falls down the middle of *The Ambassadors*.

* See p. 32 above.

THE GLOVES LINE

The second of the three lines in *The Ambassadors* with potential significance is that set by the slantwise straight edge (diameter) bounding the pendant semicircle of the torquetum. It is on the line joining the mid-point M of the nominal 80-inch square and the gloves (G) carried by de Selve. It is the recurrent use of the mid-point that seems to guarantee that the line is a special one. The gloves do not, needless to say, define a point precisely, and they may even be thought an insignificant addition to the painting. A reason for setting some little store by this rather arbitrary alignment is that the gloves seem to come into a later configuration, and that gloves did have an important symbolic function within the Catholic Church. They were generally the prerogative of the pope, cardinals and bishops, and played an important part in religious ritual, as they still do. Here they are carried. They were worn in general only at the celebration of mass (but not at a mass for the dead). At a bishop's consecration they were put on the new bishop immediately after the mitre, with the wish that the sacrifice of the mass might be as pure as the gift of venison which Jacob, his hands wrapped in the skins of kids, brought to Isaac.[155]

The colour of gloves was usually matched to the liturgical colour of the day, and that was almost certainly the case here, since the day is Good Friday and the gloves are black. The brown cast that Holbein gave them presumably conveys an effect of the light. There is no liturgical colour brown. Black is used relatively rarely in the church year, being reserved for offices for the dead (except children) and on Good Friday, when it is apparently traditional only to use it in the first part of the *afternoon* celebration – welcome support for the day and the time of day.[156] On the question of colour, it is of some interest that there are vestiges of a bright red paint beneath the surface of the lower part of de Selve's robe, most probably indicating a change of mind as to what dress was appropriate for the hour or even the day represented in the painting. It is conceivable that the bishop was painted with an earlier hour of Good Friday in view, since red was commonly – although by no means universally – worn then.[157] On the other hand, the great complexity of the composition, and so the time required to plan it, may be thought to speak against the idea.

THE ST MICHAEL-ROME LINE

A third alignment in the painting is that from the head of the crucified Christ through the head of the saint on the medallion of St Michael, worn by Dinteville. This third line runs along a diameter of the terrestrial globe, and through *Rome at its geometrical centre*. The repainted handle is only slightly off this line. The line continues through the peg of the lute that belongs to the broken string and on to the point *Q* on the lower axis of the painting 20 Tudor inches from its right hand edge, that is, a quarter of the nominal square. Before reaching *Q*, it passes through the auricle of the skull (*D*), the skull which would no longer hear the lute string even if it were not broken.

This line embodies what is without exception the most satisfying piece of *geometry* in the entire painting, and it seems right and proper that it should pass through the angle of that geometrical instrument, the set-square, that holds open the arithmetic book. This is very fitting, since the result depends on the decomposition of a square into three right-angled triangles. To show the underlying geometry it is best that we detach it from the picture and place it within a true square on which are drawn only it, a line at the 'one in two' angle (about 27°), and a construction line to aid our demonstration (Fig. 33). To keep to small numbers, the side of the square will be taken as 4 units. *M* is the mid-point of the right hand side *AB*, and *N* divides the base *BC* into segments of 1 and 3 units, as does the St Michael-Rome line in the painting. What those who planned the design appreciated was that the angles *ADM* and *MDN* are equal. In words that relate to the painting: the St Michael-Rome line also makes the familiar angle of close to 27° with the viewer's sightline up to the eye of Christ. To express it in this way, however, might be to make it sound almost accidental. Far from it. Noticing the property must have been nine-tenths of the battle, for the proof is simple enough. Here is one version:

DM is of length $2\surd 5$ units, *MN* is $\surd 5$ units and *DN* is 5 units (all by Pythagoras' theorem). By the converse of the same theorem, *DMN* is then a right angle, and therefore the gradient of *MDN* is simply 1 in 2 (or one might say that triangles *ADM* and *DMN* are equiangular since their sides are proportional).

Transferring this elegant result to the picture, the artist would have had a few awkward facts to accommodate, such as that Christ's eyes cannot be on the very edge, either of the top or of the left side. This is surely a major part of the justification for the strips at the left side and foot. Those who take the trouble to do so will find that the geometrical figure has been adapted to the plan of the painting with an error in the upper angle of the order of only half a degree, as explained earlier, and a negligible error in the middle angle. More important is the fact that the 'theorem' inherent in the painting at last provides us with a solution to the hitherto unsolved problem of why, on the quadrant scale, *angles above 54° were hidden from view* at the lower end, just as angles below 27° had been hidden at the other. The angle that is the double of 27° is simply the angle made by the St Michael-Rome line. But is that the whole story? What else could it signify? It looks like an altitude (consider the angle *DNC*), but even the noon altitude of the Sun in London on this day was not as high as 54°. The answer is patently obvious. It is the angle submitted at the viewer's eye by the two lines of sight, one up to Christ and one down to the skull.

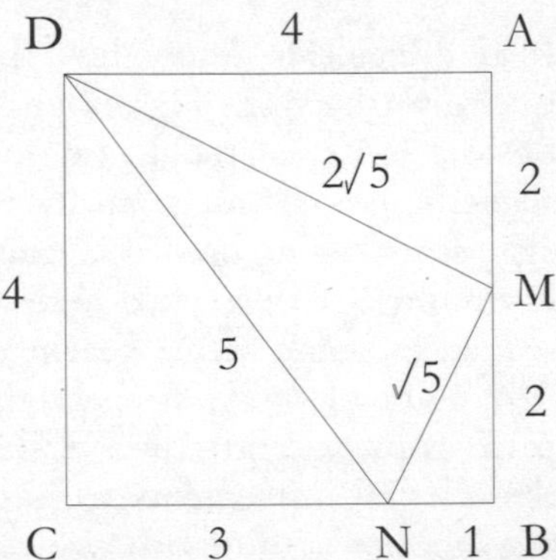

33. A figure of which the painter seems to make use, showing how a right angle can be divided into two angles with gradient 1 in 2, and a third with gradient 3 in 4.

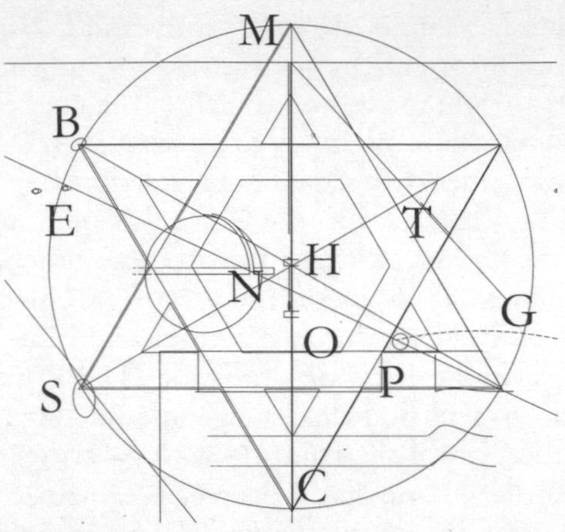

34. The hexagram fitted to the upper central area of *The Ambassadors.*

The St Michael-Rome line (corresponding to *XQ* on the simple figure) is almost tangential to a circle that will be introduced next. The circle is centred on the centre of swing of the plumbline of the compound solar instrument (Fig. 34) and is important because there is a hexagram that begs to be inscribed within it, in a way that will need to be explained at length.

THE ORB OF INSTRUMENTS, SOLOMON'S SEAL AND THE WHITE STRIP

It is difficult to know how best to introduce the circle in question (shown in Figs 34 and 35), since it does not have the obviousness of a straight line of sight. How such a thing first suggests itself to us is hardly relevant to an argument for or against its having been deliberately planned. However lame its beginnings, it does yield a series of entirely unexpected consequences, some with a bearing on other areas of the painting. The point of swing of the central plumbline seems a natural place to put a centre for a circle that will gather together all of the celestial instruments within its orbit. Regarding it in this way, its size is more or less determined and makes it more or

35. The hexagram in its relation to the painting.

less tangential to the St Michael-Rome line. It necessarily passes through the medallion of the order of St Michael; but then we notice that it passes through the golden cap badge with its silver skull motif, and that those two badges have an extremely interesting property. They turn out to be positioned at sixty-degree intervals around the circle, reckoning from its uppermost and lowermost points. Taking the circle as one that was deliberate and was required to have that as a property, we choose its dimensions to give the best fit, only to find to our surprise that one vertex of the imaginary six-sided figure suggested by the badge property lies almost exactly on the sightline up to the eye of Christ. What then of the other three vertices? One of them is the true centre of the basic 80 by 80 square (as explained previously). The uppermost vertex is off the picture but is (trivially) bound to be on the central axis. The sixth vertex of the hexagram is on the curtain and has nothing notable near it. The bounding circle passes through the gloves carried by de Selve in his right hand, but that is a very imprecise datum and may be ignored.

Having been led along this far from compelling route to the idea of a hexagonal figure, we can surely draw some confidence from the fact that Holbein's painting already includes a six-sided figure, namely a 'Solomon's Seal' or 'Shield (or Star) of David', half-hidden in the innermost circle of the pavement.[158] With the pavement to show us the way, we then discover that the upper figure makes far more sense if it is interpreted as a repeat of the floor design, a hexagram (a 'star') rather than a hexagon, and a banded design rather than a simple line figure. Before a similar banding can be added to the upper hexagon, however, its width has to be settled. If we choose *the same proportional value* for it in the upper hexagram as we find in the pavement, then several unforeseen properties of the scheme emerge immediately. They are as follows.

The edge of the table runs along the inside of one component triangle, and the polyhedral dial fits snugly into one angle of it.

The first white line of the turkey rug below the table edge defines the outside of that same triangle.

Two of the inner vertices of the triangles are fixed on other clearly defined lines of the turkey rug.

The vertical diameter of the circle (the plumbline of the compound instrument) passes through the middle of the horizontal 'S' motif on the turkey rug.

The rucking of the carpet on the right hand side of the painting seems to have been deliberate, for it follows the line of the bounding circle.

More compelling reasons for accepting this construction are still to come. Not only does the floor on which the two men stand have a Solomon's Seal motif worked into it, but when we calculate the relative sizes of the two hexagrams – one on the real floor, the other that we believe to be hidden on the oak panel – we find that they are almost exactly in the ratio of two to one. (The precise ratio depends on a complicated analysis of the perspective of the painting, something to which we shall need to return, but by measurement and calculation I deduce 23.1 and 46.4 Tudor inches respectively.) These lengths seem at first quite nondescript, but on the contrary, the dimensions of the two hexagrams are of great interest, for *the sides of the triangles out of which they are constructed have lengths of 20 and 40 inches*. (This is true to within a fifth of an inch. Conversely: triangles of exactly those dimensions would have yielded 23.1 and 46.2 inches for the diameters of the two circumscribed circles.)[159] Needless to say, this is a remarkable confirmation of the basic principle that the painting was constructed as far as possible around submultiples of its 80-inch outline square.

HEXAGRAM AND MOON

There are more than geometrical arguments for the reality of the upper hexagram, however. When we first identified the line from the torquetum that passed through the zero of its upper scale and through the Moon mark (on 'hour 2') down to the mid-point of the base of the painting, it seemed to fall at a thoroughly nondescript angle – no longer one of 27 or 45 degrees, for instance. Its angle to the vertical is approximately 11.7°. The line so drawn fits perfectly into the hexagram, passing very precisely through one of its 'inner' vertices. What if we supply its counterpart, up to the corresponding vertex on the left (Fig. 36)? It will meet it on the left side of the horizon ring of the globe, but where it will do so is hidden from view, because Dinteville's black sleeve is in the way. It is nevertheless possible to calculate that the line in question will mark *the place of the Moon on the celestial globe* (for which see Fig. 37).

This statement can be made with confidence, although a discussion of a few finer details is needed if we are to appreciate

36. The key sighting lines in *The Ambassadors.* Small triangles have been added at ten places where the angle nominally equal to 27° is to be found. Also shown here are the Moon lines (coming down to a point at mid-base), the St Michael-Rome line (quartering the lower axis), and the hexagram that relates to all of these.

properly how Holbein and his adviser must have proceeded. (Numerical detail is relegated to a note.)[160] Holbein made the *lower* face of the horizon ring pass through the centre (O) of the globe as it is presented to our view, rather than the upper edge (centre M). It is usual to read the scale on the *upper* edge, when using a globe, but what Holbein has done is perfectly correct, for the point of view of the painter – at least when he was making his preparatory drawing – was slightly below the level of the centre. (His sightline was about 3° to the horizontal.) Where any lesser artist would have drawn a straight line for the edge of the horizon ring, he has given it a very subtle curve, for this reason. The astronomer wanted the Sun to be on the main 27° line of sight as well as at the correct (negative) altitude of -14° (see the last note). To have taken Holbein's prepared drawing and to have measured the latter angle from 'centre' *M* would have been mistaken. The geometry of the case is too complex for a brief discussion, but it helps to remember that however one views a sphere, its true centre is always in line with its apparent centre, which in this case is *O*, exactly where Holbein put it. If we could see under the ring on the right edge and measure 11° down the apparent rim of the globe, we should be in approximately the correct place for a Sun with the required negative altitude. *B* shows the resulting position. Putting the Sun where the line of sight up to Christ crosses the edge of the globe would give a Sun at *A*. The two points *A* and *B* are separated by less than a centimetre.

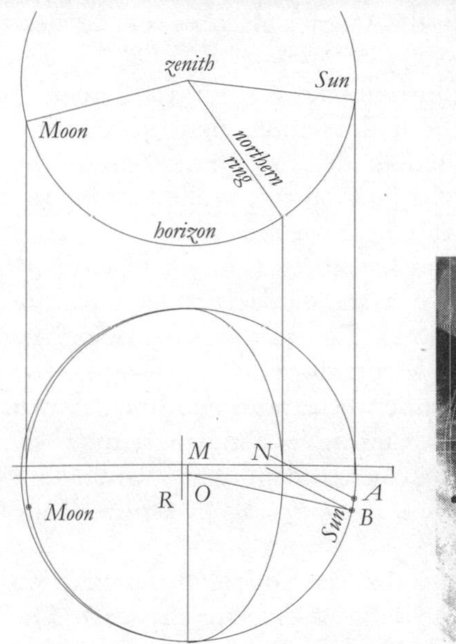

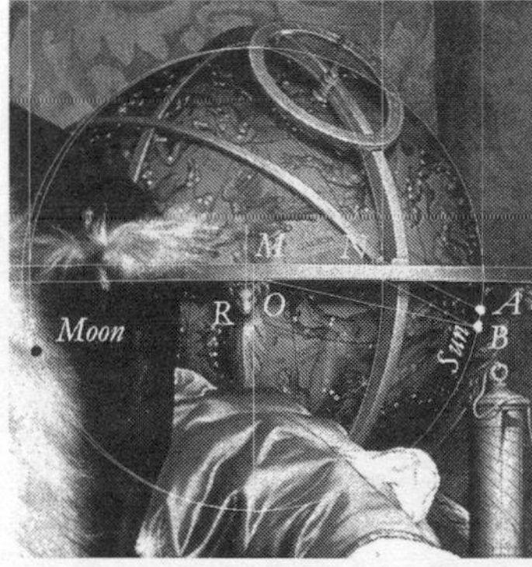

37. The positions of the Sun and Moon on the globe, assuming only that the day is Good Friday 1533 and that the Moon is in its afternoon position against the stars. Certain simplifying conventions are used in the superimposed figure, as explained in the text, but taking the Sun as at *B* and the Moon as marked they will certainly be (on the painting) within a few millimetres of what was clearly planned.

Our superimposed scheme (shown in the left hand of the figure) is drawn as though the globe is seen from a great distance, that is to say, it is in orthogonal projection (see the plan view at the upper left of the figure), but from a viewpoint slightly below the ring, as explained here. Had Holbein painted from a viewpoint about 75 cm from the centre of the globe (about 30 inches), *both Sun and Moon would have appeared on their respective edges of the visible hemisphere*. It seems quite likely that this was done. He could hardly have seen the fine detail of the stars from a very much greater distance, however good his eyesight. The distance is a minimum, since both Sun and Moon cannot be seen simultaneously from a lesser distance. Varying the distance can make only a few millimetres' difference to the Moon's 'painted' position, and even less to the Sun's. (But we repeat that in the final version the Moon's place was deliberately concealed by Dinteville's sleeve.)

This result shows the consummate skill of (presumably) Kratzer many times over, for it does more than merely link together the two 'Moon references'. It brings the Moon on the globe as close as possible to the horizon ring while keeping the Sun on the line of sight up to Christ on the right hand side of the globe. The Sun and Moon have been brought to virtually the same level, as they are in a standard crucifixion picture (see, for example, Fig. 68 below). The method of placing the 'V' of lines that 'point' to the Moon allusions, however, is even more ingenious, for the angle between those two lines, drawn up from the very base of the painting, is almost exactly 23.5°, which every medieval or Renaissance student of arts would have known to be *the angle between the ecliptic and the equator* ('the obliquity of the ecliptic').

The ecliptic, which runs through the middle of the band we call the zodiac, is the path of the Sun through the stars. The Moon is never more than five degrees or so away from it, and astronomers often ignored the discrepancy, that is, the Moon's ecliptic latitude, which was on this Good Friday about 5° N. With or without that adjustment, the left hand leg of the ecliptic 'V' points to the place of the Moon on the globe to a high degree of accuracy, and yet it is doubtful whether this 'V'

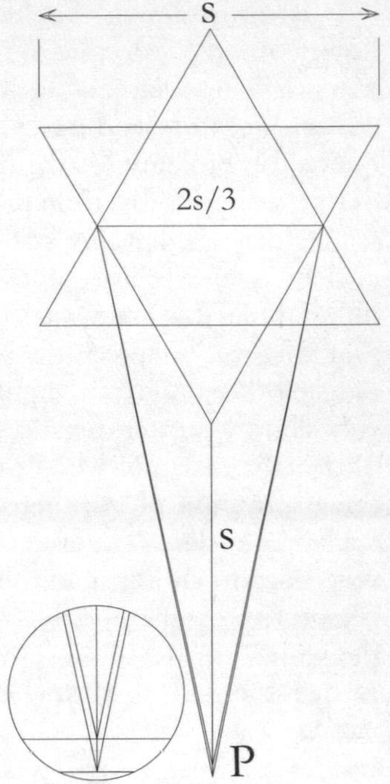

38. The construction by which the two lines to the Moon's places yield a fair value for the obliquity of the ecliptic (23.9°) that is improved by increasing the distance of *P* (giving 23.4°). This is effected in the painting by adding the bottom strip, as indicated in the enlarged detail of the diagram.

was being regarded as a purely lunar indicator. From Fig. 36 we can see how the 'V' contains within it all of the instruments on the upper shelf, and they are largely solar in character. Whatever else the painting contains, it is certainly not weak on solar symbolism.

How Kratzer – or any other astronomer, for that matter – came by such a construction for the obliquity we shall probably never know. At first sight it rests on a piece of pure geometry. Here is the construction:

> Two equilateral triangles, each of side *s*, form a regular hexagram. A point *P* is taken outside the first figure, on an axis at right angles to a diameter of the inner hexagon (that formed by the triangles) and at distance *s* beyond a vertex. The diameter of the hexagon will then subtend the required angle at *P*. (See Fig. 38.)

It is easily shown that this formula would produce an obliquity of 23.86° (double the angle with cotangent $3+\sqrt{3}$). This is marginally too large for the figure generally adopted in the sixteenth century, although it is astonishingly close to the figure quoted by Ptolemy for the obliquity. (It differs from Ptolemy's 23° 51′ 20″ by only four parts in ten thousand, which makes us wonder whether any such construction is to be found in an ancient source.) The most commonly quoted value for the obliquity at this time was (in decimal format) 23.56°. It seems that whoever adapted the geometrical scheme to the painting reduced the 'Ptolemaic' figure to about 23.4° by moving *P* to a very slightly greater distance, aided and abetted by the addition of the lower strip of white on the painting. (This claim rests on the assumption of symmetry around the central plumbline, as explained earlier. The line from the torquetum cuts this at the very bottom of the painting.) This gives us an entirely new perspective on the possible reasons for Holbein's having added the white strip to the fore-edge of the painting. It might seem to mar the perfect 80 inches, but apparently with compelling reason.

THE TURKEY RUG

The Apelles line and the upper hexagram are related in a simple way, and the latter is related to the turkey rug twice over, in its horizontals and in its fold. There is another property of the painting, however, that binds all three together, and that does so in a way that leaves little doubt that we are dealing with a religious allegory. To introduce it we must look into the history of oriental rugs bearing Christian motifs, for they are certainly present on the rug in *The Ambassadors*. Mention was made earlier of the religious use of a turkey rug, so called, at St Paul's. Later in the sixteenth century the English would begin to manufacture comparable carpeting of their own, learning from Flemish immigrant weavers, who in turn had learned to imitate styles that entered Europe through Italy, Bavaria and especially Vienna, where Armenian and other oriental traders operated, and where they also wove their own products. Some imported carpets were from the Islamic world, where styles fall into two broad classes, one in which the patterns have stiff, geometrical and generally abstract forms, the other in which the forms are freer and more obviously based on botanical, animal or other natural originals. The pattern of the rug in Holbein's painting might be thought to fall into the first, more orthodox, category, but it is not a Muslim product at all. As Volkmar Gantzhorn has shown, in a comprehensive study of Christian oriental carpets, Holbein's carpets as a whole belong to a different tradition, one that went back to the high middle ages and that would continue into the eighteenth century and beyond. It belongs to an Armenian Christian culture, especially that of western Anatolia.

The Armenians in question were at various stages in their history forced to move elsewhere – to Greece, to Persia, to Central Asia – and some groups even went to the West, but somehow they managed to preserve their techniques and styles of weaving, which were generally more welcome than their religion. The Armenian Monophysite church – they took the name since they believed that Christ has only one nature, divine and not human – was widely condemned as heretical by the Catholic and Orthodox churches, but some similarities with the faith of Islam helped to get them the protection of certain Muslim rulers. As a result of their dispersal they adopted a few new elements of design, some of them traceable back as far as the first millennium BC. Their most easily recognised motif, howcvcr, is that of thc cross, symbolising thc cross of Christ. (They used the 'Greek' cross, which has its four arms of equal length.) They wove it into their designs in innumerable ways, but the end result can usually be analysed in terms of a relatively small number of basic categories. Among the most important themes were rosettes of crosses built out of crosses – some of these are evident in the rug in *The Ambassadors* – and stars of crosses. They also introduced highly stylised cosmic diagrams, with colours of wool carefully chosen to represent the four elements. In some rugs they used a spiralling Sun motif. In other words, Anatolian rug making had become an art form that encoded the language of religion – of God, of Christ and of God's created world.

Several of the standard components are detectable in Holbein's painting, without being obvious, but what are very plainly present are two even more important shapes, the S- and E-symbols. The former is very conspicuous below the plumb-line on the solar instrument, the 'Apelles line', which more or less bisects it. There is only one such letter-form on the visible part of the rug, which is appropriate, since it denotes God Almighty, being the first letter of the corresponding Armenian word. The E-shape, which is harder to make out, resembles a Greek ε, and has a cross worked into the cleft. It is the old Armenian short form for 'HE', with which the name of Jesus begins, although it can also mean 'Almighty'. The E-symbol is repeated many times over, but again one instance of it is in the Apelles line. There is good reason for thinking that this line was meant to be taken together with a horizontal through the middle of the hexagram as a symbol of Christ's cross. A highly influential book of Christian cabalism by Pico della Mirandola, which had been reissued in 1532, explains how a crucifix is to be seen in exactly this position in the Shield of David. Perhaps the 'S' and 'E' were together taken to denote Christ. Whether or not this is so, however, the Pico text makes it seem highly probable that Holbein was placing a crucifixion scene in the very middle of his painting.[161]

On the question of the symbolism adopted by the Armenian weavers, it is of course not enough to know their original intentions: we must persuade ourselves that these could have been transmitted to the West and to Holbein. The use of such rugs in western Christian ritual, as well as the symmetries in the placing of the Holbein carpet, strongly suggest that Holbein and his collaborators had some knowledge of the symbolism originally intended by the weavers. Presumably there were Christian merchants who could have transmitted that knowledge. Commerce apart, there are several ways in which western churchmen might have learned the rudiments of it. The Armenian church sent a delegation to the Council of Florence, for example, when an attempt was being made to bring eastern and western churches together (1439–45). This part of the story is something we cannot supply, but our original suspicion that

39. The symbols S and E in the turkey rug.

the rug was placed on the upper, 'celestial', shelf of the stand for spiritual or cosmological reasons is certainly supported by what is known of the intentions of the rug makers.

THE ABBEY PAVEMENT AND THE FORM OF THE UNIVERSE

It is a curious fact that the cosmic forms in Armenian carpets and in the Westminster abbey pavement share a common ancestor, that is the philosophy of Plato and Aristotle. Mary Hervey drew attention to the importance of the design of the 'Cosmati work' in the painted pavement, and to the fact that it appeared to be closely modelled on the once famed pavement in the Westminster abbey sanctuary – the sacred area in front of the high altar. Judged by its prototype, the hexagram in the pavement is anomalous: there is no such thing at the centre of the pattern in the abbey, although there is a small-scale hexagon motif that patterns the entire surface. That the two pavements are related is not, however, an illusion.

A more recent study of the abbey pavement than Hervey's was made by Richard Foster, and much of the following account rests on it.[162] The pavement was constructed in 1268, some years after the abbot, Richard de Ware, had been confirmed in his abbacy by the pope. The pope was then at Anagni – a papal stronghold to the south of Rome. As it happens, Thomas Aquinas, the greatest Christian philosopher of the age, was teaching there at the time of the abbot's visit. Whether or not the Englishman was as impressed by that fact as by the floor decoration is not on record, but Anagni had the best Cosmati work in Italy – it has the best to this day – and he was determined to embellish his London church in a similarly magnificent way. The abbot's new pavement has to be seen in the context of Henry III's lavishly funded programme of rebuilding and decorating Westminster abbey. The vast sums then being spent were in preparation for the transfer of the body of Edward the Confessor to the abbey, which took place in 1269. What had begun life as an ordinary convent of Benedictine monks gradually acquired a peculiar status and a special place in English history. It owed allegiance – as it has done ever since – to the crown rather than to Canterbury.

No photograph of the pavement can do justice to the richness of its elements or its overall colouring. The schematic plan made of it by the Royal Commission on Historical Monuments in 1924 (Fig. 40) is neither coloured nor complete, but it does give an excellent impression of the sheer complexity of the work. The pavement, 7.57 m square, is created out of cut tiles of various sizes. (For this reason it is best described not as mosaic but as *opus sectile*.) The tiles are of coloured stone and glass, obtained from various widely separated places: many of the materials are of British origin, but some come from as far afield as Egypt. Much of the coloured glass was seemingly from Rome, but some might have come from the Islamic world. The work was done by Italian workmen under the direction of the master artist Oderic.[163] It is now for most of the year out of sight, protected by a carpet.

40. The Westminster abbey pavement, after a plan published by the Royal Commission on Historical Monuments (1924).

Various writers over the centuries have left records of what they saw or did not see of inscriptions that had been let into the pavement at the time it was laid. The *Chronicle* of William Rishanger provides us with a text as early as 1310. The letters, which in a few isolated cases still survive *in situ,* were individually cut rather than put on a continuous brass strip. Foster, with the help of an assortment of historical records from many periods, was able to piece together the inscription that originally ran in brass letters round three bands of the design, and the Latin version used below is due to him.

The square outermost band corresponds to the fore-edge of the Holbein painting and its unseen continuation. In the abbey it carried this statement of the circumstances of the work:

+ XPI MILLENO BIS CENTENO DUODENO
CUM SEXAGENO SUBDUCTIS QUATUOR ANNO
TERTIUS HENRICUS REX URBS ODORICUS ET ABBAS
HOS COMPEGERE POPHYREOS LAPIDES

In the year of Christ one thousand two hundred and twelve
and sixty minus four,
King Henry III, the Church of Rome, Odoricus and the Abbot
laid down these porphyry stones.

The way of expressing the date is quite typical of the numerology that was common among medieval and Renaissance scholars. A weak example could indeed have been found at the beginning of the Latin poem on Kratzer's Oxford University dial, mentioned earlier, which in English runs as follows: 'To fifteen hundred years and three add double ten, / You'll have the year in which they put me here.' This sort of thing had been common in Neoplatonic writings on cosmology from the early centuries of the Christian era. There it tended to be an elaboration of the account of the World Soul in Plato's *Timaeus*, which in turn owed something to the followers of Pythagoras of an even earlier period.[164] Every part of the number being built up was chosen for a meaning that all who were privy to this type of mystery were likely to appreciate.

Whoever composed the abbey lines knew the game well. The *thousand* years were the millennium that some – before it was safely passed – had thought would mark the end of the world. After the first millennium of the Christian era there were explanations in plenty for God's postponement of Christ's second coming, and theories too of how it might be brought about speedily, for instance by participation in the crusades. There were many, for example, who accepted the ideas of Islamic astrologers that history was cyclical and that the movement of the heavens (and a great conjunction of Saturn and Jupiter in particular) would bring about the downfall of the Saracen sect around the year 1264.[165] But this date too had passed by 1268. There is nothing to hint that such 'advanced' astrological ideas were tacitly expressed in the Westminster pavement, but there were certainly scholars around at the time who would have known of them. There were others who thought that the entire history of the world might be *seven* millennia long. Our abbey pavement author had other ideas, as we shall see.

The mention of *twelve* hundred years in the inscription picks up the 'twelve' in the same line. Twelve is a number pregnant with cosmological meaning, for it is both the number of months and the number of signs of the zodiac, and derivatively the number of hours in a day or in a night. Theologically it was a reminder of Christ's twelve disciples. *Sixty* was a number in regular use by astronomers, following in a tradition that had first seen the light in ancient Mesopotamia. Among other things it was the number of minutes in an hour, and of minutes of arc in a degree. It had many other astronomical uses – for example it could be the number of parts in a radius of a standard circle.

In suggesting such meanings for numbers it is usually easier to know where to start than where to stop. Thus, in view of the hexagon motif that is found across the entire surface of the pavement in many different forms, it might be observed that there were astronomers at this time who divided the zodiac not into twelve signs but into six, each of sixty degrees. This was an ultra-modern tendency in 1268, and it had not reached England, so the coincidence is best dismissed as fortuitous. On the other hand, the pavement's central circle is surrounded by a ring of exactly sixty lozenges of stone, each of them therefore covering an angle of six degrees. Six-degree divisions were common on astronomical scales. Does this mean that the circle emulated an astronomical diagram? The idea is not easy to square with the philosophical context to which the pavement almost certainly belongs. Are we to look to those seemingly endless medieval works on the 'theology of numbers'? Take, for example, the reading offered by the great contemporary scholar

Albertus Magnus to explain the yield of the seed sixtyfold in the parable of the sower. He saw it as a reference to the level of chastity attained by people who are continent, and explained it all in terms of six works of mercy done in obedience to each of the ten commandments.[166] Faced with numerology at this level – the existence of which certainly cannot be denied – in the absence of a text we can only despair.

Finally, the *four* in the formula for the pavement's date draws our attention to the square form of the entire pavement, which is directed precisely to the four cardinal points, north, south, east and west, thanks to the eastern alignment of the abbey church. There are four roundels surrounding the central circle, and four more outside the trapezium-square containing them. This is exactly the situation in the floor of the painting, and it draws our attention to another similarity: as we earlier demonstrated, those viewing the painting are facing due east, exactly as they would stand in the abbey.

The sort of thirteenth-century texts in which this type of diagram was commonly found would have stressed other simple correlates of the number four. It is the number of the seasons and of the ages of man (childhood, adolescence, youth and old age), the number of terrestrial elements (earth, water, air and fire), the number of astrological triplicities (groupings of the signs of the zodiac by threes, spaced at 120-degree intervals), and many other things too, especially if we branch out into the human condition or theology. Thus Paul Alvarus's exegesis of the Book of Daniel divided up world history into four empires that Christians traditionally interpreted as the Roman, Assyrian, Persian and Greek. A painting of pre-1464 in the St Lorenz church in Nürnberg has the four evangelists in the roundels and the new-born Christ in the square at the centre.[167] The list is seemingly endless.

If we are prepared to look into alchemy we can find many other parallels – thus in his versified *Compound of Alchymy* the fifteenth-century English alchemist George Ripley drew his cosmologically inspired 'wheel' in a form very similar to the Westminster design.[168] In a chapter on 'putrefaction' in the same work he spoke ironically of those alchemists of dubious character who congregated at Westminster abbey daily. We should dearly like to know the nature of an alchemical painting in the abbey that may have been part of their reason for attending. Elias Ashmole reported on it in 1652, but it is now lost. While we must certainly resist the use of such parallels unless they stay close to the brief texts that were once to be read in the floor, they need to be mentioned, if only as a corrective to cool modern attitudes towards cold tiled church floors hidden under carpets. It is quite likely that only the simplest of the cosmic associations mentioned here were present in the mind of the *designer* of the pavement, but mysteries do tend to multiply with time. The pavement as it was known when Holbein took his inspiration from it in the 1530s – we shall show that he almost certainly did so – would have accumulated new meanings and have lost old ones.

The next inscription followed along the quadrifoil band around the four circles of the central quincunx. (Is there a history of the four-leafed clover?) In the painting, Dinteville's left heel rests on a circle in the corresponding group. Finally there is a circular band around the innermost ring in the abbey floor, with another short text for which it is not difficult to find a very broad context. (The corresponding part of the Holbein painting is partly covered by the inverted lute case.) It seems likely that all of these inscriptions were more or less intact in Holbein's time, judging by John Weever's guide to the abbey of 1631.

The quadrifoil inscription was broadly cosmological, but it made use of a strange analogy:

> SI LECTOR POSITA PRUDENTER CUNCTA REVOLVAT HIC FINEM PRIMI MOBILIS INVENIET / SEPES TRIMA CANES ET EQUOS HOMINESQUE SUBADDAS / CERVOS ET CORVOS AQUILAS IMMANIA CETE / MUNDUM QUODQUE SEQUENS PREEUNTIS TRIPLICAT ANNOS
>
> If the reader go carefully round all this he will come to the end of the *Primum Mobile.* A hedge is three years, you add dogs and horses and men, stags and crows, eagles, a wild sea monster, the world: each triples the years of the one before it.

Following this tripling process – 3 years for a hedge, 9 for a dog, 27 for a horse, 81 for a man, and so on – the age of the world will amount to 3 raised to the power of 9, or 19,683 years. Various parallels for this formula are known, but apparently none from a strictly academic context.[169] The reference to the *Primum Mobile,* the First Mover that drives round the sphere of the stars and all the planetary spheres below it, makes a shadowy allusion to the system of the world bequeathed to posterity by the Greek philosopher Aristotle, but the tenor of the inscriptions as a whole is Neoplatonic. This is true also of the inscription around the central circle, which tells us that it represents the Macrocosm – the universe as a whole, in contrast to mankind within it, the Microcosm:

> SPERICUS ARCHETIPUM GLOBUS HIC MONSTRAT MACROCOSMUM
>
> This spherical ball shows the Macrocosmic archetype.

The language is that of very many commentaries on the *Timaeus* of Plato, for whom the 'archetype' is the original pattern of forms, of which actual things are merely copies.

So short and aphoristic are these snatches of Latin that finding a unique textual source is a hopeless task. The same applies to the general style of placing text within roundels, an arrangement used for many other purposes, as well as for the naive representations of the cosmos that were common to Christian authors in the centuries before more advanced Islamic and Greek scientific texts arrived in western Europe. Those texts were arriving in ever-increasing numbers in the thirteenth century, and the Westminster pavement was being laid down at a time when rapid intellectual change was being brought about with the help of the new texts.

The beautiful central disc of Egyptian onyx marble in the abbey pavement has veining that makes it look somewhat like a figure of the earth, but we must obviously not ask too much of a slab of natural stone. In his annotations to John Flete's text on the pavement, Richard Sporley (1450) regarded the central disc as revealing the pattern of the universe, as the inscription promised, 'because it contains within itself the colours of the four Elements'.[170] The colours of the onyx are not such that one would expect to find them mentioned in any thirteenth-century text. In fact it would be hard to put a name to them even in our own colour-rich age, but the pavement was obviously then as now capable of moving the imagination. Around the central onyx of the abbey pavement there comes a circular band, predominantly of sky blue, in which darker blue hexagonal stars are set. Beyond that is the *Primum Mobile*, the 'First Mover' of the universe, as the inscription tells us.

Such highly stylised images were of a type soon to be outmoded in the higher reaches of learning, although not entirely. There are textual parallels, and one would have no difficulty in tracing them in a continuous line to the seventeenth century. The author of the inscriptions might have been influenced by the work of Hugh of St Victor (early thirteenth century), or by the commentary on Plato by the still earlier writer Honorius of Autun (early twelfth century).[171] An even more influential work by Honorius including snatches of the same vocabulary was his *Imago mundi*,[172] on which Walter (Gauthier) of Metz based an extremely popular French encyclopaedic poem, *L'image du monde*, just two years before the pavement was laid. William Caxton, the first English printer, prepared an English version of that work and published it at Westminster in 1481.

Academic writers continued to produce simple pictures of interlocking squares with roundels conveying rather trivial information on tetrads, foursomes of concepts – the elements, the humors of the body and the like. Holbein, Dinteville, de Selve, or Kratzer could easily have come across any one of a dozen examples, some of them traditionally strait-laced, others positively arcane – as in the contemporary writings of Charles de Bouelles, for instance. But to whose taste would they have been? It is hard to say, but surely not to Holbein's. Although it was printed in 1542, a few years after Holbein's painting was done, a woodcut from a work on the celestial sphere by the French scholar Oronce Fine may be taken here to illustrate the older academic tradition (Fig. 41). It introduces a bit of university logic into the simple theory of the four elements. At its centre it portrays a crowned dolphin, making allusion to Fine's native region, the Dauphiné. We have already come across the dolphin on the celestial globe at Dinteville's elbow in *The Ambassadors.* Fine's symbol of the dauphin of France is also linked in a remote way with the Westminster pavement, as we shall see.

HOLBEIN'S PAVEMENT

The pavement in *The Ambassadors* is not an immediate representation of the abbey pavement. What then are we to make of the relation between the two? Most recently, P. C. Claussen, an authority on Cosmati pavements, has proposed an elaborate interpretation that rests on the idea that the two ambassadors are standing on 'double ground', the territories of London and Rome, so to speak.[173] Richard Foster had not accepted that Holbein's was a copy of the Westminster pavement in any sense. Mary Hervey had admitted long before that the two differed somewhat, since the painting gives a mirror image of the real pavement – in fact this is not true of the inner quincunx, quadrifoil plus central disc – and because both differ in colouring and in other respects; but she leaves us with the general impression that artistic licence was the only cause of variation. Foster noted that the mosaic strips that Hervey believed Holbein had copied from the outer region of the pavement (those outside the range of the painting) are the only elements that match the present pavement. It could have been added that the sizes of the patterns in the two pavements are very different. All of this serves as an absolute refutation of the idea that the painting was an *immediate* representation. But it certainly does not prove that the two pavements are unconnected.

Foster made an interesting suggestion, that the floor on which the two men stand in the painting was one in either the palace at Bridewell, where ambassadors were housed, or the palace at Greenwich. He favoured the second, since a record

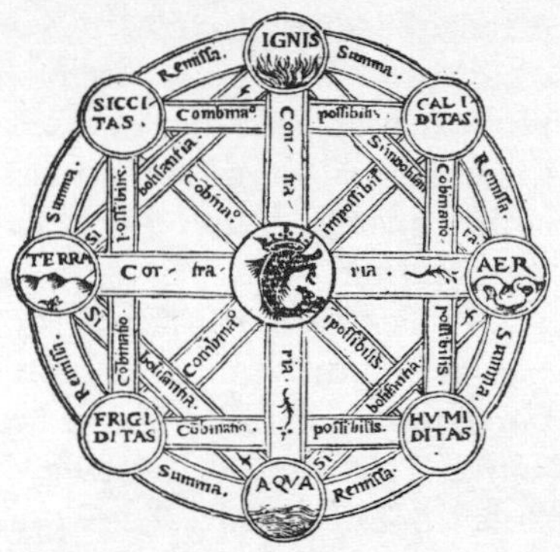

41. A typical scheme of the four elements. From Oronce Fine, *De mundi sphaera* (Paris, 1526).

survives of two named painters (Andrew Wright and John Heythe) having painted the courtyard to resemble coloured stone, with 'orbys and antyke work', and this in 1533, the year of *The Ambassadors*.[174] He remarks that it is not unlikely that the floors of the palace received the same treatment, and a closer look at the painting does, as he says, suggest that the real floor was of wood painted to look like stonework. There are, for instance, dark dividing lines where one would expect mortar of a light colour. So much for the painting as a contribution to our understanding of the Westminster pavement. But still it is going too far to dismiss the latter as a contribution to the understanding of the painting, and this for four main reasons.

The first reason is that both floors have a plainly cosmic significance, supplementing their strong similarities in general plan. The plans of both, with circles produced by endless banding, is characteristic of Cosmati work. Whether at Westminster it was ever associated with the toing and froing in the motions of the planets around the central Earth, their progression and retrogradation, it is impossible to say, but it would have made a good story. The second reason is that the Westminster pavement must have been known to Holbein, and probably what had been preserved of its meaning too, in view of the continuing interest shown in it by London scholars long after his time. The third reason is that Holbein's painting seems to draw on that strange bit of cosmic calculation presented in the middle inscription of the abbey pavement. And the fourth is that the abbey pavement, considerably larger than the other, seems to have been *exactly double the scale* of that which Holbein was painting. We recall that the hidden hexagram in the upper half of the painting also has this property of being at approximately double the scale of the hexagram in the floor of the painting.*

The last two points will be postponed for the time being. For the moment, Foster's conjecture as to the painting of the Greenwich palace floor can be provided with a tentative alternative. Holbein and Kratzer were themselves not above large-scale work of the sort that would have been involved in painting a wooden floor in the intricate manner shown in *The Ambassadors.* Holbein is not only to be seen as an artist whose every painting can be dissected into miniatures. He had decorated the exteriors of complete houses in Basel with frescoes, and on occasion in London was engaged in temporary paintings for ceremonial purposes.[175] We recall how at Greenwich in 1527 he and Kratzer had together designed and painted an astronomical allegory on the ceiling of a splendid but temporary building erected by the king for the entertainment of the French ambassadors.† It will be remembered that the occasion was the visit of an impressive train of gentlemen, led by *grand maître* Anne de Montmorency, Jean du Bellay and the chancellor of Alençon, who had come to seal Henry's good will in the matter of the league against the Emperor Charles v, bringing with them the royal order of St Michael for the king. (Note that our conjectured hexagram in the upper painting is linked to the order of St Michael.) By the time Holbein was painting his double portrait of the two later ambassadors that visit was more than five years past, but it is not impossible that the painted floor in the portrait was left over from the 1527 celebrations. Even if it were not, its cosmic character makes it more likely that he and Kratzer, rather than untutored artisans, would have been responsible for it, whether or not they had assistance.

As announced by its inscription, the abbey floor had at its

* See p. 197 above and 237 below.

† See p. 21 above.

centre a circle representing the Macrocosm. It was at the centre of the floor in his painting that Holbein added a barely visible six-pointed star in the form of a double triangle. The abbey pavement is bestrewn with hexagons and hexagrams, where the meaning is cosmological and tacitly theological. The inscriptions did not need to spell out the fact that a six-sided figure was a symbol of God's having created the world in six days, as well as a Christian symbol of the Trinity twice over. All men of religion would have known as much. Several early sixteenth-century printings of the Bible in Dutch, for example, have a large woodcut on the first page in which each segment of a six-sided figure contains an illustration of God's work on one of the six days of creation; and in each of them God has a six-pointed halo around his head. There was a text by Rabanus Maurus on the mystery of the number six that was still widely known and quoted. Some, recalling the apocalyptic vision of St John the Divine, might have seen in it the six ages preceding the Last Judgement. The geometer Charles de Bouelles, having discovered that six equal circles exactly enclose a seventh of like diameter, related it to the mystery of creation. (He was even more excited by the idea that twelve equal spheres may exactly surround an identical sphere, suggesting that twelve is 'the measure of all corporeal plenitude'.) It is impossible to prove specific influence when we are in the presence of such an all-pervasive tradition. Any or all of these things might have been understood by the six-pointed star in the painting. The abbey inscriptions did not need to emphasise that the heavens were replete with six-pointed stars, for they were portrayed in the pavement for all to see. Whether those in the Holbein circle were of a mind to make use of this kind of imagery is another question. One might comment endlessly on the Platonic background here, without showing even remotely that Holbein and his friends were aware of the nature of the stream that was carrying them along, as they plotted with threes and sixes. But this they did, and we shall later consider other ways in which they may have justified themselves.

TEN

HINTS OF ASTROLOGY

. . . if they [the monks of the religious orders] intend to recount the mystery of the cross, they'll happily begin with Bel, the Babylonian dragon. If fasting is to be their subject they make a start with the twelve signs of the Zodiac, and if they would expound the faith they open with a discussion on squaring the circle

Erasmus, *Praise of Folly,* trans. B. Radice, pp. 168–69

Quite apart from the hexagram, there appears to be another figure concealed in *The Ambassadors*. It is one that would have carried more scientific weight, while linking the heavens with human fortune in a more familiar and determinate way. We have seen how, by ignoring the lower strip of white marble and a corresponding strip on the left, a square of eighty Tudor inches remains; and we have seen that this is perfectly divided by the vertical of the plumbline on the compound solar instrument. All of this makes good sense of the two geometrical constructions embodied in the painting, one for the doubling of the angle of 27°, the other for the obliquity (Figs 33 and 38 above). But it also makes the painting admirably suited to the standard astrological figure used for a horoscope.

Holbein had collaborated with Kratzer on the Greenwich ceiling shortly after his first arrival in England, a ceiling with plainly astrological overtones. He had drawn for Sebastian Münster's technical publications, and in that connection he must have acquired a smattering of astronomical knowledge. There is no reason to think that Holbein was expert in astrology, but neither – in view of his friendship with Kratzer – did he need to be. He lived and moved in circles where astrology was honoured. There were a few dissenting voices, but generally speaking the subject was as deeply respected by the reformers as by the established church. Martin Luther believed firmly in many facets of astrology, although not as firmly as his strongest supporter, Philipp Melanchthon, professor of Greek at Wittenberg. Melanchthon was portrayed by Holbein, although the painting in question – an ornamental roundel only about 12 cm across – is now thought not to have been done from life.[176] A man does not become an astrologer by painting one, but that Holbein was at least aware of the symbolic value of astrology can be seen from his early *Dance of Death* series of woodcuts, dating from around 1525.[177] The overall message of those illustrations is that death has dominion over the affairs of all mankind, rich or poor, sinful or virtuous. A subsidiary theme is that of the wickedness of the clergy. Holbein introduced the theme of astrology there only casually and incidentally, but in one small respect the way in which he did so reflects on *The Ambassadors.* An astronomer sits at a table, on which rest a book and a quadrant, and he studies an armillary sphere suspended from the ceiling. His companion is a skeleton, standing with its back to an open arch, and holding in its hands a skull which it scrutinises in much the way that we are expected to study the skull in the Dinteville painting (Fig. 42). This sort of composition required scarcely any prior astronomical or astrological knowledge – which is just as well, judging by the penultimate item in the series, a Last Judgement that depicts a sphere with completely muddled zodiacal signs. (Perhaps the errors were introduced by the man who cut the blocks.) In the case of *The Ambassadors* there is far too much concealed expertise for Holbein to have worked alone.

Before turning to the painting itself for evidence, we might consider the intrinsic likelihood that astrology, as opposed to simple positional astronomy, would have been added to it. *The Ambassadors* has a religious theme for which time is central. Would the fact that Holbein wished to represent time in the painting not have been reason enough for introducing astronomy? Perhaps so, but it would not have been reason enough for excluding its sister science, which for so many of Holbein's contemporaries was the chief justification for astronomy and its instrumentarium.

Astrology was undergoing a threefold renaissance throughout Europe when Holbein was at work. What had for so long been

42. A woodcut from Holbein's *Dance of Death* series (designed *c.* 1525).

an art that was thought proper and even necessary to kings was spreading throughout the higher and wealthier echelons of society. Scholar-astrologers were becoming aware of the healthy income it could provide, especially when combined with medicine. Its gradual spread into the lower reaches of society took nothing off its edge in royal circles. The French court was flattered to learn that according to Flemish astrologers the victory of François I at the battle of Marignano was connected with a fiery comet seen in the Low Countries on the day of the battle (15 September 1515) and the following two days. For good measure, it was also connected with the day of the Exaltation of the Holy Cross (14 September). Louise de Savoie kept a journal which had astrological arrangement and content. When her son was pressing on with his army towards the catastrophe at Pavia, she wrote asking him to return, since 'our good angel has deserted us and your horoscope foretells disaster'. Such examples of a deeply felt belief could be easily multiplied. For about twenty years, Jean Thenaud provided the French court with horoscopes and prognostications and the year 1533 found him casting a horoscope for the king himself. This was the situation that Jean de Dinteville had left behind him. In London, the situation was much the same. An Italian astrologer-physician, William Parron, had made a lasting impression on the court of Henry VII years before, and expert university astronomers were regularly giving astrological judgements, as they had been doing on a lesser scale for centuries. Within the orbit of his court, Henry VIII could have found ready advice of this sort not only from Nicolaus Kratzer but from the royal physician William Butts. An even more likely consultant at this period would have been the royal chaplain John Robyns, who wrote assiduously on astrology, addressing some of his writings to the king. Robyns tells us in his writings on the astrological significance of comets that he discussed their natures and their powers with the king when at the royal residences of Woodstock and Buckingham. This was after the appearance of a comet in 1532.[178] The praise Robyns lavishes on Henry's mathematical knowledge no doubt reflects less on its object than on the writer's wish for royal patronage.

Among the lower orders, cheap almanacs and broadsheets with 'prognostications' were becoming increasingly popular, and printing was bringing some of the cruder claims of astrology to the notice of an ever-wider circle. English printers were slow to find native authors, and for many years they were driven to publish translations of works written in the Low Countries. Some of those by the Laet family, a dynasty of astrologers whose works appeared annually in the southern Netherlands between 1469 and 1550, were translated into English and printed in London by Richard Pynson, the king's printer. It seems not to have mattered that the forecasts in a work by Gaspar Laet published for the year 1533 dealt with not a single English town![179]

A third place in which the study of astrology was promoted was in the more rarefied atmosphere of humanist debate, often where the initial intention had been to attack it. The most powerful onslaught from this quarter had been launched by Pico della Mirandola, a convert from the art. Prompted by his writings, several scholars of a humanist persuasion took a fresh look at ancient and modern dissensions about astrology's plausibility and acceptability, and many seem to have liked what they found. Even among the humanists there were those who felt too strongly about a subject they had learned to love in their student years to allow it to suffer defeat. By all means let the pure texts of ancient authors be recovered, they thought, but let it be shown that they can be reconciled with Christian morality and the theology of divine providence. Several scholars of the first rank – Paul of Middelburg and Petrus de Rivo were two of them – spent an inordinate amount of time on establishing the chronological details of Christ's birth and crucifixion, first using astronomical knowledge and then investigating the astrological consequences of their findings. (The task was not easy. De Rivo had to admit that he was unable to calculate planetary positions using the Alfonsine tables, and he left this task to an assistant. Holbein would have fared no better without help.) This sort of exercise, one that started with the very roots of the Christian faith, could easily be extended to its branches: we have already mentioned certain types of 'great conjunctions' of the superior planets that were traditionally supposed to herald momentous religious change. Such conjunctions seemed to have a direct bearing on the rise of the Lutheran movement. We must not underestimate the strength of feeling about such things, even on the part of scholars who were not particularly well schooled in the ways of astrology.

The upshot of all this is that strength of feeling about such questions mattered more in the end than logic and reason. Those who today are unaware of this historical situation will no doubt consider it outrageous that we should be arguing, in effect, that the plain evidence in the painting for astronomical thinking means that astrology too will not be far to seek. Such sceptics will find that the best medicine for their condition is to search for literary or artistic evidence of any astronomical allegory that *lacks* an astrological ingredient. Certainly the Holbein painting seems to give evidence for astrology, in the form of a horoscope square.

1. Hans Holbein the Younger, *The Ambassadors.* Oil on oak, 207 cm by 209.5 cm. The two men are Jean de Dinteville (left) and Georges de Selve (right). Between them is a stand carrying numerous artefacts, mostly scientific. A distorted skull appears to stretch across the foreground. Note the crucifix in the upper left corner, partly hidden by the curtain, the intricate pavement and the lute case in shadow under the stand. In shadow on the floor on the left is a signature and date: IOANNES / HOLBEIN / PINGEBAT / 1533. *(National Gallery, London)*

2. Hans Holbein the Younger. Miniature on vellum, 4.2 cm diameter. Probably by Lucas Hornebout after a supposed self-portrait (now in Florence) from 1543, the year of Holbein's death. The Florence portrait shows no hands. Holbein was left-handed. *(The Wallace Collection, London)*

3. Jean de Dinteville, bailly of Troyes.

4. Georges de Selve, bishop of Lavaur.

5. Fine copy of the portrait of Nicolaus Kratzer by Holbein now in the Musée du Louvre, Paris. The inscription on the paper gives the sitter's age and the year, 1528. He holds a polyhedral dial and dividers. The disc near his right hand belongs to the solar instrument in the niche behind him. All of these have counterparts in *The Ambassadors*. *(National Portrait Gallery, London)*

6. The celestial globe on the upper shelf of the stand. The central constellation above the horizon ring is Cygnus, although it resembles a cock and has often been presumed to allude to France. Pegasus is conspicuous below it. To the right of this detail is the cylinder dial that provides us with a precise day and hour. Note the slightly curved shadow cast by its gnomon.

7. The compound solar instrument and the white quadrant behind it. The disc with spike in the foreground is for use on the pivoted arm. The plumbline on the left is of importance to the composition of the painting as a whole. The criss-crossed lines on the quadrant are the hour lines, limited by inner and outer scales. Below them is the scale of *umbra versa*.

8. The polyhedral dial to the left of the book, with the torquetum behind them. The edge of the book records the age of Georges de Selve.

9. The hand-held terrestrial globe, with the arithmetic book by Peter Apian, propped open with a folding set-square. Marked on the globe is the name of Polisy.

10. The eleven-stringed lute with its broken string, the dividers in its shadow, and the Lutheran hymnal and case of flutes. At the top of the left-hand page of the hymnal is the number XIX.

11. The dagger lightly held in Jean de Dinteville's right hand. The sheath and handle are in a style typical of Holbein. Dinteville's age is indicated on the sheath (ÆT[atis] SVÆ [ANNO] 29).

THE HOROSCOPE SQUARE

The common method of drawing such a square is easy enough to follow, and while not universally favoured was used in the great majority of horoscopes. (There was much more disagreement about the method of calculating how the zodiac should be divided up into 'houses' at the crucial moment, but that is a separate question.) Starting with any square, the astrologer joins the mid-points of its sides (producing an inner slantwise square) and then joins up the mid-points of the latter. This automatically produces a square with sides half as long as the first. The vertices of the first and third squares are then joined. There is no ambiguity in the result, if this procedure is followed. It could be illustrated a thousand times over from finished horoscopes. A topical example would be one of several done for the occasion of Martin Luther's birth, which some were then using to show that Luther was the new Messiah, others that he was the Antichrist. (This ambiguity was helped by the failure of his mother to remember the time of his birth. His leading Catholic opponent, Johannes Cochlaeus, or Dobeneck, claimed that Luther was a bastard conceived when his mother copulated with the Devil in a bath-house. A horoscope could be used to heat up the steam in such cases.)[180] The most common outward form of horoscope may be illustrated from the version published by Jerome Cardan at Nürnberg in 1543 (Fig. 43). The drawings of Fig. 44 lend themselves to a more general introduction to this subject. They come from a book of 1488, one that was published as it happens in Holbein's birthplace, Augsburg. Its purpose was to help the inexpert astrologer to determine the division of the zodiac into the astrological houses.

The zodiac is divided into twelve houses in two quite different senses. The thirty-degree signs of the zodiac (Aries, Taurus, Gemini, and the rest) are houses of fixed extent, and it is useful to avoid ambiguity by referring to them as *domiciles.* They are reckoned from the vernal point, the zero of ecliptic longitude, where the Sun crosses the celestial equator at the spring equinox. No calculation is needed to specify them. Each planet is supposed to have different strengths and debilities according to the domicile in which it finds itself – indeed even certain subdivisions of the signs play their part in deciding on a planet's 'dignity', according to an elaborate system that need not be considered in detail here. This system gives what were known as the 'essential' properties of the planets for a particular time, properties that are the same for all geographical places.

A horoscope diagram (or 'figure' or 'square') is meant to register house divisions of a very different sort, corresponding to a particular geographical latitude and time. Calculating the variable house divisions was a tiresome matter, and was part of what justified giving an astrologer his fee, his respect, or both. The starting point of this variable division was the ascendent, the point of the ecliptic rising above the horizon at the time of interest. (One might say that it is the rising point of the zodiac, although the zodiac is strictly a band of sky, with the ecliptic circle through its middle.) Reckoning from that point, there were various rival mathematical rules for performing the division, most of them fairly difficult to apply. The Augsburg book was meant to save the common reader the trouble. It gave the house divisions, according to the most common system of all, for every ascendent degree, that is for every one of the 360 degrees in the zodiac as they rose over the horizon. The user

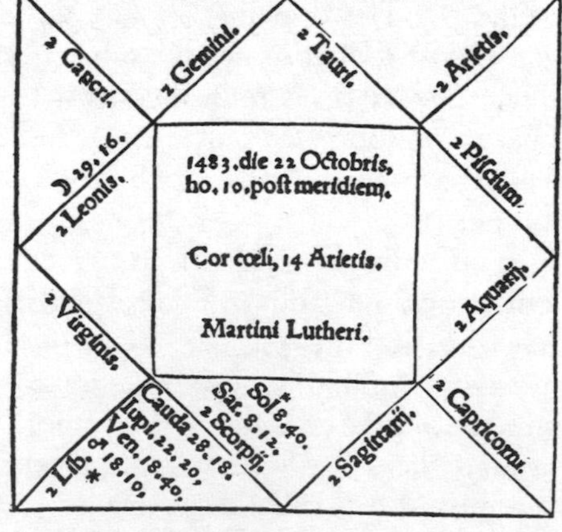

43. A horoscope (or 'figure' or 'square') cast by Jerome Cardan for Martin Luther, published at Nürnberg in 1543. It is included here chiefly to illustrate what was by far the most common form of geometrical pattern into which a summary of the state of the heavens at the moment of interest (for example the time of birth) was inserted by the astrologer.

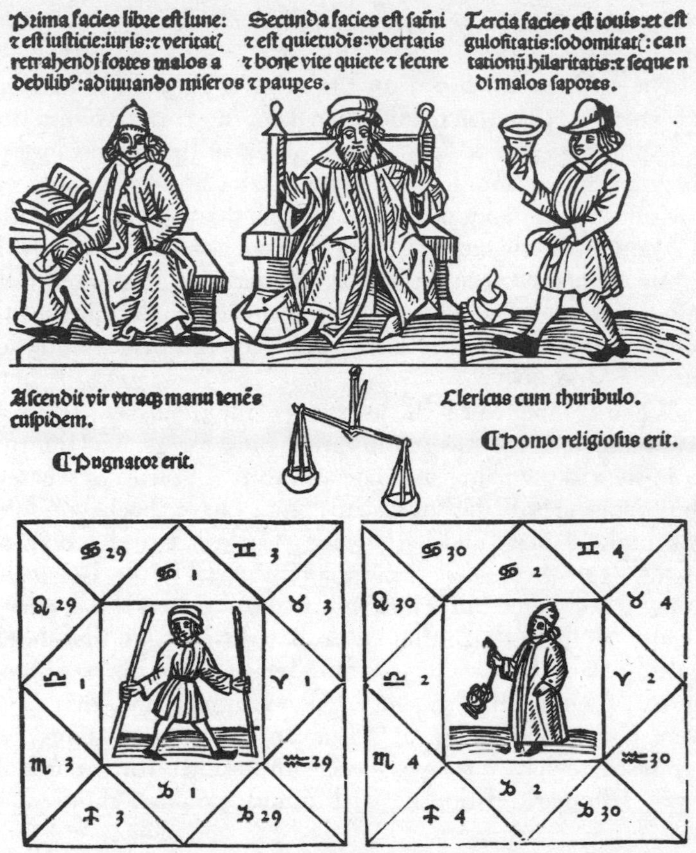

44. Two horoscopes, pre-calculated only as far as the division of the zodiac into houses is concerned, and printed in the popular work by Johann Engel, *Opus astrolabii plani* (Augsburg, 1488). That on the left is for the rising of the first degree in the sign of Libra (the Scales), that on the right for the rising of the second degree. The former is said to characterise a warrior, the latter a religious.

was saved the trouble of calculating the houses, but only at a certain cost: the latitude of place used in the calculation was appropriate to northern Italy.[181] This fact does not seem to have limited sales of the Augsburg edition of the book, which was also much copied in manuscript, in some cases with a German rather than a Latin text (the so-called *Heidelberger Schicksalsbuch*).

The two figures shown on the printed page illustrated here may be considered as blanks that have the correct house divisions but that do not yet have the places of the planets inserted for the chosen moment of time. Calculating the planetary positions was an even more tedious task than that of calculating the houses. With luck, one might have access to an almanac, listing planetary positions at daily intervals. That would certainly have been good enough for most people, although it might have given rather poor results in the case of the fast-moving Moon.

When completed by the astrologer, the innermost square of a horoscope figure was usually used only for general information, such as the name and date and time (of birth, or whatever the occasion of the horoscope may have been) and the geographical place and its latitude. The outer twelve divisions of the figure were what really mattered, that is the astrological houses, numbered anti-clockwise from I to XII. If we were to regard Holbein's painting as a horoscope, the first house, starting from the ascendent, would be drawn in the neighbourhood of Dinteville's dagger. The ascendent and first house were taken to be of great significance, but every house was supposed to have its own special importance for a particular type of human relationship – brothers, parents, children, illness, etc.[182]

The Augsburg illustration selected here shows the division of the houses for the case when the very beginning of the sign of Libra (the Scales) is ascendent, as it would have been at the time deduced earlier for *The Ambassadors* portrait. Without putting great store by the numerical data in the illustration,[183] we observe simply that when the first degree of Libra is rising, the character of the subject is said to be combatant (he is a *pugnator*). He is described in the printed book as 'a man holding a javelin in each hand'. (Strictly speaking, *cuspis* is a word that could be used of almost any spiked weapon.) A minute or so later, when the second degree of the sign rises over the horizon, another division of the horoscope is needed. The subject of the horoscope is in this case described as religious, and is portrayed on the right as a cleric with a censer. What reason might have been offered at the time for this second idea? Perhaps there was an association with the known belief, not altogether common, that Christ was born when this degree of the zodiac was rising. That doctrine links Christ's birth and death. In what is perhaps the best-known evaluation of Christ's natal horoscope, cast in 1532 but published in 1555, Jerome Cardan put the ascendent at Libra 2° 43′, and noted that Jupiter was near by. The idea is certainly much older. Tiberio Rossigliano seems to have been ascribing it to 'the Arabs and Egyptians' when he compared different opinions on the question in the second decade of the sixteenth century.[184]

It might be entirely fortuitous that the two characters in this Augsburg illustration from what had become a best-selling book correspond in a curious way to the two ambassadors in the painting, the one seigneurial and knightly, with sword and dagger, the other clerical. Is it entirely illusory that the dagger in the painting bears a rough similarity to the beam of the balance in the standard representation of the scales (to which the woodcut is entirely true)? Was Dinteville not bailly of Troyes, a man with judgemental responsibilities? He holds the dagger in a most uncombative way, rather as scales are held (Plate 11). Of course, how he holds it might be nothing more than an indication of his personality. Holbein's portrait of Charles de Solier shows a compatriot of Dinteville's – indeed his successor as envoy to the London court – with a much more determined and forceful grasp of a similar dagger.[185]

Whatever weight we are to give to these seeming resemblances between the Augsburg horoscopes and *The Ambassadors,* the fact remains that *the first degree of Libra was rising at London latitudes at the time we assigned to the scene portrayed.* This astronomical fact may be without deep significance, but it cannot be denied merely on the grounds that one dislikes the various parallels suggested here.

Had Holbein connected the time of Christ's death on the first Good Friday with the local – and astronomically inappropriate – state of the sky, he would not have been the first

45. The crucified Christ and the curtain selvedge.

to do so, as we shall see in due course.* Of more immediate importance are the reasons for likening the painting to a horoscope figure in the first place. It is not simply that by trimming two of its edges, as explained earlier, it becomes a square figure. Holbein has shown us that he attaches importance to the midpoints of its sides, and when we connect them as required by the astrologer the resulting figure does seem to pick out important lines in the painting. But why did Holbein not use a perfectly square panel in the first place? We have already given geometrical reasons for painting a picture that needs to be trimmed at the left-hand side and foot, but there is another possible reason. It could simply have been that the image of the crucified Christ was to be kept outside the horoscope. There were brave or foolhardy souls who were prepared to astrologise Christ, but they were few and far between, and some of them came to a sticky end.

* See p. 337 below.

If we are to trim the painting in our imagination, so as to yield a horoscope square, where will the edge of that square be? Measurement of the vertical distance (with the white strip removed) gives us the length of the square's side. Measuring off the same distance across the top from the upper right corner tells us where to place the other dividing line. On the strength of present-day evidence, it turns out to be precisely where the selvedge of the curtain, curving up from Dinteville's right elbow, reaches the top of the panel (Fig. 45). This fact makes it very easy to locate the point of division at a glance.

There are other convincing lines in the painting that fit well with the horoscope figure (Fig. 46). The central plumbline inevitably marks its meridian line. The line dividing the tenth

46. The matching of the horoscope square to the painting.

house from the inner square (as superimposed by us on the painting) runs along the horizon ring of the celestial sphere, an appropriately astronomical line of division. The lower edge of that inner square is delineated precisely by the lower edge of the bottom shelf of the central stand, and the visible leg of the stand reaches exactly to the III/IV house division. The turkey rug that is laid over the stand reaches exactly to the edge of the inner square, and does not enter the 'zodiac' part of the horoscope at all. In fact the figure of de Selve defines quite accurately the limits of the houses on the western side and upper corner (houses VI, VII, VIII, and IX). The dagger reaches exactly to the right-hand edge of the house of the ascendent Libra, and points accurately (backwards) to the cusp of the house, inclining us to the view that it somehow corresponds to the beam of the scales. Finally, the torquetum seems to fit nicely into house X, and almost defines its right-hand edge.

This sort of coherence is gratifying, but there is another that in its way is even more surprising. There is no reason why Holbein should not have built a horoscope square and a hexagram into his scheme in ways that were quite independent of one another. They need not have been geometrically related at all, but they turn out to be intimately linked, as can be easily appreciated from Fig. 47, which should be in need of no commentary. (Reference was made earlier to the harmonious

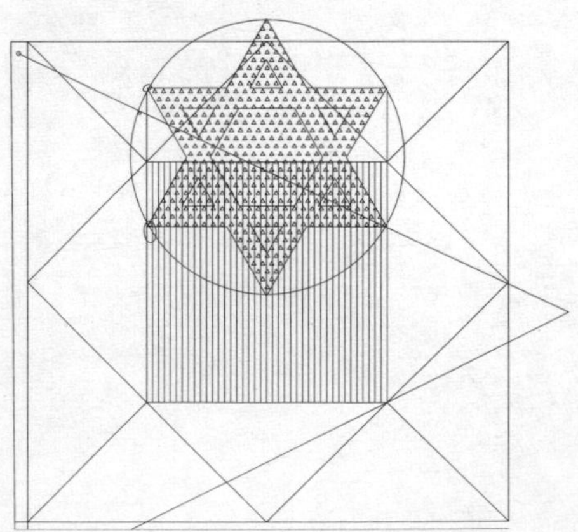

47. From this drawing of the two together, it would appear that the hexagram was geometrically placed with reference to the horoscope square.

dimensions of the two hexagrams.)* This entirely unexpected link through size and placement surely raises the probability that the two constructions are not illusory. The link will eventually prove to be reinforced by another consideration, for the medallion seems to have a dual function, once in the hexagram and once in the horoscope.

THE HOROSCOPE'S DETAIL

The introduction of a horoscope square into a portrait is not common, but neither is it unique to Holbein. A horoscope, tied as it is to a specific time as well as to human fortune, makes a natural addition to any portrayal of the private self – although it may have other uses. There are, for example, two plainly visible examples of simple personal horoscopes painted by the artist Christoph Amberger on his separate 1542 portraits of Matthäus Schwarz of Augsburg and his wife Barbara. (The details of the first have usually been misread, and hence their implications for Schwarz's personality have been misunderstood, but that is by the way.)[186] Holbein did not adopt such an obvious approach. There is nothing in his painting that is a blatant outline of a horoscope square. How then are we to be sure that the horoscope plan is there at all?

We have seen how well fitted the details of the painting are to the lines of a standard horoscope, but one particular property stands out from the rest. The astrologer uses the central area of his square to record details of the circumstances under which the thing was cast, and in particular the place, its latitude, and the local time. That is precisely what the painter has done. The central square contains the local story, so to speak, and remarkably little spills out into the surrounding area – just half of the globe and a part of the torquetum.

To try to prove the existence of a horoscope by construction lines alone would be to disregard a stronger argument for its reality, namely the compelling nature of what it would of necessity have been found to contain, bearing in mind the

* See p. 197 above.

mentality of the age. We know the place, the date and the precise time of day, and therefore the least we can do is consider the fine detail with which an astrologer would have filled a horoscopic figure for what was a deeply significant moment in the Christian calendar.

On the face of things one would not expect to find much worthy of note in such a scheme. It is just one among an endless number. Holbein, Kratzer, and any others who had a hand in the design, had very little control over its content. They had none over the movements of the planets and the heavens, and only a little over the precise time chosen on this Good Friday. What they could do, however, was make use of something astrologically apposite when it had caught their attention. There is good reason to think that this is exactly what happened, even though we need only consider the end-result. If this is true, it has strong implications for the act of artistic creation. We have already seen how many details of the painting there are that could only have been planned by a trained astronomer. If it was the same astronomer whose attention was caught by astronomical circumstance, then the very form of the painting must be assigned not to Holbein but to him.

With knowledge of the astronomical procedures of the age, we can say very precisely where the Sun, Moon and planets would have been placed. The points of division of the houses of the horoscope give rise to some slight ambiguity, since there were various systems in use, and since we need to know the geographical place for which the supposed horoscope was cast. With the possible exception of the quadrant, everything points to London. We might guess that the house-system that had been adopted by Regiomontanus was in use here, especially since one of the rings on the celestial globe in the painting was designed to be used with it. (German astrologers often referred to the system as that of 'our Regiomontanus', unaware that it was not of his own invention.) By reason of a certain symmetry in the scheme, this uncertainty makes no difference whatsoever to the three most striking facts of the astrological situation as it would then have been judged (compare Fig. 48).[187]

The first is that the beginning of the sign of Libra is rising

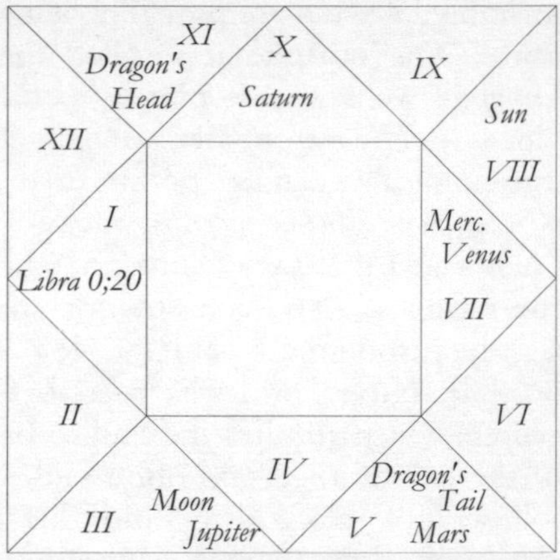

48. The horoscope square with planets assigned to the astrological houses. Roman numerals mark the houses, beginning with the ascendent house (I). Especially significant are the ascendent point itself (only 20 arc minutes into the first degree of Libra) and the positions of Jupiter and Saturn.

above the horizon, an incontestable astronomical fact. As will be explained, this event had great symbolic force relating to the crucifixion, although it was something that did not occur at the same time every Good Friday. How frequently it happened at four in the afternoon, for example, depends on how narrowly we define 'the beginning of Libra'. Even if, for example, we are generous enough to admit dates on which a point in one of the first *three* degrees of Libra is rising,[188] it happened on average only about one year in six at this period.

The second fact is that Jupiter, the planet often associated with Christ, is at the foot of the painting (seen as a horoscope) and in an astrologically unfortunate position, being in the third house and within 3° of the lowest point of all, the beginning of house IV.[189] It so happens that Jupiter is in much the same position as in one of the *Canterbury Tales* by the fourteenth-century poet Geoffrey Chaucer. There, in the *Man of Law's Tale,* it is described as 'falling into the darkest house'.[190]

As if that were not bad enough, the malevolent planet Saturn, in the ninth degree of Cancer, is overhead and near to mid-heaven. It is in the tenth house, which in this instance begins in the first degree of Cancer. The presence of Saturn in this position signals a gloomy situation, well befitting a most depressing hour of Good Friday.

The other astrological details relating to the houses are not unambiguous and are probably best ignored, with a few exceptions. What astronomers called the 'Head and Tail of the Dragon' were pseudo-planets commonly marked on horoscopes.[191] The astronomer's dragon actually represents a pair of astronomically defined points in the heavens that were used when calculating eclipses of the Sun or Moon. It is, and was, often stated that the crucifixion, when 'darkness descended on the earth', was the occasion for an eclipse, although from a strictly astronomical point of view this was known to be impossible. (Good Friday is near to full moon, so that a solar eclipse, which requires the Sun to be behind the Moon, is out of the question.) It was often said, even so, that a *miraculous* eclipse took place then, and this idea was well known to university-educated men, since it is expressed in the closing words of the standard astronomical text by Sacrobosco. There were various tales woven around the event in medieval commentaries on that basic text, such as that the philosophers in Athens were so impressed by the remarkable event that they erected an altar in the temple of Athena to the unknown god who had just suffered death. Christian scholars certainly had few qualms about discussing this most sacred of events in measured astronomical and astrological terms.[192]

Had an astrologer included the Head of the Dragon in our proposed horoscope it would have been in house XI, which in relation to the painting is where Holbein places the cap badge with its skull, its Death's Head. The image of St Michael killing the dragon – on Dinteville's collar of the order of St Michael – might have been thought a more potent symbol, but that is at quite a different place in the painting. It accompanies the dagger and the end of the sword in the first astrological house, where the Augsburg woodcut speaks – not inappropriately in this case – of a combatant with a spiked weapon in each hand (Fig. 44). How minute are the details of the painting that we may reasonably take into account in our search for such symbolism? The fine detail of the instruments does nothing to discourage the idea that great care was taken in the placing of the medallion. An X-ray photograph of it before the recent restoration showed that none of Holbein's paint survives to guarantee its detail. Two medallion-like drawings of St Michael by Holbein are still preserved in Basel, and they are generally supposed to have been sketches for the medallion in the painting. Not only do they differ from one another, however, but they differ in one significant respect from the medallion as it is presently found in the painting and in other portrayals of knights of the order from the same period. In the Holbein sketches, St Michael is spearing not a dragon but a human form, a more obvious representation of Satan. It is true that some latitude was allowed in the design of the collar as a whole, but the use of a Satan figure seems rather unlikely, in view of the fact that the painting was restored before 1797 on the orders of the descendants of Dinteville's niece by a painter who had probably seen enough of the original to reconstruct it. A sceptic might argue that that painter was probably simply copying the image of St Michael killing a dragon as it was found on a common French coin, the golden *angelot*. Holbein was familiar with the image on its English equivalent, the angel (Fig. 50). It was the coin presented by English kings when they touched those suffering from scrofula, 'the king's evil', to effect a cure: they hung it round the neck of the sufferer. To the French it was a reminder that Joan of Arc had seen St Michael in a vision, and that the English were never able to capture the seat of the order, Mont-Saint-Michel.[193]

As for the position of the medallion in the painting, St Michael's lance is inside the first house, like the dagger. St Michael himself was separated from the point of his weapon by the line of the horoscope construction. While the archangel is therefore mostly in the neutral central square, there is a strong reason for associating the saint astrologically with the first house, the house occupied by the sign of the Scales. He was regularly personified as Justice, and assigned the task of weighing souls. In many illustrations he carries a sword or lance in his right hand as he holds the balance in his left. Perhaps the most famous examples of this portrayal are Rogier van der Weyden's retable for the hôtel-dieu in Beaune (Burgundy), where it is still to be seen, and that by his pupil Hans Memling, on a triptych now in the National Museum in Gdansk. This once common

49. Holbein's drawing of St Michael, in his dual role of righteous combatant and weigher of souls.

image is still to be seen in a painting on the wall of the church of St Jean in Dinteville's own town of Troyes. It was known throughout western Christendom, from the Mediterranean to Ireland, but it seems to have been especially widespread in Germany, where churches were very commonly dedicated to the warrior saint.[194] Not only did Holbein know of the tradition, but on at least one occasion he drew a perfectly typical representation of it, with the winged archangel holding a sword above his head in his right hand, while in his left he holds a pair of scales. The good of a cherub on one side outweighs the evil of a horned satanic fiend on the other (Fig. 49).[195] In short, the placing of the St Michael medallion fits very well with the idea of an ascendent Libra (the Scales) in the horoscope.

The painted pavement, which seems to have been inspired by that in Westminster Abbey, although on a smaller scale, favours this reading. Forgetting for a moment the six-pointed star motif, we see that the central part of the abbey pavement on which Holbein has concentrated his attention – judging by the floor of the painting – also bears a certain similarity to the frame of a standard horoscope. It is not that its makers thought

50. The English gold coin known as the angel. Erasmus suggested that Holbein came to England to pick up just such coins. The example illustrated was struck in the 1480s, but the same pattern was still in use in the reign of Henry VIII. It was copied from the French triple golden angelot of 1469, which took its name from its portrayal of the archangel Michael and commemorated the newly created royal order of thirty-six knights.

of it in this way, but that a sixteenth-century astrologer who had drawn it would have seen the resemblance immediately. The central square of the abbey pavement 'horoscope' (Fig. 51) is roughly two and a half times as large along its sides as the 80 Tudor inches of Holbein's oak *panel*, but what of the *pavement* he was painting? Recalling our earlier discussion of Holbein's various perspective viewpoints, in the context of the drafting of the celestial globe as well as the painting as a whole,* we can say that taking the perspective of the pavement as our starting point, the side of the basic square was within an inch or so of 104 in (264 cm), inclusive of the boundary strip. From the 1924 plan of the Royal Commission on Historical Monuments we find that the corresponding dimension of the Westminster pavement (its inner square) is 209 in. There can no longer be any serious doubt about the Westminster connection: the floor on which the men stand was drafted to exactly half the scale of that in the abbey. This is an especially gratifying discovery, since we earlier decided quite independently that the hexagram circle hidden in the painting is exactly double the scale of the hexagram circle on the (actual) floor. Holbein the measurer,

* See p. 112 above.

51. The weak similarity of the geometry of a horoscope square to that of the Westminster sanctuary pavement.

Holbein the draftsman, had probably made a scale plan of the abbey pavement. Scaling it down, and then up, for his floor, would have made him very familiar with it. Alternatively, he might have started from plans prepared by someone else, possibly annotated plans. In either case, it would not have required Kratzer to see the resemblance to a horoscope figure, for that was something with which everyone in their circle would have been familiar.

A final word about the abbey floor 'horoscope'. It is here being claimed that several elements in *The Ambassadors* are closely fitted to a horoscope square. Can this be an illusion, a coincidence that follows only because the painting is patterned after the abbey pavement? The suspicion can be laid to rest at

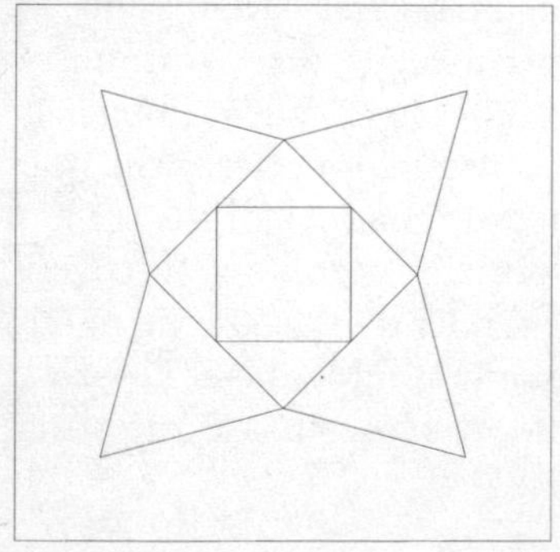

52. The centres of all but the innermost circle in the abbey pavement (see the previous figure) are on the vertices of the equilateral triangles in this figure.

once. The painting only fits the plan of the pavement at all well in respect of those of its properties that resemble a horoscope. The circles on it do not fit with the painting, a fact that can be seen from the pattern that was followed, according to Foster's analysis, when the centres of the various pavement circles were laid out. The centres of all the abbey circles, apart from that at the very centre, in fact lie on the vertices of the equilateral triangles in Fig. 52.

THE HEXAGRAM AND THE PLANETS

Looking for meaning in the hexagram that seemed to be hidden in the painting, it was natural to consider the best known of all interpretations, those based on biblical and other spiritual traditions. There is another place in which such figures are commonly found, namely in the astrological doctrine of what are known as *aspects.* Imagine a zodiac circle on which all the planets are to be found and at the centre of which is the Earth. When two planets are separated by sixty degrees in the zodiac – that is when the angle they subtend at the Earth is sixty degrees – they are said to be in friendly aspect, and to regard each other favourably. (This particular aspect was technically known as 'sextile'.) When the separation is ninety degrees, the aspect is supposedly unfriendly ('quartile'). There are various other aspects, and there are related principles that involve not only their separation but the characters of the planets themselves. We have already seen that Saturn and Jupiter were in the aspect of opposition on Good Friday, 1533 – the rules allow a little leeway, and 'opposition' does not have to correspond strictly to a separation of 180 degrees. There is no need to set out the rather intricate rules for the astrological meaning and use of aspects, but it would be a mistake to underestimate their attraction for astrologers, for they rested on a simple analogy with the human act of 'regarding', and were easily manipulated without much mathematical expertise, despite the harmonious geometry used to express them. In fact hardly sixty years had passed from the time of Holbein's painting before Johannes Kepler, prompted by this bizarre astrological doctrine to investigate

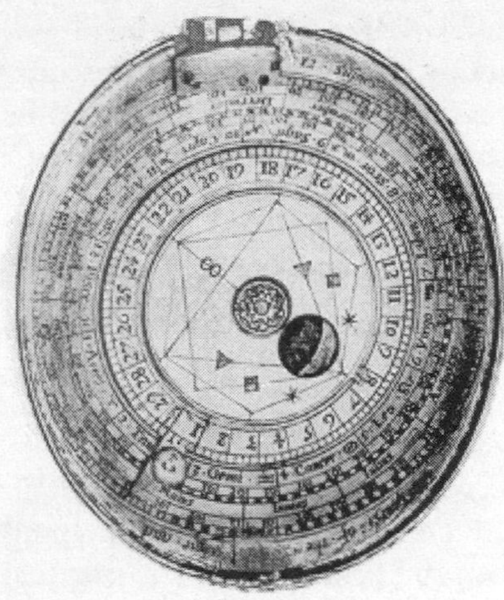

53. One of the sections of a pocket compendium made by Humphrey Cole and dated 1569. (Now in the National Maritime Museum at Greenwich, it may once have belonged to Francis Drake.) The central part of the instrument illustrates the principle of the aspectarium. It offers an easy way of spotting astrologically meaningful aspects (angular separations) of the Sun, Moon and planets, the positions of which are supposedly first marked on the peripheral zodiac scale in some way. Thus the tiny double circle (8) indicates opposition, the tiny triangles register 60 degrees separation (sextile aspect), the squares 90 degrees (quartile) and the crosses 120 degrees (trine).

the harmonies of the planets, was led to revolutionise the mathematical theory of planetary motion.

To spot aspects quickly and painlessly, without the need to calculate all possible angular separations of the planets by subtraction, there was a simple instrument available, known as an 'aspectarium'. This is commonly found in books and on astrolabes of the period. The astrologer calculates the planetary positions – not a trivial task, of course – and marks them on a zodiac circle. Pivoted around the centre of the zodiac circle there is a disc with all the aspects marked on it, radiating from a single point (Fig. 53). The disc is rotated, bringing that point up to each planetary position in turn. Whether or not there are planets in aspect to any particular planet will be immediately obvious.

In the context of astrology a hexagram is strongly suggestive of the doctrine of aspects. The Sun at the time represented in the painting was in sextile aspect to Saturn. Mars was near to conjunction with the (heavenly) Dragon's Tail, something that might easily have been interpreted in terms of St Michael, the knightly archangel, killer of the dragon of Christian legend. The Sun was virtually sextile to Mars and the Dragon's Tail, and they in turn were sextile to Jupiter. The geometry of the heavens is a more or less incontrovertible matter, which is not to say that the aspects were indeed calculated. The most we can say is that the number of significant aspects is unusually large, and well fitted to the six-pointed figure in the painting. The state of the heavens on Good Friday 1533 would have lent itself to a discussion in which the idea of a mystical hexagram in the heavens would have occurred quite naturally. What is not straightforward is how we fit it to the painting, and decide on the starting point of the zodiac and its sense of rotation. It could have been drawn in two ways, one corresponding to the sphere of stars as we see it – the horoscope convention – the

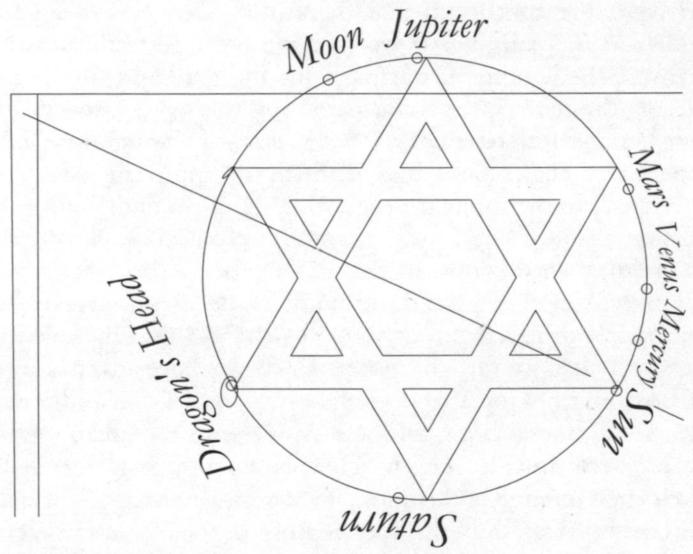

54. The circle circumscribing the hexagram is here taken to represent the zodiac, the general sense of circulation of the planets being clockwise and the zero-point of the zodiac (the head of Aries) at furthest right. The planets are placed in the positions they occupied in the afternoon of Good Friday 1533. It is quite possible that the hexagram idea was first suggested by these several sextile aspects, perhaps orientated differently.

other to a God's-eye-view, so to speak, in which the imagined sphere of stars is regarded as viewed from the outside. The aspects themselves, angles between the planets regarded as points on the zodiac circle, are the same in both cases, but not the correspondences of the planets with points on the painting. (One arrangement that seems not implausible is shown in Fig. 54).The Sun is on the line of sight leading up to Christ, and the Dragon's Head (the ascending node of the Moon in reality, that is) corresponds to the medallion of St Michael, with its dragon. Jupiter is directly overhead and Saturn directly below. Another arrangement would switch all planets to diametrically opposite points. The number of possible astrological interpretations of the aspects is legion, and none will be suggested here.

The account given here follows the order in which I first arrived at the conclusion that there might be a set of aspects hidden in the painting. It would have been perfectly possible to invert the argument, starting with the date and time, considering the state of the heavens, noting the sextile aspects and then looking for some figure in the plan of the painting with sixty-degree angles built into it. Such an approach may have been closer to the thought processes of Holbein and Kratzer, or whoever planned the painting, and who may have chosen the hexagram to encode the aspects.

There is another procedural point to be mentioned. It has been tacitly assumed throughout this chapter that the relevant time was that in the afternoon, since we have given strong reasons for thinking that the globe was not set to indicate a time at all, but to bring Sun and Moon into the reckoning in the way explained at length. The planetary aspects would be much the same for both times, since even the Moon will have moved less than three degrees against the stars, but there is another reason for taking the afternoon situation. It has an important historical precedent, and this will be explained in our final chapter. To lay the matter to rest once and for all, however, we note that the night horoscope is a mediocre affair. Of all the planets, only Saturn is above the horizon, and no planet is in a memorable place. There was never a horoscope cast from which a good astrologer could not extract something worthy of a fee, but this would have taxed the patience of most.

A NOTE ON GOLDEN SECTION

The outline figure of the standard horoscope, based on the simple division of a square, was very widely known. There is another geometrical figure based on a square that will jump to the eye of a reader well versed in Euclid's geometry, and it will be as well to dismiss it without more ado. Much attention was paid in the middle ages, and even more in Holbein's century, to the ratio commonly known as 'golden section'. The figure that Euclid used to construct it is strongly reminiscent of the basic pattern of the Holbein painting, for it not only involves a square, but a square divided into two equal rectangles.[196] The ratio is closely linked to the construction of a regular pentagon and other regular figures related to it, and it may even be found in a scheme underlying Piero della Francesca's *The Baptism of Christ.* *

By selecting suitably artificial elements from Holbein's painting it is possible to extract lengths that are more or less in the desired ratio of golden section, but it is hard to see how this could ever have been done at all naturally. (The most promising starting point might be the side of length $\sqrt{5}$ in Fig. 33.) The six-pointed figure in the pavement might also be thought to speak against it. There is no clear sign of any regular pentagon, star pentagon, pentagram or pentacle – to use names beloved of mystics ancient and modern – in *The Ambassadors.* Hexagons are another matter.

* See also Chapter 6 above and Appendix 1 below.

PART THREE

The Meaning

'But let us argue. I imagine . . .', said I.

'I won't imagine,' said he. 'You poets imagine,
and every word is a lie.'

'Grant then, . . .', said I.

'I won't grant,' said he.

'Let's assume, then, . . .', said I.

'But it is not so,' said he . . .

Erasmus to Thomas More (September 1520), on his
Louvain debate with the Carmelite Nicolas of Egmont

ELEVEN

SHADOW AND TRUTH

> [*Folly*] 'What difference is there, do you think, between those in Plato's cave who can only marvel at the shadows and images of various objects, provided that they are content and don't know what they miss, and the philosopher who has emerged from the cave and sees the real things?'
>
> Erasmus, *Praise of Folly*, trans. B. Radice, p.137

Of all Plato's myths, that of the cave in book 7 of *The Republic* is the most famous. In it he describes men who, able to see only shadows on the walls of a cave, judge them to be the only reality. Erasmus made frequent use of the image, and it would be hard to find a humanist scholar of note in Holbein's time who did not refer to it. It is a highly appropriate text for Holbein's painting. The day is Good Friday, 1533. The skull casts its shadow at an unnatural angle, judged by the rest of the painting, but it is an angle that correctly represents the time recorded in various ways in the painting for that Good Friday. Any person who is positioned so as to decode that distorted emblem may look up at the same symbolic angle, the angle to the Sun at that moment, and see the shaded countenance of Christ. The gloom is meant to be untrue to reality, which the Christian believer – following an earlier verse in Matthew's Gospel (17:2) or any one of a thousand texts thereafter – likens rather to the Sun itself.

For those who in 1533 were apprised of the painting's crucifixion theme, what for most modern onlookers counts as nothing more than a puzzle in perspective technique was a sombre reminder of the most doleful point in the Bible narrative. It is much more than that, however, for the perspective carries a promise of its own. The observer, in looking up to Christ, becomes part of a spiritual world outside that of the two ambassadors and the worldly instruments of the quadrivium. Looked at in this way, the earthly world shows itself to be less than fully real. This is the fundamental message borne by the underlying perspective, and is one to which all others conform. It is a pious message that supplements the painting's many reminders of Christ's promise of salvation, and it is reinforced many times over in different ways.

But are we ascribing too much to Holbein and to those who helped him to craft *The Ambassadors*? It is as well to remember how extremely sophisticated medieval and Renaissance theories of artistic and literary purpose and exegesis were, theories that had grown out of the ways devised earlier by the Church Fathers to teach their followers. Four levels of meaning were commonly distinguished in each reported biblical event. There was first the literal meaning, where the text was concerned with a simple historical occurrence. The text was also supposed to be capable of bearing an allegorical or metaphorical meaning – a useful idea when a commentator wished to explain a text in the Old Testament as anticipating another in the New. The third type of meaning was taken to be on the moral plane, with a message concerning the way in which we should conduct our affairs; and the fourth was the anagogical (mystical) interpretation, which to all intents and purposes drew a parallel between this life and the next. To quote William Tyndale, writing in the year 1528, the year in which Holbein first left London: 'They divide the scripture into four senses, the literal, tropological [moral], allegorical, and anagogical. . . . The allegory is appropriate to faith; and the anagogical to hope, and things above.'[197] Whether or not the intelligent artist, who had rubbed shoulders with members of the literary profession without being one of them, would have been aware of this much-repeated fourfold division, his sitters and Kratzer would have known of it. They might even have known of the scorn Erasmus had poured on some who were fond of parrotting it.

We have no textual evidence for Holbein's or their intentions in *The Ambassadors*. His exercises in perspective are no more than a starting point in the search for them. The angle of the skull and its shadow offers a key to much of the painting's temporal meaning, and leads by other paths to other dimensions – numerological, astrological, and so on. The first concern of the painter and those who helped to guide his hand is less likely to have been with them than with eternal religious verities. They constitute the spiritual backdrop to the painting, but it is not they that make the painting so unusual. For that quality we must look to the foreground, where painted forms render Christian belief, and perhaps more besides. It is in discovering the meaning of the foreground that our chief difficulties lie.

THE PLACE OF THE SKULL

> And when they were come unto a place called Golgotha, that is to say, a place of a skull, They gave him vinegar to drink mingled with gall . . . And they crucified him.
>
> Matthew 27:33–35[198]

The theme of Christ's suffering and death was by no means new to Hans Holbein the painter. His father had led the way with several Passion cycles, and so highly prized was the younger Holbein's *Passion of Christ* altarpiece, painted around 1524, that the seventeenth-century painter Joachim von Sandrart persuaded Duke Maximilian I of Bavaria to offer the Basel government an extremely large sum of money for it. The offer was unsuccessful, and it remains to this day in the city. At first sight it is a conventional enough work, although, as Oskar Bätschmann points out, it makes use of unusual lighting effects: the first three scenes of the upper panels portray events taking place at night, while various carefully contrived light sources provide illumination and shadow.[199] There is absolutely nothing, however, apart from the figure of the crucified Christ and the experiments with light, that can connect this earlier work with *The Ambassadors*.

From what is known of Holbein's biography there is even less that can connect him with the tacitly academic side of the London painting. There is a wide gulf between the structural readings of the painting offered here and those that rest on symbolisms that any intelligent man-about-court might have applied or recognised. The surest way of banishing this uncomfortable thought is to acknowledge that there is in *The*

Ambassadors the hand of one or more scholars who knew the sciences of the quadrivium well. The person – or persons – chiefly responsible for its mathematical aspects needed to have more than mere sympathy with Christian astrology. The distorted skull leads inevitably to that conclusion. From the key line of sight along it we have been led to others, and on to a fitting horoscope that commemorates the immediate aftermath of Christ's death. The malevolent Saturn is culminating while Jupiter, the planet of religion, has sunk to its lowest.

Since the planning of such matters was surely well beyond Holbein's powers, it is worth comparing what we are claiming to detect in *The Ambassadors* with what is to be found in the work of other astrologising painters. Most trivially, there are the portraits that have had horoscopes added in order to supplement biography – they are often on tombs, for example – but theirs is a different function entirely, and the calculated square would simply have been handed over by the astrologer to the painter for copying. More interesting are the various painted ceilings, especially in Italy, that take the form of explicit allegories, with personified planets and zodiacal signs, hopefully so accurately placed that they may be dated and analysed. Such things also needed more knowledge than most untutored painters would have had, but by their very openness they would probably have been obnoxious to Holbein's sitters. The figure of Jupiter – a common astrological substitute for Christ – would have been considered in barbarous taste if placed openly in a Good Friday scene.

There seems to be no known example of another painting structured around a concealed horoscope square, but by the very nature of the exercise one cannot expect such a thing to be easily identified. There is a painting now in Kassel that at first glance seems as though it might follow the same pattern. It does not, but it well illustrates what a painter could do with minimal technical help, and it has some strange points of contact with the London painting. It is a table top by the Ulm painter Martin Schaffner (1477/8–1546/9). Not only is he said to have studied with Holbein's father, but the work was done in 1533, the year of *The Ambassadors.* Schaffner as an artist was no match for the younger Hans Holbein, but his work is exquisitely done in oils, looking almost as though taken from an elaborate manuscript illumination, and its subject is equally bookish. It is an allegory of the seven liberal arts, each represented by a seated woman – grammar, rhetoric (here with a crucifix in her hand), logic, arithmetic, geometry, music and astronomy. Each is under the influence of a conventionally chosen planet, and each is correlated with a colour, a metal and a day of the week. A red-robed male scholar (Ptolemy?) makes an eighth, and he is under the tutelage of the sphere of fixed stars.[200] Inevitably there is some overlap between the instruments in Schaffner's painting and Holbein's, but in the last analysis the two are as far apart in intellectual depth as in artistic merit. That they share certain qualities is to be explained not by some ineffable *Zeitgeist* but by the network of serious-minded scholars practising astrology with whom both were in touch, directly or indirectly – such men as Philipp Melanchthon, Johannes Stöffler, Peter Apian and Nicolaus Kratzer.

There is more to be said about the Holbein horoscope, and it follows logically, or rather astrologically, in the wake of what has been said already. There is a point of standard doctrine that relates to the planetary domiciles – the signs of the zodiac that are 'houses' in the simpler sense of that word, as the Ram is the house of Mars, and so on – and to what are known as the 'essential' properties of the planets that were mentioned earlier.[201] Astrologers had a way of taking the set of planetary positions for the moment of interest and then adding up the 'dignities' of planets and subtracting their 'debilities'. When we do this for Jupiter and Saturn, for the time represented in the painting, we find something very surprising. While it is true that Saturn was near to culminating, up high and strong, the planet was actually in Cancer, the sign known as the 'exaltation' of Jupiter. And while Jupiter was in a depressed state, 'falling into the darkest house', he was also in its own domicile, Sagittarius. Adding up the dignities, the astrologer would have found that Jupiter (often associated with Christ) reached a very high score and that Saturn (planet of melancholy and misery) had many debilities. The methods of calculating these things varied, but all astrologers would have agreed with these general statements. In other words, while the 'accidental' properties of the planets in the horoscope are depressing, their 'essential' properties are a cause for optimism. Any Christian astrologer looking for a situation that spells out the message of future salvation, and the conquest of evil by good, would have been hard pressed to find a better situation.

There is another piece of astrological doctrine that might have gone along with the painting. Again it has strictly nothing to do with the implicit horoscope, but only with the positions the planets Mars, Jupiter and the Moon occupied. The knightly Mars, perhaps representing the noble Dinteville, was in Pisces, while Jupiter and the Moon, potentially representing a man of religion such as de Selve, were both in Sagittarius. These two are the only zodiacal signs painted on the lowest torquetum disc, as noted earlier.

THE THEME OF TWENTY-SEVEN

Astrology, however, is a fickle guide. If any one thing points to the religious meaning of *The Ambassadors* it is the recurrence of the theme involving the number 27. The angle of 27° – we may now put aside all talk of 26.56° – was the altitude of the Sun at a few minutes past four in the afternoon, the time that would have been shown on the cylinder dial had its gnomon headed more precisely for the Sun on Good Friday of 1533. That is precisely the angle at which the foreground anamorphosed skull is drawn, so that the skull may be treated as a visual record of the shadow cast by the Good Friday Sun at the end of the hour following Christ's death on the cross. The angle is marked off on the quadrant scale by the arm of the solar instrument. The only words on the quadrant that are open to view are those labelling the scale of 'VMBRA VERSA', the 'facing shadow', normally denoting the shadow cast by a horizontal gnomon on a vertical wall. The shadow cast on the cylinder dial by its gnomon is likewise an *umbra versa.* The quadrant itself does not register anything on its scale of *umbra versa.* Nothing so obvious. It registers rather the angles of 27° and 54° in a most devious way, as explained earlier.

And then there are the other occurrences of the angle of 27°, on the two dart gnomons; on the 'wrong' edge of the alidade for the 'ecliptic crest' of the torquetum; and in the angles of the two books on the lower shelf, for example. Whether or not anyone was ever conscious of the fact, 27 was also the average of the 'years' of the two men as added to the portrait itself, 25 and 29.[202] As a pure number, 27 is a factor found three times on the open page of the arithmetic (Fig. 19). As a pure number, 27 is thrice thrice three, and three is the number of the Trinity. An association of that cumulation of threes with the Holy Trinity begs to be made, but there are many other potential associations with the number three and its powers. The crucified Christ would rise from the dead on the third day. The theological virtues were often said to be three in number. Some spoke of the Three Ages – the first under Adam, the second in Christ, and the third with Christ. There are triads wherever one looks in early sixteenth-century literature. Holbein himself was not averse to including, in one of his metal-cuts, an image of God's hand emerging from a cloud and holding the triple-headed symbol of the ancient Egyptian solar deity Serapis. Many 'trinities' will take an unprepared modern reader by surprise – as for example, the three naked Graces standing by the throne of Apollo with his lute (lyre), at the place normally occupied by God or Christ in a conventional illustration of the spheres of the universe.[203] (Apollo was a usual analogue of Christ, and Jupiter of God.)

Putting threes aside and restricting ourselves to a complete 27, there are meanings to be found in the class of literature that the humanists of the age most admired. We may perhaps dismiss such numerological ideas as Plutarch's, that 27 is the first masculine (odd) cube, but we cannot ignore Plato's doctrine of the World Soul as presented in the *Timaeus*. As the abbey floor reminded us, Plato was much influenced by the followers of Pythagoras, and many of their doctrines were passed on to Christian theology by Neoplatonist philosophers in the early centuries of the Christian era.[204] Plato based his arguments for the World Soul in the first place on a notion of *numerical* harmony – rather than musical harmony, as is so often claimed. He believed that there were two sorts of existence, that of the objects of reason (such as the Forms) and that of the entities we perceive. A soul, to comprehend both, must have a type of existence that is a mixture of the two. This, he said, is a truth that applies to the soul of the universe as well as to the human soul. He explains the creation of the world with the help of a famous myth which represents sequences of numbers as the very stuff of creation.

In this myth he blended two sequences of numbers (each a so-called geometrical progression): 1, 2, 4, 8 and 1, 3, 9, 27. Why stop at 27? Because it was a cube number, which somehow Plato thought capable of encompassing three-dimensional reality. Early medieval philosophers in the West found this idea much to their liking. To take only one example: the youthful twelfth-century Neoplatonist William of Conches took the numerical relationship of the Platonic 27 and the number of the Trinity as an argument for the identity of the World Soul and the Holy Spirit, even though he was duly criticised for his boldness. Neoplatonism is the ultimate context for the pavement in Westminster abbey, where the age of the universe is spelled out in the inscription on the abbey floor, three raised to the power of nine. There had been a generous inflation of the Neoplatonic mystery over the centuries, for the factor 27 is tacitly placed on the abbey floor three times over, just as on the open page of Apian's arithmetic in Holbein's painting. The number of Neoplatonic texts on this subject, from any one of which a good humanist might have drawn inspiration, is very great, and we shall later come across a powerful theological movement that inflated the sixteenth-century total even further.

MEMENTO MORI

This interpretation of *The Ambassadors*, in terms of Redemption and the creation of the world by God, is a far cry from the usual ecumenical and political schemes, most of which can ultimately be traced back to the pioneering study by Mary Hervey. Since we have here already found several architectonic layers of meaning in the painting, however, we should hesitate before ruling out others that may prove to be perfectly compatible with them. Hervey put much emphasis on the way in which so many of the things in the painting – the lute with its broken string, the skulls, the crucifixion, the hymnal, and the instruments for recording time – seem to constitute a complex *memento mori*. In a simple form, such a thing typically showed a skull, or other sign of human decay, and carried an inscription to the effect 'I was once what you are, and you will one day be what I am. Pray for me'. Elaborated upon by Mary Hervey and others, the *memento mori* is now considered as reminding the onlooker of how vain are *scholarship and power* when we are constantly faced by the inevitability of death. This additional rider has proved to be irresistible to many commentators on the painting, but I need not survey this particular vein of scholarship any further.[205] Hervey was even persuaded by 'the Arms of Death' woodcut in Holbein's *Dance of Death* series that his renewed use of the skull motif indicated that the melancholy Dinteville, often ill, had adopted the Death's Head as his personal badge or *devise*. Here she placed herself in a difficult position, since a *devise*, properly speaking, had two parts: an emblem and a motto. She tried unsuccessfully to read certain miniature brushstrokes on the sheath of Dinteville's dagger as a motto, but her conjectures owed more to a Holbein design now in Basel than to the London painting.[206] There is much to be said for seeking a motto, since mottoes were in vogue throughout the century. Why not the words on the quadrant? *Umbra versa* might be thought an unpromising motto, but such a clipped phrase would not have been at all unusual. It can be closely paralleled by an *Umbra tantum* from the emblem book of Camerarius, for example.[207] The phrase *Umbra versa* might have been taken to mean 'The shadow reversed' or 'The shadow overcome', and so have carried a Christian message of the hope of redemption. Perhaps it was regarded as a simple description ('inverted shadow') of the line that directs our eyes up to Christ. However melancholy its owner, any of these readings would have made a worthier *memento mori* than a trite reminder of death's inevitability.

Soon after Hervey's book first appeared, William Lethaby argued that the *memento mori* theme was compounded by the symbolism of the pavement: 'I believe it was selected by Holbein', he wrote, 'because it symbolized Time on which death throws its recurring shadow, as in the picture the skull forms the gnomon to the dial of the pavement.'[208] The idea of the skull as a gnomon is ingenious, but it cannot be accepted in any but the most general way, if the anamorphosed skull was truly involved in the ubiquitous theme of 27. A gnomon that heads into the Sun is useless. The evidence for 27 is overwhelming, and the Lethaby reading does not lend itself to being combined with it.

Others have allowed the skull's shadow even greater powers. 'The fact that its shadow falls in the opposite direction to others in the painting', Susan Foister maintains, 'may serve to indicate the presence of an object from a dimension beyond the temporal.'[209] If suitably rephrased this is an idea that might not have been beyond the reach of a medieval or Renaissance theologian, especially one who had read his Augustine. It is at the other extreme of the naive reading of the anamorphosis – which is simply that a clever trick has been played on us by the painter. But how deep are we to allow those concerned to be in their philosophy of time? A trick has been played, a trick that others were happy to play on the faces of emperors, kings, and friends, as well as on mundane objects. Recognisable skulls are not uncommonly included in the foreground of paintings of the crucifixion scene at Golgotha. They are a token of that place. This representation had been found throughout the middle ages in books of hours, on altarpieces and other devotional paintings in churches. From at least as early as the third century there had been a tradition that Adam had been buried at Golgotha – contradicting the tradition that he was buried at Hebron. Following Byzantine tradition, Adam's skull was often set in the foreground to crucifixion scenes, reminding the onlooker that Christ had the role of Second Adam. The New Testament includes a genealogy of Christ's descent from the first man (Luke 3:23–38). A skull, in other words, is far more than simply a stark reminder of the human condition. Given the right frame of mind, as Hamlet proved, it may prompt a soliloquy: but with what conclusion? To interpret the skull in Holbein's painting as carrying a message from another dimension seems to go well beyond the evidence, and uses a language entirely alien to the sixteenth century.

The strongest reason for rejecting the idea that the skull on the badge was a personal *devise* adopted by the melancholy Dinteville is that the day is Good Friday and the hour is after Christ's death. There was a reasonably constant common stock of customs adopted on that day, and the use of such a badge may not have been among them, but the church allowed for much latitude in local tradition. The great variety permitted within the standard guidelines of ritual – such as those standardised at Sarum (Salisbury), Hereford, Bangor, York and Lincoln – was emphasised in Thomas Cranmer's preface to the 1549 *Book of Common Prayer*, and doubtless there was a tendency throughout Christendom to consider a little judicious deviation as a mark of superiority. At all events, it seems not unlikely that Dinteville wore his badge as a token of the fact that the hour of Christ's death had passed, and that de Selve's dress indicated exactly the same thing.

The latter would have been conventional enough. After the hour of Christ's death, vestments were usually changed to the black that was appropriate to a mass for the dead. There were relatively few places where convention differed. In England – following the Use of Sarum – it was common but not universal during all of Passiontide, Good Friday included, to have vestments of red, and oddly enough the same custom was and is still kept in de Selve's Milan.

Good Friday did not belong to the clergy alone, and the skull motif need not be sought only among them. Passion Plays during Lent and Holy Week were popular and made use of it. Local confraternities of lay men and women acted out their devotion to particular aspects of the Passion of Christ in towns and villages throughout Europe. Often the day began with a searching for Christ, when white was worn. In some places

Christ's cross was ceremonially carried up to a local 'Calvary' by a person wearing red. After the Passion was over, for example in dramatised ceremonies of lowering the body and taking it to the tomb, black was the colour usually worn, and it was at this stage that some groups put on a badge with a skull. The cross seems to have been usually present, but in some instances it was completely dwarfed by a skull and crossbones, representing of course the mortal Adam. To take one example: just such a custom was adopted by the Confraternity of Prayer and Death, a group that traces its origins to the Sack of Rome in 1527. Their Good Friday customs were almost certainly older, but in them at least we have evidence that we are not guilty of anachronism in suggesting that Dinteville's badge may have been simply a token of the fact that the day was Good Friday and that the hour of Christ's death had passed at the moment caught by Holbein in his painting.[210]

Whether this is right or wrong, it is clearly no truism to say that the skull is 'a conventional *memento mori*', and turning for help to other works by Holbein will not make it one. As long ago as 1857, R. N. Wornum remarked on a strong similarity between the overall composition of *The Ambassadors* and Holbein's woodcut *Die Wapen des Thotss (The Arms of Death)*, with which the *Dance of Death* series culminated.[211] There a contemporary man and woman of high social position stand as supporters to a decrepit shield on which there is only a skull, while on the crest above the shield there are skeletal arms in the attitude of one person stoning another – a favourite biblical scene. There is also an hour glass, reminding the onlooker of the transience of human life (Fig. 55). There is certainly a fleeting similarity between the two Holbein compositions, but only that. If our French ambassadors are to be seen as in any way analogous to supporters in a coat of arms, the arms are certainly not to be equated to the vile nihilistic centrepiece of the woodcut, which cannot by any stretch of the imagination have occupied the thoughts of Holbein and the others for more than a fraction of the time spent on planning the 1533 double portrait. The messages carried by the two works are very different. Whatever else it may be, the painting stands in a tradition

55. Holbein woodcut: 'The Arms of Death'.

of full-length commemorative double portraits, which is not true of the woodcut. The painting offers hope of redemption, while the woodcut is primarily a reminder that, noble trappings and riches notwithstanding, all of us will be consumed by worms, all of us will come to dust. These are the two extremes favoured by so much of medieval theology, and between them, in medieval religious art, there is surprisingly little to be found. But not for Holbein the grim and anguished alternative image of Death the Leveller when he came to portray the two ambassadors.

The contrast is one that brings to mind a little treatise written by Sir Thomas More at some time after 1520, called *The Four Last Things.* The title is an allusion to death, judgement, heaven and hell – the 'last things' of the apocryphal Book of Ecclesiasticus.[212] Even the logical More, the rational and analytical lawyer, was prepared to play the 'dance of death' card, although he broke off after dealing with only the first of the 'four last things', death. He handled this subject in a flesh-creeping way worthy of the worst horror-inspiring sermons of the middle ages. The loathsomeness of death, the pains of death, and even more frightening, the imaginings surrounding the anticipation of them, were introduced for much the same reason as in previous centuries: people were to be led away from sin through fear of the idea that no sinner could expect any compensating bliss after the agony of death. More refers to a painted dance of death that was to be seen in St Paul's cathedral in his own day, and only regrets that it does not chill the observer as much as it should. He does his utmost to remedy this state of affairs, and in doing so puts himself at the same emotional level as the early Holbein, despite the intellectual and theological differences between them. By the time Holbein painted *The Ambassadors*, he had seemingly risen to a higher theological plane. With the help of others.

TWELVE

TOUCHED BY THE OCCULT?

> The brooches that our courtier must wear in his cap must be very rich, and excellently wrought, and his device or word that he will have about it such that every man may read it, yet few shall understand what it means.
>
> Don Anthony of Guevara, *The Diall of Princes* (Seville, 1528), trans. Sir Thomas North (London, 1535)

It has been shown probable that the skull in Dinteville's cap was conceived to fit into a hidden hexagram on the upper level of the panel. By analogy, it may have been linked in Holbein's overall plan to the skull that obscures the hexagram on the painted floor. Even those who reject the idea will need to decide on the meaning of that figure on the floor. Half-obscured by shadow and the distorted skull, it is unlikely to have been added casually, or as a purely decorative device – it is almost as difficult to make out as the distorted skull. If we have correctly discerned a second example in the patterning of the painting, it raises by a very great margin the probability that both were important to its plan.

It is out of the question that the half-visible figure was included in the painting merely because it was already to be found on the floor where Dinteville and de Selve stood. Its placement in relation to the rest of the painting is too contrived for that. Examined carefully, the geometrical centre of the hexagram on the floor is found to coincide with the centre of the elongated skull *as perceived by a person looking at it from the correct viewpoint at the side of the painting.* This *perceived* centre is not the *geometrical* centre of the flat figure – say the rough ellipse outlining much of the skull – but a point in the very middle of the skull conceived as a three-dimensional object. It is a point that presents itself to the viewer of the restored skull as being in line with a point just over the left eye socket (Fig. 56). That Holbein should have gone to such pains in producing

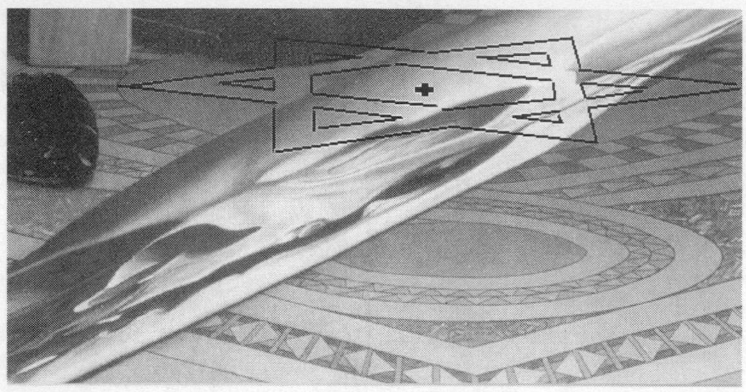

56. The half-concealed hexagram in the floor of *The Ambassadors*, here completed, with a cross marking its geometrical centre.

his final composition is entirely in keeping with the morass of fine scientific detail in the painting generally, and with the trouble he took when drafting so many of his other paintings. Not to mention the skull's involvement in the theme of left and right eyes.

Lest the significance of this geometrical property be overlooked, it may be expressed in other terms. The anamorphosed skull does not merely lie athwart the pavement hexagram, it is to be *seen* as centred on it, that is, as intimately related to it, by those contemplative observers who, from the same place at the side of the painting, by raising their eyes look up directly to the crucified Christ. No matter how we interpret Holbein's hexagram, it was at the very least a focus for the regard – vision, thought, attention – of such observers. This was no peep-show. But why this particular figure?

A purely astrological explanation in terms of sextile aspects has already been offered here, and we have also hinted at philosophical and theological doctrines of creation to explain the six-fold symmetries. There are other possibilities, more easily described than put into neat pigeon-holes. There is little in the known biography of Holbein himself that allows us to speculate about his likely attitudes to what may be loosely described as the world of spiritual forces. He was a practical man who busied himself with most of the applied arts, a man with his feet on the ground, but one who lived at a time when the occult arts were much debated – in demand in some quarters and reviled in others. If the painting is making conscious use of them, we should be looking for an explanation beyond the painter's personal experience and wishes.

MAGIC AND ANGELS

In one of its more notorious manifestations, the hexagram was to be found inscribed within a circle drawn for magical purposes.[213] The resulting figure was perhaps most commonly used for necromancy – the art of obtaining knowledge, especially of the future, by communicating with the dead. It took on many forms, but commonly had a band around the edge in which were inscriptions; and there might also have been triangular bands within for the same purpose. Richard Kieckhefer mentions a medieval example with five bands and the words *Salve crux digna* ('Hail, noble cross') within it.[214]

A painting with a religious theme must seem an unlikely and unwelcome place for an image associated with magic, and yet magic as a means of discovering the future was on the verge of acceptability in some academic as well as theological quarters in this period. One of the most notorious of all early sixteenth-century practitioners of dubious magic, Johannes Trithemius, was an abbot. Even the reputations of saints could be touched by occultism. Dinteville's collar, with the insignia of the order of St Michael, is a reminder that one of the roles of the archangel in Christian thought was to allow access to that part of the old magic which was compatible with the faith. When St Augustine compared angels with the demons of which Plato had spoken, the differences he found between them were of power and farsightedness rather than of reality. Broadly speaking, the message of this highly influential churchman to posterity was that both types of being could assist in divination and prophecy, although the angels would perform a much loftier and more reliable service.[215] With such credentials as these, it is not surprising to find that the names of the archangels –

occasionally written in Hebrew characters – were commonly added to a Solomon's Seal within a magic circle. Indeed, if the nineteenth-century romantic practitioner of magic Francis Barrett is to be believed, a necessary accessory for the evocation of spirits was a circular plate known as the 'Holy Table of the Archangel Michael', inscribed with Michael's name inside a hexagram.[216]

Despite the potential links between the cult of St Michael and arcane practices, the Holbein painting probably had nothing whatsoever to do with them. It is not that the hexagrams can be safely cleared of suspicion, but that St Michael's character was more often read in a different way. Several church councils in the middle ages had to warn against overzealous devotion to St Michael, but that was because they were disturbed at the ways in which angels were being given the attention due to God. Michael was supposed to be second in command to the archangel Gabriel, but he was often given pride of place in angelic devotions. Renowned for his sheer strength, he was a natural ally for kings and their supporters. The saint whose insignia Jean de Dinteville wears is that archangel who in the Book of Revelation fights the heavenly battle against the Devil or dragon.[217] Throughout the middle ages, and well into the seventeenth century in Germany, soldiers prayed to St Michael for help in battle.[218] But Michael was also the archangel of light, and was associated with the Sun.[219] In the Roman liturgy for the dead, the prayer is 'May Michael the standard-bearer lead them into the light . . .' The ambassador's medallion, chief token of Dinteville's membership of the most prestigious royal order of France, may therefore have meant something more to him and to the many other educated Christians who pondered his portrait. It is less likely to have been a symbol touched by magic than yet another reminder of the Sun, the focus of the astronomical instruments on the upper reaches of the table, a symbol both of shadow and of illumination.

The dividing line between magic and religion in the middle ages and the succeeding period was nevertheless a very fine one, and there is a considerable literature on the subject of the Seal (or Key) of Solomon that places it on one side or the other of that line. The 'Shield of David', *Magen David*, was used as a Jewish printers' device from 1492 onwards, especially in Prague, and its distinctively Jewish associations probably contributed to its mystical appeal, at a period when the Cabala was beginning to attract much attention. Solomon's reputation was multi-faceted. His reputation for wisdom often led to his being associated with the seven liberal arts. The items on the shelves of *The Ambassadors* represent four of the traditional seven, at least. (Hervey was so anxious to find all seven that she suggested the two ambassadors as representing the other three, those of the *trivium*.) The hexagram could have been no more than a pointer to knowledge of the sort vouchsafed to Solomon, had the symbol not already taken on such a distinctive life of its own.

This had begun long before Holbein's time, although it is much easier to find relevant literature from a later period. So much of what we have was inspired by the rise of the cult of freemasonry from the eighteenth century onwards that our modern perception of the image has been greatly corrupted. Most of those who think of it at all probably view it as relating to magic and the zanier sorts of spirituality alone. One of the texts responsible for this perception – which is not without roots in the past – almost seems to be tailored to our pavement. While it is known in several languages, it is a work that was circulated widely in a French eighteenth-century version with the title *La clavicule de Salomon Roy des Hebreux*, purporting to have been first translated from Hebrew into Italian.[220] There is talk in it of a magic circle surrounded by a square ('directed to the four quarters of the globe'), the square having four more circles at its corners – in other words, an arrangement somewhat like that of the Westminster abbey pavement. The master is to stand in the large circle and his four disciples in the others, all of them dressed in linen, and along the sides of the square they are enjoined to inscribe 'the terrible names of the Creator'.[221] The route by which such debased mystical doctrines reached the eighteenth century does not matter here. It is enough that the crude ideas at its core are to be found at almost every period between antiquity and then. Amulets from Christian Byzantium, at least as early as the sixth century, name the hexagram as Solomon's. From the time of the Church Fathers onwards, Solomon and Christ had been closely associated and yet, at the same time, even in the same writings, Solomon's name is found linked with trite magical tricks. Talismans of the Salomonic sort were often also described as belonging to Arabic magic – as indeed they did – without attracting obvious disapproval, strongly suggesting that hope was more important than the means of attaining it.

The hexagram associated with Solomon entered European literature through one especially influential text, one that will be found cited at regular intervals over a period of almost a thousand years, but that to modern eyes must seem quite bizarre. It was a collection of poems by the German archbishop and abbot, Rabanus Maurus (*c.* 780–856). His work, entitled *De laudibus sanctae crucis* (*On Praise of the Holy Cross*), is an extraordinary combination of Christian theology with numerical and geometrical symbolism. Rabanus contrived ways of writing out his poems so that ancillary poems are to be found hidden within them, taking on geometrical shapes. One such poem incorporates a set of hexagon poems.* The fact that this well-known work combines the themes of the calendar, the Sun, time, hexagons and the crucifixion gives it an especial interest for us, but the chances that its immediate influence is to be seen in Holbein's painting are very slender.

The theme of the mystic hexagon clearly brings together an odd assortment of activities. It encompasses those in which Rabanus Maurus indulged, Christian rites such as those enacted around the Westminster pavement and the episcopal throne at Anagni, and English coronation ritual. It is fed by Neoplatonic mystical writing and cabalistic magic. As already intimated, very many of those who used books of necromancy to invoke evil spirits while standing in magic circles – like those Pope

* For further details see the second half of Appendix III. The first part of the appendix touches on Rabanus' commentary on biblical references to Solomon's throne.

John XXII accused of trying to kill him – were clerics, as of course were most of those who attacked them for behaving as they did. Magical practices by the clergy and other hangers-on in the world of Christian learning were not rampant, but they existed, and they were thought by many to be justifiable. That the hexagram could so easily draw together theologians and alchemists, magicians and writers on the cosmic order was quite simply because it was seen by all of them as a sign of some sort of power, a power that was largely unknown and in that sense mystical, but a power that was nevertheless considered to be real and *physical*. Above all, it could be discussed in a familiar language, that in which they were accustomed to speak of the Holy Spirit.

METAPHORS OF SPIRIT

The Holy Spirit had been an object of Christian worship from the very first. It was believed to be passed on through anointing with oil or water, or by the laying on of hands. Consider how Piero della Francesca's painting *The Baptism of Christ* shows a central figure of Christ with the dove of the Holy Spirit hovering centrally over his head while John pours the baptismal water on Christ's head – down the central line of the painting. Scriptural texts tended to emphasise that its way of working is not magical but moral, and that it takes place within the enlightened consciousness of believers. The Holy Spirit was nevertheless often spoken of as a real substance – whether a wind, an outflowing of the divine essence, the essence of the sacraments, or some similar quasi-material thing. This is why it lent itself to a quasi-scientific treatment that readily shaded into magic. The Holy Spirit was often taken to be transmitted in the form of light – hence the way of speaking of the baptised as *illuminati*, a nomenclature picked up by freemasonry but not of their making.

Whether a belief in such things is to be put on the same level as a belief in astrological or magical influences is partly a matter of definition, but certainly there were such ingredients in the texts of the Old Testament and eastern mystery religions.

57. Cosmati work. The episcopal throne in the cathedral at Anagni, with elements modelled on Solomon's throne and with a Solomon's Seal in the back.

Abstractions are not easily grasped. People continued to need an image of that spiritual thing, and a focus for its working. The king was to stand inside the Westminster circle as the Holy Ghost descended upon him – that sort of thing was easy enough for everyone to grasp. Similarities between the various ways in which people speak of things of the spirit tell us much about the deep psychological need for crude symbolism. We should not be too hard on magicians for their delusions.

The Cosmati workers at Westminster knew and delighted in the six-fold symmetry of the hexagon and the stellated hexagram, which they used repeatedly in the pavement and around the tomb of Edward the Confessor, just as they had done in other churches. They did not choose it for its geometrical properties alone, however. One of the most striking of all surviving examples of six-pointed stars created by those Italian craftsmen is in the shape of a Solomon's Seal at head height behind the preacher in a pulpit at S. Andrea, Orvieto. An even more magnificent example is on the back of the bishop's throne in the cathedral at Anagni (Fig. 57). The latter is positioned so as to appear as a halo around the bishop's head when he sits in state. The throne in question was plainly meant to imitate Solomon's, for it had a lion on each side and a rotund back, as did his.* 'King Edward's Chair', the oak throne used in the coronation ceremony at Westminster, probably also once had a pair of lions or leopards, and might originally have had some geometrical decoration in its back, but not for long, and not when Holbein saw it. Long before Holbein's time in London, a painting of an enthroned king, perhaps Solomon, had been put there.[222] Did it cross Dinteville's mind as he watched the coronation of Anne Boleyn in 1533 that it was taking place above what had served as a model for the pavement in his painting? Hervey reproduces an account Dinteville wrote of the occasion, in which he refers to the fact that the throne was on a dais covered in red cloth. Unfortunately that is as far as he goes. There is nothing in his remarks to justify an idea that one hears mooted from time to time, that Anne's coronation was the *raison d'être* of *The Ambassadors*, but to take any such claim seriously one would in any case have to demolish the highly consistent evidence given here for Good Friday, more than seven weeks earlier than the coronation. I can see no astronomical evidence whatsoever for the Whit Sunday alternative.

It is unlikely that Holbein could ever have seen a hexagram at the centre of the Westminster pavement. There seems to be no precedent for exactly this arrangement in Italian Cosmati work, although strangely enough it would have chimed rather well with the creation theme that is writ large on the Westminster floor. There is, as it happens, an instance of this usage far closer to *The Ambassadors* in time and culture: Peter Apian used the symbol in a widely read but now rare book of 1524, to mark the centre of the world (Fig. 58), which is more or less what the abbey pavement's magnificent central disc represents, symbolising the six days in which God created the universe and all within it.[223] Perhaps calls were being made on Apian not only for the arithmetic book and the design of the torquetum but also for the idea of a central hexagram.

The centre was considered to be the very focus of the creative

* For an explanation of their hidden meanings, see again Appendix III, below.

act. It was there that God was shown placing the point of his dividers, in a common medieval depiction of the act of creation. The pavement disc, as we recall, is of precious Egyptian onyx. That it was thought to be a place of great spiritual power is why it was made the focal point of the coronation ritual. It was over that centre of power, seated in the oak chair, that the monarch was anointed with holy oil, so receiving divine right, after the singing of the hymn 'Veni creator spiritus' and the words of 'Zadok the Priest'. (They commemorate the anointing of King Solomon in 1 Kings 1:39–40.)[224] However unpalatable the comparison, there were undeniable similarities between the functioning of the central disc and that of the hexagram in magical ritual. There were sixteenth-century theologians anxious to contest such parallels. Many were aware of scholars – Petro d'Abano had been the most notorious – who were even prepared to find a connection between magic and the eucharist. The general idea of an inflowing of spiritual powers, focused on a geometrical figure, was very small beer by comparison with this particular comparison.

With the Reformation, and the new emphasis on the personal experience of believers, the Holy Spirit gained rather than lost in importance. Luther wrote much on the subject. For him the Bible was its word, and through the Holy Spirit the word was written inwardly in the heart. The Latin hymn writers had helped to stabilise theological language and imagery, and here they did so most conclusively with that hymn 'Veni creator spiritus' and its later partner, 'Veni sancte spiritus'. In short, at least one text of the sort we are seeking is in the painting itself, in the form of the open Lutheran hymnal on the lower shelf of the stand, with its Lutheran version of the Catholic hymn invoking the Holy Spirit to enter our hearts. We should perhaps be looking to this, and even to the Lutheran preamble to the Ten Commandments with which the hymn is associated, for the image – an entirely innocuous one – sealed by the hexagrams. Hervey was perhaps looking at these printed works too objectively. She speaks of them as complete texts, as material entities, as something taken over from Catholicism by

Libri Cosmo. Col. 63.

Media nox.

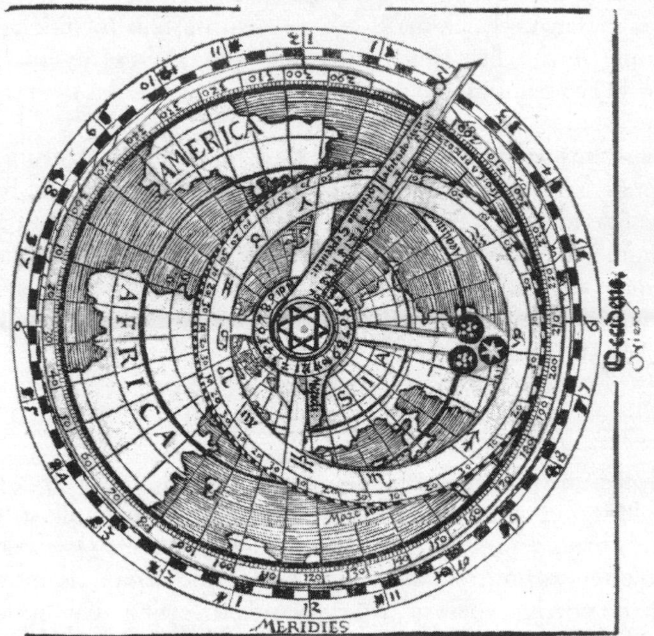

Meridies.

58. Apian's use of a hexagram to mark the centre of the world, on an unusual volvelle in his *Cosmographicus liber* (Landshut, 1524). The design of the zodiac ring (the eccentric ring with the familiar signs marked on it) is inspired by that of the ordinary astrolabe. The north pole is at the centre and the Earth's equator is above the name of AFRICA. It is *Southern* America that we see drawn with both east and west coasts. Europe is largely hidden under the zodiac ring, as here arranged. The long pointer is graduated in degrees of latitude, north and south. The small pointer is attached to the 24-hour clock and points to midday at the bottom of the page. Midnight is at the top. When Holbein and Kratzer put up the temporary Greenwich ceiling for the entertainment of the French ambassadors in 1527, they may have been basing their design on this instrument, which we might today describe as a world clock.

the Lutherans – in other words, as symbols of a much needed reconciliation between Christians. It seems more likely that attention was being drawn to the traditional *message* of a text that could be shared by Christians of all persuasions. It was a message that Luther himself coupled with a plea for tolerating learning. In his first preface to what was the very hymnal on show in the painting, he writes these words:

> That it is good and pleasing to God for us to sing spiritual songs is, I think, a truth of which no Christian can be ignorant. Besides, I am not of the opinion that all sciences should be battered and annihilated by the Gospel, as some fanatics would have them. I would rather see all the arts, and music in particular, used in the service of Him who hath given and created them.

HUMANISM AND MAGIC

Scarcely anyone in Holbein's vicinity would have regarded astrology with complete disdain. While it had many illustrious critics, they were not typical of the age and their own beliefs were often inconsistent with their criticism. Magic was another matter entirely. There was a widespread feeling that popular Christianity was debased through magic and superstition. It was seen as the reverse of the coin of vulgar piety, the religiosity of the thoughtless herd, with its pilgrimages, its worship of relics and its carefully computed penances that could be done even by proxy. A horror of these things was shared by men as far apart as Pope Leo x and More, Warham, Colet and Fisher, and no attack on them was more pointed than Erasmus's. To take just one chilling story from his *Letters*, he tells of a magician in Orléans who bought the body of Christ from a priest and kept it under his bed. With his wife and daughter he used it in a ceremony to produce a Triple Monad – note once more the love of the triad – which he worshipped to such effect that Satan appeared and gave him money. But not enough. He consulted a scholar who then betrayed him to the church authorities, and he was relieved of the Holy Thing. It was carried off with great ceremony to the church of St Cross in Orléans, and a fuller story was drawn out of the unfortunate magician and his wife on the rack.

Such events are too tragic to be treated simply as amusing cases of gullibility and make-believe, but they were not rare. They reflected beliefs that often came to the surface, even at the French, Burgundian and English courts, despite notable writings directed against them long before Erasmus and his like added theirs. Nicole Oresme had spoken out against this kind of thing in the fourteenth century, for example, and Laurens Pignon in the fifteenth.[225] They would not have preached had there been no practice. What was called the 'notory art' (the word means notorious) or the 'art of Toledo', was a form of magic which according to legend was revealed by God to Solomon through an angel. It was still much practised in France in the time of Dinteville and de Selve. Their close contemporary François Rabelais, the foremost French satirist of the time, mentions it in *Pantagruel* as a French speciality, but in practice it had become a hotchpotch of doctrines ranging from playing with symbols to the raising of spirits. Mary Hervey long ago claimed to detect Hermetic symbolism in the architectural detail of a house built by Jean de Dinteville's brother the bishop near the château at Polisy, although she seems to have had in mind no more than a rather tame symbol of Fortune.[226] Necromancy, which – by definition – required communication with spirits of the dead, was another matter entirely, and many were put to death for practising it. It had given magic a bad name, but it came in many different forms, and there were well-respected humanists who found certain of them irresistible. Three or four scholars deserve especial mention for their contributions to a broad movement on the fringe of theology that at times came uncomfortably close to the cruder extremes of beliefs they claimed to be opposing.[227]

The first was Marsilio Ficino (1433–99), the founder and guiding spirit of the Platonic academy of Florence. A philosopher and ordained priest, Ficino made Latin translations of Plato's dialogues and various key Neoplatonic works, the first reliable versions of them that were accessible to western scholars in general. He spent much effort reconciling Platonism and Christianity. The first widely circulated translation he made from the Greek was that of a collection of works of occult philosophy attributed to Hermes Trismegistus: it found an eager audience, especially among people anxious to enlarge the spiritual and contemplative traditions of medieval Christianity. Ficino's interests ranged over fundamental Christian theology – he contributed some extremely influential writings on immortality – and astrological medicine. What he wrote shows a strong bias towards Neoplatonic mysticism: he regarded the universe as a living and in a sense divine thing, enlivened by an influence emanating from God, passing through the heavens and the elements, and ending up in all forms of matter here on Earth. Secondary influences from the stars and planets were assigned responsibility for the way the world is, at every level, and not only in matters of personal fortune. Thus to take just one example from Ficino: the focusing of the rays of the Sun and Jupiter were taken to account for the medicinal properties of the plant spearmint.

Ficino took those earlier analogies that we found in the Westminster pavement between the universe and mankind, macrocosm and microcosm, and modified them. The division of the universe into material and immaterial realms – the latter lying beyond the sphere of the Moon – was one that he paralleled by the distinction between man's body and soul. With his grandiose metaphor of an emitted supernatural spirit in mind, it comes as no surprise to find that he was an enthusiastic proponent of the old idea that by inscribing images on things one might dispose them to receive astral influences. The humanists were above all else wordsmiths. Words, songs and sounds were considered to be especially fitted to attract the influence of the Sun. Ficino used 'Orphic hymns' for drawing astral powers, hymns not entirely out of key with the message of 'Veni creator spiritus'. (The painting too has its words.) In all this he defended himself against the charge that he was invoking the help of demons. Not so, he said, his magic was natural, harnessing the powers of nature. He had a healthy respect for demonic powers, but that was not the point.

Ficino had much to say about numbers and geometrical figures, which he viewed as intermediate between divine and natural things. He took the human soul to be analogous to a triangle. Demons have mastery over a world of light, and they may inhabit a world of plane figures – squares, triangles, and so forth. Only the crudest of them inhabit three-dimensional figures. Here too he thought it possible to use his own spirit to harness the powers of demons, by numbers and geometry.

It would be impossible to give an account of Ficino's mystic utterances in a short space. Most of his numerology is undisciplined, and for page after page he spins a visionary yarn out of simple numbers. We are astonished that he had so many avid followers, until we recall how many people still delight in discovering deep truths in simple relations between numbers. (And the painting too has its numbers.) It is often supposed that Ficino's 'magic' in general was pagan and un-Christian. There were, admittedly, Platonists who spoke of the Sun in a theologically dubious way as the creator of all things, but Ficino would have defended himself strongly against any charge of impiety, saying that when you sing a hymn to the Sun you are not worshipping the Sun as a god, or trying to make the Sun do something miraculous and unnatural, but merely making your own spirit more Sun-like, and so more receptive to the *natural* powers of the Sun. His physics was not ours, but still it was for him physics.

The religious reformer Jacques Lefèvre d'Etaples (1450–1536), mentioned earlier for his connection with the French court and the fact that Jean de Dinteville was his sometime patron, was another humanist scholar of the first rank with leanings towards Hermeticism. This might seem strange, in view of his frequent criticism of the Pythagorean mystics and Platonists and his dedication to the study of Aristotle, both text and meaning. He hinted, however, at the existence of hidden secret analogies running through the whole of Aristotle's natural philosophy. Inspired by the Holy Spirit, he decoded, as he thought, Aristotle's *Physics*, finding there a portrait of the Creator and evidence for the Trinity. He thought well enough of Nicholas of Cusa's treatise on divine numbers to produce an edition of it. Lefèvre d'Etaples imparted his tastes to many of his followers – the circle-squarer Charles de Bouelles again deserves passing mention here. A competent mathematician who wrote on such topics as star polygons and the so-called 'perfect numbers', de Bouelles corresponded with both Lefèvre d'Etaples and Budé on the relations between mystic numbers and angels, men, memory, body, soul, the heavens, and the world – intellectual and physical. Erasmus judged his writings to be unreadable, but later in the century Conrad Gesner described him as 'polished with the liquor of rhetoric, poetic variety, and most sparkling splendour of all philosophy, and an outstanding geometer'.[228] The humanist movement clearly allowed for a wide spread of tastes.

GEMATRIA AND THE CABALA

On another mystical excursion Lefèvre d'Etaples cautiously combined magic with astrology and gematria. Gematria was the cabalistic art of setting up correspondences between names and numbers. It was not a Parisian invention, but it too had a sizeable following among Parisian intellectuals in the 1530s. Dinteville and de Selve must at least have heard of it. It was in this very period that Rabelais used it as an idiosyncracy on which he could lampoon the intellectual pseuds of the day. In his story of Gargantua and Pantagruel he tells of how the great English scholar Thaumaste sought out Pantagruel, on account of his fame in magic, alchemy, the Cabala, geomancy, astrology and philosophy. Thaumaste was allowed to dispute with Pantagruel's rascally subordinate Panurge, and when he did so it was entirely in obscene or ludicrous gesture and sign language, although both parties to the debate made promises that they would later publish it in verbal form.[229] While Rabelais' first aim was to mock medieval learning and literature, as well as ecclesiastical authority, and while he was generally in sympathy with humanist values, he could not resist the temptation to burlesque a number of recognisably humanist foibles. A fashionable obsession with the Cabala was not the least among them.

The Cabala had begun as an oral tradition claiming secret knowledge of the unwritten divine revelation (Torah) that God had spoken to Adam and Moses. It was supposed to be a way of approaching God directly, although it was frowned upon by many Jews, who thought it inclining to heresy. It nevertheless gave rise to an important theological movement in Christian Europe, based on two simple ideas. One was that the great depth of religious meaning in the Bible was due to certain qualities that were peculiar to the Hebrew language; the second was that words not only denote things but exert powers which are connected with those things. In that direction lay various forms of magic, but of a more ethereal brand than crude necromancy and different again in character from Ficino's.

No one caused more of a commotion over the Cabala than the great Hebrew scholar Johannes Reuchlin (1455–1522). He too was fascinated by the magical power of music, but his lasting influence on the European world of learning was through his own cabalistic writings on the power of words and the mystical significance of numbers that could be derived from them. (Music, words, numbers. He would have admired Holbein's painting.) His first book on the subject appeared in 1494, and was reprinted in 1514, but his most influential work – dedicated to Pope Leo x, no less – was his *De arte cabalistica* (*On the Cabalistic Art*) of 1517. It is in the form of a discussion between a Greek philosopher representing the Pythagoreans, a Muslim and a Jew. Its contents were not especially original, but their Hebrew sources were at that time mostly unknown in Christian circles. Reuchlin's writings soon began to spawn many others, for example those by his old friend Lorenz Beheim and by various converted Jews. One of them, Petrus Galatinus, in 1516 wrote a defence of Reuchlin and dedicated it to the Emperor Maximilian. These writers often met with powerful and bitter opposition, much of it voiced by academic writers who believed that the Cabala would undermine the philosophy and theology of the universities. As a result, the Cabala began to have all the attractions of forbidden fruit.

Nowhere is its impact on Christian thought better illustrated than in the account offered of the names of God and Jesus.

Before Reuchlin reaches that theme, at the culmination of his treatise, he presents his reader with a veritable mass of material, on letters, numbers, seals, voices, the names of the seventy-two angels and their pronunciation, the ten steps to knowledge, the celestial and terrestrial Adams – Christ and the skull in the painting, one could say – and a great many other topics. The crowning principle, however, is that which explains the mystery of the so-called Tetragrammaton, the ineffable 'word of four letters' used for God, written in Hebrew *yhwh* or *jhvh* (vocalised as *yahweh, jahveh*, or *jehovah*). Here knowledge of God, and in principle of all theological mysteries, is reached through an association of numbers with words through the science of gematria. The method is to begin with the number yielded by turning each of the letters of the word into a number, according to its place in the alphabet, and then taking the sum of all. Thus *IHVH* yields 26, the sum of 10, 5, 6, and 5. The name of Jesus is the ineffable name of God with an 'S' (*shin*) inserted, making the ineffable audible, and so representing the Incarnation. The method was extended to other persons in the Bible story, and by combining and transforming numbers and their 'meanings' in various ways it must have seemed that almost anything was possible. That should have worried people, but of course it had exactly the opposite effect.

Erasmus's character Folly, who as always manages to throw a welcome dash of cold water over empty numerology, takes a broad swipe at gematria on one occasion. Folly speaks of grammarians who have made a grammatical triad out of the parts of speech 'in the way mathematicians draw triangles'. An octogenarian scholar is mentioned who has discovered the triple nature of Jesus in the inflexions 'Jesus, Jesum, Jesu', and who saw in the word-endings 'an inexpressible mystery'.[230] There must have been many non-octagenarian Christian Cabalists who wondered whether Erasmus had them in his sights.

While it would not have taken any competent apprentice in the arts of the Cabala more than a couple of minutes to turn 26 into 27, it seems on balance unlikely that the 27 in *The Ambassadors* would have been explained by those who planned it in quite this way – even assuming that it was explained cabalistically at all. There is a far more natural explanation, which is simply that 27 *was a number that according to the Cabalists characterised the universe itself.* This can be very briefly explained.

The Cabala is said to have flourished in the Middle East only after the first century of the Christian era, but the earliest Jewish text on magic and cosmology in this tradition, *Sefer Yetzira* (*Book of Creation*), did not appear until two or three centuries later. That work effectively created an easy alternative to the account of the cosmos offered by Plato in his *Timaeus* – a point that did not escape the notice of several sixteenth-century writers when they seized on Plato's name to make the numbers game more acceptable to their colleagues. As we have already seen, 27 was the 'solid' number at one foot of the 'lambda' that summarises the Platonic account of Creation.* Creation was presented in the Cabala as a process involving the ten divine numbers (in sets 1–9, 10–90, 100–900) and the 22 letters of the Hebrew alphabet with certain additions to bring the number up to 27. God of course lies outside the system of the three separately created worlds, the angelic, the celestial and the corruptible. Since each of those worlds has nine divisions (the 'enneads'), *God's creation comprises 27 divisions in all.*[231]

If there is any hint of cabalistic magic or simple gematria in Holbein's painting, this extension of the Platonic idea was probably at the root of it. That certainly does not rule out the more obvious notion of the Trinity, the triple godhead – on the contrary, it was elaborately woven into the story of gematria to strengthen its appeal. The cabalistic claim to 'declare the secret and the mystery of the soul and of the world' was not hidden in some obscure doctrinal crevice. It was one that meshed fairly comfortably with Ficino's ideas but went further, causing a great stir in its time and arousing much hostility. Broadly speaking, one may say that magic was growing increasingly demonic, picking up more and more of such medieval traditions as were to be found in Roger Bacon and Petro d'Abano. Schools of the Christian Cabala began to appear on the scene,

* See p. 254 above.

especially in Italy. Since the subject was taken up by Heinrich Cornelius Agrippa of Nettesheim, who was for a time at the French court, it became a point of discussion there. It is no surprise to find the French king, François I, commissioning a work in French on the subject in 1536, from the Abbé Thenaud.[232]

AGRIPPA AND THE LUXURIANCE OF OCCULT BELIEF

In trying to locate scholars who might have helped to form the world view that comes to the surface in *The Ambassadors*, the French connection means that we cannot safely leave Agrippa out of the reckoning. Not only was he an extremely influential writer on the occult arts, but Holbein, Kratzer, Dinteville or de Selve could all have met him in person. Agrippa was a university man, a notable lawyer, alchemist, astrologer, occult philosopher, illicit physician and hanger-on at courts. He was a flamboyant individual, but one who wrote serious pieces on theology and was concerned enough about his faith to have read Luther carefully and sympathetically. The fact that he had travelled widely gave his ideas much currency – he had, for example, lodged with John Colet, dean of St Paul's, when as a servant of Louis of France he visited London in 1510. (It is often supposed that he was there to sow seeds of mistrust of the pope in Henry's mind.) Perhaps Erasmus had him in mind when, in Folly's caricature of national characteristics, the Germans are said to boast of their height and their knowledge of the arts of magic. In the 1530s Agrippa was still remembered in London in humanist circles. Of the four men most concerned with Holbein's painting, Jean de Dinteville is likely to have known the magus best. Just before he received his first appointment at court, Agrippa was astrologer and physician to the queen mother, Louise de Savoie, and at that time Jean's brother François was her almoner. Agrippa was employed by her when she was regent at Lyon (from 1524) during her son's imprisonment. For reasons at which we can only guess, she left the astrologer there without pay when she went back to Paris. He suspected that she had discovered the fact that he had criticised her in correspondence with friends, on account of her superstition and belief in astrology. He thought he had also failed her in his use of astrology to predict the success of the renegade constable de Bourbon. His puzzlement suggests a poor knowledge of human nature, but there must have been more to the story than we shall ever know.[233]

In 1510 Agrippa had begun to draft an ambitious scheme for the restoration of magic, but he did not really make his mark through his writings until around the time that Holbein was painting *The Ambassadors.* The first part of his greatest work, *De occulta philosophia* (*On Occult Philosophy*), appeared in 1531, publication was resumed in 1532, and it was finished in 1533 (Fig. 59). Agrippa's writings are often presented as an incoherent mixture of credulity, fervid belief and scepticism, but that is a mainly modern judgement. The image his contemporaries had of him was confused, with good reason. Convincing himself no doubt that the best astrologers were all things to all men (and to almost all women), in 1530 he published a refutation of the work he had prepared earlier, work that was still mostly awaiting publication. The refutation is to be found in his *De vanitate scientiarum et artium* (*Of the Vanitie and Uncertaintie of Artes and Sciences*, to give it the title of its 1569 translation into English). Even in the *De occulta philosophia* he added a few unconvincing sentences to the effect that he was there merely reporting what was done in the occult sciences, rather than recommending it.

There is pathos in this change of heart, to the extent that he had advocated occult philosophy as the way to a knowledge of God. After the change, one hardly knows what to make of him. As D. P. Walker points out, while the 1530 volume is to a large extent evangelical, it is in many respects a rhetorical set-piece, with a display of destructive scepticism of a type that was never meant to be taken too seriously.[234] This is doubtless an accurate diagnosis, but a modern one. Astrology and alchemy did come in for telling criticism of a kind that only a convert could purvey, and it is a mark of the relative academic respectability of those subjects that his attack earned him the bitter hostility of the university of Louvain and of the Sorbonne in Paris.

HENRICVS CORNELIVS AGRIPPA.

59. Agrippa, from the title page of his *De occulta philosophia* (Basel, 1533). Under the portrait was an apt quotation from Matthew 10:26, which in the Authorised Version of the Bible becomes 'there is nothing covered, that shall not be revealed; and hid, that shall not be known'.

Erasmus in one place remarks that everyone is talking about the 1530 book, and that he hopes to get a copy. Despite Agrippa's having made clear his support for Catherine of Aragon – which caused the imperial ambassador in England, Chapuys, to write to invite him to defend her in his capacity as a lawyer – the *De vanitate* nevertheless helped to lose him his imperial patronage. He found alternative protection at the court of the archbishop of Cologne.

Cornelius Agrippa illustrates perfectly the dangers of looking for cultural and intellectual influence in a subject as luxuriant as magic. Not for nothing did he get a colourful reputation as a black magician – as a sorcerer who went around accompanied by the Devil in the form of a dog, for instance, and later as the guide to Mary Shelley's Frankenstein, by which route he reached Hollywood. He was a more serious thinker than his tawdry reputation might suggest. There was scarcely any branch of learning that he failed to criticise for its inconsistent and ephemeral character, but still he could recount its details with glee. He loved the search for symbolic meaning in biblical texts, but so did hundreds more. He was prepared to take over and promote the cabalistic theory of three created worlds divided into 27 – the world of the elements, that of the stars, and the third of the angels. His often bizarre but influential writings include a lengthy exposition of Ficino's ideas, and lean heavily on cabalistical writers of a quieter temperament than his own. Drawing on the latter they make much use of such geometrical figures as the pentagon, hexagon and heptagon, all for mystical as well as numerological, alchemical and astrological purposes.[235] In a work such as his *De occulta philosophia*, however, two or three hundred thousand words long, it is possible to find almost anything to match a number, a geometrical figure, a colour, a musical tone, a planetary configuration, or the cabalistic translation of a sacred word into number and hidden meaning. Angels and demons and magical ritual are of course all waiting in the wings. From the stretched out human body, geometrical figures can be created: the human figure within a pentagon as drawn by Leonardo is the best known of all, but there are others, and a square with a horoscope-type figure within it is one of Agrippa's examples (Fig. 60). Among the geometrical figures with the greatest magical force he gives the example of the cross, and relates it to the numbers five, seven and nine. For every number up to 12 he can fill two or three pages with interpretations: three and nine connect with everything holy that one would expect of them, and much more besides. The lunar dragon is to be found there – with an anecdote about the magical force it had when incorporated by a

60. A man's body fitted into a horoscope square. From Agrippa, *De occulta philosophia*, book 1 chapter 27. This deals with the 'Proportions, Size and Harmonies of the Human Body'.

Jewish savant into a girdle presented to a Spanish king by his queen. There are many things in this colourful patchwork that it would be easy to imagine as elements of Holbein's painting, but the great redundancy of esoteric elements in Agrippa's works takes away all confidence in the idea that we have pinpointed one of Holbein's sources. The fact that similar ideas can be found in the writings of other less ostentatious scholars of the time merely adds to our difficulty, and the most we can say is that Agrippa is a potential source. To decide how likely a source he was we should have to know much more than we do about the influence on our two ambassadors of the many criticisms he made of French theologians in his writings, after leaving Louise de Savoie's service. He had some French allies, for he had long been a defender of the opinions of Lefèvre d'Etaples.

Despite the hopelessness of proving influence from this quarter, the case of Agrippa does at least show us how different our own way of looking at the world is from that of so many of Holbein's contemporaries, even those at the more disciplined end of the academic community. It was not uncommon at this period for respectable writers to treat of the theology of the Christian sacraments, demonology and the various arts of divination, including astrology, in a single text. Agrippa does so with complete abandon, even recommending a mingling of prayers to God with invocations to angels, stars or saints at astrologically favourable times. 'Choose the hours and the days for your works, for it was not without cause that our Saviour spoke thus: Are there not twelve hours in a day?'[236] Agrippa was an extreme case, but he was not an isolated one. Far from being perceived as incongruous, each of these subjects could be seen as an aid to the others. They were taken to differ greatly in spiritual danger, and also to be founded on theories of very different scientific status, but each had a sizeable following. It is not difficult to believe that magic and the Cabala would have come into the reckoning of either Dinteville or de Selve, or even of Kratzer and Holbein. Does that seem intrinsically likely, in a Good Friday context? It seems more than likely that behind the symbolism of the painting there is some sort of

'Platonic' notion of a real spiritual influence at work, while full-blooded necromancy seems entirely outside the realm of probability. The same cannot be said of the more refined arts of the Cabala. The theme of 27 in the painting, which relates so closely to them, was surely more than a question of shadow angles alone.

AN ALCHEMICAL IMAGE?

Detecting symbolism in an undocumented painting is bound to be a much more impressionistic affair than its counterpart in written texts. Let us suppose nothing more than that the hexagram motif was meant to signal some sort of spiritual transmission. It is hard to believe that it was meant to be anything less than that. The idea of heavenly influence, the inflowing of a spirit which penetrates, nourishes, gives life, and resembles the light and heat of the stars or of the Sun, was an idea with a long history behind it and was easily grasped. When influence was symbolised as radiation from a star, it was usually six-pointed, and this is how it was commonly represented, well into the eighteenth century. Such cosmic metaphors were not likely to offend the theologians, but it was all a question of degree. One final instance on the verge of respectability that was being bandied around in Holbein's time deserves mention. It comes in a series of alchemical images – in fact there were several closely related series – aimed at explaining the production of the 'philosopher's stone'.

There is no denying that the alchemists, like respectable Christian practitioners of the safer sorts of magic, could safely bring religion into their art. Certain Christian motifs begged to be provided with alchemical translations: the resurrection of Christ from the dead, for example, and transubstantiation of the eucharist (the supposed changing of the substance of the bread in holy communion into the substance of the body of Christ, leaving its appearance unchanged). There are numerous medieval examples of Christian writers who were not afraid to use the crucifixion of Christ to help them encode their procedures, parallels being drawn between Christ and the philosopher's stone. There is one notorious German manuscript of the fifteenth century, *Das Buch der heiligen Dreifaltigkeit* (*The Book of the Holy Trinity*), in which extraordinary liberties are taken with the crucifixion image for alchemical purposes.[237] Between 1490 and 1516 there was an even more daring work, dedicated to King Ladislas II of Bohemia by Nicholas Melchior, in which an alchemical procedure was given the form of the Christian mass.[238] By comparison, the blend of alchemical and cosmic imagery to be mentioned here was very tame.

Near the beginning of each set of images in each of the series in question there may be one with a king standing on the Sun and a queen standing on the Moon. They are usually presented as both man and wife as well as brother and sister. The allegory makes use of familiar and ancient correspondences between the Sun, gold, the Lion (Leo) and kinghood on the one hand and between the Moon, silver, the Crab (Cancer) and the feminine on the other. In an example drawn from the most widely distributed text of this type, *Rosarium philosophorum* (*The Philosophers' Rosary,* see Fig. 61), the king and queen hold flower stems, and with the help of a falling bird in whose beak is a third stem they produce a six-pointed figure. Above the bird is a large six-pointed star. The allegory is one of a sacred marriage and derives from much earlier Arabic Sun-Moon allegories.[239] It is no accident that the number six was known to the Pythagoreans and Neoplatonists as the 'marriage number', the product of the first male and female numbers, three and two.

Here is an entirely different reading of the six-pointed figure from those considered earlier, and yet these illustrations are strangely reminiscent of *The Ambassadors* in several obvious respects. In the *Rosary* there are two figures flanking a hexagonal scheme, as we found to be the case in the painting. The bright, Sun-like, colouring of Dinteville contrasts with the darker, lunar, appearance of de Selve, whose neckcloth even has something of a crescent shape about it. The left eye of the king in the woodcut is for some reason deliberately encircled, at least in two copies I consulted. The white and red of the flowers on the stems are not only the colours often assigned to the Moon and

Sun but they may also represent physical elements, as in the Neoplatonic schemes that inspired the Westminster pavement. The bird in the *Rosary* at first sight bears comparison with Noah's dove, as portrayed on innumerable occasions throughout the middle ages, when it carries with it an olive branch to Noah's ark. It is then the dove of the Holy Spirit, and it is labelled as such in the next woodcut of the printed *Rosary.* In these illustrations the bird is given a *crest*, reminding us perhaps of the fowl on the celestial globe in the painting. The cock was a solarian, Sun-like, thing – like heliotrope and honey, Orphic prayers and music – which could be used to bring down the Sun's influence on oneself, in Ficino-type magic.[240] Perhaps this detail of the illustration was not added with serious purpose, but it seems plain enough in the end result.[241]

If the parallel with the image of Sun and Moon is not illusory, and such images as those from the beginning of the *Rosary* were in the mind of those concerned with the painting, what of the images that follow? The series continues with sexual

61. *Rosarium philosophorum* (Frankfurt, 1550), fol. C II recto. This, the first printed version of a work aimed at showing the way to produce the philosopher's stone, is based on earlier manuscripts of a type that had become widely diffused by Holbein's time.

62. *Rosarium philosophorum* (1550), fol. C II recto. The king and queen have shed their clothes and some text is added, including an indication that the bird is the spirit that gives life. The king is proposing marriage and the queen promises to be faithful. In the woodcut that follows in the book, the king and queen sit in a similar relationship in a hexagonal bath, the bird above them still.

embrace, copulation, the production of offspring, a lion with the Sun in its mouth, and much else besides that seems quite out of key with the Good Friday theme of *The Ambassadors*, even though it ends with the crowning of Mary by the Father and the Son, and an image of Christ rising from the tomb. The moral here is that it is wrong to think of two cases – alchemical theory and religious narrative – as parallels. Doing so makes them seem co-equals, but that is not the right approach. Here one side of the analogy is taken as understood, so that the other can then be explained in terms of it. The alchemical examples were not designed to carry a theological message in any sense. They were simply making use of familiar Christian doctrine in order to convey alchemical knowledge.

The case of *The Ambassadors* is likely to have been very different. If there is an occult element in the painting, it is far more likely to have been meant to make a theological or moral or political statement than to teach some sort of esoteric doctrine by means of well-known Christian doctrine. The only likely alternative is that the painting began as an exercise in some sort of scientific imagery, whether astrological, alchemical, or of some other sort, but that a theological statement was grafted on to it at a later stage. In this case Dinteville might be envisaged as having begun by commissioning a portrait of himself and his friend in the style of the king-queen illustration from the *Philosophers' Rosary*, for reasons known best to himself, but without thought for Good Friday symbolism. There is red paint under the bishop's red cassock, later overpainted by Holbein. If it was not put there to give the brown a special hue, it could conceivably have had something to do with that original plan. After a change of plan, the original theme might have been suppressed as far as possible. Such an argument is not very convincing, simply because the astronomical substructure of the painting seems to be far too deeply embedded for us to contemplate the idea of a change of plan during the execution of the work. The hidden hexagram is intimately related to the viewing lines, which are emphatically astronomical. This kind of objection, on the other hand, does not stand in the way of the idea that the prime redemption message of the painting was consciously supplemented with a mild blend of theology and the occult. The hexagrams and the potentially cabalistic 27 make this more rather than less probable. It is not inconceivable that biographical research will one day reveal what brand of the occult it is likely to have been.

THIRTEEN

AIR ON A BROKEN STRING

KING RICHARD: Harp not on that string, madam; that is past.
QUEEN ELIZABETH: Harp on it still shall I till heart-strings break.

Shakespeare, *King Richard III*, IV. iv. 365–66

Mary Hervey believed that when the painting was done it would have conveyed a plainly ecumenical message, a call for religious *concord.* The idea is not implausible, even though there were many in both English and French court circles in 1533 who would have been unhappy at the idea of allowing the reforming party an identity of its own. In favour of her thesis there is the stance taken by de Selve later in life, proving his ambition to heal the religious schism that was tearing Europe apart. No good Catholic could have demurred, although most would have viewed the exercise as one of bringing the secessionists back into the light of truth. We recall that the main evidence for de Selve's wish for reconciliation with the Lutherans is a document which Hervey argued was delivered by the fledgling bishop to the reactionary Diet of Speyer in 1529.[242] Holbein's having included in his painting German texts that were well known and widely used in their original Catholic (and Latin) forms by all early Protestants might be a pointer to the ambition of one or both ambassadors, but it is going too far to say that de Selve and Dinteville were demonstrably ready to accept 'characteristically Lutheran elements' in their portrait. The texts were theologically neutral, as far as the Lutheran divide was concerned. The hymns were clearly making some point or other, since they were brought together in the painting, whereas in the printed book they are separate. They could certainly have been regarded as pleas for spirituality and reasonableness. They could have carried a message of hope for the unification of the Christian churches through the agency of the Holy Spirit – a hope that was not one-sided – but we cannot forget the plainer and more enduring messages we found for them, connecting them with Good Friday, creation and redemption.

What then of a suggestion that some have made, that *discord* is being consciously symbolised, discord as a lamentable fact, rather than as a threatened consequence of a failure to achieve the harmony of reconciliation? The distinction is perhaps too subtle to be read from a painting in the absence of supporting symbols. In both cases the first port of call is now almost invariably Hervey, who read the symbolism of the lute with its broken string in terms of Alciati's book of emblems, first published in Augsburg in 1531.[243] Andrea Alciati (1492–1550) was an authority on Roman law, which he taught in Avignon between 1518 and 1522 and in Bourges from 1529 to 1533. His pupils founded an important 'Romanist' school of French legal historians, and it is quite possible that Jean de Dinteville had met him. A later French translation of his book of emblems was dedicated to a friend of the Dinteville family. There is a less widely appreciated possibility of Alciati's influence, albeit still remote, but through Holbein now. A friend of Erasmus, the Basel publisher Bonifatius Amerbach, was also Holbein's patron. Amerbach made Alciati's acquaintance in Avignon in 1520 and kept up a regular correspondence with him up to the time of his death. There is also some evidence that the man who cut the blocks for a 1534 edition of Alciati's *Emblemata* was influenced by Holbein's own design for a printer's insignia.[244]

Such circumstantial evidence for an Alciati connection is extremely tenuous, but it has been made to bear the weight of many an argument about Holbein's use of the lute. Hervey's

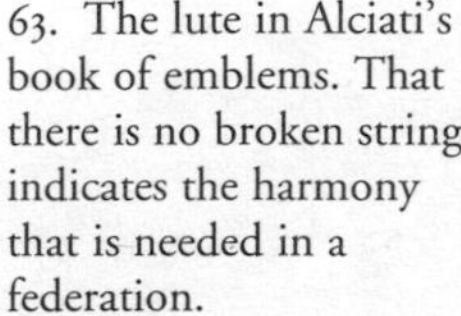

63. The lute in Alciati's book of emblems. That there is no broken string indicates the harmony that is needed in a federation.

argument begins with the Latin poem that illustrates Alciati's lute emblem, and which has the theme of *federation*, having apparently been addressed to Francesco Sforza, the last duke of Milan (Alciati's native city). Sforza is preparing to enter into new alliances. He is warned to fear nothing if harmony ensues, but that if any member defects the alliance will come to nothing, just as harmony is lost when a lute is out of tune or a string is broken. Hervey therefore saw in Holbein's lute a symbol that could be turned against the perfidious Sforza, in the very year in which the Milanese had murdered Merveilles:

> The very hand [Sforza's] in which Alciati had placed his exhortation to peace had roughly snapped the string of the lute.[245]

This reading requires that Alciati's book was provided with this interpretation – one that he did not intend – by the time Holbein was at work on the portrait. The Milan murder was not known in French court circles until June, two months after the date we assign to Holbein's portrait of the two friends. This all seems to imply a very tight chronology, but Hervey has an answer to the difficulty, although she tucks it away in a footnote:

> The picture had of course been begun earlier in the year, but it must have taken a considerable time to think out all the elaborate accessories, and still longer to execute them.[246]

This type of open-ended argument is virtually irrefutable, but it has one grave weakness. Of the London group connected with the painting, the authority on Milanese politics was de Selve. He would not have been available for consultation in June, and this special reading cannot possibly have been one that he planned in advance, without second sight. If there is reason to think it likely that he was involved in planning other themes of the painting, for instance the central Good Friday theme, then doubt is surely cast on the idea that Sforza was the reason for the breaking of the string.

It has gradually become accepted that the Alciati connection was so firmly established by Hervey that it can be taken as an unquestionable starting-point for a political reading of the painting. It is frequently forgotten that hers was a very specific historical point, concerning Alciati and the Sforza episode, and not a general point about lutes and harmony. Anthony Colantuono is one of those who accepts without more ado that Hervey showed the lute to be 'unmistakably linked to one of Alciati's emblems'. He holds that in view of the proximity in time of the publication, its popularity, and the fact that our sitters were diplomats, 'it can hardly be doubted that Holbein's portrait of the lute with the broken string is a visual expresssion of rhetorical metaphor, that is, the likening of a lute with a broken string to an alliance in which one of the members has broken his promises'. He goes on to criticise those who in the recent National Gallery book interpreted the evidence solely in terms of the historiography of art collecting and not in terms of the diplomatic aims that Dinteville 'was pursuing in England when he conceived and commissioned' the painting. He might well be right to claim that it was not just an object made to be collected and enjoyed by Dinteville but that it was also an instrument of diplomatic persuasion, a means by which the English were to be apprised of the importance of universal Christian harmony; but how is that to be proved on such a slender basis? It cannot. The painting's metaphorical argument, we are told, like that of Alciati's emblem, is specifically addressed to a ruler, namely Henry VIII, who alone could be moved by such conceits in 1533, since it was only he, and not the two ambassadors, 'who stood in a position to re-tune the chords of Anglo-French relations at that moment'. This is true enough, but it does not prove that the object was commissioned as an implement of diplomatic persuasion. Colantuono admits that we do not know where, when or even whether the king ever saw the painting. It is hard to believe that he did not, but even if we knew where and when he saw it we should still not know whether it was made with the intention that he should see it and have his thoughts prompted by it. The argument here is that its pacifistic imagery must have been an expression of what the two ambassadors were telling the king at that moment. This, however, is to assume that Hervey was right in her diagnosis of its imagery, which is not at all self-evident. Oddly enough, Colantuono goes on to say that we cannot understand the broken string – *pace* his Herveian starting-point – but that the two ambassadors must have known what they meant by it, and that they were there to explain it.[247]

Sceptical as one must be about an argument that rests on such a slight foundation and that draws any plausibility it might have from the known functions of the two sitters, it does make a useful point. It is at least conceivable that the painting was used as claimed, as a rhetorical device by which the topic of political harmony could have been introduced to the English king. Unfortunately the same could be said of almost any respectable message that is to be read into the painting. The Christian message associated with Good Friday and Easter – to take what is by far the most certain of all readings – could itself have been applied without difficulty to almost any political situation, as long as the ambassadors steered clear of Machiavellian Realpolitik.

What then are the alternative political readings of the broken string? We have already seen how frenzied life at court was during the week before Easter, Holy Week, one of the most exhausting in Henry's entire life. Queen Catherine was confined to a private house with the new title 'widow princess'. Cranmer had asked to be allowed to decide on the question of marriage, in view of popular unrest. From the time when she so irritated Chapuys by flaunting her pregnant self in the Chapel Royal on Easter Eve, 12 April, most at court paid lip-service to Anne Boleyn's title as queen. As the imperial ambassador wrote, 'All the world is astonished at it, for it looks like a dream, and even those who took her part know not whether to laugh or cry'. The king had other things on his mind, such as the pope's resistance to his marital wishes, the increasing seriousness of Scottish raids, and the confiscation of English goods in the border country.

Whether or not Chapuys was right to think that Henry was also worried about the prospect of civil insurrection on account of popular dislike of Anne and his treatment of Catherine, he was certainly anxious about the possible wavering of the French in support of his cause. It has been said that the broken lute string is a call for Anglo-French solidarity, and even for solidarity with the German princes. The flutes have been seen as flutes of war and so as a warning to heed the message of the broken string.[248] But whose painting was it? Not Henry's, and these sentiments do not seem very likely to have been Dinteville's. Are we really to see war in a case of flutes? I doubt it. It has been said that, from classical times, the idea had survived that there is a tension between 'high', 'ethical' and 'rational' stringed instruments on the one side and 'low' and 'intoxicating' wind instruments on the other, but the fact remains that there is no necessary connection. Flutes were in plentiful supply at Henry's court – there was even a case of ten named in the royal inventory as 'pilgrim staves', which tells us about at least one peaceful use of the instrument.[249] Flute cases were carried by military pipers, but they were also a common commodity wherever flutes were played professionally, for instance at dancces. Flautists were not all men. The Pageant Arch designed by Holbein for Anne Boleyn's entry into London as queen (May 1533) included five instrumentalists, all female, of whom two played wind instruments.[250] In one of the best known of all late medieval books of illustrations, in a genre known as 'children of the planets', the page portraying the children of the Sun shows worshippers kneeling before a crucifix while, outside the chapel, musicians play on wind instruments.[251]

The difficulty with all interpretations that draw on long and undefined tracts of history is that there is no clear means of verifying or confirming them. It is not hard to spin a story out of these ingredients, even mutually inconsistent stories, as in the case of the lute string. Had it not been for the fact that Holbein seems to have preferred to go along with political currents rather than resist them, those who see it as essentially his painting might have argued that he meant it to show French solidarity with Henry in his quarrel with the church of Rome. The idea would be that we have here a call not to arms but to armed federation, Alciati-style. (There was an apparent stalemate in Henry's game. Efforts made in 1533 by Thomas Howard, duke of Norfolk, to persuade King François I to follow Henry's example and create a national church had utterly failed to produce the desired result.) Once again, however, it has to be said that this was not Henry's painting, and that what counted as a desirable state of affairs would have been something for Dinteville to judge. It might even be argued that the musical instruments were not an expression of a diplomatic ideal at all, but were merely symbols of political and ecclesiastical realities. Thus the broken string might have been meant to represent an imperfect state of affairs, one beyond human power of correction, but a state of affairs that could be put to rights with God's help.

ROME AND THE LYRE

To appreciate the ease with which one may tip the scales in such matters of interpretation, consider two properties of the globes, terrestrial and celestial. On the terrestrial globe, Rome is painted more or less precisely at the geometrical centre, as it is presented to our view. Rome, in short, is presented as the centre of God's earthly realm in some sense. Jerusalem is not entirely ignored – in fact it seems that Dinteville's dagger points to Jerusalem rather precisely – but Rome, not London, Paris, Wittenberg or any other such place, is at the centre of things. What things? Spiritual, perhaps, and possibly political, but if so only in second place. That cannot be the end of the statement being made in the painting. The line from Christ through the medallion of St Michael and Rome goes through the peg with the broken lute string and the unhearing auricle of the skull, before meeting the lower side in a point 20 inches from the right. The studied symmetry of this line shows that, no matter what point was being made about Rome, it was one that was carefully planned. Was Rome perhaps placed centrally in order to declare Rome's supremacy in matters of faith? Was it merely placed there to emphasise that the painting as a whole was making a statement about Rome? What might it be? That Rome is deaf to Christ's message? It would not be difficult to

64. The constellation of the Lyre as drawn by Albrecht Dürer in 1515, combining the image of a lyre with that of the 'falling vulture' or 'falling eagle'.

embroider such an idea, weaving St Michael into it. Was the archangel-warrior, leader of the heavenly host, being asked to raise an army against the forces of evil, Lutheran or imperial or whatever? Or was St Michael being called upon to give judgement in some sense? It is hard to know where to begin, faced with the many plausible options.

One celestial symbol not previously considered is the constellation of the Lyre – *Lyra*, or *Vultur Cadens*, as Holbein labelled it. This seems to contribute a point (the star Vega in the head of the bird) to the main line of sight up to Christ. For Ptolemy, the constellation had simply been a lyre, and Vega he labelled 'the bright star in the shell', that is, by implication, the shell out of which Apollo's lyre was made. By Holbein's day the various catalogues in use were influenced by an accumulation of glosses acquired in the fourteen intervening centuries. 'Vega' is a corruption of an Arabic word for 'falling', and in eastern sources the constellation is drawn so as to correspond to the literary description of a *falling eagle*. When in 1515 Albrecht Dürer drew maps of the northern and southern constellations for Johann Stabius, from notes by the astronomer Heinfogel, he drew Lyra as a bird, but he was following in an established tradition when he added a stringed instrument to its body (Fig. 64), so working both images into his representation.

Does Vega carry any message? It was by name a *falling* bird. Can it have been meant as the Imperial Eagle? At about the time he was engaged on *The Ambassadors*, Holbein was undertaking commissions on behalf of Anne Boleyn. The bird was presumably not meant to be her badge, the White Falcon. (There was one amusing occasion on which the imperial ambassador Chapuys mistook the White Falcon for the Imperial Eagle.) Astronomically speaking, the bird falls down to the horizon daily in the ordinary way of things. At the time of the Good Friday horoscope that we offered for consideration in a previous chapter, Vega had sunk more or less as low as it can go.[252] Are we then to suppose that Kratzer and Holbein were conniving in simultaneously glorifying the Gallic Cock and denigrating the Imperial Eagle? It is hard to believe that they set out to do this, not because the message was unpalatable, but because arranging the globe to bring the Sun, Moon and Cygnus into the splendidly apt positions they occupy would have brought Vega into place more or less inevitably. As in every other kind of human activity, meaningful symbolism may occur by sheer serendipity. Vega presents itself in a prominent position, and the schemer suddenly realises its potential as part of the grand allegory and trims accordingly. Whether or not such a thing happened it is quite impossible to say – in which respect it is no different from the opposition.

Even a theological reading of Vega is not out of the question. The lyre is Apollo's instrument and, in the analogy between Orphic (and thus pagan) theology and Christian theology, Apollo was taken to correspond to Christ. This is not an obscure doctrine found in an obscure source that no one but obscure scholars have read. It was an idea that had been given a certain publicity a generation earlier, for example, by the imperial poet laureate and humanist Conrad Celtes (or Celtis).[253] Having the eye of the fallen Vega on the line up to the eye of the crucified Christ may have been thought fitting. In the same general analogy, Pegasus represents the Dove of the Holy Spirit. These correspondences are not especially compelling, and they are certainly very unsubtle by comparison with what was being done at the same period by the Italian humanists, for example, but no one can say that they are utterly implausible. They show how difficult the task of interpreting the fine detail in a painting of such enormous variety and complexity as *The Ambassadors* is, in the absence of written materials, or strong symbolic traditions. It is as well to keep the complexity of the painting in our thoughts, as an antidote to complacency. Inner coherence in an interpretation is a minimum requirement. There is little merit in offering a reading of the broken string that is merely coherent. The most satisfying solutions are the most comprehensive. The bald political readings of the painting are not impressive in this respect – which is not to deny that they may be partially true.

DIVISION AND THE HARMONY OF THE WORLD

It is unlikely that Holbein or Kratzer would have slipped dark meanings into the portrait without Dinteville's knowledge. A book of commercial arithmetic is most unlikely to have been used to signify the commerce of the Steelyard, for example, in a painting done for the French ambassador. As we have already seen, Hervey certainly saw the arithmetic in a very different light, imagining it to have been chosen for its use of a single German word, *dividirt*, signifying 'divides', to draw attention to religious or political divisions. True, the notion of division is commonly encountered in the political writings of the day – politics without division is barely conceivable – but one may speak of other sorts of division than were in Hervey's thoughts. A few months before the painting was done, Christopher St German had published a notable polemical work with the title *A Treatise Concerning the Diuision betwene the Spirytualtie and Temporaltie*. When he used the word 'division' here, he was pleading for unity of quite a different sort from that which Hervey had in mind.[254] St German wanted a unity of spiritual and temporal, in other words one that took away church privileges. This would not have been Dinteville's wish, much less de Selve's, and their views on any religious statement would have been paramount, but the same could be said about divisions of the sort Hervey had in mind. The point to be made is that her reading, which may be expressed as 'Division – a sorry state of affairs', is far from simple. Indeed, one might even make out a case for regarding any ostentatious plea for Christian unity in the London of 1533 as an act hostile to Henry VIII – and that was presumably far from the ambassadors' plan.

Needless to say, entering into a discussion of those alternative readings will not seem especially urgent to those who are convinced by what we have already discovered about the page of the arithmetic, namely that the division of numbers on the open page results in the key number 27, not once but three times over, and that this number offers a direct entry to the Good Friday theme.

What is true of arithmetic's *dividirt* applies equally to the lute. Suppose that we start in a simplistic way and try to gloss individually the various items in the painting that it is possible to associate with the quadrivium, the sciences of arithmetic, geometry, astronomy and music. Suppose then that we begin to notice idiosyncracies, blemishes such as those that seem to be present on the astronomical instruments. The fact that they may, as there, turn out not to be blemishes at all shows how much the meaning that is extracted may depend on the biography of the spectator and on how closely the case is studied. Close study is not without its dangers. Are we perhaps being tricked twice over by the lute and its broken string? Is it not just what it seems to be? In view of the general context of skulduggery, almost certainly not. Recognising that fact does not take us very far, for even the theme of disturbed harmony can be understood in many different ways. To the religious pessimist, the message of the lute might be nothing more than that all is not well with God's creation. To the optimist it might be that while death is inevitable, the perils of death are countered by God's redeeming grace, symbolised by the image of the crucified Christ. As for expressing these ideas in words, if we knew a hundred times more about the biographies of its creators than we do, we should still hesitate. And so it is that we fall back on texts, which have an authenticity of sorts, but which also bring along with them their own problems and ambiguities. They may fit perfectly with our preconceptions and yet have been rare or entirely unknown. These points may be well illustrated from a single text, not for any demonstrable relevance to the lute in the Holbein painting, but to show how difficult it is to reach even moderately firm conclusions in a case of this sort.

There is a work by Honorius of Autun – whom we met earlier in connection with the Westminster abbey pavement – in which he sets out to prove twelve theological theses, some concerning angels and demons and some with a rather plainer Neoplatonic character.[255] He shows that the sensible world is a *shadow* of the archetype created by God (note the form-giving but shadowy lute case in the painting, the shadow of the skull, and so forth), and he points out that in the church there are nine orders of the just, corresponding to the nine orders of angels. The second and fourth of his theses actually concern the instrument that Holbein has included in his painting, the lute. Honorius argues that *the universe is arranged in the form of a lute*, and that different things in the world harmonise in exactly the ways that chords do in music. Every student of arts who had remained awake during lectures on Martianus Capella's *Marriage of Philology and Mercury* would have known how excited university musicians could become on discovering how the perfect number six, the number of God's creation, could generate the musical concords: the octave (the ratio 6:12), the fifth (6:9) and the fourth (6:8).[256] As for Honorius, he has a theological axe to grind. He goes on to argue that the elect are themselves responsible for their entry to heaven, but that those who are rejected are sent to a suitable place *like dissonant chords.* What some have thought a political statement, and others a statement of an ecumenical ambition, seen in this light would take on the complexion of a much more basic statement of Christian theology: the dissonant chords amongst us shall not inherit the kingdom of heaven.

This is an old text but one of a type that was still in vogue in the sixteenth century. At the heart of very many analogies of this general sort there was the notion of an earthly music, a *musica mundana*: the idea was that ours is a universe in which each planet is associated with a given musical note, and that all their notes are in harmony. This commonplace, with its roots in the doctrines of the Pythagoreans of antiquity, was extended to include the idea that the human body could respond sympathetically to heavenly music, making for a corresponding human music, a *musica humana.* In a curious way, this ancient doctrine was embodied into the very history of the lute, which in its western forms owed much to the Arab world. Medieval Arabic and Persian texts on the short-necked lute, which was so often used to demonstrate musical theory, reveal a fascination with the symbolism of the number six – after the style of Martianus Capella – as may be seen at a glance from the fact that the roses drawn on their lutes are commonly in the form of hexagrams that are said to symbolise the meeting of visible and spiritual worlds. Unlike most other stringed instruments, as R. H. Wells has pointed out, the western lute retained the geometric motifs of its Arab origins, with the result that the most frequent of all Renaissance rose patterns remained the hexagram, albeit often obscured by other decoration. (A typical example of a western rose pattern cut in a distinctly Arab style is shown in Fig. 65.) Not only was the basic pattern transmitted, but its meaning was remembered. It would be hard to find a more suitable proof of this than in Wells's quotation from the Scottish poet William Drummond of Hawthornden, writing in the early seventeenth century: 'This LUTE's round Bellie was the azur'd Heaven,/The Rose those lights which Hee did there install'.[257] There is plainly a possibility that the rose of the lute in *The Ambassadors* incorporated the painting's third hexagram. If this is the case, and if we are to accept the idea that there is a hexagram hidden in the design of the upper part of the painting, then it possesses this very beautiful property: looking along each of the three principal sightlines – through the skull, through the lute, and up to Christ – one is looking through the middle of a hexagram.

It is because there was a whole class of texts embodying the 'mundane music' doctrine, many of them with theological embellishment, and because so much of the doctrine had by

65. The not untypical rose pattern of a sixteenth-century lute, incorporating hexagrams. In style it owes much to the Islamic world. Drawn after an ivory lute made by Georg Gerle, now in the Kunsthistorisches Museum, Vienna.

Holbein's time become almost platitudinous, that we find it quite impossible to be more specific about what was in the mind of whoever decided to include a lute with a broken string in his painting. Of course one can make intelligent guesses as to the meaning, as Hervey did when she suggested that we consult Alciati's book of emblems. At much the same time in history, however, we find Cornelius Agrippa – and those he was copying – setting out a detailed theory of the relationship between strings and the universe, something that is quite alien to the style of Alciati's published book of emblems. When Agrippa recounts the history of the number of strings on the lute, he is not talking about politics and federation at all. According to his widely read *Occult Philosophy*, the ancient tetrachord corresponded to the four elements, the lowest note to earth, then water, air and fire.[258] Later, he says, Terpander of Lesbos increased the number of strings to seven, each emitting a note corresponding to a planet. (He includes here a passage on correspondences with medicine.) Then came an instrument with nine strings. At this point Agrippa finds it necessary to weave the muses and the celestial spheres into his story, and he sets down the various correspondences at some length. Finally, he relates tones and half-tones to the planetary distances. To understand the broken string, we may therefore need to look to Agrippa's cosmology, or others like it, rather than to Alciati's book.

Other writers tell the cosmic story differently, but the

differences are too subtle for them to be taken into account in what is bound to remain an impressionistic rendering of this side of the painting's meaning. Holbein's instrument has the eleven strings of the most fashionable lutes of his day, as does the lute in another portrait by him, one of an unknown gentleman from about the same period.[259] Perhaps the eleven strings were suggested by the spheres of the four elements and seven planets combined – as they were combined in some later representations. If symbolism there was, of the kind suggested here, then it is the element earth which corresponds to the string on the lute that is actually broken. It might be said that this is not so very different from the simple political readings: all is not well with affairs on earth. The element earth, as it happens, is the twenty-seventh and last of the subdivisions of the created worlds, as purveyed by cabalistical contemporaries!

While some of these readings can be made to converge in a rough and ready sort of way, it should by now be apparent that we are in a state of ignorance – ignorance of the identity of the person who planned the symbolic scheme, of its desired complexity, and of the relevant literary sources and other influences on that person. On the one hand, we are bound to acknowledge that Holbein or Kratzer or Dinteville or de Selve, or others in their circle, may have helped to devise a highly complex series of correspondences between message and image. The sheer complexity of the painting's design supports this idea. On the other hand, we have to admit that the inspiration for some of its simpler symbolism may have been Holbein's, a painter with neither the scholarship to work out an elaborate story nor perhaps even the time or inclination to work one out. 'Lute?' – 'Harmonious universe!' 'Broken string?' – 'Universe in disarray!' 'A disordered universe? All of it?' – 'No, just a part, but that's what disharmony is!' Need the message of the broken string have been any more complex than that? In view of the extraordinary astronomical complexity of the painting, it seems very probable that it was much more complex, but whereas the geometry of shadows lends itself to a fairly determinate outcome, this is not so in the case of complex human affairs. There are times when discretion is the better part of valour. It is only unfortunate that those times have often been wrongly identified. To insist that Holbein was indifferent to the scientific paraphernalia on the stand except for their decorative function is a counsel of despair with nothing to recommend it.[260] The skull and the theme of 27, the hexagram and the horoscope – all speak for careful planning. The broken lute string takes its place by their side, as something that can only be partly understood.

FOURTEEN

THEOLOGIES OF THE CROSS

This divine mysterie is more true than plaine.

Richard Hooker, *Of the Lawes of Ecclesiasticall Politie* (London, 1597), v. chapter 52, section 1

Even as Holbein was preparing the portrait of the two ambassadors, the problem of finding acceptable religious symbolisms was being seriously and systematically addressed by a number of writers, either on behalf of Reformation theology or in defence of tradition. Thomas More was the most important thinker in Holbein's immediate vicinity, but it is instructive to begin with Dean John Colet, who had died in 1519 but whose reputation lived on. Colet in fact left an important legacy to those who were destined to debate the Protestant revolt. He had provided one of the main channels through which the English had learned to admire Italian humanism in general and the Florentine version of Plato's philosophy in particular. For centuries, large numbers of theologians had found the metaphors of the Neoplatonists irresistible. They admired Plotinus when he equated darkness with matter, and both with evil. Such ideas were not new on the intellectual scene, which made them doubly welcome. St John's Gospel makes much use of a metaphor of light, and tells us how Jesus made use of it to his disciples: 'I am the light of the world: he that followeth me shall not walk in darkness, but shall have the light of life.' And again, 'Are there not twelve hours in the day? If any man walk in the day, he stumbleth not, because he seeth the light of this world'. We have seen how Agrippa twisted this to his own ends. In Holbein's day, there was a fresh enthusiasm for metaphors of light and Sun and for the idea that they apply to all creation. They were regularly applied to the cosmos as a whole, for instance to fantastic theoretical superstructures like that of the ancient writer now known as Pseudo-Dionysius, whose scheme for the ranking of the angels was plundered by the Cabalists.

He maintained that they were arranged in three threes – seraphim, cherubim, thrones; dominions, virtues, powers; princedoms, archangels, angels. Like the doctrines of the ancient astrologers, these ideas were generally taken over unquestioned.

COLET, MORE AND THE SUN

Colet followed in the footsteps of Marsilio Ficino and Pico della Mirandola – whom he introduced to Oxford audiences in the 1490s – and like them he made use of an analogy between God and the natural Sun. We have already considered how Ficino would have answered those who thought him to be playing with paganism in this respect.* God was the 'divine Sun', the 'Sun of truth', who sends forth 'rays of grace'. Colet went on to extend the metaphor to Christ, 'the Sun of righteousness' whose redeeming role he thought Dionysius had tended to overlook. Through 'the rays of the celestial Sun, Jesus Christ', the soul is reformed. A good way for mankind to start, as he believed, is by imitating the highest order of angels.[261] Colet combined elements of Plato's *Republic* and of St Augustine, as well as of other Platonists of the day, and if Neoplatonic mysticism shone somehow into the portrait of the two ambassadors, the fact may well have owed something to him, with Thomas More a possible intermediary.

Long before the painting was done, after Colet had been appointed dean of St Paul's by Henry VII in 1504, More had listened to Colet's blend of Platonism and Christianity and had fallen under his spell. He described Colet as 'the director of my life'. He later published a condensed version of the life of Pico written by Pico's nephew Gianfrancesco, and according to Cresacre decided to model his life on Pico's.[262] (More too was once young.) Erasmus was one of the many affected by Colet's message. Since Colet believed that everything that is true can somehow be found in scripture, he gave his followers a liking for biblical exegesis – not to mention the habit of finding things in threes everywhere they looked, starting with the Trinity.

* See p. 275 above.

Searching early literature for the revelation of mysteries that Christians shared with pagans became a Renaissance sport, and so many different triads were uncovered by writers of the time that it would be almost impossible to list them. (We have already come across numerous examples.) Colet, like More and Erasmus after him, was in love with concealed meanings in literature, comparing the concealed meaning to the spirit and the obvious meaning to the body. This explains in part why they were enchanted by the Pythagoreans and the Platonists: like Augustine, they thought that those Greek mystics had used language allegorically and figuratively, in a manner reminiscent of the Holy Scriptures themselves.[263] In this way the triad of scholars helped to create an atmosphere that was highly conducive to the tacit imagery of *The Ambassadors.*

MORE AND THE CRUCIFIXION

If More's influence is to be seen elsewhere in the painting, it will be in a form far removed from an allegory of light and shadow. There was no strong disagreement about the commemoration of Good Friday and Easter as such: the mass, derived from the Last Supper preceding the crucifixion, was one of the three sacraments that Luther considered valid.[264] Zwingli, on the other hand, was pressing the point that the mass was a commemorative event rather than a sacrifice, and Holbein's stay in Basel from 1528 to 1532 means that he almost certainly heard this question debated on numerous occasions. He must have felt very much at home when he learned on his return of More's heated debate with Lutheran theologians on the sacraments. Just before Easter in the year of the painting, 1533, More published his *Apology*, much of it an attack on Luther's English ally William Tyndale, and much of it a general defence of the universal church.[265] It was then nearly a year since More had resigned the office of chancellor, and as things turned out it was almost exactly a year before his imprisonment, leading up to his execution. Tyndale was himself executed for heresy a year after More, but in this case Henry VIII was denied the pleasure. Betrayed by an English Catholic who had feigned friendship, Tyndale was put to death at Vilvoorde near Brussels, under imperial law administered by Margaret of Austria, regent of the Netherlands.

The *Apology* was in some respects a defence of its author's own record in office. The books of Tyndale and his friends, rather than the men themselves, were all that had been burned up to that time. This is no reflection on More's weakness of will. It was chiefly because the men had been on the Continent, and out of his reach. Against one of them, John Frith, alias Richard Brightwell, More had written a separate tract on the doctrine of the eucharist at the very end of 1532. Frith was a man whose commonsense outlook began with a disparaging of beliefs about angels, demons and fairies, and ended with a denial of Christ's physical presence in the mass. He was a disciple of Zwingli – Holbein must have been given pause for thought – and as matters turned out was burned at Smithfield in July 1533. While the supremacy of parliament and the limits to be set to the power of the church and the pope were uppermost in the political consciousness of most of these people, they felt deeply about the theological subtleties surrounding the mass. They debated on whether Christ is truly present in the bread and wine at mass, and they refined their doctrines of transubstantiation and consubstantiation, and all their unutterably subtle offshoots. So contentious was this general issue that attempts made later to reconcile the Protestant and Catholic churches (at Ratisbon in 1541 and Poissy in 1561, for instance) seem to have foundered mainly over its interpretation.

More and Erasmus had debated doctrines of the eucharist vigorously in London years before, when More apparently held what was to become a notorious Lutheran heresy, that whether Christ was truly present in the elements of the bread and wine depended on the faith of the person receiving them. Erasmus took a more orthodox view of the Real Presence, but in his *Praise of Folly* gives a pointed and impatient criticism of the worthless logic-chopping of scholastic theologians on the matter. It is not surprising that when he was thrown into prison for his obduracy, his thoughts turning inevitably to death, More should have written a new tract, *A Treatise upon the Passion*, touching on many of the old familiar points of dispute.[266] There are five or six pages on calculating the feast correctly – hardly a matter of great moment in the eyes of a modern observer, which only goes to show how great the gap is between our mental constitutions and theirs. There is much in the tract that is likely to be found more interesting today – for instance on the psychology of the mass, the continuing debate over what the sacrament signifies, and a rather philosophical question of how it gets its meaning. More organised his book as a Bible commentary. He never got as far as the crucifixion as such, for reasons that are not difficult to understand. Superficially, his style is very different from that in his earlier work on the 'four last things', but beneath the surface of both there is the idea that the agony of Christ on the cross is analogous to that of every human being who is suffering for a high moral principle. He never underestimated his own moral value.

LUTHER'S 'THEOLOGY OF THE CROSS'

It is as well to remember these things when considering the meaning of Holbein's painting, for while it figures the crucifixion in what to us seems an almost apologetic way, it was painted in the midst of a very violent conflict between opposing systems of belief, one that enmeshed people who were intimately known to one another and to all concerned with the painting. The painter could count himself fortunate if he was allowed to keep his thoughts to himself. A crucifixion is a crucifixion. If the scheme of the painting was decided by others, then his thoughts on the underlying theology, as he painted, mattered little to its form. But did he and his sitters never discuss that important episode in the early history of Lutheranism now known as the 'theology of the cross'? Some Lutheran historians have gone so far as to see in this the true spark that ignited the Reformation. Martin Luther was a member of the Augustinian order of hermits from September 1505. In 1518 he accepted an invitation by Johannes von Staupitz, the leading Augustinian at Heidelberg, to address his old order there. Luther's 'theology of the cross' was presented in a public lecture on 26 April 1518, probably for the first time, and less than six months after his notorious Wittenberg theses had come to the notice of a wide public.

The tenor of his new message was that those who derive their theology from 'things visible' are merely fools, and that the true theologian is one 'who comprehends the visible and manifest things of God seen through suffering and the cross'. He cites Exodus, chapter 33, where God explains to Moses that no human being can see God's face and live. We may see his back, but not his face. The majesty and glory of God are beyond human comprehension or endurance.[267]

Why this seems so appropriate as a potential text for *The Ambassadors*, with its half-hidden crucifixion and its numerous concealed meanings, is that in it 'the visible things of God' are consistently placed in opposition to the invisible. This is Plato's cave, in a sense, but on a different theological plane. Luther makes continued use of the language of concealment and of God's hiding himself in the humility of Christ. There is no point in recognising God in His glory and majesty, he argues, unless we recognise Him in the humility and shame of the cross. He repeatedly falls back on a language that contrasts appearance and reality, and behind it all there is the desire to castigate those who seek God in visible glory and power, 'theologians of glory'. They call evil good and good evil, whereas it is 'the theologian of the cross' who calls these things what they actually are.

A crucifixion is a crucifixion. It carries no overtly sectarian theology until it is discussed, explained or interpreted. Its simple and uncommented use carried no great risk of reprisals, even though it must have stirred up uneasy thoughts of doctrinal dissension on the part of some of those who contemplated it. By comparison, the message carried by the image on Dinteville's collar was a simple one in which all, for the time being, could share. As he leads up to the events surrounding Christ's death, Sir Thomas More quotes at length from St John's Book of Revelation (ch. 12), concerning Michael and his angels and how they fought with 'that great dragon the olde serpent which is called the deuill' and threw him out of heaven and 'downe into the earth'.[268] On the identity of the devil on earth there was likely to be much disagreement. More wisely left it to the reader to supply the name.

FIFTEEN

SYMBOLS OF THE MILLENNIUM

> Since everyone knew that the French king had invaded Italy with his forces, when I began my sermon with these words, 'Behold, I will bring flood waters upon the earth', suddenly many were astonished and thought that this passage of Genesis was furnished by God's hidden will for that moment in time. Among these was Count Giovanni della Mirandola, a man unique in our day for talent and learning; he later told me that he was struck with fear at these words and that his hair stood on end.
>
> Girolamo Savonarola, *Compendium of Revelations*, referring to the year 1494[269]

The Ambassadors was a painting done for a special occasion, not for a glorious state occasion but to commemorate the most desolate time on the first Good Friday. This it does by reference to the corresponding hour in 1533. There was nothing new in the use of scriptural history to illuminate the present, but how seriously the exercise was taken naturally rested on the perceived gravity of the current state of affairs. Was the hour of Christ's death in 1533 different enough from the corresponding hour in any other year to have made an erudite Florentine humanist's hair stand on end? Or a French ambassador's? The year 1533 was indeed unusual, but the question will best be answered only after we have cleared away a number of lesser problems associated with it. Some of them are connected with ritual and tradition. What of the relevant symbolism of the painting on a smaller scale? Why four and not three o'clock, for example, which the ordinary well-read Christian of the age would have known to be the time of the climax of the crucifixion story, the time when Christ cried out to God asking why he had been forsaken, and soon after which he died?

There are two ways of approaching the question of timing. The obvious one is to start from the scriptural account, and customs known to have been based on it. The other will have regard to the special circumstances of 1533. Since the artist has invoked astronomical methods to convey the timing, the second method suggests that some astrologically significant state of the heavens may have caught his imagination, or that of his friends. Such a thing would of course have needed to be broadly compatible with the scriptural account, or at least to have conformed to some established custom. In chapter 16 it will be shown that at least one other person, namely the poet Geoffrey Chaucer, made artistic use of precisely the same hour on an earlier Good Friday. This fact does not greatly simplify our problem, but it weakens the force of the most obvious objection to our solution.

There were many long discussions of the timing and chronology of the crucifixion in the middle ages, as indeed before and after, but none of which I am aware that offers this hour of the day in exactly this context. Some of the greatest biblical commentators – Thomas Aquinas, for example – were resigned to noting the imprecision of the gospel accounts of the timing of the first Good Friday. Dante even argued that the Gospel of St Luke implied that Christ died at the sixth hour of the day, that is noon.[270] The gospels do not yield a precise time for the moment of Christ's death, but all imply that it was at about the ninth hour, which is usually taken to mean that Christ died shortly after three o'clock, in modern parlance.[271] According to the gospel account, between the sixth and ninth hours (between noon and three o'clock) 'there was darkness over all the land' (Matthew 27:45). It was at the end of this time that Jesus cried out to God, asking – in the opening words of Psalm 22 – why he had been forsaken, whereupon one of the onlookers ran for a sponge, filled it with vinegar, put it on a reed and gave it to Jesus to drink. Others said, 'Let be, let us see whether Elias will come to save him'; and at this Jesus cried out yet again and 'yielded up the ghost'. There were yet more unnatural events:

> And, behold, the veil of the temple was rent in twain from the top to the bottom; and the earth did quake, and the rocks rent;

> And the graves were opened; and many bodies of the saints which slept arose,
>
> And came out of the graves after his resurrection, and went into the holy city, and appeared unto many.
>
> Now when the centurion, and they that were with him, watching Jesus, saw the earthquake, and those things that were done, they feared greatly, saying, Truly this was the Son of God.
>
> Matthew 27:51–54

There were many women watching from a distance, including Mary Magdalene and Mary the mother of James and Joses, and 'When the even was come' a rich man, Joseph of Arimathaea, begged the body from Pontius Pilate and laid it in a tomb he had prepared for himself (Matthew 27:57–60).

Four o'clock, the end of the tenth hour (as it would there have been expressed), is not mentioned in the gospel accounts of the crucifixion, but it cannot be easily brushed aside. It was derived in earlier chapters not only from the cylinder dial in conjunction with every other instrument on the upper shelf, but from the symbolism of the recurrent 27, which indicates the Sun's altitude at that time. We have seen that a time around four would have made good sense by the lights of the astrologers. It does not actually conflict with any scriptural account: the three hours of unnatural darkness had passed and the dead Christ was left on the cross until evening. It is conceivable that they had come across a medieval English source that makes the darkening of the Sun last for an hour after Christ gave up the ghost, but a very different solution has been suggested to me by Mr Peter Nockolds. In view of the symbolism of the Lamb of God in the painting, he notes the potential relevance of the first chapter of the gospel of St John. There Andrew and Simon become followers of Jesus, described to them by John the Baptist as the Lamb of God, and this at 'about the tenth hour'. The opening verses of that same gospel would indeed have made a fitting text for the painting, especially the fifth: 'And the light shineth in darkness: and the darkness did not comprehend it'.[272]

The setting of the globe might be thought to require no justification beyond what we have found for it already, but we shall shortly discover in it a tacit reference to Christ's descent from the cross. Twilight has just ended, night is beginning, and a starry crucifix is tilted so that it rests on the horizon.

Of equal interest is the use made of the ram as a Sun-marker and symbol, tacitly in the painting of the globe and explicitly in the supporters of the horizon ring. We are clearly confronted with some kind of symbolism of the sacrifice of Christ. There has always been plenty of room for differences of theological opinion on the precise relationship of the Last Supper to the feast of Passover (*Pesach*), which was instituted to commemorate Israel's deliverance from Egyptian slavery. The rules laid down then for the sacrifice of a lamb were 'to be kept by the law forever'. That particular sacrifice was not to atone for sin, as was the case with other lamb sacrifices in the Old Testament, but was a prelude to marking the houses of the Israelites with blood so that God would avoid them when striking down the first-born of the Egyptians. In the Christian account, however, the death of Christ was presented as being like the sacrifice of a lamb – an atonement, but now for the sins of mankind generally. In the words of St Paul, for example, 'even Christ our Passover is sacrificed for us' (I Corinthians 5:7). The word 'lamb' is not used by St Paul here, but was generally taken to be implicit in what he said, and many analogies were later drawn between the Passover lamb and Christ – for instance on the rules for the preparation of the lamb for the Passover feast and the way Christ's body was treated.

There can be no doubt of the fact that the line of sight leading up to Christ passes through the Sun's place on the globe in the constellation of the Ram. The supporters of the globe's horizon ring are rams' heads (Fig. 27). The Passover sacrifice was not a ram, but the constellation of Aries was, and there is relatively little variation in the manner of depicting it over a long period of history. Dürer's is entirely typical

66. Albrecht Dürer's image for the constellation of the Ram (detail of Fig. 7). The Sun, on Good Friday 1533, was in the second degree of Taurus, on the ecliptic (the scale) and below the muzzle of the ram. The supporting rams on the globe seem to be meant to draw attention to this.

(Fig. 66). On what grounds might Holbein's advisers have used the ram as a symbol of Christ?

RAM, CROSS AND CREATION

There are numerous theological precedents for the change from lamb to ram. One might even ask why the point is important. If Holbein could turn the Cygnus-hen into a cock, could he not turn a ram into a lamb? That would be to support one weak argument with another. There are frequent references to Christ as a ram in the writings of the Church Fathers. From early Christian times onwards, when Christ is represented as the Lamb of God – usually with the lamb holding a cross – the animal is often depicted with seven horns (following the Book of Revelation, see Fig. 67) or with an ordinary ram's horns.[273] As for an astronomical reading of the scriptures, there are many sources that might have come to the mind of a trained theologian. In some Jewish Rabbinical literature, for example, it is claimed that it was Moses who chose the lamb as a sacrificial animal for the Passover, for reasons connected with Egyptian idol worship and the fact that in the month of Nisan the Sun was in the zodiacal sign of the Ram. One of the most widely respected of all Christian theologians, Thomas Aquinas, connected these events with the Christian paschal meal and its timing, in his most famous work, *Summa Theologica.*[274] It is possible that Maimonides was his immediate source.

There were other doctrines that found general acceptance

and that linked the constellation of Aries with God the creator. All the planets were said to be there at the time God created the world. Perhaps that is why the *zodiacal sign* of Aries is occasionally depicted in 'Lamb of God' style, with the animal supporting a long cross, often with a flag. And as a token of interchangeability, we find the poet Dante on several occasions in his *Divine Comedy* associating the planet Mars not with a ram (Aries is the domicile of Mars) but with a lamb. There is an allegorical painting by Jan Provoost bringing these ideas together. It is now in the Louvre and is perhaps a decade or two older than *The Ambassadors.* In Provoost's complex work, a typical lamb and flag are depicted above a sword-carrying Christ, to our left. In the middle of the painting there is a large heavenly sphere on which are a Sun, Moon and Earth, and the sphere is surmounted by a cross. To our right is the Virgin, carrying a lily and the dove of the Holy Spirit. There is a symbolic eye above the globe and another eye below it. The

67. Detail from Dürer's woodcut 'The Adoration of the Lamb', included in German and Latin editions of a series illustrating the Revelation of St John the Divine (1498). This is depicted as a heavenly apparition. The image of a cup being held to catch blood from the lamb's breast follows the tradition of depicting cups that catch the blood from Christ's wounds. The multiple horns and eyes correspond to the scriptural reference to 'a Lamb as it had been slain, having seven horns and seven eyes, which are the seven Spirits of God sent forth into all the earth' (Revelation 5:6).

parallels with Holbein's painting may not be close, but they do share an allegorical Christian language.

Why did Holbein so arrange his globe that the line of sight up to Christ passes through the most northerly point of the horizon (Fig. 27, fourth segment)? One reason might have been to make it easier for Kratzer to situate the globe correctly, in keeping with the calculated (negative) altitude of the Sun. There were certain constraints on the placing of the globe, in view of the need to place the Sun – in principle invisible – on that line of sight. Of the need to do that, we can be reasonably certain, since it *was* done, and to such good purpose. It would have been easy to swivel round the globe to put the Sun elsewhere, for instance nearer to a ram *supporter*, but doing so would have fixed the time of night so that the Moon was no longer in the wonderfully symmetrical position that had been found for it.* That the cock showed to advantage when Sun and Moon were rightly placed may have been serendipitous, and perhaps the same goes for Vega in the Lyre, as mentioned earlier, but the potential symbolism of both, as discussed in the following section and elsewhere, seems to me to have been simply too compelling for it to have gone unnoticed. And we should not forget that it is the *brightest* stars in both constellations that are on the line up to Christ. With the Dolphin, matters were just too difficult for it to be given prominence. Fitting the two bright stars to the line virtually removed all room for manoeuvre in placing the globe on the painting, keeping both Sun and Moon on the near side of the ring. (While neither was meant to be seen by us, they had to be placed correctly, separated by roughly 159° of azimuth. Holbein was able to vary what was in principle visible to the viewer of the painting, obstructions apart, up to something approaching 180°. It was simply a question of how near he placed his point of view from the globe when he painted it.)

One possible reason for making the line pass through the northern point of the horizon precisely, in view of the crucifixion theme, would have been to create yet another cross out of

* See p. 200 above.

68. Manuscript illustration of a characteristic cross within a halo, showing also the Sun and Moon above the beam of the cross and the rent curtain in the temple. The original from which this comes, the twelfth-century *Hortus deliciarum* of Herrad of Hohenbourg, is now destroyed. The present copy was made in the nineteenth century.

the rings of the globe. In the mind's eye, the observer may have been meant to conjure up a composite image, with a circle, a cross, and Christ's head at the centre of the cross – in short, a very common representation of Christ in medieval art, even though in Holbein's day it was passing out of use among painters in favour of a rayed nimbus. Another possible image, in view of the Sun's place, may have been that of the Lamb of God – compare Dürer's version in Fig. 67 – but it seems far more likely that a cross was intended. In the early middle ages a small head had often been depicted at the centre of a relatively large cross, sometimes with a circular halo surrounding Christ's head, but in time the whole thing was combined into one and reduced in size (as in Fig. 68).

Whatever the intended mental image, the idea of a cross created out of the circles of the celestial sphere is strongly reminiscent of an image used by Dante in the first canto of *Paradise* (the last of the three books of his *Divine Comedy*). The passage in question (lines 37–48) is famously difficult, and what follows is more of an explanation than a translation:

> The lamp of the world, the Sun, rises to our view over different places on the horizon on successive days, but when it rises through a point that joins four circles with three crosses it has better effects. It has a more propitious course, and moulds the wax of the world more after its own way. The Sun rose over a point near to this at the time in question, and half the sphere was white and half dark when I saw Beatrice turn to her left side and look up at the Sun. Never did eagle do this more fixedly.

There has been much disagreement over the centuries about Dante's 'four circles with three crosses'. It seems almost certain that the optimum place of the Sun's rising was meant to be when it was in the first point of the sign of Aries (not the constellation), where the ecliptic and celestial equator meet. But it is not at all necessary to know anything much about these circles, or to discuss the various ways in which they may cross, to appreciate the simple point that Dante is making.[275] He creates crosses out of fundamental circles of the celestial sphere, just as Holbein's painting may have been considered to do, even though their circles are not all the same.

There was an important precedent for doing this sort of thing that would have been much better known outside Italy than the Dante passage. Plato in his *Timaeus* – which as it happens was the only work of Plato with which Dante was familiar – describes the creation of the world using the celebrated myth that we touched upon earlier, in connection with the number 27. Beginning with two long strips of 'soul-stuff', the creator (the Demiurge) is said to have put them together at their middles to form a cross, before bending the arms round to form hoops and so produce what amounted to the beginnings of a cosmic sphere. Since the arms were meant to make up the equator and the ecliptic, they were not at right angles as in Christ's cross, but Plato's image nevertheless caught the imagination of many of Plato's Christian commentators, who saw in it a prefiguring of the crucifixion. The wooden cross of Christ was the equivalent of Plato's 'X', and there was an extensive literature likening the Old Testament creation to the New Testament story of redemption through Christ's death. This, after all, is the context for the idea that Christ was the second Adam.[276] The symbolism of the cross merely strengthened that theological association. Indeed, it was strengthened in another way, as Dante's allusion to the creation of the world in the above passage (the moulding of the wax of the world, and so on) reminds us: creation and crucifixion were linked through the sign of Aries. We have just mentioned the strong tradition according to which the creation of the world took place when all the planets were congregated in the sign of Aries. The dates of the annunciation (by the angel Gabriel to Mary) and the crucifixion (after Passover) were also conventionally related to the entry of the Sun into Aries at the beginning of spring.

For all of these reasons, a cabalistic or Neoplatonic understanding of the occurrences of the number 27 in the painting, making it a reference to the creation of the world, is entirely compatible with the main crucifixion theme.

There is another astronomy-inspired cross, later in the same work by Dante. When, under the guidance of Beatrice, the poet reaches the heaven of Mars in canto 14 of *Paradise*, he briefly catches sight of a cross that leads his thoughts to Christ. It is made, he says, as though by the joining of quadrants into a circle. In other words, it has the short equal arms of a 'Greek cross', such as that on a hot cross bun. The cross was not on this occasion likened directly to the intersecting circles of a globe, but was pricked out by swarms of moving souls in lights, greater and smaller, voicing divine harmonies and songs of victory that were hard to make out. This additional passage seems to have a different basis from the first, but it likens the swarms of lights, 'gleaming white between the poles of the world' to the Milky Way, the Galaxy, *Galassia* (line 99). Holbein's globe shows us the Milky Way ('Galacia' for the Latin word *Galaxia*) in a position that makes it just as conspicuous as the supposed gallic cock or Pegasus.

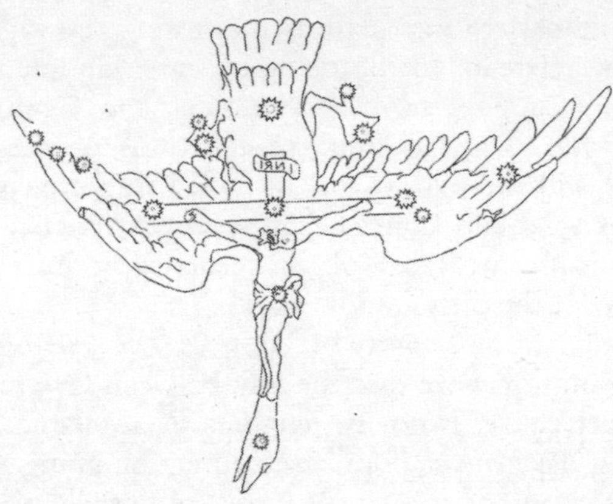

69. The constellation of Cygnus with the crucifixion of Christ superimposed on it. After Wilhelm Schickard's *Astroscopium* (1623), and drawn here in mirror image to make a comparison with Holbein's Cygnus easier. Schickard's globe was in three segments that could be dismantled. As an aid to star recognition, the constellation figures were on the *inside* of these, and so showed the constellations to the student as they are actually seen in the night sky. Most globes are like Holbein's, showing a 'God's eye view' of the heavens.

CYGNUS AND THE CROSS

The key line on the painting, that goes from the eye of the observer at the side of it up to the head of Christ, passes as we know through the brightest star in the most prominent constellation of all on the globe. The star is Deneb and we may continue to call the constellation Cygnus – it is unnamed on the globe – since that is its present conventional name. Whether or not the bird was meant to be symbolic of France, there is ample evidence that the constellation was traditionally associated with the cross of Christ. Its stars form a very pronounced 'Latin' cross (†), and it is not surprising that those teaching constellation recognition in recent centuries have often referred to it as the 'Northern Cross'. This name does not belong to mainstream astronomy, but it does have ancient precedents. There is literary support from as early as the sixth century, for example, that has been presented by Steven McCluskey. It is in a work by Gregory of Tours, who was giving his monastery instructions for timing the night offices of prayer by reference to the rising of stars. He refers to what we can only suppose to be Cygnus as 'the Greater Cross' (*Crux Majoris*). The flanking constellations of the Dolphin (*Delphinus*) and the Lyre (*Lyra*) he called respectively Alfa (or the Lesser Cross) and Omega. Those Greek letters are shown suspended from the cross of the crucifixion in a standard iconography of the early middle ages.[277]

It is a far cry from Gregory of Tours to *The Ambassadors*, but there is reason to believe that the link between Cygnus and the cross was kept alive, if not in religious or academic circles, at least among the general populace. It may be going too far to invoke depictions of the starry cross supposedly seen in the vision of the Emperor Constantine and recorded by many a later writer. It may even be unsafe to invoke as evidence the constellation figure for Cygnus as drawn in the work entitled *Astroscopium*, first published by the great Tübingen Hebrew scholar, theologian, astronomer and technician Wilhelm Schickard in 1623. The reason for hesitation is that the book came out at a time when many western astronomers were trying hard to Christianise the pagan constellation figures.[278] Five years later, for instance, Julius Schiller's atlas turned Cygnus into St Helena with the true cross of Christ that she is reputed to have rediscovered. The Schickard illustration nevertheless shows graphically what earlier artists may have been content to leave to the imagination. The flying swan is retained, but a crucified Christ is superimposed on it (Fig. 69). The head of Christ – made to coincide more or less with the 'new star', *stella nova*, that had appeared in 1600 – is near the crossing of body and wings, while his feet are towards the bird's head.

Was this simply the rediscovery of an old idea, or was it still current in Holbein's day? There are two sorts of reason for believing that the image had not been forgotten in the early sixteenth century. The first printed European atlas showing individual constellations – but without any pictorial content beyond the individual stars – was published by Alessandro Piccolomini (1540). He speaks of the five brightest stars in Cygnus as forming a cross. At the end of the century Johannes

Bayer, in the notes on Cygnus that he added to his great star atlas (*Uranometria*, 1603), makes a categorical statement that an inclined crucifix in the arrangement of the five brightest stars in the Swan had long been recognised by farmers.[279] Firm evidence as to folk belief of this kind is notoriously hard to come by, but Bayer studied at Apian's Ingolstadt and lived most of his life in Holbein's Augsburg, and his knowledge of common custom may shed light on what was known to the artist himself or to Kratzer. Cygnus is one of the three or four most conspicuous of all northern constellations. Its common names would have been widely known, and not only to a small circle of astronomers.

As it happens, we know that the leading astronomer of Bayer's time, Johannes Kepler, was also aware of the crucifixion image. Kepler hailed from the same part of the world. Writing about a new star (nova) in the constellation of the Serpent in 1606, he used the crucifixion image and the position of Christ's head and breast within it, to remind himself of exactly where there had been a nova in Cygnus in 1600.[280] Three generations had passed since *The Ambassadors* had been painted, and still Kepler did not consider it incongruous to write a book of more than two hundred pages (*De stella nova*) in which theology, astronomy and revisionist astrology were intermingled from beginning to end. This illustrates the force of the system of belief that informed the Holbein painting, and adds a grain or two of sand to the balance of evidence for our hypothesis that Holbein's Cygnus was a crucifixion image.

There is a second sort of evidence for this, however, which depends little on texts and which seems overwhelming. It is that when we take any reasonable drawing of the Schickard type, turning the stars into a cross, and add it to the celestial globe in the painting, the foot of that cross will be on the horizon and one of its arms will rest on the ground. The brightest star in the constellation will lie fair and square on the line of sight from the observer to Christ in the folds of the curtain, and the angle made between the cross and the horizon will be 27° (see Fig. 82 in Appendix v). What could be more apt?

THE RITUALS OF GOOD FRIDAY

It is probably wise to suppose that the resemblance between Dante's image and the way in which that upper sightline seems to nail together the crossed rings of the globe is purely coincidental. There are other ideas in the same cantos, however, that resonate with Holbein's painting as convincingly as any political allegory. Dante makes mention of the small circle of the Holy Spirit, he has symbols of the mystical number three, and references to the wisdom of Solomon. Such things are probably best seen not as signs of direct influence but of the use of a pool of common religious ideas. Not that Dante was an unknown author. His work, especially in the best-selling commented editions printed by Cristoforo Landino (1424–1498), had become familiar to a large audience by the early sixteenth century, and the relevant passages were already much debated. If *The Ambassadors* does indeed make calls upon either of the two poetic images of the cross, then the person most likely to have introduced them to Holbein and the others is the young bishop Georges de Selve, Italian-speaking and of Italian ancestry.

There are other points on which de Selve may have made suggestions in his priestly capacity, but how are we to single them out? If one were to stick the proverbial pin in the painting, and ask a theologian to interpret what was there, so comprehensive is the Bible that this would present no great difficulty. The tip of the spike for the solar instrument? Does it denote the lance with which the Roman soldier Longinus pierced Christ's side? (There was a legend that he was blind, and that his blindness was cured by the blood that fell on his eyes.) Or failing that, what about an allusion to the scriptural image of the wounded Lamb of God, as captured in Dürer's woodcut? (The tip of the spike may be thought to pierce the breast of the ram as viewed along the upper line of sight in Fig. 28, third segment). Or does your pin hit one of the birds on the globe? Then what about St John the Divine's vision of an angel standing in the Sun who cried with a loud voice 'to all the fowls that fly in the midst of heaven' (Revelation 19:17–18)? From the

Book of Revelation one may prove almost anything – as history amply testifies.

There are points where the ground is firmer, and where we may imagine that de Selve would have wished to express a theological opinion. On good historical and astronomical grounds, we have connected the imagery of the painting with the weighing of souls, and we shall come back to this question in our penultimate chapter.* It is not for us to ask whether it was good theology or not to give Christ this function before he had ascended into heaven. For at least five centuries, European literature, drama and art had been much influenced by the story of Christ's having descended into hell before rising from the dead at Easter. It is true that some Christians found the idea hard to accept, and theologians – confronted by Luke's Gospel which places him in Paradise – often debated the doctrine at length. There was more agreement over the fact of the descent than over its purpose. At the very time that Holbein was painting the dual portrait, Martin Luther was preaching a sermon at Torgau in which he argued that the mystery of Christ's descent into hell cannot be understood by blind reason. It was a familiar doctrine, however, to all who sang or said the Apostles' creed or the Athanasian creed, and would have been well known to all in Holbein's circle. They would have known of the doctrine according to which Christ brought away from hell the souls of the righteous who had been held captive there since the beginning of the world. This, called in English the 'harrowing of hell', might just possibly be part of a message the painting was meant to convey. We are, perhaps, being invited to look upwards to contemplate Christ after he has made the ultimate sacrifice, and to look down to a symbol of death and the place of death, to which Christ has for the time being descended, and which by that sacrifice he will vanquish.

It seems very probable that there is an allusion to the rending of the veil of the temple, in the division of the green curtain, a third of the way along the top. The temple curtain was depicted

* See pp. 236 above and 341 below.

at the side of the cross in many a medieval crucifixion scene.[281] It is not difficult to imagine other allusions in the painting to the services and ceremonial of the church, although that to the veil is most compelling. There were actually two different veils used in the ceremonials of Holy Week, in English distinguished as the 'Lenten veil' and the 'rood cloth'. The first veiled the altar or sanctuary, and corresponded to the veil of the temple in the biblical account. The second covered the crucifix, and was removed from it by degrees in the ceremony of Creeping to the Cross. If the green curtain in the painting alluded to either of these, it would have been to the first. But how typical was the colour green? There was great variety in the colouring of both types of covering, both in England and elsewhere, but throughout the middle ages white and red were commonly combined. From the sixteenth century onwards, however, there are increasing numbers of records of the use of green, a notable example being that from Westminster abbey around the year 1540, which speaks of the Lenten veil as 'a travers of grene silk'.[282] Green was the colour of hope, and was associated with the hope of resurrection.

Good Friday began, as did Wednesday and Thursday of Holy Week, with the ceremonial of *Tenebrae* (Darkenings), enacted by the priest through a gradual extinguishing of the candles in the church.[283] Some derive this custom from the supposed eclipse of the Sun at Christ's passion, and say that the three nights represent his three hours on the cross. The number of candles varied greatly between churches, but twenty-four or more are commonly mentioned, making for a comparison between them and the hours of the day, with Christ corresponding to the Sun. (The Moon is the church.) The Good Friday services usually incorporated a veneration of the cross, and in some cases this began with the priest uncovering it by withdrawing in stages the rood cloth. In a later service there were threes (the so-called 'Trisagium', with its three repetitions of the adjective 'Holy') and nines (in the form of prayers known as the nine 'Reproaches'). After this there was a 'Mass of the Presanctified'. (The name refers to the use of the bread and wine sanctified on the previous day.) There was much variation in the timing of such services. Perhaps four o'clock was deemed to be when the *Tenebrae* were sung for the last time. In some places they were not sung until after another service, in which Christ's burial was represented, but the timing of this too is uncertain. The cross that had earlier been venerated was in this case washed in wine and water and placed in a mock sepulchre, such as a niche in the wall or a wooden chest, adorned with curtains and hangings. The lute case, deep in shadow? The possibilities are endless. The sepulchre was to be ritually opened on Easter Day.

This was a period of rapid change in the ritual of the English church, but the greatest changes, brought about by Protestant revulsion at what were seen as Romish superstitions, were still in the future in 1533 – and in any case, any hints of ritual in the painting would presumably have reflected on the thoroughly Catholic practices of the two Frenchmen. Even in Protestant England some of the old practices were surprisingly continued, such as that in which the monarch blessed a basinful of rings which were to act as cures against 'cramp' – epilepsy, palsy and other diseases. The ancient and almost universal Catholic ceremony of Creeping to the Cross continued for some years. Following the final removal of the rood cloth, the clergy first crept barefoot on hands and knees to kiss the foot of the cross, and the laity then followed suit. Popes and kings did this, including Henry and his queens, until Cranmer persuaded him to abolish the custom in 1546. It did not disappear finally from the practice of the English church until the time of Elizabeth. By injunctions of 1538, most ceremonial lamps and candles were banned, but even then not the sepulchre light. Finally, under Elizabeth, bonfires were made of the old wooden sepulchres.

FEARS FOR THE MID-MILLENNIUM

Whether or not it is wishful thinking to find reference to any of these things in *The Ambassadors*, the shadow of Christ's death on the first Good Friday, and the manner of it, had some clear parallels in England in 1533. In an age when number mysticism was rampant, it would not have passed unnoticed that 33 was the age of Christ at his death, and that just fifteen centuries, a millennium and a half, had passed since the day of his crucifixion. The constellation of Aries belongs to the millennium discussion, for it relates to the dating of creation and God's plans for world history. The Westminster pavement makes allusion to the same. It is quite possible that for this very reason the pavement was being introduced into the ongoing discussion of the imminence of Christ's second coming.

The doctrine of a millennium was already being advocated in the first two centuries of Christianity. After Augustine preached caution, it was discussed in relatively subdued tones, but the idea resurfaced on numerous occasions during the middle ages. Broadly speaking, the apocalyptic view of history took two forms. In one of these, a sense of dread predominated, dread of the coming of the Antichrist, or of the Day of Judgement, for example. The Italian dread of French invasions in the 1490s, the Sack of Rome in 1527, the dread of Turkish invasion of the empire, and on a larger scale the dread of Lutheran reform, were all fuel to the greater fear. Countering the pessimistic vision, however, there was the expectation of the second coming of the Messiah, which would be preceded, according to some, by a golden age. To many, this meant a universal Catholic church, incorporating the eastern church at the very least. To some Catholic writers, the conquests of the Portuguese and Spanish navigators promised the advent of universal Christianity. Even some of those humanists who saw a coming golden age in the recovery of ancient texts were able to persuade themselves that this token of history's cyclical nature was yet another reason for religious optimism.

Many of these ideas eventually found their way into the teachings of the Reformed sects. In Holbein's time the subject was giving rise to heated debate, even civil revolution, in parts of Germany, although the worst excesses were still in the future in 1533. No matter what it was that was thought likely to herald the end of the world, there remained the thorny question of when this would happen. In 1532 Frederick Nausea, a Württemberg theologian who was generally sceptical about astrological prediction, had preached sermons in Mainz and elsewhere in which he interpreted numerous strange happenings in the heavens as signifying that the world's end was close at hand. He was wise enough to refrain from setting a precise date.[284] In 1533 the celebrated Anabaptist visionary Melchior Hoffman preached that Christ's second coming was imminent, that it would dawn in Strasbourg, that 144,000 people would be saved (true to Revelation 14:1), after which the rest of the world would be consumed by fire. He was arrested and imprisoned in that city, whereupon leadership of the Anabaptists passed from him to the revolutionary Jan Matthys of Haarlem. What had begun as a relatively peaceful movement – one that took its name from its advocacy of adult baptism – quickly turned into an aggressive campaign in which the righteous were told to take up the sword against the ungodly, and so to prepare for the millennium. Matthys announced that it would materialise in 1534, at Easter. In February 1534 the forcible rebaptism of Lutherans and Catholics in Münster led them into war, and to even further spiritual excesses.[285] But again, this was in the future in 1533. There were, however, other predictions of Christ's imminent return in which the date was set in either 1532 or 1533, and they are of interest, since they were well known in circles with which Holbein maintained contact.

The predictions were made by Michael Stifel (c. 1487–1567), who was destined to become the leading German algebraist of the sixteenth century. A member of the same order of Augustinian hermits as Martin Luther, Stifel followed Luther's example and quit the cloister. He was eventually installed by Luther in the parish of Lochau (since renamed Annaburg). Stifel made a minor reputation with evangelical tracts in support of the reformer (1522–23), but when he published two books in Wittenberg in 1532 with apocalyptic subject matter, even though the first was anonymous, Luther became alarmed.[286] They were based not on astrological or astronomical considerations but on what Stifel called his *Wortrechnung* (word reckoning), his personal version of the cabalistic gematria, by which he assigned numbers to letters of the alphabet in various non-traditional ways. Thus in the first of his two books – many knew that he was the author – he took the roman numerals out of the Latin description of the crucified Christ (*Jesus Nazarenus Rex Judeorum*, Jesus of Nazareth, King of the Jews) and created a number equivalent to 1532 (that is, out of IVVXIVDVM, duly rearranged). In another example, he connected the Latin for 'behold the cross of Christ' with the battle of Heidelberg (1462). Using these techniques, almost anything was possible – when short of a thousand he was quite capable of introducing an M for *Mysterium*.

Luther advised him against continuing, but in vain. In the second work, *Vom End der Welt* (*On the End of the World*), he took a sentence from John 19:37: *Vid*eb*u*nt *in* *quem* trans*fix*er*u*nt, 'They shall look on him whom they pierced'. This follows the account of Jesus's death, and refers to the incident in which the Roman soldier pierced the side of the dead Christ. By rearranging the letters italicised here, Stifel derived the year 1533 (MDXVVVVIII). He decided that the world would end on a date in either September or October, and eventually settled on 19 October at 8 o'clock in the morning. He advised his congregation to prepare for the occasion, and no doubt the highly specific hour strengthened the conviction that he should be taken seriously. Labourers neglected their work, in preparation for the final day of judgement. Stifel and many of his flock gave away their possessions, some even burning down their houses, freeing themselves of all they owned so as to make the path to salvation easier. Crowds flocked to Stifel's parish church from far off places to greet the dawn of the fateful day, but he and they were disappointed. An hour after he had been proved wrong, he was arrested by the civil authorities, angry at the economic chaos in the region but not confident enough to arrest him sooner. Fortunately for the course of mathematics, he was freed at the request of Luther – whom at one stage he had characterised as Pontius Pilate – and Melanchthon. They eventually moved him to another parish: he was never entirely cured of his 'word reckoning', but it later took on more modest forms. By the time the sorry episode of October 1533 had played itself out, Holbein had presumably completed his dual portrait of the two Frenchmen, but the millennium, and Stifel's books and personal statements, seem likely to have been topics of

70. The crucifixion scene on the title page of Michael Stifel's *Vom End der Welt* (*On the End of the World*, Wittenberg, 1532). Stifel predicted that the world would end in 1533.

discussion in the Holbein–Kratzer circle during the very months in which the painting's complex scheme was being planned.

If there was ever any apocalyptic alarm expressed in London, it was uncalled for. The second coming of Christ did not occur during Easter 1533; and yet even retrospectively, Good Friday must have been regarded as a day of great symbolic moment, a millennium and a half after the first Good Friday. Dinteville and de Selve may not have had direct dealings with those who were voicing their millennial expectations in Germany, but had they known of them, it is unlikely that they would have remained indifferent, especially before Easter. Like all Christians they lived in hope of heaven. As educated men they would have framed their hope in the commonly accepted celestial imagery of the scriptures. In 1533 it so happens that the lesson for the day would have included the well-known *tibi dabo* passage from Christ's words to Peter, with a distinctly celestial colouring. In the text in which Christ promised Peter the keys to the kingdom of heaven, the same word (*coelum*) was used for God's heaven and the heaven described by the astronomers (Matthew 16:18–19).[287] Even the best theologians took a view of heaven much less abstract than that of later centuries. When the cross is laid on the earth, says one famous text on the discovery of the true cross, it points to north, south, east and west, the four corners of Christ's dominions. And when set upright, its arms distinguish right from left, good from bad, its foot is rooted in earth and its upright points directly to heaven.[288] Heaven was simply 'up above', and the cross could without any strain on meanings be made to serve as a cosmic symbol.

This kind of thinking is now largely outmoded, if not forgotten, but Holbein's painting owes more to it, and to the cosmic outlook of the middle ages, than is generally recognised. We have seen how the floor in the painting was derived directly from a pavement which was known to link human and celestial elements. A part of the meaning of that had always been Christ's role as saviour of the world. This we know from a large painted wooden panel, still to be seen in the south ambulatory of Westminster abbey, which stood as a retable at the back of the medieval high altar. Christ is there depicted holding a globe of the world as it was created by God in the beginning, with the waters, the firmament, the earth, vegetation, lights in the heavens, and living creatures on land, in the sea, and in the air. As was first pointed out by Paul Binski, the iconography is unusual, in that the Virgin and St John, both attending Christ, hold palm leaves. This is typical of scenes in which Christ is the Lamb of God, *Agnus Dei*, through whose death comes human redemption.[289] The retable is no crucifixion scene, but it could have shifted, however slightly, the mind of anyone perusing the pavement in Holbein's painting, for it was a part of what a visitor to the abbey saw in conjunction with the pavement there.

The visitor would no doubt also have known of the abbey's claim to have a piece of the true cross, housed within the altar. When Holbein and the others saw the pavement, that was yet another fact that might have reminded them of the salvation message. If the pavement in *The Ambassadors* was ever a talking point, by dint of its having been a scaled-down version of that in the abbey, then talk, or thought, may have spilled over into the realms of throne and retable. We are now in the land of meaning by association, a somewhat lawless territory. Discretion recommends that we do not press for one specific focus of meaning, even for a simple 'saviour of the world' reading. We must accept a blurring of focus. The painting is not a rigorously defined intellectual study of the constitution of the universe and its God-given harmony, of the sort that had been preached by the philosophers and theologians for centuries. Despite all its astronomical legerdemain, it conveys its human message, the central message of the Christian faith, in a partly evocative way – in that respect it shares its style with most religious sermons. It has expressive and emotive qualities that will remain hidden as long as we concentrate only on the academic disciplines illustrated at its centre.

SIXTEEN

ON PAINTERS AND AUTHORS

> You demonstrate nothing to anybody but those who understand your symbolic tongue.
>
> Thomas Hobbes, *Six Lessons* (1656), in *Works* (London, 1845), vii, p. 264

There is something more, concealed beneath the outwardly honest exterior of *The Ambassadors*, than the layers of meaning uncovered here – the half-hidden skull, the pavement and the two hexagrams, the three to the power of three, the lines of sight and hearing, and the horoscope. The additional element will be of little consequence to the ordinary spectator, and would have seemed of even less moment when the painting was done, if it were ever revealed by its author. In many ways, however, it is the most intriguing component of all. The painting seems to contain yet further pointers to the middle ages, and in particular to the work of the poet Geoffrey Chaucer.[290]

Chaucer's habit of concealing complex astronomical situations in his poetry remained largely unrecognised for well over five centuries, and even now the idea is resisted by many who are unable to accept that their hero's character differs from their own. Between the poet's death in 1400 and the late seventeenth century there were others who tried to imitate his astronomical style of allegory, although none put up a very convincing show. If we were to judge the case by the astronomical expertise shown in English poetry from Holbein's century, only one solitary poet would lead us to suspect that any deep and specific knowledge of Chaucer's technique had survived at all. The survival relates to Chaucer's *Parliament of Fowls*, which has a structure that rests heavily on the state of the heavens at or around the time of its composition. As Victoria Rothschild has shown, Edmund Spenser (1552/3–1599) imitates Chaucer's *Parliament* at several points in his long allegorical poem *The Faerie Queene* while in the 'Mutabilitie Cantos' he goes further, and openly invokes the aid of his master 'Dan Geffrey' – which is to say Geoffrey Chaucer.[291] Spenser refers explicitly to the 'Foules' Parley', the Birds' Parliament, and uses the calendar in half-concealed ways that are so similar to Chaucer's that one must suppose either that he worked it out for himself by careful analysis of his famous predecessor, or that he had access to some sort of key. The second seems the more likely.

Why this is a matter of such interest is that since some traces of Chaucer's astronomical technique are now known to have been passed on to an Elizabethan author, we need not be resolutely sceptical of the idea that others were known to Holbein, or to one of his group, in the intervening period. The reason for suspecting that this was so is that the horoscope uncovered in an earlier section of this book has an uncanny resemblance to one introduced surreptitiously by Chaucer near the end of his *Canterbury Tales*. The pilgrims have reached Canterbury, the Manciple has finished his tale, and the pilgrimage is coming to an end with the Parson telling what is to be the last tale of all – in reality it is a long sermon in prose, in character quite unlike most of what has gone before. *The Parson's Tale* is prefixed by a verse prologue, beginning with a dozen lines that simply cannot be understood except with reference to astronomy. In those lines the time of day is given obliquely, in terms that would have baffled the ordinary listener. It would all have been plain to any good astronomer of the period, however, granted a reliable text.[292] The poet announces the time by reference to the length of his own shadow. He leaves us with no explicit information as to the date, but gives us clues enough for it to be shown that the day may have belonged to one of a handful of specific years towards the end of the fourteenth century. I believe that the day was Good Friday, 16 April 1400. Chaucer died later in that year. More important than the year for us now is the astronomical and literary use that Chaucer made of a shadow.

As between the moment chosen for the scene in Holbein's painting of 1533 (a moment in time set by a date and a shadow) and that in 1400, or possibly an earlier year, to which Chaucer was drawing attention in equally precise terms (he actually states the altitude of the Sun quite explicitly), two key properties of the Sun are very similar. One is its position in the zodiac, near the beginning of Taurus, and the other is the point of the zodiac that is ascending over the horizon, the point that matters most to an astrologer. In both cases, this 'ascendent' is the very beginning of the sign of Libra, the Scales. Do such coincidences not need to be explained?

The easy way out is to say that one or the other is illusory, perhaps both. Having given arguments for both, and having heard no intelligent argument to the contrary, I cannot offer that primrose path. Another way of explaining the similarity of the two situations would be to say that the configuration of the heavens to which Chaucer was drawing attention (the Sun's place, the rising Libra, and some other points) could have been easily copied. This might have been so were all of Chaucer's astronomical data expressly quoted, but they are not. Only with some effort can they be extracted from his words.[293] He makes no explicit reference to the fact that it is Good Friday or to the year, for instance. A third way out might be to claim that there is a certain inevitability in the resemblance between the astronomical situations at four o'clock on Good Friday in those two years, 1400 and 1533, and that there was no other interdependence at all. May it not have been by sheer chance that two similar situations were hit upon?

Such a thing is possible, but the chances are not especially high. Good Friday can vary between wide limits in the calendar, giving utterly different astronomical configurations in different years, even in regard to the Sun, and even granting that special importance was ascribed to the hour of four o'clock on that day. (And where do we find evidence for that?) Just how similar were the two situations? Briefly, the similarities relate to the position of the Sun, which is on the point of leaving the eighth house, the house of death, in the horoscope. Within the zodiac, the Sun is in a place known to astrologers as the Moon's 'exaltation'. Also, as explained, both Chaucer and Holbein have the first degree of the sign of Libra ascending over the horizon. Such coincidences depend on similarities in the Sun's position in the zodiac and a common time of day, but Good Friday is not on a fixed date, so that such coincidences are far from inevitable.

To give an idea of what is involved in the claim of chance coincidence: we have already seen that there were four occasions between 1500 and 1533 when Good Friday fell between 10 and 13 April, to take a generous spread of dates within the year.[294] In those four special cases where Good Friday fell close to the day Chaucer chose, then something roughly similar would have been found as regards the Sun and everything having to do with matters of timing and the rising point of the zodiac.

But there is more to the coincidence we have found than this. There are also marked similarities of artistic expression. Both men 'state' the situation by reference to *a shadow with very special properties*, specified explicitly in Chaucer's case, and tacitly – through the distorted skull and the theme of 27 – by Holbein. Both schemes involve horoscopes, in the sense of astrologically remarkable configurations, even though one is a literary product and the other not.

It is undeniable that a standard horoscope square may be fitted precisely over the painting. It is also undeniable that if a horoscope was ever systematically calculated, it would have had several properties that a sixteenth-century astrologer would have judged to be very striking. If the planning of the square was deliberate then the calculation is very likely to have followed, yielding a complete set of positions for the Sun, Moon and planets. The astronomical details of all this follow quite automatically. Everything hangs on whether the horoscope square was ever deliberately superimposed. If we were dealing with only one instance, we might examine the resulting horoscope and ask whether it relates closely to the theme of the painting – or in Chaucer's case the poem. We have already touched on this question briefly, and have found that it does. But now we are in a new situation, for we can make further comparisons between the two supposed Good Friday horoscopes, those for 1400 and 1533. When this is done, it is found that their general resemblance goes far beyond the similarities already mentioned.

In both, the planets Saturn and Jupiter are in highly significant places, so much so that the decision to use the horoscope for artistic purposes would have been in both cases a very natural one. This is true despite the fact that the planets are in different positions. Saturn, the malevolent planet associated with melancholy and misfortune, takes nearly thirty years to go round the zodiac, and Jupiter takes almost twelve, so that their positions in the zodiac cannot be the same on dates that are 133 years apart. If we are to accept a date of 1400 for Chaucer's example, then Saturn is at its very lowest point. On the other hand Jupiter, planet of hope and judgement, has just come above the horizon, close to the rising head of Libra, the sign of the scales and another symbol of judgement. In Holbein's case, the planet Saturn is virtually overhead, while Jupiter is at the lowest point. The potential interpretation of this latter situation has already been given. The two cases are different, but they have enough in common for it to be quite plausible that the one inspired the other. Such similarities do recur, but over intervals of the order of decades, not years.

The two situations may be easily compared by showing their key elements as they would have appeared on an astrolabe. Both Chaucer and Kratzer were at home with this type of representation. It is not necessary to explain it in detail here. Suffice it to say that an astrolabe presents a graphical representation of the daily rotation of the stars, Sun and (with additional help) Moon and planets, not in three dimensions, as on a globe, but on a flat surface. It has a rotatable part of pierced metal (called the 'rete') carrying the stars, and behind the fretwork of the rete may be seen various local features such as the fixed local horizon and the vertical meridian line. On the moving rete there is a ring representing the zodiac on which are marked the signs of the zodiac, and on which one might place temporary marks for the positions of the planets within the signs. There is also on the rete of the astrolabe a natural cross-like structure. These elements are shown in Fig. 71 in the positions they would have occupied at four o'clock on Good Friday, first for Chaucer's 1400 and then for Holbein's 1533. The planets most important to the scheme are shown too on the drawing. It will be seen that Libra, the sign of the scales, appears to hang from one arm of the cross, rather as it does in the manuscript illustration of Fig. 73, to be considered shortly. Compare Fig. 72, which illustrates an unusually simple astrolabe, but one

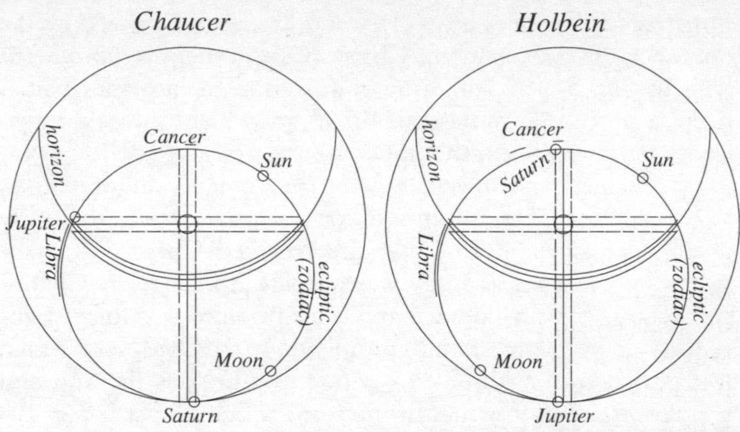

71. The configuration of the heavens as shown on an astrolabe, for Good Friday 1400 (left) and 1533 (right). Note how the sign of Libra seems to hang from the cross.

that picks out exactly the point being made here about the cross.

If the astronomical and stylistic resemblance of the poem and the painting did not come about by chance, did it perhaps come about through reliance on a shared source, or a broad common tradition, rather than by direct influence? Potentially shared sources there were, even though there is reason to think that the connection with Chaucer was much more immediate. We begin with tradition.

A SHARED TRADITION?

That Christ's crucifixion was historically associated with the rising of the sign of Libra, the Scales, has already been touched upon.* The association was not commonplace, but neither was it rare. Francis Wormald drew attention to a connection between the cross and the balance in medieval religious art when he discussed two early fifteenth-century south German miniatures depicting scales hanging from one arm of the cross.[295]

* See p. 236 above.

One pan of the scales bears sins, and is counterbalanced by the other bearing the passion of Christ. (One of them is reproduced here in Fig. 73.)[296] An earlier illustration he provides comes from a so-called 'moralised Bible' in which there are two associated medallions, the upper having an image of Job holding a balance, the lower showing the crucifixion of Christ. Wormald was able to find literary support from the early middle ages for the idea that the crucified Christ was to be seen as a balance. His study was reinforced in 1970 by Chauncey Wood,[297] who noted that Pierre Bersuire – a fourteenth-century encyclopaedist and commentator on Ovid, and a man intoxicated with symbolism – wrote of Christ as the Sun and *the ascendent Libra* as the throne from which Christ judges the

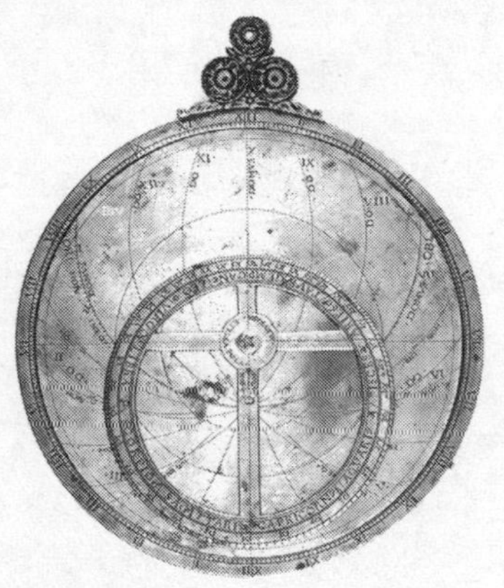

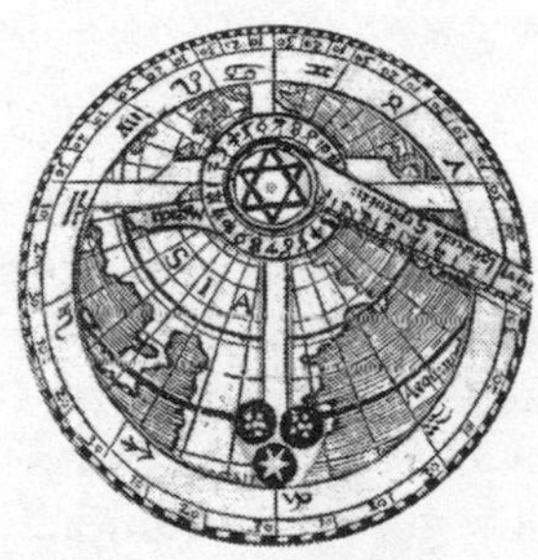

72. An astrolabe by the German maker Johannes Wagner, dated 1538, here shown with its zodiac ring and (unusually pronounced) cross placed exactly as in the previous figures. The instrument has lines to calculate the astrological houses and carries no star pointers. It was evidently for mainly astrological use. The figure on the right is the zodiac ring abstracted from Apian's paper terrestrial instrument, showing also its central hexagram boss. As on the astrolabe, the sign of the Scales seems to hang from the left arm of the cross while the Ram sits above the arm on the right. This figure could also have been used to reinforce the suggestion made earlier in connection with Fig. 40, that the concealed hexagram and cross in the painting may have been related in position. The pointer is by chance shown at approximately the same angle as the line of sight to Christ's eye. (Astrolabe: *Museum of the History of Science, Oxford*)

just and the unjust. A manuscript by the fourteenth-century political writer Opicinus de Canistris – a priest from Pavia who probably knew Bersuire – twice drew the crucifixion in the position of Libra in the zodiac.[298]

There are many other medieval precedents for these ideas, which some astrologers were pleased to be able to connect with their belief that Libra was rising when Christ was born.[299] In an allegory of the zodiac written early in the twelfth century, Philipp of Thaun identified Libra with the judgement of souls. At the end of the next century Arnald of Villanova, writing on zodiacal imagery and engraved images – that is, writing at the very edge of magical practice – mentions the hour of Christ's death with an explicit symbolisation of the crucifixion by the sign of Libra. Early in the fourteenth century we find the Oxford theologian Robert Holcot explaining how Libra is 'the balance of sin'. This is in chapter 61 of his book *Super sapientiam Salomonis* (*On the Wisdom of Solomon*), where the life of Christ is placed in the context of a universal world history based on the imagery of the zodiac. In other words, astrological materials relating Libra to the crucifixion of Christ are not at all rare, and we should not be surprised to find that the image was still in use in the early sixteenth century. Indeed, seventeenth-century writers, seizing on an analogy used by the ancient astrologer-poet Manilius, who had compared Libra and the constellation of the Lyre, created out of it a triple analogy involving *the crucifixion, Libra and a lute*. I know of no use of that particular idea prior to Holbein, but there can be no doubt about the moderately widespread awareness of the simpler parallel. There is a case to be made out for a concealed application of it in a crucifixion by the painter Raphael, often called the Mond Crucifixion, but this speculation is tentative, and should not be allowed to draw attention away from the plain evidence we have from other sources.[300]

Should we expect any such association in an image used by Holbein, one with an evident link with shadows? Holbein's painting does make use of an astronomical artifice that is completely out of character with what we know of him. We are dealing here with markedly academic knowledge, and not

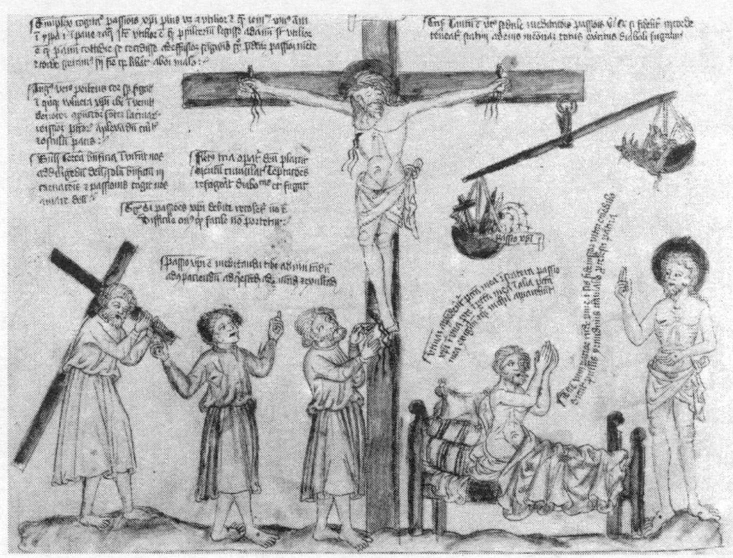

73. The scales in which sins are weighed, in a fifteenth-century south German manuscript illustration of the *Ars moriendi* (*Art of Dying*), London, Wellcome Historical Medical Museum and Library, MS 49, fol. 62v.

merely the use of techniques for perspective painting, whether by central projection or anamorphosis, that he might have worked out from his own experience. Once again, the solution surely lies neither with Dinteville nor de Selve, for while both of them were well educated, neither is likely to have been long enough in an English environment to have come across the Chaucerian device. Nicolaus Kratzer, on the other hand, who was familiar with Chaucer's London, and with astronomy's Oxford, could perhaps have acquired knowledge of it in the way that Spenser acquired a knowledge of some of Chaucer's other ruses. It need not have come from a reading of Chaucer's poetry at all, but might have been found hinted at in a document by Chaucer, or closely connected with him. The basic idea is simple enough to a person trained in astronomy, and could have been explained to him in only two or three lines. Once in possession of the idea, Holbein's astronomer friend would have explained it to the painter along with his various schemes for building it into the instruments, and knowing Holbein's concern with shadows.

CHAUCER AT THE COURT OF HENRY VIII

No such document is known, but there is an intriguing link between Kratzer and Holbein and the man who in their day knew more about the poet than anyone else. Chaucer's first scholarly editor, William Thynne, was an Oxford-educated Shropshire man who had entered service in the household of Henry VIII by at least 1524. By 1526 he was chief clerk of the kitchen, with control of banqueting, and he had an official residence at Greenwich. Thynne rose steadily in the royal service, and died in 1546. (A memorial brass in All Hallows church, Barking, still survives to mark his burial.) The dissolution of the monasteries and the scattering of their libraries was a blessing to Thynne, who had long before begun to collect all the Chaucer manuscripts he could lay his hands on. The year previous to the painting of *The Ambassadors*, 1532, saw his first published edition of them, issued from the press of Thomas Godfray: *The Workes of Geffray Chaucer Newly Printed, with Dyvers Workes Whiche Were Never in Print Before.*

That edition actually has a title page with a border after a design by Holbein, something of which the painter was presumably not ignorant (Fig. 74).[301] The edition itself was a product of national pride, dedicated to a king who was in need of national support, a king with 'the glorious tytell of Defensor of the christen faithe'. By the time he produced a second edition of Chaucer's works, Thynne chose to include in it a spurious anti-papist work, *The Plowman's Tale.* His son claimed that he wanted to include another, *The Pilgrim's Tale* – also a thinly-veiled attack on the Roman church – but that opposition by Cardinal Wolsey prevented it.[302] Muddled though this story is, it helps us to form a picture of the rapidly growing esteem in which Chaucer's name was held at the very time of the painting. Blinded by the image we have of humanist learning around Henry's court, we might have been inclined to suppose that for Holbein or his advisers to have picked up a trick or two from Chaucer would have smacked of unacceptable medievalism, but that is plainly untrue. For every Thomas More at court there were in this respect no doubt a dozen Thynnes.

The potential Holbein-Chaucer link does not end with a title page, or with the fact that Thynne and Holbein were both in their different ways satellites of the same court. There is another educated royal servant of Holbein's acquaintance who might conceivably have entered into the planning of *The Ambassadors*, namely Sir Brian Tuke. The king's antiquary John Leland tells us something about Tuke that is confirmed by a statement penned by the man himself, in a copy of Thynne's Chaucer that is now in the library of Clare College, Cambridge. It was evidently Tuke who wrote the preface to it:

> This preface I sir Bryane Tuke knight wrot at the request of Mr Clarke of the Kechyn then being tarying for the tyde at Grenewiche.[303]

Tuke was certainly well known to Holbein, for not only was his portrait done on several occasions by the artist but it was Tuke, treasurer of the household from 1528 onwards, who was responsible for administering payment to the painter from the royal accounts.[304] Kratzer would have been even better acquainted with him.

If Chaucer's astronomical scheme for Good Friday was known to anyone at this time – for example from some brief explanatory statement about it by Chaucer or a third party – it would have been known to Thynne, the assiduous collector of Chauceriana, and possibly also to Tuke. The preface written by Tuke is phrased in such a way that he probably meant the reader to think that Thynne was its author – thus he writes as though it is the author of the preface who has sought out Chaucer manuscripts. It is for the most part a platitudinous essay on the growth of literary language, and certainly gives us no real clue as to what, if anything, was then understood of the finer points of Chaucerian astronomy. There is in it no more

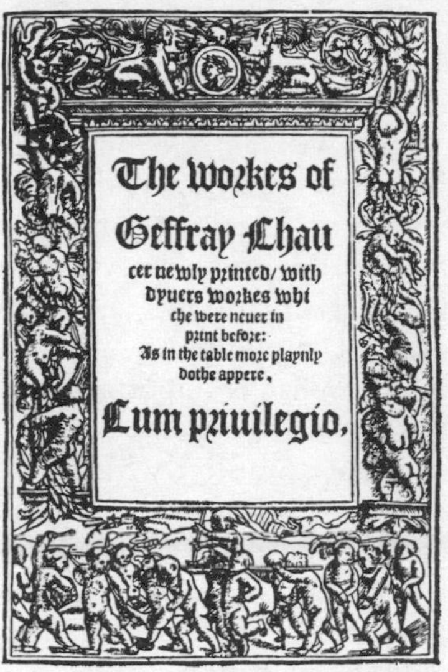
The workes of
Geffray Chau
cer newly printed/ with
dyuers workes whi
che were neuer in
print before:
As in the table more playnly
dothe appere.
Cum priuilegio.

74. The title page to Thynne's 1532 edition of Chaucer's collected works. Woodcut after a design by Holbein.

than a passing allusion to Chaucer's 'excellent lernyng in all kyndes of doctrynes and sciences', but that is better than nothing. It is hard to assess the expertise of these two senior royal servants on their own account. Tuke's eloquence was praised by Leland in nine Latin poems, and he is said to have written against Polydore Vergil, the Italian humanist long resident in England,[305] but this does not turn him into a decoder of Chaucerian astronomy. He was a deeply religious man, and one of Holbein's portraits of him contained three of the key ingredients of the portrait of the ambassadors. In it Tuke wears a large crucifix on a chain and over his shoulder there appears a skull as part of a full-scale skeletal figure that is drawing his attention to a timepiece on the table in front of them, a timepiece in the form not of a sundial but rather a sandglass.[306] It cannot be said that this Tuke portrait has any deep allegorical promise, beyond its obvious intimations of mortality and its call to piety.

Thynne seems a likelier candidate for handing on the Chaucerian clue, even if he was ignorant of its finer points, but the evidence is all too slender. His son Francis (1545?–1608) displayed a passable astronomical understanding, but if it came from his father – whom he can hardly even have remembered – it came not directly but through his books and papers. Whether or not William Thynne ever recognised as much, his son Francis certainly knew that Chaucer had not been using astronomy for merely decorative effect. As Francis states at one point in his commentary, he corrected the text 'accordynge as Chaucer sett it down . . . that yt may stande with alle mathematicall proportione, which Chaucer knewe and observed there'. What is important is not that he made a hash of the text but that he seems to have had enough in his possession to encourage him to try his hand at Chaucer's game. Francis tells of a manuscript owned and used by his father that seems to have been actually checked by Chaucer.[307] If William Thynne had materials so close to the poet then he may also have had an astronomical note or fuller explanation now unknown to us, indicating Chaucer's plans.

To repeat a point made earlier: Kratzer, or whoever was responsible for Holbein's complex set of astronomical schemes, did not need more assistance than could have been put into a short marginal note. Indeed, we must if possible produce an explanation consistent with the fact that Thynne's printed text at the relevant place in the prologue to the *Parson's Tale* is a very inferior one. Thynne's edition makes the Sun's height approach 25 degrees, and not 29 as it should be, according to the best manuscripts. He makes the time ten o'clock, and the height of the shadow-casting person five and not six 'feet'. This is a travesty of Chaucer's intentions, but we can make something of even this text.

Let us suppose that Kratzer saw or learned of a note in which it was stated that a passage in Chaucer set the scene for four o'clock on Good Friday by quoting a shadow length in round numbers. He might also have been told that there were symmetrically placed Saturn and Jupiter positions corresponding to it – rising, setting, culminating, or at lower mid-heaven. He would have needed nothing more than that, two or three sentences at most, to have been inspired to check for a similar arrangement. Were he also to have been given a date of 1400, however, he would inevitably have argued in a different way. He would not have needed to check year by year to find a parallel. He would have argued that since there were exactly seven Easter cycles of 19 years between 1400 and 1533, he might reasonably expect to reach a similar *solar* configuration as Chaucer had done. In either case he might simply have said that if Chaucer could express the time and date in shadows, so could he. As I am sure he did. And in doing so he would have discovered the very apt positions of the superior planets Saturn and Jupiter.

At present this is as far as the argument can be taken, but at least we can say that both Thynne and Tuke knew Kratzer, and that if either had needed an explanation of any manuscript with an astronomical gloss on Chaucer's text, Kratzer would have been the man to provide it. On balance, the 27 degree angle of the Holbein shadows, and the horoscope in *The Ambassadors* for the afternoon of Good Friday in 1533, seem to point to Kratzer's having been introduced to the mysteries of Chaucer's *Prologue to the Parson's Tale* by one of the two editors. The only probable alternative, granting that the 1533 horoscope was consciously introduced into the painting – its 'existence' is incontrovertible – is that we are dealing with a case of independent invention. To opt for a coincidence of this order, in view of the 1532 link between Holbein, Thynne and Chaucer, seems to me to be mildly perverse.

THE TRUE AUTHOR

The argument, if it is accepted, cannot be allowed to stop there. Kratzer is our strongest candidate by far for the drafting of the 'rising Libra' horoscope and for all other astronomical 'shadow' aspects of the design. He must have had much responsibility for selecting the time *and even the day.* Dinteville and de Selve were perhaps offered the day, Good Friday, only after Kratzer had discovered that it was going to possess astronomical properties that would be potentially useful for their symbolic value. Working out astrologically propitious times in advance was an important part of a Renaissance astrologer's task. Casting an 'election' horoscope was an especially common occasion for this type of calculation, done when a person of note was selecting the right moment to embark on an important journey or to begin a great building project – such as when Pope Julius II embarked on his scheme to rebuild the basilica of St Peter's, Rome, in 1506. It is surely to Kratzer that we should assign credit for not only anticipating the striking state of the heavens but for realising the properties of a gradient of one in two, that is, its proximity to 27°, with all that the number implies numerologically and geometrically for the layout of the panel. Holbein would have been able to cope with the page of the arithmetic text, but on the whole the number 27 occurs so often in a 'shadow' context that once again it seems most probable that Kratzer deserves the credit. And the same goes for the upper hexagram and the complex setting of the globe. Who else but Kratzer could have planned such things? Judging by his choice of eight biographies from the fifty in Plutarch, Georges de Selve was more fascinated by public and military life than by the contemplative arts. Dinteville's career seems to offer no period when he could have acquired the necessary skills. Such things were not mastered in a day.

Here we come up against an unavoidable problem. The artist must, to a greater or lesser degree, reach a compromise between his own wishes and those of his patron and any onlooker he may wish to address. Assuming that hidden meanings were meant to be concealed from all but a select circle, we are left looking to the probable attitude of Dinteville and the likely compliance of the young but high-ranking cleric de Selve. We cannot be absolutely certain that the painting was not commissioned by the bishop as a gift for his friend, although on balance that seems unlikely. On the fundamental Christian message of Easter it is unlikely that there was real disagreement among them. Holbein at this stage in his career owed his fame above all to his portraits, but he had undertaken religious pictures over a long period, and had an intimate knowledge of Catholic convention. Christ's Passion was a recurring theme, and there is no reason to doubt his religious sincerity or to interpret even his notorious *Body of the Dead Christ in the Tomb* as anything other than an act of piety. We certainly do not need to take seriously the view of André Suarès that the painting proves that Holbein was an out-and-out atheist.[308] Was Holbein's frightening reminder of the reality of Christ's death any different in character and motive from the innumerable aids to devotion to be found in medieval churches and books? John Ruskin would have said it was, for he abhorred the art of the Renaissance for its use of the science of the sepulchre to exalt the skill of the artist rather than to exalt God. One would like to have had Ruskin's reaction to the idea that Holbein could use science to *hide* devotional content.

The esoteric beliefs likely to have been held by Dinteville, which Holbein may have been persuaded to incorporate in the painting, are another matter. It is whispered that the young ambassador interested himself in the occult, but no direct evidence has as yet been published. There is no reason to think of him as a scholar of note, but like so many in his time he may have played the part of flotsam in a sea of fashionable Neoplatonic mysticism. Perhaps the hexagram in the picture was added in a response to a request from Dinteville that the order of St Michael to which he belonged be given a place deep in the allegory of the painting. And perhaps there is more vanity in evidence in the medallion than was entirely proper to the solemn day. The painting was destined for Dinteville's Polisy château, and unless it was a gift from his friend we must suppose that he commissioned it.

Of the four men, Dinteville seems to be the one most likely to have played the lute, but it is most unlikely that his personal fortunes were connected with the broken string, unless we have completely missed the point, and the dual portrait was in part a symbol of dual unhappiness. Musical harmony is to music and the sense of hearing what perspective is to the painter and the sense of vision. The pragmatic Holbein and even the scholar-virtuoso Kratzer do not strike us as the sort of men to have thought of them as purely abstract disciplines. Music and painting would have been tacitly considered by all concerned in this enterprise as practical disciplines informed by art, in the more modern sense of the word. Was it in character with any of the four men to have considered penning a treatise on the allegorical and the literal, on plain and hidden truths, on truth and falsehood in representation? The very existence of a painting like *The Ambassadors* shows that one or more of them, or of their circle, confronted just such problems. It is of very doubtful relevance that an astrological note on the first leaf of Kratzer's 'Maurbach' papers associates Libra with men who play on musical instruments such as pipes and lutes, and with the element air. This was part of a standard astrological doctrine of the elements. It seems more likely that there is some sort of allusion being made to theories of harmony and perspective. Those theories provide a foundation for a rational analysis of the relations between the world outside us and the senses of hearing and of vision by which we learn of it. The distorted perspective of the foreground skull is really no different from the break in the lute string, in the sense that both disturb the established order. Each is a distortion, and when properly considered each seems to offer paradoxically an insight into a truer world. What at first sight is no more than a series of tricks played on the senses turns out in the end to be a solemn religious statement. It is as though Holbein is telling us to correct our moral judgement by reference to Christ's, in the way that we correct the distortion of the skull.

SEVENTEEN
APELLES AND CLIO

[*Duke*] 'One face, one voice, one habit and two persons;
A natural perspective, that is and is not.'

Shakespeare, *Twelfth Night*, act v, scene 1

To suggest that there was more than one person behind the planning of *The Ambassadors* is not to detract in any way from Holbein's final responsibility for it, or for the genius that lies behind its execution. He was a product of his age, conforming to the often strange rules of his time, but there is an honesty and a vitality in the painting that comes from him alone, and to most of those who marvel at his work those qualities have an infinitely stronger appeal than his concealed designs are ever likely to have. His paintings, however, were the product of hand and eye and mind. To call *The Ambassadors* a 'painting' tends to suppress that idea, as though the paint was what mattered most. It is rather as though one were to describe all works of literature as 'inkings'. The double portrait offers proof, if any were needed, that unequalled though he was as a painter of what he saw, Holbein was not above collaborating with others in affairs of the mind. It is proof that he was never more successful than when he did so. History is now wary of the notion of the Renaissance mind, since it seems to carry with it the notion of a dominant intellectual and creative pattern that is in truth very hard to find in sixteenth-century life as a whole, whether in London or in Florence. There is certainly something odd about applying a nineteenth-century French label to an earlier Italian cultural movement, and then adapting it to an entire European historical period, during which a small minority – some of the best of them from northern Europe – happened to have fallen in love with classical antiquity. No matter how it is defined, most 'Renaissance thought' has medieval streams flowing into it and through it. And no matter how we look at paganising European artists and writers of the period running from the fourteenth century to the sixteenth, we shall find it impossible to conjure away entirely the bedrock of Christianity, which was in no sense new, Protestantism notwithstanding. *The Ambassadors* tells us as much.

Despite such qualifications, there was much that was new and exciting afoot when Holbein was at work, and of which he was certainly conscious. Religious art was suffering a decline, given the spiritual uncertainties associated with the Reformation. It was a diagnosis offered by several critics in the nineteenth century that art as a whole suffered in Holbein's time, with the decline of religious inspiration. Holbein, however, was not one to allow the grass to grow under his feet. He did not need to be either a religious reformer or one of a select group of scholarly initiates to feel that he lived in an age that owed much of its vigour to the opportunities it offered to individuals of merit. It was an age that positively encouraged self-definition. He must have felt it on his own behalf and on behalf of those he served. His portraiture served the new cult of the 'dignity and excellence of man', to use a phrase common among the humanists. Young and inexperienced as they are, the bailly of Troyes and the bishop of Lavaur are shown to us as men of rank and moral stature, men who lived in a three-dimensional world, with feet on the ground but with thoughts in tune with the divine. Or that, at least, was the theory. In practice, as Holbein through his art shows us equally plainly, they were men of their time, taking delight in some of the great intellectual diversions of the time, which could carry their thoughts away from the uncertainties of the moment. New worlds were meeting with old, new forms of scientific and human understanding were being mingled with old – gematria with theology, alchemy with astrology, perspective with the techniques of astronomical instrument making, anamorphosis with 'true' perspective, and so forth. Intriguing and even awe-inspiring new ways of encoding familiar truths were being canvassed. It does no harm to label them as facets of 'Renaissance thought' but, whether or not we do so, Holbein's portrait of the two French ambassadors seems to give credence to a number of them. These things had the power to startle and excite. No matter that Kratzer was needed, as an expert scriptwriter. Most of us today would be hard pressed to create the things we value most as symbols.

The use of symbols in a painting could make it profoundly fascinating. Patterns show a deeper truth than atoms of paint, however sensitively applied. 'And though painting bee a diverse matter from carving, yet doe they both arise of one selfe fountaine [namely] of a good patterne.' The opinion was that put forward by one of the leading characters in Baldassare Castiglione's *Libro del cortegiano* (*Book of the Courtier*) of 1528.[309] It was an opinion voiced as almost a truism, for the simple reason that it had been actively discussed by so many others at the time, and in this instance was very probably derived fairly directly from Leonardo. We should not allow ourselves to be misled by the seemingly endless Renaissance discussion of the importance of 'pattern' and 'design' into confusing two sorts of pattern. One is calculated to make a painting aesthetically pleasing, the other is a pattern concealed in the placement of the elements, which might have no consequences whatsoever for its beauty. The first was a favourite idea, much discussed, since it had been sanctioned by Plato and Aristotle, not to mention many other classical writers. Stimulated by some of Socrates' ideas, Plato in his *Philebus* had proposed a distinctly intellectualist theory of beauty that gave pride of place to formal and structural properties. This linked aesthetics with geometry, often alluded to as the geometry of divine proportion, since the harmonies could be likened to those in God's first creative act. It gave the more thoughtful painters and sculptors – who were often unduly sensitive to the common idea that they were merely rude mechanicals – cause for pride in their profession. Once their status was widely acknowledged, they felt free to squabble over whether painting should take precedence over poetry, sculpture over painting, and so forth. Leonardo, a naive empiricist when it came to understanding astronomy, even tried to make that subject a daughter of painting.[310] Such questions of aesthetics are no longer fashionable, but they are in any case entirely distinct from the themes of this book, even though they also have to do with geometrical composition and form rather than content. It is a moot point whether hidden mysteries of form have anything to do with beauty as such. They may stir the emotions in a rather similar way when they are revealed, and they may come under the heading 'art' in certain traditional senses of the word – Aristotle's, for instance – but not in any common modern sense.

The remark taken from the debate recounted by Castiglione went with other platitudes. One was that the arts were good because the ancients valued them; another was that a prime reason for portraiture was commemoration. The two ambassadors know that they will soon be going their separate ways, and they wish to have a record of their meeting. A scheme with a solemn allegorical meaning will enhance the value of that commemorative act. On the other hand, the painting is destined to be an ornament. What better than an ornament with a hidden dimension that one may discuss with guests? It will surely enhance its owner's prestige. What better way of ensuring this than by having it painted by Apelles, a specialist in portraiture and a servant of the English king? With a painting of this quality, would Dinteville not rise in the estimation of his cousin Anne de Montmorency, that consummate collector of great art? 'The painting adorns my château, just as great paintings adorn royal palaces and just as I adorned the English court.' It is a message we can imagine Dinteville conveying obliquely to his guests at a later date, suppressing all mention of the cold winds and rain, and of absent friends. It is a commemoration. Each ambassador seems to show a measure of confidence in his role in life, and yet neither is caught by the painter in the sort of situation that tells us about his daily life. In this it differs from the Kratzer portrait, for example. On the other hand, neither sitter is acting out a part, such as might have been created either by himself or by the artist for him. The acting, such as it is, has been left to the 'still life' – to use that conventional but very unsatisfactory term. This is no exercise in wanton display, although there is perhaps just a soupçon of intellectual flattery in it.

It is its hidden patterns that make *The Ambassadors*

exceptional – 'unique' is a dangerous word, although the temptation to use it is strong. Speaking of it in this way, however, is not without its problems. As soon as we classify it, say as a 'still life friendship painting', we have begun to half close our eyes to its hidden depths. 'The instruments show the vanity of the sciences', we hear, and we close our minds to the truth, which is that they show exactly the opposite. There is nothing vain about them: they are necessary instruments of understanding, but of understanding more than simple scientific truths. Taxonomy, in short, can be a deadly art, especially when it is designed to suppress the supposedly debasing scientific element. Our devout nineteenth-century forebears had the same way of dispensing with paganism, classifying it out of existence.

If we wish to make use of the painting to prove a wider thesis about northern Renaissance art and thought, then an exceptional or unique painting makes a poor foundation. Generalising from a single instance is not without its difficulties. There was no shortage of artists in the fifteenth and sixteenth centuries, especially in Italy, whose imaginations were fired by the mystery cults then being uncovered by students of classical learning, especially of Neoplatonism, cults that persuaded artists to create opaque allegories out of pagan deities and myths. *The Ambassadors* does not fall easily into any of the standard Renaissance categories, because it contains hard calculation. It does, however, have certain elements in common with other products of the time, and this is not a platitude: in many a general study of humanist themes in Renaissance art, Holbein's name is conspicuous by its absence, except in his role as the portraitist of Erasmus.

A scholarly love of classical antiquity took different people in different ways. We need only mention the names of Ficino, Pico, Lefèvre d'Etaples, Reuchlin, de Bouelles and Agrippa to see how different they could be. The tensions to which a Christian upbringing subjected them all could have strange effects – as when Lefèvre claimed to gain an insight into Aristotle's works with the self-proclaimed help of divine illumination. There are in *The Ambassadors* no classical characters, historical or mythological, acting out their parts, for above all else this is a Christian allegory. Holbein did not introduce obviously pagan characters, but still he gives us a taste of a pagan world, for instance in the Christianised Greek cosmology in the pavement, and in the related hexagrams. Humanist scholars with their noses in Neoplatonic texts – and we have already met many of them – were able to taste these illicit delights, using the excellent excuse that they were furthering classical learning. In theological debate the problem was acute enough. Ficino and Erasmus were not above elevating Socrates to sainthood. The title of Ficino's *Theologia platonica* announces his wish to integrate Platonism with the Christian faith. Some scholars, such as Dinteville's probable acquaintance Guillaume Budé, agonised over the fundamental disagreement between pagan Greek and Christian belief, in the end grudgingly recognising that each might supplement the other.

The humanists gave less of their time to natural than to moral philosophy, with its emphasis on personal and social values. This was not the best tool for unveiling cosmic truth, but the natural and exact sciences had too weak a foundation in letters for them to be high on the humanist agenda, and astrology was in a strange category: it did not require to be rediscovered, for it had never lost its academic status or its fascination. Like Hermeticism it was perceived to antedate Christianity and to hail from the East, which gave it a cachet of mystery. It had only weak literary credentials from Greece and Rome, and yet it was established in both cultures. It had fallen foul of some of the great theologians, and yet it had a secure place in artistic life. Writers and artists had learned to weave their materials out of planetary characters, according to rigorously controlled but mainly arbitrary pseudo-astronomical rules. The rules were often respected, it seems, for no better reason than that they were difficult to apply. If, as claimed here, they were applied in the planning of Holbein's painting, the act would not have earned unqualified approval.

No one will deny that *The Ambassadors* invokes mysteries of some sort, but it is important to distinguish two very different ways in which it does so. The Christian symbolism of a torn curtain, the skull of Adam, the archangel Michael, Sun, Moon and Cross; the Christianised pagan symbolism relating to the Sun and to the creation of the world; the more or less neutral symbolism of the broken lute string: all of these are mysteries on which the painter draws, but they are all distinct from the compositional mysteries. It is in its carefully orchestrated design that the painting is truly exceptional. Those who revile outlandish ideas of the first kind, perhaps horrified at the idea that Holbein could have entertained them, might consider the words of a kindred spirit, the no-nonsense Henry Hallam, who tacitly acknowledged that if nonsense was history, then it was his job to relate it:

> It would be trifling to give one moment's consideration to this gibberish, were it not evidently connected with superstitious absurdities, that enchained the mind of Europe for generations. We see the credence in witchcraft and spectral appearances, in astrology, in magical charms, in demoniacal possessions, those fruitful springs of infatuation, wretchedness and crime, sustained by an impudent parade of metaphysical philosophy.[311]

Hallam is no longer read today, but in his crude way he put his finger on a simple truth that is often overlooked. The process of 'enchaining the European mind', to the extent that this is not an exaggeration, was possible because it had a basis in reasoned rather than reasonable argument. The systems of thought which we have touched upon in these pages were real. Their existence can be demonstrated even when in some cases their use can only be conjectured. They were real enough – rewarded by money for example, by satisfaction, by glory, even death. They were real, but whether they are truly to be found in the painting needs supporting argument. Suppose that, one by one, its separate esoteric symbols are dismissed, as figments of our imagination. There will still remain the mysteries of design – if that is the right phrase – that start very obviously with the anamorphosed skull.

In dealing with 'pagan mysteries' that were mostly of the first sort, Edgar Wind noted how so many Renaissance humanists picked up the mocking tone of the ancients when they spoke of mysteries. Perhaps there was an element of 'playing seriously' in Holbein's painting too, but if so it is not obvious. What can be said is that it fits well into the category of what Wind describes as 'conceited art', which as he says, quoting E. M. Forster, has not met with much sympathy from men of experience. Forster's point was that if a work of art parades a mystifying element, then to that extent it is not a work of art, 'not an immortal Muse but a Sphinx who dies as soon as her riddles are answered'.[312] Wind admits that there are symbols which fit this description. 'They disturb us', he writes, 'as long as we do not understand them, and bore us as soon as we do'; but he insists that great symbols are the reverse of the Sphinx, more alive when the riddle is answered. There were at least four men privy to the riddle of *The Ambassadors* when it was painted, all of whom would have agreed.

APPENDIX I

PIERO DELLA FRANCESCA'S BAPTISM OF CHRIST

The painting is generally acknowledged to be entirely by Piero's own hand. Opinion is divided on the matter of date, but it is perhaps from the period 1450–55 (Kenneth Clark), and some argue for a date before 1451. There is little to be gained by systematically reviewing here the many attempts made over the years to determine the scheme of Piero's painting, but it is instructive to contrast the instinctive approach of Clark with the contrived precision of B. A. R. Carter's analysis.[313] Clark's 'few seconds' analysis' allowed him to write that 'The horizontal divisions come, of course, on the line of the dove's wings and the line of the angels' hands, Christ's loin-cloth and the Baptist's left hand; the vertical divisions are the pink [central] angel's columnar drapery, the central line of the Christ and the back of St John'. He went on to mention a triangle having its *apex* at the dove and its *base* at the lower horizontal, in other words a triangle the inverse of Carter's. Clark calls his own reading of the pattern of the painting 'the kind of simple geometric scheme which Alberti used in his façades' and adds that 'it is questionable if Piero calculated many of the minor relationships; more probably once the main scaffolding of proportion was established the details fell into place as a result of his own instinct for the general harmony'.

We only have to read Piero's mathematical works, however, to appreciate how much he was obsessed with precision in calculation, and so to suspect that Clark's free and easy analysis in terms of an instinct for general harmony fails to do justice to the formal side of the painting. (His sparkling general critique of the painting is another matter entirely.) Carter made real progress when he worked a pentagon construction into his account, and those few art historians who are prepared to entertain the idea of a hidden geometry – and are not too timid to declare their views – seem now prepared to take at least parts of his construction on board. Just as the dove was a conventional symbol for the Holy Spirit (Matthew 3:16: 'And Jesus, when he was baptised, went up straightway out of the water: and, lo, the heavens were opened unto him, and he saw the Spirit of God descending like a dove, and lighting upon him'), so were various five-pointed figures often used to symbolise the five wounds of Christ and so Christ himself. But Carter's account, like Clark's, goes beyond a few fairly conventional symbols. Both consider overall harmonies in the placement of the parts of the painting. The upper part of Christ's body is well fitted to the upper vertex of Carter's pentagram. He tries to account for the height of the image of Christ in terms of a figure closely related to the pentagram. He adds together the lengths of three sides of a regular *fifteen*-sided polygon. This seems to me to be too artificial, for there is no immediate connection between the (imagined) sides and Christ in the painting; but my chief reason for doubting whether Carter arrived at Piero's complete plan is that his two key geometrical figures (the star-pentagon and the equilateral triangle, Fig. 75) are themselves not related to one another in a very strong geometrical sense. That such figures can be strongly related should be clear from my Fig. 76, which has the mathematically appealing qualities of generality and simplicity. For this reason I feel sure that Piero would have taken pride in them, if they were indeed his. But that, alas, does not prove that they were.

The lower (roughly square) section of Piero's poplar panel, as Carter noted, is almost exactly two Florentine braccia wide, which suggested to him that the overall *width* of the panel is the right starting point. (The standard Florentine braccio was about 58.4 cm, or almost exactly 23 imperial inches.) The dove and the tip of Christ's right foot fit well into the equilateral triangle he proposed, and if there is a geometrical plan in the painting at all, beyond the obvious features (bird's wings, central vertical, division into quarters) then this triangle seems secure. The 'shoulders' of the painting seem to suggest a narrow imaginary

75. Piero della Francesca, *The Baptism of Christ* (*c.* 1450), on a poplar panel, 116 x 167 cm. Added to this reproduction are some of the overlays suggested by B. A. R. Carter, with only minor changes in their positions. Note the large equilateral triangle thought to symbolise the Holy Trinity, bounded at the top by the wing-line of the Dove of the Holy Spirit. Notice how the star-pentagon within the smaller circle frames Christ's arms. Its five vertices were thought to signify the five wounds of the crucified Christ. Carter noted that the height of the Christ figure is three times the length of the side of a certain fifteen-sided figure (that inscribed in a circle circumscribing the large triangle). A simpler explanation, not necessarily correct, is offered with the next figure.

frame for which, ideally, we ought also to be able to account. I shall shortly mention two slightly different ways of getting such a frame. (Fig. 76 gives only what I consider to be the better option.) Carter noted that the line of John the Baptist's leg lies close to a diagonal of the square, and this idea too seems entirely acceptable. Perhaps Léon Rosenthal was the first to remark on Piero's habit (especially clear from the frescoes at Arezzo) of using human limbs to carry the eye to significant points, even to places on *adjacent* panels; and the angle Rosenthal singles out is also 45° (or 135°).[314]

Since there are apparently inner and outer squares to be drawn on the panel (in view of its 'shoulders'), there is some problem with the precise positions of diagonals, but the way in which our frame is constructed makes the diagonals of the inner square pass through the corners of the wooden panel, and so in a sense they are diagonals twice over. They would obviously have intersected on the circle of which the upper semicircular arc (bounding the painting) is a part.

The chief advantage of the two alternatives to Carter's scheme is that (in each of them) the unique circle inscribed within the triangle can have a pentagram (star-pentagon) inscribed within it such that it is possible to draw an arc through two vertices of the pentagon, with arc-centre at Christ's foot, so that it will exactly cover Christ's head. The 'bow' sits approximately on the common diagonals of the squares – more closely so in the second of my constructions. (The middle of the arc will then be $(\sin 72° - \cos 72°)/\sqrt{3}$ braccia above the crossing of the diagonals.)

Christ's upper arms are held at such an angle that they will be trapped within the sides of *any* star-pentagon radiating from the dove, no matter what the size of the pentagon's circumscribing circle. This should give us some confidence in Carter's introduction of a pentagonal figure, whether or not we accept his version of it. That Christ's arms are exactly enclosed in our other versions is of no special merit, although that the centres of the star-pentagon (and the pentagon on which it is based), the circle that circumscribes it, and the equilateral triangle, *all coincide in a point at the tips of Christ's fingers* does

76. An alternative to the scheme of the previous figure. Once the line across the shoulders of the panel has been set, every other line drawn in this scheme, as well as the framing strip, is rigorously determined. No attempt has been made to move lines so as to make them fit the *details* of the painting. The limits of the strip are set by the large circle, following a construction I have taken from Piero's treatise on the abacus. It is drawn only in part here. Notice the circular arc that seems to define Christ's height. In this scheme, the circle inscribed in the equilateral triangle exactly circumscribes the pentagon and the star-pentagon inside it. The centre of all of them is at the tips of Christ's fingers, marked here by a small circle.

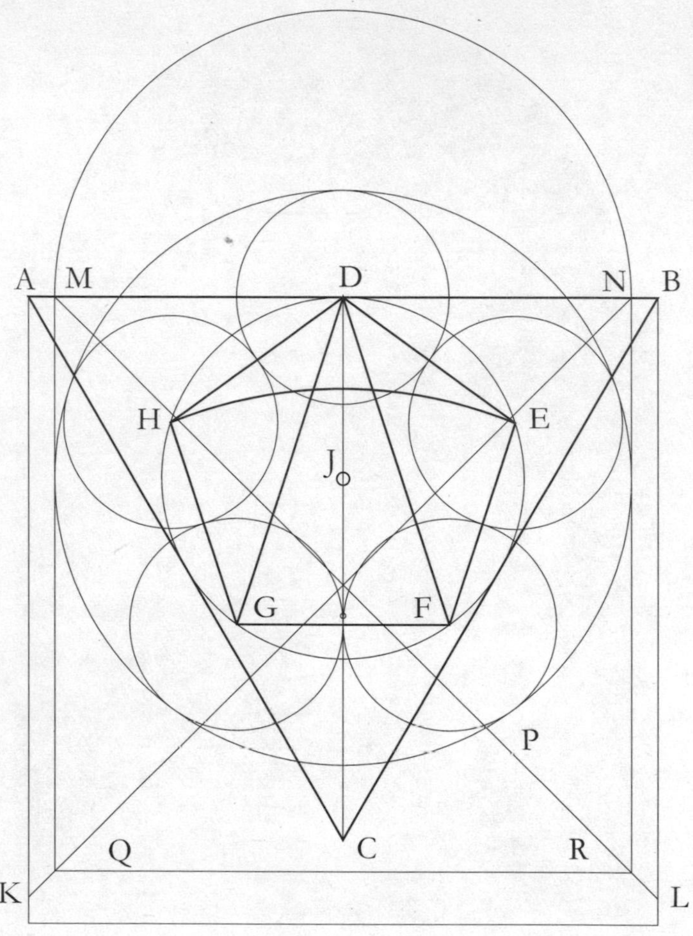

77. Our preferred scheme for the plan of Piero's painting. The star-pentagon is not fully drawn, for the sake of clarity. (Its two sides *GD* and *DF* are shown, since they mark the limits of Christ's arms.) The basic pentagon *DEFGH*, with the small circles at its vertices and the larger circle circumscribing them, is exactly as in Piero's abacus treatise. It is that large circle by which we define the framing lines *MQ* and *NR*. The actual limits of the panel are set by *K* and *L*. The central point *J* marks the tips of Christ's fingers. The arc *HE* (limiting Christ's head) has centre *C* (the tip of his right foot), while *PL* on the lower diagonal marks the line of John the Baptist's leg. The two lower small circles are not quite tangential to the diagonals.

seem to speak strongly in favour of them, on the grounds of mathematical simplicity.

All of the properties of our two schemes are arrived at by rigid geometrical design, as illustrated in Figs 77 and 78. They were of course devised with an eye to the layout of the painting, but given the rationale of the schemes and a starting line across the shoulders of the painting, *each of the complete plans may be superimposed without any further reference to the details of the painting*, and without any fine adjustment. The constructions are simple enough, and both begin in the same way. An equilateral triangle is first constructed below the initial side of two braccia, the line above the bird. A circle is inscribed in that triangle, and a pentagon and/or a star-pentagon within that, all by the usual techniques of Euclidean geometry. (Unlike most modern readers, Piero knew them well. They are easily found in geometry texts, and need not be explained here.) From here on, the two methods diverge.

In the version I favour (Fig. 77) I draw five small circles at the vertices of the pentagon, each with a radius equal to half the length of a side. A circle is then drawn circumscribing the five small circles. (Obviously only one of the five is needed.

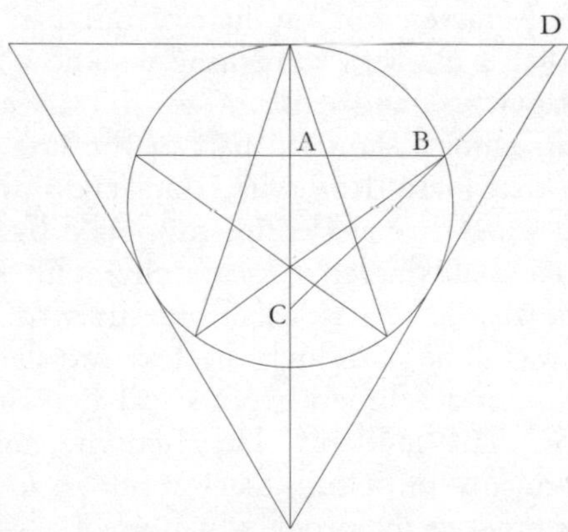

78. An alternative construction for the central part of the scheme, leading to the size of the bounding strip around the painting in another way, as explained in the text.

The reason for mentioning five will be explained shortly.) The large circle is then taken to give the dimensions of the upper semicircle; which is another way of saying that it defines the strip down the side of the painting in our imaginary frame. The inner edges of this (*MQ* and *NR*) set the key diagonals of our inner square, namely topped by the line above the dove's wings.

Another way of setting the size of the imaginary frame is shown in Fig. 78. The point *A* is where the vertical crosses the horizontal side of the star-pentagon. The point *C* is then marked below *A* on the same vertical so that *AC* is equal to *AB*. The line *CB* produced meets the upper side of the triangle at *D*. This determines the width of the bounding frame, that is, the short distance from *D* to the end of the horizontal. With this particular width the 'bow' will rest on the diagonals and mark out the top of Christ's head in the painting. There are various other properties of the scheme that might be held to have significance, such as that the resulting large circular arc passes through the eye of one of the angels. On the whole this construction seems more arbitrary than the former scheme. I can offer no textual authority for it, but like the first, and unlike Carter's, it does set the dimensions of the 'frame'.

One of the attractions of the first of our two variant constructions is that it fits with something we know about Piero's mathematical practice, and it is not as arbitrary as it might at first appear. It is not a standard part of the Euclidean canon, but we know that Piero drew what I am taking to be the key figure, that in which five circles are enveloped by another, and that he calculated all the lengths carefully. This he did in his treatise on the abacus,[315] a work admittedly written long after the painting was done, although the text reveals an obsession with calculation and a broad geometrical knowledge that we know did not come suddenly. He cited the mathematician-astronomer Ptolemy for a subsidiary result in his calculation, and did not reproduce the proof, which was not his concern. It is instructive to consider what his purpose was in the relevant text. As he made plain from a whole series of constructions, he was concerned to find numerical answers to the following

79. Diagrams that are used by Piero in his treatise on the abacus, for his calculation of the size of a circle ('roundel', *tondo*) such that several identical circles (3, 4 or 5 in number) can be fitted into a larger circle of given size.

problem: what is the diameter of the largest circle such that *n* similar and non-overlapping circles can be fitted inside another, larger, circle, of given size? He calculated the cases in which *n* is successively 3, 4 and 5. (They are here illustrated in Fig. 79.) It should be emphasised that he was concerned with measurement, that is with numerical solutions to these problems, rather than with proofs of geometrical equivalences. In short, he wrote as a practitioner, a writer whom architects designing rose windows could use, shall we say, rather than as a theoretician. But he knew the theory well.

There is another side to the question of Piero's scheme about which I have said little, beyond mentioning the symbolism of the dove (the Holy Spirit) and the supposed triangle (the Trinity). There was in Piero's time a considerable body of doctrine on the radiation of influence. This crops up in various contexts, including the theory of optics, astrology (where the influence is celestial) and even theology.[316] There were some who followed Robert Grosseteste in regarding the universe as having been created out of radiation emanating in the form of a sphere from a point source. It is not hard to imagine the circles centred on the tips of Christ's fingers as having been inspired by such a doctrine. The rays enfolding Christ's arms likewise beg to be looked upon as rays of influence.

It is impossible to prove that Piero saw them in this way, but it is worth noticing that the painting has been recognised as making clever use of simple optical principles in regard to the reflections in the River Jordan, in which Christ is shown standing. (And Grosseteste, as it happens, is one of the classic medieval writers on optics.) When one determines the view-point of the observer, taking a level mid-way between the distant horizon and its reflection, it turns out to be at exactly the mid-point of the bottom side of our pentagon, that is, the base of the 'radiation triangle' from the dove.

APPENDIX II

THE COMPOUND SOLAR INSTRUMENT

The adjustable dial, introduced earlier in a general way,* is illustrated in the two portraits with its sliding disc stored on a wooden block and not in use. That disc is an essential part of the instrument. It is not in use in *The Ambassadors*, except in the sense that the tip of the rod is an indicator of the (solar) point on the quadrant, on the line up to the eye of Christ.† Engraved with four offset quadrants, the sliding disc is redrawn in schematic form here (Fig. 80, right-hand side). In each quarter of the day a different edge of the arm on to which the disc is slotted acts as the shadow-casting 'gnomon', in what thus becomes a dial of equinoctial type. The hour divisions are equally spaced radial lines (numbered 1 to 7, etc.), not drawn in our figure.

In the Kratzer portrait, the outer semicircular scale of the main frame is blank, but here it has skew graduations through different centres. (Its scale will be called *A*.) The two series of graduations seen there, of altitude and depression, go from 0° to 90° (scales *B*). In the Dinteville portrait the upper part of the inner scale (scale *C*) is offset by 5° relative to *A*, but that is not a mistake, deliberate or otherwise. It is to be read in conjunction with the lower eccentric edge of the pivoted arm. The lower half of this inner scale is blank.

The wooden block, on which in both pictures the slider is shown resting, was perhaps to offer protection to a lower extension of the fine metal rod protruding from the disc. The rod might have been a stop to ensure that the slider could be put instantly in the middle of a scale of ecliptic longitude (scale

* See p. 123 above.

† See p. 175 above.

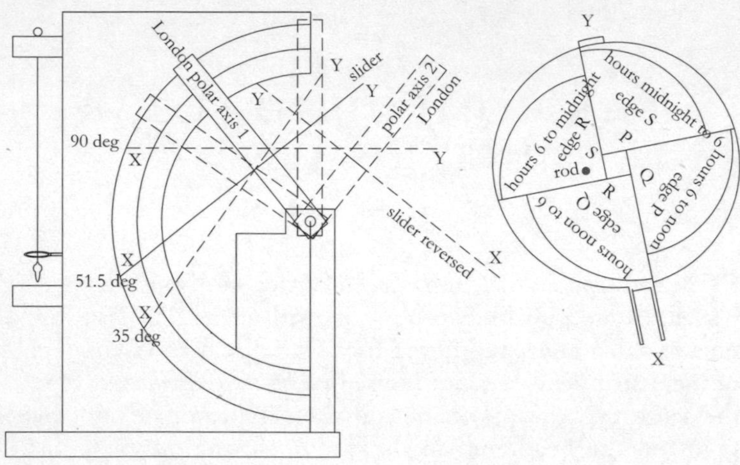

80. The compound solar instrument, with its accessory disc. That disc is drawn in plan view on the right: it is pierced with a square hole *PQRS* into which the polar axis fits. Compare the instrument as painted in *The Ambassadors* (Plate 7) and in the Kratzer portrait (Plate 5). *X* is a slotted finger on the disc that may pass over the semicircular scale of the main instrument. Since the disc has a certain thickness, a side-view of its various positions on one diagram might be confusing. For this reason only the upper surface of the disc (*X Y*) is represented. The disc and polar axis are here shown in four different positions. Note how the slider (the disc) is reversed in one instance.

D) on the pivoted wooden arm, or it might have been inserted in a hole in the vane at the upper end of the arm to hold the disc in position by friction. Friction in the square hole at the centre would by itself have provided rather indifferent control, and would have rubbed the scale on the arm. That scale of solar ecliptic longitude is crude, and too short to have more than the zodiacal signs inscribed on it. With the slider on the arm in the position marked 'polar axis 1' on our figure, the shadow cast by the edge of the disc at noon would have shown a value for the place of the Sun on the instrument's 'zodiac', and so the time of year, but to an accuracy of no better than the equivalent of a week in time, and much less at the solstices.

To put the slider in place, the arm had first to be removed from the main instrument – hence the protruding peg at its pivot. Friction at the pivot would have been needed to keep the arm in its chosen position, a weak point in the design. The peg was no doubt tapered. With the slider in mid-position (at the equinoctial points of scale *D*), the tongue *X* of the slider is set at the local geographical latitude on scale *A*. (The slider is drawn without thickness in my figure, to avoid a proliferation of lines. It is a matter of no consequence whether the scales are read from its upper or lower edge, as long as the scales are suitably offset.) This ensures that when the plane of the body of the instrument is in the meridian, the pivoted arm is parallel to the polar axis. One of the four edges of the arm then serves to cast its shadow on the appropriate quadrant of the slider. A different edge comes into play, and a different quadrant, according to the quarter of the day.

The side of the slider shown in the Kratzer portrait and schematised in our drawing has hours marked in a way inconsistent with this explanation. The reason was presumably that the disc was double-sided, and that we are seeing the side presented to a person using the device in a *second* position (see 'polar axis 2') in the figure. The slider has two potential 'pointers', *X* and *Y*, and in the second position *X* is made the lower of the two. To set the device in this case it would have been necessary to move the slider to the central position (reversing the rod) and to set *Y* to twice the colatitude of place (say 77° for London) on scale *C*. The frame of the instrument as a whole would have been turned through 180°. For normal use, Kratzer might well have marked the line of the meridian on his wall or window ledge.

There is another potential use. In a useful study of the instrument, Peter Drinkwater regards the 'skewer' as having been painted to the wrong side of the slider, and to have no use – although both paintings, done years apart, have it in the same position.[317] He imagines the hole in the disc in which it is lodged to be a sighting hole, or rather a hole through which an image of the Sun could be cast on the protruding peg. If so, the hole in the vane at the end of the arm would need to have been very perfectly aligned with it. What seems to me much more probable is that the arm, moving over scale *C* on the semicircle (and note that this scale only needs to cover the upper quadrant), without the slider in place, was used alone to cast a pinhole image of the Sun on the peg, so yielding the altitude of the Sun quite effectively. The body of the instrument would first have been turned out of the meridian so as to head for the Sun.

One further use for the instrument was mentioned earlier in connection with the polyhedral dial, a device that could have been used at all geographical latitudes, given some means of directing its rod gnomons and the edges of its dart gnomons to the poles. This would have been effected very easily, using the compound solar instrument as an auxiliary device, by simply pushing one of the rod gnomons into the hole in the radial arm and ensuring that the polyhedral block was sitting with its top edges perfectly horizontal, while moving the arm to the right setting.

APPENDIX III

RABANUS MAURUS AND SOLOMON'S THRONE

Rabanus Maurus (*c.* 776–856), born in Mainz, was a highly influential encyclopaedic writer, and one much quoted in the middle ages. He was a pupil of Alcuin, the scholar and poet who introduced Anglo-Saxon humanism to Charlemagne's Europe. In his commentaries on the Fourth Book of Kings, Rabanus helped to establish the aura surrounding the number six, and contributed an allegorical reading of the biblical passage on Solomon's throne. The following excerpt is translated from the Latin version of those *Commentaria in libros IV Regum* as printed in Migne, *Patrologia latina*, vol. 109, cols. 195–97. The scriptural quotations on which he comments are here taken from the Authorised version of the Bible.

1 Kings 10:18. 'Moreover the king made a great throne of ivory, and overlaid it with the best gold.'

> By 'the throne which Solomon made' is meant holy Church, in which our ruling Peacemaker makes known his judgements – for the soul of the righteous man is the seat of wisdom. The throne was well to be made of ivory, for not only is that a suitably precious material, but the elephant from whose bones it comes is a creature of especial chastity. It is an animal of unusual intelligence, is united with its mate temperately, and does not know a second mate. This is suitably fitting for modest spirits, since they are as it were ivory when they have followed the precepts of Christ Our Lord in matters of chastity. The throne was overlaid with the best gold to make the splendour of Solomon's glory evident and to signify his power through marvels.

1 Kings 10:19. 'The throne had six steps, and the top of the throne was round behind: and there were stays on either side on the place of the seat, and two lions stood beside the stays.'

[The throne had six steps] because the perfection of good works may be clearly demonstrated in that way. In six days God created the world. Moreover the number six is the first number which is perfect in all its parts. Half of it is three, a third is two, and a sixth one. One, two, and three add up to six. [The Greeks called a number perfect when it was the sum of its factors.] Since the world passes through six ages before it is finally perfected, let us therefore also hasten to ascend to our Heavenly Father by way of good works.

[The throne is round behind.] What does this rotundity of the back of the throne mean if it is not the eternal rest which will come after this life, where whosoever labours well will enjoy for ever the wages of his work. Wherefore also in the Song of Songs [3:9–11] concerning this same throne under another heading it is said 'King Solomon made himself a chariot of the wood of Lebanon. He made the pillars thereof of silver, the bottom thereof of gold, the covering of it of purple, the midst thereof being paved with love, for the daughters of Jerusalem.' [Rabanus interrupts this somewhat irrelevant passage to quote Bede at length, and John 15.]

[On the 'two hands on either side holding the seat', Englished in the King James version as 'stays on either side on the place of the seat'.] What do they mean if it is not the solace of divine grace, which raise up holy Church to the Kingdom of Heaven? These are well described by the binary number, since in both testaments [divine grace] is preached and greatly commended. [Rabanus then quotes 1 Corinthians 3, Philippians 2, and John 15.]

[On the two lions:] What do the lions symbolise if not the fathers of the two testaments, who by force of character learn to be ruled by themselves and others? [Rabanus quotes Psalm 144, 11 Corinthians 15, Jeremiah 9, 1 Corinthians 1.]

1 Kings 10:20. 'And twelve lions stood there on the one side and on the other upon the six steps: there was not the like made in any kingdom.'

> What is meant by the twelve lions unless it is the order of preachers that follows the apostolic doctrine? They therefore stand on both sides of the six steps, since on all sides they take pains to build up good works by their doctrines and examples, and lest pious labour well begun should waver in its working they vigorously uphold righteousness as they advance in virtue.
>
> ['There was not the like made in any kingdom'] is a reference to holy Church . . . (etc.)

Some of the doctrines developed by Rabanus here help to explain an even more remarkable exercise in mysticism for which he is responsible. It must be by far the most elaborate of all allegories of the cross written in the middle ages. This work, entitled *Praise of the Holy Cross* (*De laudibus sanctae crucis libri duo eruditione, versu, prosaque mirifici*, printed in Migne's *Patrologia latina*, vol. 107, cols 133–294), combines theology with mystical mathematical symbolism. While in outward form it is a literary work, it has a strong figurative element. It is further removed in time from Holbein than he is from us, but it speaks clearly for a type of thinking that was still very common in Holbein's century. It has much in common with the rationale of the Westminster pavement, and it is conceivable that, perhaps through Georges de Selve, there are distant echoes of it even in *The Ambassadors.* It combines the themes of the calendar, the Sun, time, hexagons, and crucifixion.

The work is a series of twenty-eight poems, each of them relating the cross to items of Christian doctrine – for example the four cardinal virtues, the seven gifts of the Holy Spirit, and so forth – and to various beliefs about the physical and astronomical nature of the Cosmos. Each poem addresses the theme of the cross, and is written out as an approximately square table, with evenly spaced letters and no spaces between

81. Rabanus Maurus' ninth poem, with its deeply symbolic creation of the cross of Christ out of four hexagons.

words. Certain of the letters are picked out, however, usually in colour, so as to create a pattern that itself has relevance to the crucifixion. The very first is a pattern representing the crucified Christ. The highlighted patterns of letters are not chosen for their overall shape alone. Within each of them the letters make up quite separate statements (some of them in verse) about the cross. And lest the reader miss the point, each is followed by a lengthy explanation, and (in a second book) what amounts to another explanation, this time in a more lyrical vein.

It is difficult to do justice in a short space to the literary ingenuity of this mathematically naive exercise in allegorical writing, but one of the poems, the ninth, may be used to illustrate it. Superimposed on a true square of letters – 41 rows and 41 columns, just a few of the letters being coalesced or contracted to guarantee a square – there is the pattern of a cross. Each of its four arms is a hexagon. The four are pinned together at a central square with the single letter C. The poem as a whole speaks of the year of 365 days and its division into four parts – the handling of the fractional parts was clearly no easy exercise for Rabanus, whose knowledge of mathematics was no better than that of the average bank clerk of the twenty-first century. The four divisions are considered to be the seasons, which of course are unequal in length, as Rabanus at first seems to assume that they are. The angles of four hexagons are said to symbolise the 24 hours that remain when the four 91-day seasons are removed from 365¼ days. The verses made up from the letters inside the hexagons refer to 365 as the 'universe of time', the 3 times 91, and 91 plus one. Just how intricate the scheme is only becomes obvious when we count the numbers of letters inside the hexagons, for they represent those same numbers, supposedly the days in the seasons, three hexagons containing 91 letters and one containing 92. In book II we are told that the scheme symbolises the passing of hours, the vicissitudes of times, the yearly circuit of the Sun and the course of the stars. Each of the four hexagons making up the cross represents six hours, so that the holy cross, glistening with miracles and casting the clear light of faith and wisdom into the shadows of infidelity, represents one day. Our modern printing of the ninth poem will give some idea of its ingenious pattern (Fig. 81). The geometrical form of the hexagons leaves something to be desired, but it could be improved by taking taller letter forms.

Structuring poetry around the number six, for reasons of religious, philosophical or cosmological belief, continued into the Elizabethan period and beyond. An especially complex instance is the sestina form, as used with great effect by Sir Philip Sydney.[318] This was usually six unrhymed six-line stanzas with a tercet envoy. The same endwords were repeated in each stanza, but in positions continually varied according to a strict rule. The patterning of the sestina could be related to the twelve signs of the zodiac. To modern readers who see this type of activity as a depressing sign that human beings admire complexity for its own sake, those who indulged in it would simply have responded that there is nothing trivial about God's created universe, and that theirs was a way of singing its praises.

Rabanus, not surprisingly, writes also on the number 27, not deriving it from the Three of the holy Trinity but from a sort of Greek gematria. See his *De universo* (cap. 3, De Sybillis), where he writes about one of his geometrised verses, in this case one of several with an embedded crucifix.

APPENDIX IV

HOLBEIN AND CHAUCER COMPARED

In the following brief comparison, *T* denotes the Chaucerian text, *C* is the half-hidden Chaucerian astronomical situation (the year and day being left to us to deduce), and *H* is the situation represented in Holbein's painting (1533).

Little weight will be placed here on the positions of the Moon and planets, since to do so would detract from the marked similarities between 1533 and 1400, the year I favour for the lines from Chaucer, that is, the last of his life. It has already been explained, however, that there is an interesting contrast in the positions of Saturn, which in 1400 was at its lowest point and in 1533 was overhead; and that while Jupiter was for Chaucer rising, for Holbein it was at more or less its lowest point. (See Fig. 71 above.) Both are astrologically significant – but both are also ambiguous. More precisely, at four o'clock on Good Friday, 16 April 1400, Jupiter was at 19° Virgo, the ascendent was 2° Libra, and Saturn was 7° Capricorn, all at London. The Sun and Moon were quartile (separated by 90°).

A bare comparison of the Chaucer and Holbein situations is as follows:

T: The Sun was under 29° in altitude.

C: According to contemporary tables, drawn up in fact by the friar Nicholas of Lynn, for the time given below, the altitude was 28°41′ on Good Friday, 16 April 1400; but on any date between 14 and 17 April those tables would set it at between 28° and 29°.

H: The Sun was under 27° in altitude (26°34′ is equivalent to a gradient of 1 in 2).

T: The time was four o'clock in the afternoon, and the poet's shadow was in length more or less eleven sixths of his height.

C: On 16 April, according to Nicholas of Lynn's tables, the length of his shadow was 10 and 59 sixtieths of those human units, those sixths of his height.

H: The time was about eight minutes past four o'clock in the afternoon, and a person's shadow was in length exactly twelve sixths of that person's height. (If he had his eyes too close to Thynne's poor text, Kratzer might have thought of it as ten *fifths* of his height. Alternatively, he might have thought in terms of the twelve units on a quadrant's shadow square.)

T: The Moon's exaltation was with the Sun.

C: At four o'clock on Good Friday in any of the years 1386, 1389, 1392, 1394, 1397, 1400, the Sun was in Taurus. The entire sign may be considered the Moon's exaltation.

H: The Sun at the time in question on Good Friday, 11 April 1533, would have been placed in the second degree of Taurus (1°11′ if it was placed according to the best authorities of the day).

T: The sign of Libra was beginning to ascend.

C: The ascendent point, the point of the zodiac on the eastern horizon, was very near the first degree of Libra in all the years named above. The third degree was beginning to ascend on Good Friday in 1400 (more precisely the ascendent was 2°05′ of Taurus).

H: The ascendent point was the first degree of Libra. (More precisely, it was 0°58′.)

In both cases, the Balance, Libra, hangs from an arm of the cross.

APPENDIX V

THE CELESTIAL GLOBE AND THE NORTHERN CROSS

There is no better way of discovering the order in which Holbein worked on the globe, and the source of the mistakes he made with it, than by comparing his globe with the ideal outline of a three-dimensional celestial sphere, complete with stars and scales. It is not easy to draw, since we can only decide on the painter's perspective viewpoint by first analysing his work, so that we run the risk of a circular argument. The evidence has unfortunately been muddied in the past by some trifling mistakes in Holbein's numbering of the brass scales of his globe, and this has obscured the fact that the disposition of the meridian ring (its north pole is the crucial point when setting it for latitude) and the other armillae are as accurately drawn for the latitude of London as are the constellations in relation to them. (The analysis in the book was based only on the disposition of the many recognisable stars.) The rings are not as true to the globe as a photograph of them would have been, of course. The problem is also complicated if we fail to appreciate Holbein's technique for producing a composite image from separate components. The painted globe was almost certainly built up by stages, as a collage, but this is something that does not appear immediately.

Holbein's mistakes in numbering the meridian ring are at the very points where they are most needed to read off the latitude (the altitude of the pole). While the graduations cannot be fully appraised without some reasonable estimate of the painter's viewpoint, high precision is not needed to detect his errors. Every ten degrees there is a graduation numbered twice, so that the scale may be read in two directions. The graduation marked 70/20 should read 80/10 (polar distance/declination), while 60/30 should read 70/20 and 50/20 should read 60/30. This last

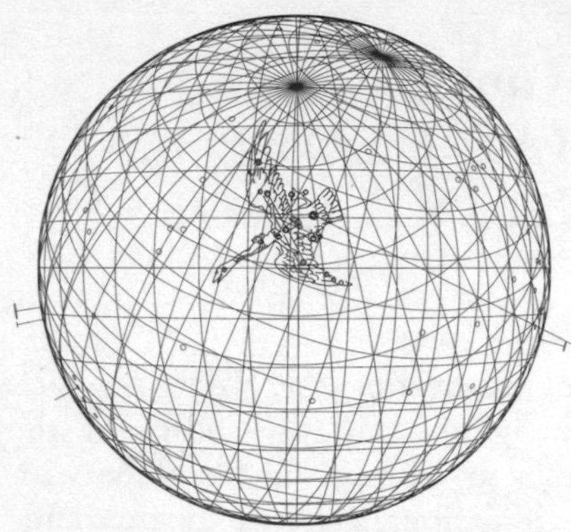

82. A reconstruction of the principal reference lines and stars on Holbein's celestial globe.

graduation (the mark, not the label) is only slightly in error, while the other two are quite accurately painted. While the 20/70 mark is hidden, 10/80 and 30/60 are both correctly painted and labelled, but the graduation labelled 40/50 is badly placed. The sheer distortion of the scale in the neighbourhood of the horizon is relatively obvious. I will not consider the errors in detail, for reasons that will soon become clear.

These errors on the globe with a pole that is set for London demand an explanation. Faulty restoration of the painting is quite certainly not to blame. There are no doubt some who, if they had noticed the errors, would have argued that Holbein and his friends wished to have a label at the horizon that was ambiguous – for example, as between London and Rome. This is equally unlikely. I think Holbein made a mistake after the 30/60 mark because he was covering up for other small inconsistencies. These are very difficult to disentangle. In the following explanation of them a useful reference line will be the horizontal diameter of the circle on the painting that bounds the visible globe. I will here refer to that diameter as D.

Holbein allows us to see the lower hemisphere right up to D, which he should not have done, whatever the viewpoint, since the thickness of the brass horizon ring would have prevented it.

The Tropic of Cancer is nevertheless correctly drawn with reference to D, as though D represents the horizon circle. The same is true for the armillae in general and possibly for some stars in the lower hemisphere. The deduced time is about 8:50 p.m.

The lines of ecliptic longitude are also related to D, but I am reasonably certain that he pricked his outlines through a paper draft, or something of the sort, and that this slipped slightly to the right as he did so. This slip might even have been deliberate, for it brings Deneb accurately on to the line up to the eye of Christ.

When he came to add the key constellations to the upper hemisphere (Cygnus and Aquila in particular) and the most conspicuous (Pegasus) in the lower, Holbein did so with reference to the 'slipped' reference lines but, more significantly, he now used the *upper* side of the painted horizon ring as his horizon. The resulting hiatus in the neighbourhood of the horizon would thus have given rise to confusion in any numbering of the scale of declination and polar distance, as soon as an attempt was made to relate it to the stars.

From the azimuth of Markab (alpha Pegasi, virtually due north) we again deduce the time as near to 8:50 p.m. Lowering the altitude of Deneb (alpha Cygni) by little more than a degree (less than 3mm on the painting) would bring a time deduced from Deneb into agreement with this. (Markab is changing with respect to the meridian faster than Deneb with respect to the horizon, so it is preferable to start with Markab.)

The accompanying figure (Fig. 82) shows an idealised celestial globe for the latitude of London, viewed from a point 5.44 radii from its centre and very close to the horizon plane. (The point was chosen to represent the perspective of the painting as accurately as I could easily do, but it is unlikely to be perfect.) Three coordinate meshes are added, for the sake of those who wish to consider the matter in greater detail, but for most readers they will be of much less interest than the disposition of Cygnus. The conspicuous pole near the central vertical is for the ecliptic, and higher on the right is the north pole. The zenith at the top is inevitably just hidden. The stars are accurately placed on the globe for 1533, following modern and not Renaissance tables. They would not have been in exactly these positions on the globe in the painting, although most would have been well within the limits of the small circles that mark them (each is of arbitrary diameter 1.15°). The pointer (resembling a nail) on the lower right edge is to the Sun, and the upper two pointers on the left are for the Moon's position as Kratzer would have calculated it, the upper with latitude (approximately 5°), the lower without. The headless pointer on the lower left edge is to Jupiter, as Kratzer would have had it. Strictly speaking, these relate to my figure, not to the painting, but the two are in extremely close agreement.

I have added a line to the figure at a gradient of 1 in 2 (approximately 27°, of course) as a reminder that the crucial line up the crucifix in the painting passes through Deneb (indeed it does), the brightest star in the constellation that is given pride of place. I have no doubt that the constellation (Cygnus, the Northern Cross) symbolises the taking down of the crucified Christ in the evening. The strongest reason, as explained above at p. 325, is the way in which the cross rests on the horizon such that the angle between it and the horizon is 27°. The cross as added to the present figure is drawn after Wilhelm Schickard's rendering (compare Fig. 69), but artistic style is of little relevance to its disposition, which is ultimately defined by the bright stars of Cygnus. The New Testament gives the time of taking down the body of Christ simply as evening, but we recall the old and still current Christian tradition of celebrating the event at 9 p.m. The time as represented in the figure is 8:50 p.m, but a few minutes make little difference to the overall pattern.

NOTES

Second and later references to any particular item use only an abbreviated title. The full title will be easily retrieved from the Bibliography at page 438 below, which lists all publications referred to in these notes.

1 Michael Levey, *The Soul of the Eye* (London, 1990), p. 90.

2 John Rowlands, *Holbein: The Paintings of Hans Holbein the Younger. Complete Edition* (Oxford, 1985), item no 47, p. 85.

3 For a study of the genre of friendship paintings of this period see H. Keller, 'Entstehung und Blütezeit des Freundschaftsbildes', *Essays in the History of Art Presented to Rudolf Wittkower* (London, 1967), i, pp. 161–73.

4 The cartoon was 258 cm high by 137 cm wide, and took in the figures of the two kings on the left side. See Roy Strong, *Holbein and Henry VIII* (London, 1967), pp. 34–54. His plate 2 shows an engraving of the whole by George Vertue after the painted copy by Remigius van Leemput, now at Hampton Court. Jane Seymour was the mother of Henry's male heir, later Edward VI. Holbein's two largest monumental paintings were not portraits. They were the *Triumphal Processions of Wealth and Poverty* and were done as a pair for the hall of the Hanseatic Steelyard in London. They ended up in Kremsier in the collection of the archbishop of Olmütz, but were destroyed by fire in 1752.

5 For more detail see Rowlands, *Holbein*, p. 140. For her crucial contribution to the convoluted history of the picture's movements, see M. F. S. Hervey, *Holbein's 'Ambassadors': The Picture and the Men* (London, 1900), pp. 5–34.

6 Alfred Woltman, *Holbein and His Time* (London, 1872).

7 In a letter to *The Times*, September 1890. Dinteville was commonly styled 'Seigneur de Polisy, Bailly de Troyes'.

8 William F. Dickes, *Holbein's Celebrated Picture, Now Called 'The Ambassadors', Shown to be a Memorial of the Treaty of Nuremberg, 1532, and to Portray Those Princely Brothers, Counts of Palatine of*

the Rhine, Otto Henry . . . and Philipp [etc.] (London, 1903). Dickes's argument rests heavily on Le Brun's sale catalogue (1787) and the supposed absence of a date on the painting at that time, but the catalogue is unreliable in this and several other respects. The ages of his two candidates fit with the indications of the ages of the sitters (as given in the painting) on the assumption that the year is 1532. The latter half of the book gives biographies of the two princes.

9 Lons-le-Saulnier, Archives Départementales Jura, E 722.

10 Hervey, *Holbein's 'Ambassadors'*. As all historians of the Tudor court must do, she makes extensive use of J. S. Brewer et al., editors, *Letters and Papers, Foreign and Domestic of the Reign of Henry VIII* [etc.] (London, 1862–1932), vi, for 1533, arranged and catalogued by James Gairdner (1882).

11 'IOANNES HOLBEIN PINGEBAT 1533' on the pavement was barely legible before the recent restoration.

12 The precise date will be discussed below.

13 I have not been able to consult Joseph Harnest, 'Das Problem der konstruierten Perspektive in der altdeutschen Malerei' (unpublished thesis, München, 1971), which is described as a study of the perspective techniques, often naive, used by all three members of the Holbein family.

14 The exhibition, in the National Gallery's 'Making and Meaning' series, ran from 5 November 1997 to 1 February 1998. Susan Foister, Ashok Roy and Martin Wyld, *Making and Meaning: Holbein's Ambassadors* (London, 1997). The first part (to p. 57) is by Foister alone. The sections by Martin Wyld on the physical aspects of the restoration are supplemented by Martin Wyld, 'The Restoration History of Holbein's *Ambassadors*', *National Gallery Technical Bulletin*, 19 (1998), pp. 4–25.

15 Generally speaking, a mid-grey primer was put on a ground of two or more layers of natural chalk mixed with animal glue, the lowermost strengthened with vegetable fibres of some sort. There is evidence of some underdrawing. Some symmetries in the design, for example in the carpet, assisted in the restoration. More difficult was the restoration of the skull, although fortunately the outer areas offered no great problem. (The nasal aperture was the most difficult region.) The general policy adopted for the restoration was one of 'deceptive retouching'. Its critics come in all shades, and include lovers of cloudy nineteenth-century varnish and haters of pink satin.

16 Essential biographical surveys will be found in Paul Ganz, *The Paintings of Hans Holbein* (London, 1950), in Rowlands, *Holbein*, which largely supersedes Ganz, and in Oskar Bätschmann and Pascal Griener, *Hans Holbein* (London, 1997). All supply biographical information and its sources. Perhaps the best short summary of modern attitudes to *The Ambassadors* is Peter Cornelius Claussen, 'De doppelte Boden unter Holbeins Gesandten', *Hülle und Fülle: Festschrift für Tilmann Buddensieg*, ed. Andreas Beyer, Vittorio Lampugnani and Gunter Schweikhart (Alfter, 1993), pp. 177–202. (It is unfortunately difficult to locate.) An important earlier work of biography in English is A. B. Chamberlain, *Hans Holbein the Younger*, 2 vols (London, 1913). A readable general study that supplements the known evidence with a few plausible reconstructions of the unknown is Derek Wilson, *Hans Holbein: Portrait of an Unknown Man* (London, 1996).

17 Carel van Mander, *The Lives of the Illustrious Netherlandish and German Painters from the First Edition of the 'Schilder-Boeck' (1603–1604)*, 2 vols, ed. H. Miedema (Dornspijk, 1994). Also *Hans Holbein. A Biography from the Schilderboeck*, trans. Constant van de Wall (New York, 1935).

18 Bätschmann and Griener, *Hans Holbein*, p. 148.

19 Ganz, *The Paintings*, plate 62, catalogue no. 30; and Rowlands, *Holbein*, colour plate 11 and plate 8, cat. no. 7. Erasmus was at this time about fifty-two. He died in 1536, and Amerbach was an executor and chief beneficiary of his will.

20 Myconius (1488–1552) occasionally goes under his earlier name of Geishüsler. For Erasmus see G. T. Jensma et al. (eds), *Erasmus: de actualiteit van zijn denken* (Zutphen, 1986), and for his relations with Holbein pp. 142–43 and 160–68 of the same work (contribution by A. M. Koldeweij).

21 Desiderius Erasmus, *Opus epistolarum*, 12 vols (Oxford, 1906–58), ed. P. S. Allen, vi, item 1740 (29 August 1526). An angel was an ordinary gold coin, originally of value 6s 8d but at this period 7s 6d. It was more or less the equivalent of a well-known French coin, the *angelot*, and it is no more certain that Erasmus was punning when he spoke of Holbein 'collecting a few angels' than that Oxford undergraduates are punning when they say they are 'going up to Jesus'.

22 On Kratzer, the subject of Chapter 4, see J. D. North, 'Nicolaus Kratzer, the King's Astronomer', in *Science and History: Studies in Honor of Edward Rosen* (Ossolineum, 1978), pp. 205–34; reprinted

with short addenda in my *Stars, Minds and Fate* (London and Ronceverte, 1989), pp. 373–400. (This was first written and circulated in 1972 as part of an introductory volume for the official history of Oxford University, a volume abandoned after the death of the editor.)

23 William Roper, *The Life . . . of Syr Thomas More*, part 1, first published in Paris, 1626. The fact that Henry and his queen made great demands on his company, and kept him from his wife, eventually became irksome to More. Erasmus's praise of the king's argument in a Latin debate with an eminent churchman (available to him in a short tract written by the king) was genuine enough. He gave similar praise to Henry elsewhere while at the same time professing openly his dislike of courts. In 1521 Henry, with some help, published a scholarly work against Luther. Some said that Erasmus had written it; but the same was said of Luther's reply. See Preserved Smith, *Erasmus* (New York, 1923), pp. 276–77.

24 Ganz, *The Paintings*, pp. 281–84; Rowlands, *Holbein*, pp. 69–72 and plates 188–90, cat. nos L.10a–c, for the annotated sketch and copies of the painting. See also Lesley Lewis, *The Thomas More Family Group of Portraits After Holbein* (Leominster, 1998). Even the best of the five versions ascribed to R[owland] Lockey (1565/7–1616), is too stiff and formal for Holbein. Now at Nostell Priory, it is wrongly inscribed 1530 for perhaps 1593. The original painting went to the Continent (Kremsier) and was destroyed by fire in 1752. The version in the National Portrait Gallery has some of the sitters removed.

25 As John Rowlands notes (*Holbein*, p. 71), it is of a type later known as a 'Conversation-Piece'. The name fits perfectly with Erasmus's description of the household.

26 The technical meaning of 'house' in this context must remain uncertain, since the ceiling does not survive, but see p. 224 below for the alternatives. The word used for masques was 'disguisings'. On the evidence for these early instances of collaboration between Kratzer and Holbein, resting on the entirely plausible identification of the latter with 'Maister Hans', see Rowlands, *Holbein*, pp. 68–69, and Sydney Anglo, *Spectacle, Pageantry and Early Tudor Policy* (Oxford, 1969), pp. 217–19.

27 The letter from Kratzer is dated 24 October 1524. Dürer's reply was written 5 December 1524. These short but important letters are printed in Moriz Thausing, *Durer: Geschichte seines Lebens und seiner Kunst*, 2 vols (Leipzig, 1884).

28 The supposed Holbein woodcut is from Johann Huttich and Simon Grynaeus, *Novus orbis regionum* (Basel, 1532). The first three are discussed and illustrated in Rodney Shirley, *The Mapping of the World: Early Printed World Maps, 1472–1700* (London, 1984), no. 67. Large reproductions of all but the 'Holbein' are also readily accessible in Peter Whitfield, *The Image of the World: Twenty Centuries of World Maps* (London, 1994), pp. 48–57. The last, from Apian, *Cosmographicus liber* (Landshut, 1524), is of especial interest since the centre of the volvelle is marked by a hexagram. See further p. 269 below on this point.

29 On the character of an astrolabe see chapter 14 of my *Stars, Minds and Fate* (London, 1989), pp. 211–21. For a planetarium within a tent (the *tentorium* of the emperor Frederick II, a very different device, but one set against cloth), see chapter 11, ibid., pp. 135–71.

30 Eduard His, 'Holbeins Verhältnisse zur basler Reformation', *Repertorium*, 2 (1879), pp. 156–59.

31 Fritz Saxl, 'Holbein and the Reformation', in *A Heritage of Images: A Selection of Lectures by Fritz Saxl*, ed. by Hugh Honour and John Fleming (London, 1957, and Harmondsworth, 1970), p. 124. The lecture dates from 1925. The three woodcuts mentioned here are plates 173, 174 and 183. It is not known with certainty what biblical text the first woodcut was originally meant to illustrate, since the Zürich printer Froschauer bought the block and trimmed it for use on a calendar by Johannes Copp for the year 1527. The contemporary Ulrich von Hugwald wrote in a letter to a friend that he suspected that it was Erasmus who gave the idea of the Hercules broadsheet (which he found very offensive) to Holbein. See Saxl, 'Holbein and the Reformation', p. 126.

32 Saxl, 'Holbein and the Reformation', p. 126.

33 This woman, widow of a former burgomaster of Basel, was the model for his painting known as the *Darmstadt Madonna* and for two others. In one of them she is Venus, and in the other she is Laïs, a Greek courtesan who was once mistress of the painter Apelles, with whom Holbein liked to be identified. Most of Holbein's biographers draw the obvious conclusion, and take the gold coin and outstretched hand in the last painting to indicate a reason for which he may have broken with her.

34 'He was a big, burly, noisy, small-eyed, large-faced, double-chinned, swinish-looking fellow in later life (as we know from the likenesses of him, painted by the famous Hans Holbein), and

it is not easy to believe that so bad a character can ever have been veiled under a prepossessing appearance.' History is duller now.

35 The standard work on the drawings at Windsor is K. T. Parker, *The Drawings of Hans Holbein in the Collection of His Majesty the King at Windsor Castle* (2nd edn, Oxford and London, 1945); reprinted with appendix by Susan Foister (London and New York, 1983).

36 W. Stechow, *Northern Renaissance Art, 1400–1600: Sources and Documents* (Englewood Cliffs, NJ, 1966), p. 132. For the text of the will, see Rowlands, *Holbein*, p. 122.

37 Nicolas Bourbon, Παιδαγωγειου: *Carmen de moribus* (Lyons, 1536), pp. 27–29.

38 Foister et al., *Making and Meaning*, and Wyld, 'The Restoration History'.

39 Giorgio Vasari, *Le vite de' più eccellenti architetti, pittori, et scultori italiani* [etc.] (Florence, 1550; 2nd edn, 1568, often reprinted and translated); ed. L. Bellosi and A. Rossi (Turin, 1986). Carel van Mander, *Hans Holbein.* For the following story see p. 14 in the New York translation.

40 'Utinam ad Galli cantum Petrus resipiscerat!' was the retort made to the bishop of Orvieto's taunt 'Gallus cantat', 'The Cock is crowing', when French delegates were attacking the Papal Curia at the Council of Trent. 'Peter' refers to the church and 'the Cock' to France. J. C. L. Sismondi, *Histoire des Français*, xi (Paris, 1836), p. 380.

41 Garrett Mattingly, *Renaissance Diplomacy* (London, 1955, often reprinted), p. 51. This classic account of the subject may be supplemented with Joycelyne G. Russell, *Peace-Making in the Renaissance* (1986).

42 On the gifts to the secretary see H. Keniston, *Francisco de los Cobos, Secretary of the Emperor Charles V* (Pittsburgh, 1960), discussed by V. L. Cañal in Elizabeth Cropper (ed.), *The Diplomacy of Art: Artistic Creation and Politics in Seicento Italy*, Papers from a Colloquium Held at the Villa Spelman, Florence, 1998 (Milan, 2000), p. 123. On the complex history of the Michaelangelo bronze see Anthony Colantuono in the same volume, pp. 55–57. On the question of the taste of the giver and the recipient see Colantuono's discussion of the contrasting views of Marc H. Smith, 'Les diplomates italiens, observateurs et conseillers artistiques à la cour de François Ier', *Histoire de l'art*, 35–36 (1996),

pp. 27–37, and J. Cox-Rearick, 'Sacred to Profane: Diplomatic Gifts of the Medici to Francis I', *Journal of Medieval and Renaissance Studies*, 24 (1994), pp. 239–58.

43 Essential sources for the Dinteville family and de Selve are the book by Mary Hervey already cited, especially pp. 36 ff, and Elizabeth A. R. Brown, 'The Dinteville Family and the Allegory of Moses and Aaron before Pharaoh', *Metropolitan Museum Journal*, 34 (1999), pp. 73–100.

44 Montmorency was named after his godmother, the notorious Anne of Brittany, consort of the French kings Charles VIII and Louis XII. He was brought up with François I. The Dinteville brothers were his fourth cousins, through both their father and their mother.

45 Hervey, *Holbein's 'Ambassadors'*, p. 40.

46 After the defeat of the French at Landriano in 1529, Montmorency helped arrange the Peace of Cambrai (the so-called Paix des Dames, since it was largely negotiated by Louise, the mother of François, and by Margaret of Austria) between France and the emperor; and yet in 1536 he again took up arms against Charles. Conservatism can take many forms.

47 James Kelsey McConica, *English Humanists and Reformation Politics under Henry VIII and Edward VI* (Oxford, 1965), p. 18.

48 Brown, 'The Dinteville Family', pp. 79–80.

49 J. S. Brewer et al., *Letters and Papers, Foreign and Domestic*, item 90.

50 Jean to his brother the bishop of Auxerre: 'Monsr. de Lavor m'a fait cest honneur que de me venir veoir, qui ne m'a esté petit plaisir. Il n'est point de besoing que Mr le grant maistre en entende rien.' Hervey, *Holbein's 'Ambassadors'*, p. 80.

51 De Selve's right elbow rests on a book edged with the words 'ÆTATIS SVÆ [ANNO] 25'. The half-concealed second figure looks rather more like Holbein's '3' than his '5', but the latter is a possible reading, and the former would require a different identity for the cleric in the painting. The cumulation of evidence in Hervey, *Holbein's 'Ambassadors'*, p.13, indicates that de Selve was born between 13 May 1508 and the end of that year.

52 *Les vies de huict excellens et renommez personnaiges grecz et romains* . . . (Paris, 1543 and 1548). It was not de Selve's translation (of nine lives) but Jacques Amyot's which became canonical. This was used for Thomas North's, on which Shakespeare relied.

53 Hervey, *Holbein's 'Ambassadors'*, p. 151.

54 His father in 1529 and his mother in 1533. Hervey, *Holbein's 'Ambassadors'*, pp. 153–54.

55 Hervey, *Holbein's 'Ambassadors'*, pp. 83–88, drawing on a document transcribed by Denis-François Camusat.

56 The text of the letter is Hervey, *Holbein's 'Ambassadors'*, pp. 79–81. The French word *compas*, like its English equivalent, first referred to a circle or its circumference, and later to compasses. It could in various combinations signify exactness. For the common use of the Latin word *compassa* (which presumably had vernacular equivalents) for what we now call an 'old quadrant', see for example Petrus Apianus, *Cosmographicus liber . . . studiose collectus* (Landshut, 1524), col. 104, and Sebastian Münster, *Horologiographia, post priorem aeditionem . . . recognita* (etc.) (Basel, 1533). For the meaning of sundial (with magnetic compass) see Elly Dekker and Kristen Lippincott: 'The Scientific Instruments in Holbein's *Ambassadors*: A Re-Examination', *Journal of the Warburg and Courtauld Institutes*, 62 (1999), pp. 93–125, at p. 117 n. 54. They refer to P. Gouk, *The Ivory Sundials of Nuremberg, 1500–1700* (Cambridge, 1988), p. 9. For devices for drawing ellipses (elliptic compasses), see P. L. Rose, 'Italian Renaissance Methods of Drawing the Ellipse and Related Curves', *Physis*, 12 (1970), pp. 371–404.

57 J. S. Brewer et al., *Letters and Papers, Foreign and Domestic*, item 212 for 8 March.

58 Hervey, *Holbein's 'Ambassadors'*, p. 78, citing J. S. Brewer et al., *Letters and Papers, Foreign and Domestic*, item 465, Chapuys to Charles v, 10 May 1533. A tertian fever is strictly one in which the fever recurs after forty-eight hours (on 'third days', with inclusive counting). All standard medical works classifying fevers distinguished (among others) between tertian, quartan, quotidian and continuous, and tertian was subdivided into three. If malarial, Dinteville's would not have been transmitted at London latitudes, but he could have brought it with him. As for sweating sickness, there were serious epidemics of it on at least five occasions in the century, mostly in England, except in 1528–29 when it was reported in the Netherlands and eastwards of there, but not in France or Italy. An account of the outbreak in 1551 written by John Caius, a Shrewsbury physician, is still the starting point for discussion of the disease. It is unlikely to have been influenza or typhus. Mortality was high.

59 Much of the report is given by Hervey, *Holbein's 'Ambassadors'*, chapter 4.

60 They included Cranmer, Cromwell, Hugh Latimer, John Dudley, Henry Knyvet, William Butts, William Boston (the evangelical abbot of Westminster), Thomas Berthelet, John Dudley (the future duke of Northumberland), his host Cornelius Hayes and his wife Margaret, Kratzer, and Holbein—the last two as reported elsewhere. Of Thomas More he wrote some callous lines that were calculated to win favour with Anne Boleyn's circle. See Eric Ives, 'A Frenchman at the Court of Anne Boleyn', *History Today*, 1 August 1998.

61 His own future was secured by his appointment as tutor to the Princess Jeanne, who became mother of Henry IV. He died with a rural living in 1550. His modest choice of title for his principal publication – *Trifles* – was turned against him by such critics as Joachim du Bellay, J. J. Scaliger and John Owen, with some reason.

62 E. A. R. Brown, 'Sodomy, Treason, Exile and Intrigue: Four Documents Concerning the Dinteville Affair (1537-8)', *Sociétés et idéologies des temps modernes: hommage à Arlette Jouanna* (Montpellier, 1996), pp. 512–32; and 'Sodomy, Treason, Exile and Intrigue: Francis I, Henry II and the Dinteville Brothers', *Sixteenth-Century Journal* (forthcoming). Sebastiano da Monteculli was executed for the alleged poisoning on 7 October 1536 and withdrew his accusation against Guillaume, who was awarded 10,000 *livres* of the culprit's property. The king granted Jean du Plessis's request for a duel, but Gaucher fled to Venice and counter-challenged him to a duel there. This so angered the king that Gaucher's property was confiscated and his arms were dragged through the streets of Paris. Soon after, he was dragged through the streets in effigy and burned, 'as if in person'. Continuing to absent himself, he was found formally guilty of the crime 'repugnant to nature', and various others, and the king ordered the symbolic punishment to be carried out in the chief town of *every* district in the realm. By mid-April 1539 François reintroduced charges of felony and treason against Gaucher's brother Guillaume, charges that were coupled with a statement to the effect that their brother François was strongly suspected of involvement.

63 Hervey, *Holbein's 'Ambassadors'*, pp. 173–74.

64 Again, if malarial this would have been contracted in France or Italy.

65 *Virtus* was usually a manly virtue such as bravery, and the motto was perhaps first seen as approximating to Virgil's 'Fortune is ally to the brave' ('Audentis Fortuna iuvat', *Aeneid*, x.284). Hervey, *Holbein's 'Ambassadors'*, pp. 130–32, seems to want to turn this into an indication that the bishop had a strong interest in Hermeticism, especially since in a window he included an emblem aping the Hermetic emblem of the Lyon printer Gryphe.

66 Metropolitan Museum of Art, New York, by an unknown artist, but ascribed in the bottom corner to Holbein. This, and a chalk sketch by Jean Clouet, as well as an oil and canvas portrait of him as St George by Francesco Primaticcio, are all illustrated in Foister, Roy and Wyld, *Making and Meaning*, p. 23–24. The portrait of Jean in the New York painting has a fuller and wider mouth than in Holbein's, and the two are not obviously of the same man. The painting is the subject of Brown, 'The Dinteville Family', where she argues that the year to which the scene relates is 1538, the year in which their brother Gaucher was charged with sodomy, and that the proclaimed 1537 was a convenient fiction. She finds support in the puzzling 'EN' and '8' on Aaron's cape. (But could this not have indicated *ennui*?)

67 Rowlands, *Holbein*, colour plate 19, plate 59, and pp. 73 and 134–35. Oil on oak, 83 x 67 cm, Paris, Louvre. This was acquired for Louis XIV by his minister Colbert. See Rowlands, pp. 134–35. A copy, formerly at Holland House and later owned by Viscountess Galway, is now in the National Portrait Gallery, no. 5254. The inscription on the portrait reads: 'IMAGO AD VIVAM EFFIGIEM EXPRESSA Nicolai Kratzeri Monacensis qui Bavarus erat quadragesimum primum annum tempore illo complebat 1528' ('Image from life of Nicolaus Kratzer, a Bavarian of Munich, done in his forty-first year, 1528').

68 This section draws on my earlier biographical essay and I shall not usually refer to other sources unless they are newer and independent. The most useful earlier source is M. Maas, 'Nikolaus Kratzer, ein münchener Humanist: ein biographischer Versuch', *Beilage zur Münchner Allgemeinen Zeitung* (18 March 1902), pp. 505–08 and 515–18.

69 Oxford, Corpus Christi College, MS 152.

70 Who was the 'Secretary' mentioned? Surely not an English courtier, or the letter would have been divulging the secret. Gillis was the secretary to the town of Antwerp, so the reference here might have been to an accompanying letter to him.

71 Moriz Thausing, *Dürer*, pp. 251–53.
72 Strong, *Holbein and Henry VIII*, p. 13.
73 Bätschmann and Griener, *Hans Holbein*, p. 177.
74 For a succinct history of perspective see the article by B. A. R. Carter in the *Oxford Companion to Art*, ed. Harold Osborne (Oxford, 1970). For a lengthy account, see Martin Kemp, *The Science of Art* (London and New Haven, 1990).
75 For a fuller account of Scepper in an astrological context see Steven Vanden Broecke 'The Limits of Influence. Astrology at Louvain University, 1520–1580' (unpublished thesis, Louvain, 2000), pp. 166 ff. and notes 102 and 103. I am indebted to him for these references to Cornelius Scepper (or Schepper).
76 Corpus Christi College, Oxford, MS 152. At least ten of the texts are known from copies in other manuscripts.
77 Now Bodleian Library, Oxford, MS Bodley 504, a small volume of seventeen leaves bound in green silk velvet of a similar colour to the curtain in *The Ambassadors*. P. S. Allen identified the scribe as Peter Meghen, Colet's scribe. There are illuminated initials, only the first of them being of any complexity – a letter 'E' rather resembling a large commemorative postage stamp in size and edging. That they were by Holbein was first argued conclusively by Otto Pächt, 'Holbein and Kratzer as Collaborators', *Burlington Magazine*, 84 (1944), pp. 134–39, with plates. Kratzer's preface (dated 1 January 1528/9) explains that the work was written in response to an almost daily request for information about the Sun's rising and setting by Henry's chamberlain, William Tylar. Kratzer, however, finally dedicated it to the king himself.
78 One of the most valuable documents of recent years relating to the material side of court life is David Starkey (ed.), *The Inventory of King Henry VIII: Society of Antiquaries MS 129 and British Library MS Harley 1419*, transcribed by Philip Ward and indexed by Alasdair Hawkyard (London,1998). The inventory was ordered by a commission of 14 September 1547, and gives a rich insight into the conspicuous consumption of a monarch who was breaking with the medieval itinerant tradition. It was unfortunately compiled by people who were often ignorant of what they were describing. Thus the 'divise of astronomye of woodd three plates of silver two parcell gilt and thother gilt' (item 3318) could be a horoptrum, but was probably nothing of the sort. It was in the 'Barbours coofer [coffer]', a box of Naples fustian sent to the

Tower, which does not mean that it was of low importance. One of the remarkable facts revealed by the inventory is that very many of the astronomical instruments were of silver or gold, and that some were bejewelled with the occasional ruby, pearl or diamond.

79 Sebastian Münster's German *Instrument über die zwei Himmelslichter* was followed by *Canones super novum instrumentum luminarium* (etc.) (Basel, 1534). The title goes on to say that it will allow the calculation of the mean and true motions of Sun and Moon, lunations, conjunctions, oppositions, the Head of the Dragon, eclipses, unequal hours, equal nocturnal hours, the rising and setting of the Sun, the ascendent point of the ecliptic, the golden number, and other things. By comparison with this bombastic and technical announcement, Holbein's drawing was rudimentary. See Fig. 5. The publications are discussed by H. Koegler, *Jahrbuch der Preussischen Kunstsammlung* (Berlin, 1910), pp. 247 ff.

80 Pächt, 'Holbein and Kratzer', p. 138, was the first to identify Kratzer's hand and to infer that the astronomical design was due to him. The design is illustrated in John Rowlands, *The Age of Dürer and Holbein: Catalogue of an Exhibition Held at the British Museum* (London, 1988), pp. 248–49. Denny was knighted in the year of the gift. The whole is on a base supported by two satyrs. Doors could be closed to conceal the hour glass, which was graduated to mark the quarters. The doors were to be inscribed (as Kratzer wrote) with new or full moons for twenty years. The top concealed a large magnetic compass that allowed the device to be set correctly for use as a sundial. The very top carried a twelve-hour dial resembling an ordinary clock, but it probably had no drive. It is more likely that a servant was meant to set the device by daylight and tip the glass every hour thereafter, moving on the pointer accordingly and so registering the night hours.

81 Bätschmann and Griener, *Hans Holbein*, p. 188.

82 Guido Bonatti, *Tractatus de astronomia* (Basel, 1550), ed. by Nicolaus Prugner (or Pruckner). See the editor's preface. Prugner's Basel edition of the works of the fourth-century Syracuse astrologer Firmicus (second edition, 1551) includes, curiously enough, a preface defending astrology addressed to the young Edward VI of England. It seems likely that he had learned of English court affairs from Kratzer.

83 'La pièce est estimée la plus riche et mieux travaillée qui soit

en France.' Hervey, *Holbein's 'Ambassadors'*, p. 20. The writer, Camusat, did not know the name or fame of the painter, and even thought him to have been Dutch ('un Hollandois'). The document from which the statement comes was presented to the National Gallery by Mary Hervey, and is a copy (made in 1654) of a memorandum of 1653 on the family and descendants of Georges de Selve's father.

84 In assessing Piero's qualities as a mathematician it is common to measure him against Luca Pacioli, a close contemporary who has always been much better known as a mathematician. (Both were natives of Sansepolcro.) Piero was the more original of the two, and Luca borrowed heavily from him without acknowledgement. See Marshall Clagett, *Archimedes in the Middle Ages*, iii, part 3, Memoirs of the American Philosophical Society, 125B (Philadelphia, 1978), pp. 383–415 (Piero) and pp. 416–61(Luca). Clagett focuses chiefly on their knowledge of Archimedes, and their sources.

85 See Fig. 75 in Appendix 1, and the caption to it, where Carter's chief principles are briefly outlined. For his study, see Marilyn Aronberg Lavin, with an appendix by B. A. R. Carter, *Piero della Francesca's Baptism of Christ* (New Haven and London, 1981). He took Clark's analysis as his starting point. See K. Clark, *Piero della Francesca* (2nd edn, London, 1981), especially p. 25. The 'Microsoft Art Gallery' CD-ROM (1993), which is effectively a guide to the collections of the National Gallery, London, opts for Clark's simple division.

86 Foister, Roy and Wyld, *Making and Meaning*, pp. 37–38.

87 Foister, Roy and Wyld, *Making and Meaning*, p. 88.

88 Petrus Apianus, *Cosmographicus liber*. The woodcut illustrating this is on the title page and is repeated at col. 47. The same is found in the Gemma Frisius edition of Apian's cosmography (*c.* 1547). This is not the only point at which the painting might hint at the contents of the Apian book. See p. 269 below.

89 For a description of an extant Schöner celestial globe see G. Bott (ed.), *Focus Behaim Globus*, ii (Nürnberg, 1992), pp. 524–25. Compare the description of the earlier Stöffler globe, pp. 516–18. Both entries are by Elly Dekker.

90 See Dekker and Lippincott, 'The Scientific Instruments', especially pp. 98–106, for their views on the celestial globe. Their well-documented account is a great improvement on that in Foister, Roy and Wyld, *Making and Meaning*, but their attempts to

unravel the meaning of the painting have much in common with it, and are rejected for reasons to be given below.

91 The vanishing point as deduced from lines on the pavement suggests a viewpoint about 480 cm from its front edge. The globe would need to have been not 28 cm (like the Weimar globe) but nearly 36 cm in diameter if drawn from the same perspective. The stand seems to have been about 4 ft high (122 cm), with lower shelf about 16 in above the pavement (41 cm). It cannot have been drawn from a normal standing position, but it is wrong to conclude (as some do) that its perspective is wrong. It was probably painted from a sitting position with the eye about 120 cm from its front edge. The upper shelf is of little help to us, since the sides are largely hidden. The lower shelf seems to have been about 2 ft wide, or 61 cm.

92 Thus F. A. Stebbins, 'The Astronomical Instruments in Holbein's *Ambassadors*', *Journal of the Royal Astronomical Society of Canada*, 56 (1962), pp. 45–52, at p. 47, holds that the globe is set for latitude 43° N, judging by the meridian ring, but nearer 53° N by the constellations. The first is a mistake, perhaps stemming from the author's having relied too heavily on his use of graduations on the meridian ring. In fact the perspective geometry of the ring and globe of stars is right for around latitude 52°, give or take a degree. London's latitude is 51.5°. Dekker and Lippincott, 'The Scientific Instruments', pp. 105–06, follow a similar line of argument to Stebbins, and conclude that the globe is set for a Rome latitude (42° N) and not for London. A second set of graduations, offering a potentially misunderstood 48° N, they consider as possibly hinting at Polisy. They conclude that the painting is not related to the sojourn of the sitters in London. 'It is not set to reflect a London sky', they write categorically, and so decide against any interpretation based on English politics – all this because they prefer readings on a scale to a globe, its stars and its rings plain for Holbein to see as he painted. As to those rings, it is doubtful whether there is any astrological significance in the arrangement, but it is perhaps worth mentioning that the ring crossing the tail of Cygnus could have been used to mark the mundane houses on the astrological system favoured by Regiomontanus and other astrologers of the period.

93 'The Scientific Instruments', p. 106, and appendix 11 (p. 125). Their lengthy criticism of the sentence and a half I gave to the subject in my 1978 Kratzer article is based entirely on their own

procedure. (That I long ago announced that I was abandoning my old assumption of a morning painting and a date around the autumnal equinox is hardly relevant.)

94 See p. 198 below. The constellation chart of Fig. 7, p. 109, may be found useful here.

95 In the sentence I devoted to the globe in my Kratzer article of 1978 I stated that the constellation was 'marked as *Galacia*', following Mary Hervey in her belief that the word referred to the French cock. (The Roman name for the Gauls, *Galli*, and the adjective *gallicanus* were associated with *gallus*, a cock, at an early date.) The putative cock is in fact placed near the word *Galacia*, which conventionally refers to the (nearby) Milky Way. Whether there was any imagined play on words it is impossible to say. *Galaxias* is late classical Latin, directly from the Greek. *Via lactea* was the older Latin alternative, and was commonly used for the Milky Way, even up to the twentieth century. On Schöner's gores, the word is spelt *Galaxia.*

96 For numerous literary references (some of them unreliable) see R. H. Allen, *Star Names: Their Lore and Meaning* (New York, 1963), originally *Star-Names and Their Meanings* (1899), pp. 192–98.

97 Hervey, *Holbein's 'Ambassadors'*, p. 210. Dekker and Lippincott take issue with Hervey's statement (and with the old statement of mine that followed Hervey's), which they say 'rests on two significant misunderstandings'. On the contrary, it rests on no particular argument beyond the plain resemblance of the constellation to a cock, the symbol of France. Admitting in the end that making a punning reference to France is conceivable, they then add that 'nothing on the surface of the globe has been manipulated in order to do so' ('The Scientific Instruments', p. 105). No one ever suggested that it had; but the *surface itself* could certainly have been manipulated to bring the symbol to face the viewer.

98 See also Hervey, *Holbein's 'Ambassadors'*, pp. 53–54, 59, 62, and Brown, 'The Dinteville Family', pp. 79–80.

99 On the notebook, which he copied out to a large extent while still in the Carthusian monastery at Maurbach, see also the Kratzer biography in my *Stars, Minds and Fate*, pp. 375, 378–79. In the royal inventory of 1547 (David Starkey (ed.), *The Inventory of King Henry VIII*), there are 'pillars' in items 3305 ('a litel pillar of astronomye of golde'), 10487, 15849 and 16680. More ambiguous are 'an hower instrument pillor fasshion enameled half blewe' (2094) and 'a clocke pillor fasshion enameled with imagerie

garnished with diamountes and rubies and a greate perle on the toppe of the handle having twoo vyces [screws or fastenings] one garnished with a rubie and a diamounte' (2095). These two were in the Secret Jewel House in the Tower. Since there are mechanical clocks in pillar form, these need not have been cylinder sundials.

100 For more on its use see my *Chaucer's Universe* (Oxford, revised edn 1990), pp. 111–16.

101 The gnomon is in the first or second degree of Taurus (painting: 11/12 April), or in the last or penultimate degree of Leo (painting: 14/15 August). The calendar scales are more accurately placed than one has any right to expect of a painter. Such scales have to serve the four years of the leap-year cycle, and are a day out of true for 1533. If we are to look closer for an accurate and significant setting, then presumably Kratzer's Alfonsine tables would have been consulted. Kratzer would have said that the Sun occupied the two degrees between noon on 10 April and noon on 12 April, or between midnight commencing 12 August and midnight commencing 14 August. There seems to be a slight space between the gnomon and the end of the line of division of the signs, making 11 April and 12 August the more probable pair of alternatives. The date of 13 August has only a slight (ecclesiastical) recommendation: it is the eve of the Annunciation of the Blessed Virgin Mary. Since Dinteville was kicking his heels waiting for Anne Boleyn to bear a child, it is worth mentioning that the future Queen Elizabeth would eventually be born on 7 September at about 3 p.m., which now seems an unlikely occasion for the painting. The August date will later be ruled out completely.

102 It is not necessary to give a full mathematical expression here for the shadow length in non-standard positions, but since its behaviour is not intuitively obvious it may be worth pointing out how the shadow lengthens. As the dial is rotated as a whole, so as to make the gnomon deviate more from the direction of the Sun (in azimuth), the shadow is of course inclined more to the vertical, but *its lower tip descends*, that is, comes closer to the table. For small angular shift the change is negligible. For the dial as painted, the drop is only about six parts in a thousand. To find a good approximation to the time of day one may simply draw a *horizontal* through the shadow tip until the line meets the vertical through the gnomon (the ideal vertical, for correct use on the day in question).

103 Stebbins, 'The Astronomical Instruments', p. 49, calls this 'an instrument for taking altitudes', which is true but not enlightening. There is an account of it in Peter I. Drinkwater, *The Sundials of Nicholaus Kratzer* (Shipston-on-Stour, 1993), 13 pp. See Appendix 1, below.

104 'The Scientific Instruments', pp. 109–12. On this tack they liken it to another 'dial-maker', as engraved on a mining compass of *c.* 1600, an illustration that is plainly allied to the text in the Kratzer notebook (Oxford, Corpus Christi College, MS 152, fol. 10v). The latter text, while not relevant here, is interesting in its own right. It is copied from a fifteenth-century original. Besides being different from the instrument in the paintings, it is much simpler in conception. Strangely enough, Dekker and Lippincott end their account with a suggestion that the instrument in the painting (which they call a 'universal equinoctial dial') might have been used to collect empirical information to enable time-telling devices to be calibrated. While it would not have been in principle impossible, they give no evidence that such a strange procedure was ever followed. No small instrument could have competed with existing astronomical tables and geometrical techniques.

105 Two common types of simple medieval horary quadrant are known, sometimes distinguished as *quadrans vetus* and *quadrans vetustissimus* (respectively old and oldest). For the early history see R. P. Lorch, 'A Note on the Horary Quadrant', *Journal for the History of Arabic Science*, 5 (1981), pp. 115–20. The so-called 'new quadrant' (*quadrans novus*) offers so much more that it should not be considered an extension of them. (It is closely related to the astrolabe and would be hard to explain to a student who had not first studied that instrument.) The quadrant in the painting is of another sort. It was perhaps first correctly identified by Drinkwater, *The Sundials*. In my 1978 Kratzer article I called it a 'meteoroscope', for reasons that puzzled Dekker and Lippincott ('The Scientific Instruments', p. 112 n. 44) as much as they now puzzle me. A meteoroscope, however, does not have to be a calculating instrument, as they apparently believe. See *OED*. Oddly enough, the name would not have been a bad one for the compound solar instrument.

106 Foister, in *Making and Meaning*, p. 36, suggests that the pinnules are wrongly placed, and she also objects that the instrument is upside down. This is not surprising: it would hardly have been in character with the painting had one of the sitters been holding it

to the Sun. (Is a cabbage in a still life not authentic because it is not being eaten?) In any case, for *computational* use, or for *showing* the hour corresponding to a given solar altitude and season, a quadrant can be in any orientation whatsoever.

107 Taking thirteen solstitial or equinoctial test points I find the root mean square error to be only 1.25°. Not bad for a painting. Kratzer's manuscript drawing is in MS Corpus Christi College, Oxford, MS 152, at fol. 92r.

108 There is a beautiful brass quadrant of the same general type, dated 1599, included as the chief feature of an instrument which is now in Florence. Bearing the name Christoph Schissler, it is for a latitude of 48.25° and its hour lines are well nigh perfect. It would be wrong to compare these three media (paper, wood and brass) but I am sure that Kratzer was not in the same class of instrument-maker as Schissler, for whose quadrant see Maria Luisa Righini Bonelli, *Il Museo di Storia della Scienza a Firenze* (Florence, 1968), plate 55. His astronomical expertise, on the other hand, should not be underestimated, as I believe this present chapter proves.

109 More specifically, the planes of the 'outer' faces all pass through the east-west line of the celestial equator, while those of the 'side' faces pass through the north-south line of that same circle of the celestial sphere. A reasonably good and intuitive feel for the layout of the hour lines can be had without much astronomical knowledge. Imagine the celestial sphere carrying the Sun, Moon and stars to be rotating around the polar axis once a day, and imagine that we are at the centre of a *fixed* grid of lines resembling the lines on the surface of a peeled orange (genetically modified, if need be) with twenty-four segments. One of the lines should be on the meridian, the central pith representing the polar axis. The Sun is not fixed on the celestial sphere but moves round it slowly, taking a year to return to any starting point. Its path is inclined at about 23.5° to the celestial equator. One might express this last property differently: the Sun's distance from the poles varies – it comes closest to the northern pole in summer and closest to the southern pole in winter. *No matter where the Sun is in relation to the pole* (something that varies with season but that may be treated as though constant over a day) *it will pass from one segment of the orange to the next every hour*. When it does so it lies on one of the twenty-four semicircular arcs separating the segments of the orange. We may call the planes between segments 'hour planes'.

When the Sun is in this position it can cast a shadow of the polar axis (which we can think of as a gnomon) precisely through the opposite interface between segments, that is, the extended hour plane. Imagine now that we slice through the 'orange' with another plane (we shall call it the 'dial plane') to carry the hour markings of our sundial. The dial plane can be skewed at almost any angle that we find convenient, and does not have to be symmetrical with respect to the meridian. (In the case of dials on buildings, for instance, one may have little choice in the positioning of the dial plane.) How the hour planes are cut by the dial plane will decide the shadow lines on it. The important point to grasp is that, given the position of the dial plane, the hour lines are given once and for all, and that *they will be correct for every day of the year, regardless of season.* To get a *symmetrical* set of hour lines one has to slice the orange in a symmetrical way, for example ensuring that the dial plane passes through the east-west or north-south lines in one's locality. (Those directions on a level surface are of course related to the lie of the polar axis.)

110 Alexander Sturgis, *Telling Time* (London, 2000), p. 12. The book accompanied an exhibition at the National Gallery, London, 18 October 2000–14 January 2001.

111 While different spellings are used, the instrument should not be confused with Ptolemy's *triquetrum*, as it has been by some who have written about *The Ambassadors*. Its medieval ancestry includes texts by Franco of Polonia and Bernard of Verdun, but they were perhaps derived from related instruments from the Islamic world. The common later spelling *turketum* (cf. *turcus* for 'Turkish') seems to stem from that belief. See my *Richard of Wallingford* (Oxford, 1976), ii, pp. 296–300; and for a possible contribution from Muslim Spain to its evolution see R. P. Lorch, 'The Astronomical Instruments of Jâbir ibn Aflah and the Torquetum', *Centaurus*, 20 (1976), pp. 11–34. The instrument is versatile, and amounts to a combination of equatorial and ecliptic mountings. In that sense one could say that its principles are still in common use. Kratzer's poor manuscript drawing of the instrument (see Fig. 16, from Oxford, Corpus Christi College, MS 152) stems from a medieval source. The superior woodcut illustration in Apian's *Astronomicum Caesareum* (Ingolstadt, 1540) is often mentioned in the Holbein connection. Note Apian's earlier use of the same cut in his *Introductio geographica* (Ingolstadt, 1533), for which see Fig. 17. An earlier illustration, perhaps the first to be

printed, is in Gregor Reisch, *Margarita philosophica* (4th edn, Strasbourg, 1512).

112 Or 'crest ecliptic'. As a noun, *cresta* could be used to denote the urn on a tombstone.

113 Dekker and Lippincott, 'The Scientific Instruments', p. 123. This notion they rightly call 'tenuous at best', but it falls in with their overall conclusion that 'none of the dials in the painting depicts a scientific instrument "displaying" time'.

114 Dekker and Lippincott, 'The Scientific Instruments', pp. 120–21, claim that, before Erasmus Habermel's modifications of the mid-sixteenth century, 'the torquetum did not allow for observations relative to all three coordinate-systems'; and they seem to be concerned at the absence of hinges between the ecliptic plane and the equatorial plane. In fact the three systems are all easily implemented. To take a torquetum of Apian type: (1) ecliptic longitude registers on the zodiac scale (using the alidade, below the four turned legs in Holbein's painting) and ecliptic latitude on the 'crest' scale (half-hidden behind the pendant scale); (2) equatorial hour angle registers on the scale on the hinged wooden base while declination is found by setting the alidade to the head of Aries, sighting the object, and adjusting the reading on the ecliptic scale by adding or subtracting the obliquity (which could be done easily with a second scale, backing the ecliptic scale); (3) altitude is read directly off the pendant scale, while azimuth could be found by the same technique as in (2), after folding down the hinged equatorial scale until it is level. A standard wedge or peg keeps it in the raised position.

115 This is a fairly precise figure. The reading is certainly nearer 6 than 7, but the point is not a critical one. The plumbline of the hinged semicircular plate appears to be not quite vertical, but this is an optical illusion created by the ten-degree lines. There is a vertical crack between two of the oak planks of the panel in this region and the corresponding planks of oak, the seventh and eighth, were very slightly misaligned in the regluing after 1891. (See Wyld, 'The Restoration History', pp. 21, 24.) A non-vertical plumbline would not affect our conclusion, which rests on dial readings.

116 The *precise* Alfonsine figures with 4:10 p.m. would mean setting the Moon at less than 2 minutes before the 2 a.m. mark on the hour scale, while the rounded figures (longitudes 31° 241° and hour 4:00 p.m) would give a Moon setting of 2:00 a.m. precisely.

One might blend the figures to provide a worse or a better answer, but these seem to be the most probable options. On the question of Kratzer's command of the more difficult parts of mathematical astronomy there is very little direct evidence, but in an addendum to my biographical essay on him (see my *Stars, Minds and Fate*, p. 399) I noted his purchase in 1535 of the severely mathematical manuscript which is now British Library MS Royal 12.G.1.

117 That the 'cosmic zone' includes the book suggests to Claussen ('De doppelte Boden', p. 180) that it has a spiritual or astronomical content.

118 'One Turkeye carpett for the Communyon table', cited from 1552 in *OED* from J. O. Payne, *St Paul's Cathedral in the Time of Edward VI* (London, 1893), p. 24. For a history of oriental carpets in the context of western Christianity, see Volkmar Gantzhorn, *Oriental Carpets: Their Iconology and Iconography from Earliest Times to the Eighteenth Century* (Köln, 1998), referred to more fully below.

119 David Starkey (ed.), *The Inventory of King Henry VIII* includes more than eighty entries with Turkey carpets, but some are for multiple items. Thus inventory item 12148 lists seventeen 'carpettes of Turquey makinge of soundrye fasshions serving for Tables and Footcarpettes'.

120 The possibility is raised in Foister, Roy and Wyld, *Making and Meaning*, p. 37. The Kratzer drawing of a torquetum, to which they refer, is of a different design, however, and is shown in a very different position from that in the painting.

121 Studies of Holbein's technique in oil painting are well summarised in Maryan Ainsworth, '"Paternes for Physioneamyes": Holbein's Portraiture Reconsidered', *Burlington Magazine*, 132 (1990), pp. 173–86. Holbein used his drawings as patterns, their outlines being transferred to the panel either by pricking and pouncing with black dust (such as blackened chalk) or by covering the verso with black chalk and tracing with a sharp instrument (rather as is done with carbon paper). In the 1530s Holbein perfected his style of drawing so as to make it more suited to the second method.

122 The Heidelberg Catechism (1563 and later), which eventually became the most commonly used in the continental reformed churches, interprets the Gospel as meaning that Christ was in hell *before* his death, not after.

123 Foister, Roy and Wyld, *Making and Meaning*, p. 91.

124 Dekker and Lippincott, 'The Scientific Instruments', pp. 93–98. On the gores from the 1550s and the offending globe (now in the New York Public Library) see A. David Baynes-Cope, 'The Investigation of a Group of Globes', *Imago mundi*, 33 (1981), pp. 9–20. Michael Levey had earlier given a useful list of better readings than Hervey's for what remains of Holbein's names on the terrestrial globe. While he believed that the objects in the still life have a collective meaning, Levey was prepared to write that 'it is conceivable that some of the names were put in merely to avoid blank spaces on the map of Europe'. See his *National Gallery Catalogue: The German School* (London, 1959), pp. 47–54. His brief comments on the scientific aspects of the painting rested mainly on Hervey and information given by A. Barclay and W. E. Pretty of the Science Museum during the Second World War.

125 David Starkey (ed.), *The Inventory of King Henry VIII*, items 17940 and 15420 respectively. Another 'great' terrestrial globe is item 11656.

126 For an account of state-sponsored piracy as a political force, see Michel Le Bris, *D'or, de rêves et de sang: l'épopée de la filibuste, 1494–1588* (Paris, 2001). The second date refers to the English privateer, Francis Drake.

127 *Making and Meaning*, p. 40. The design, now in the British Museum, is in black ink and wash and is about two inches in diameter. It includes a pair of dividers, a pair of serpents, a pair of dolphins (or grotesque fishes of some other sort) and a pair of cornucopias. Foister reads the motto as '*Prvdentement et par compas incontinent tu viendras*' and translates it as 'You will come back immediately in a prudent and measured way', which she says 'might be read as a suitable motto for a diplomatic mission'. The last three words, however, read '*incontinent rich viendras*'. Taken together with the cornucopias, they suggest a more transparent personal message, wishing a friend a lucrative journey.

128 Musea voor Schone Kunsten van België, item 6950. It was painted under the influence of a series of prints (Hieronymus Cock, 1565) based in turn on a series of seven painted canvases on that same theme by Frans Floris (1557). For an illustration and sources see Tineke Padmos and Geert Verpaemel (eds), *De Geleerde Wereld van Keizer Karel*. Catalogue of an exhibition: Wereldwijs: Wetenschappers rond Keizer Karel, 23 September to 3 December 2000 (Louvain, 2000), pp. 22–24 and 127. Astrology (*sic*) is represented by a celestial globe, and music by a lute.

129 It has a folding 45° hinge, interesting in its own right, but not likely to have made it very reliable.

130 Petrus Apianus, *Eyn newe unnd wohlgegründte Underweysung aller Kauffmanns Rechnung* (Ingolstadt, 1527).

131 They are 27 x 27 x 112 and 27 x 70000 respectively.

132 M. Rasmussen, 'The Case of Flutes in Holbein's *The Ambassadors*', *Early Music* (February 1995), pp. 114–23. There might conceivably be six tubes, but five seems more likely.

133 Worms, 1525; 1st edn, Wittenberg, 1524. For the very convoluted publishing history of Luther's hymns, and the numerous editions, see Markus Jenny, (ed.), *Luthers geistliche Lieder und Kirchengesäng*, Archiv zur Weimarer Ausgabe der Werke Martin Luthers, iv (1985).

134 Johannes Lichtenberger (astrologer to Frederick III) made play with the number 19. He predicted the birth of a prophet who was later identified with Luther. See my *Stars, Minds and Fate*, p. 80. *The Book of Common Prayer* has the hymn under 'Ordering of Priests', in very free translation. This 'Veni Creator Spiritus' is traditionally ascribed to Charlemagne. The first stanza of the Lutheran version of 'Veni Sancte Spiritus', the hymn illustrated in the painting, is translated from the Latin hymn ascribed to King Robert of France (AD 991), and has been traced to a service-book of the church in Basel of the year 1514. The two last verses of it are Luther's own. The common modern melody is from 1609 (Erythraeus).

135 Hervey, *Holbein's 'Ambassadors'*, p. 203, gave this idea currency, but seems to have thought that while the painted image was *produced* with a distorting mirror it could be *viewed* slantwise without one. For a more recent attempt to solve the problem optically see E. R. Samuel, 'Death in the Glass: A New View of Holbein's *Ambassadors*', *Burlington Magazine*, 115 (October 1963), pp. 436–41.

136 J. Baltrusaitis, *Anamorphic Art*, trans. W. Strachan (Cambridge, 1977), pp. 104–05. This general survey was earlier published in French (1955, 1969, and later 1984). Leonardo's known sketches are from the Codex Atlanticus (1483–1518). Especially interesting are literary references to other specimens by Leonardo, now lost, and also two items in the Lipschitz Collection in New York (Charles V and St Anthony of Padua, from 1533 and 1535 respectively). Baltrusaitis argues that this general movement owes much to some geometrical experimenting on perspective technique by

Dürer, dating from 1525. The connection does not seem to me to be very clear.

137 Foister, Roy and Wyld, *Making and Meaning*, pp. 52–55, 94–96; Wyld, 'The Restoration History', pp. 22–23, 25.

138 Ganz, *The Paintings*, catalogue no. 128, plate 169; and Rowlands, *Holbein*, plate 243, cat. R. 35. The New York version is from the Lee of Fareham and Bache Collections. Some still follow a traditional assignment to Holbein, but R. Strong, *National Portrait Gallery: Tudor and Jacobean Portraits*, 2 vols (London, 1969), suggests the studio of Willem Scrots. The prince is in his sixth year, so the original belongs to the last year of Holbein's life. There is a generally similar but very weak drawing of the prince by an unknown hand in the Royal Collection. See Parker, *The Drawings*, plate 85. Richard Foster and Pamela Tudor Craig, *The Secret Life of Paintings* (Woodbridge, 1986), p. 89, referring to Baltrusaitis, note that the Scrots painting hung in Whitehall Palace, where the Company of the Lord Chamberlain's men (to which Shakespeare belonged) often performed. They make the intriguing suggestion that these words from *Richard II*, act 2, scene 2, may refer to it: 'For Sorrow's eye, glazed with blinding tears, / Divides one thing entire to many objects; / Like perspectives which, rightly gaz'd upon, / Show nothing but confusion, eye'd awry, / Distinguish form!'

139 There is a slight complication in any discussion of the original size of the painting, since J.-B.-P. Le Brun's sale catalogue of 1792 illustrates it in a poor engraving as though it then carried above the present scene an appreciable area of curtaining that is no longer there. It cannot have had the stated dimension of 54 pouces width (63 English inches or less, according to the pouce used). Dickes, *Holbein's Celebrated Picture*, p. 8, says that he had seen copies of Le Brun's *Galerie des peintres* (1790), where 54 had been altered by pen to 84. If it was truly 96 pouces in height, as the catalogue has it, then I can only suggest that at some stage a vast extra piece was added to fit it to a new location. The entire composition is out of keeping with the extra curtaining, and the old paint was applied so as to stop at the upper edge. The existing curtaining and crucifix had been crudely overpainted in a dark heavy green, however, which could just possibly have been intended to blend in with an added panel. Another possible explanation would be that the engraver added the curtain when he noticed that his preparatory sketch did not match the

(wrongly) stated dimensions. On this question see also Hervey, *Holbein's 'Ambassadors'*, pp. 5–10.

140 From the 'lower axis' to the top right corner is about 2022 mm, making 80 units of 0.995 imperial inches. The Tudor standard yard, used between 1497 and 1588, is accurately known. It is 0.037 inches less than the modern imperial standard, so we can take the English inch of the time to be 0.999 imperial inches, the equivalent of 2.54 cm to the nearest 0.01 cm. See R. E. Zupko, *British Weights and Measures: A History from Antiquity to the Seventeenth Century* (Madison, Wisconsin, 1977), p. 77. The many other units of potential historical importance include the *Zoll* used in Prussia, equivalent to the 'Rhineland inch' (1.03 in, 2.62 cm) and the Austrian *Zoll* (1.04 in, 2.64 cm). See Zupko, *British Weights and Measures*, p. 174, for others. These were thus appreciably larger than Holbein's unit. The Bavarian inch was actually *smaller* than the English.

141 Thus in the verses in which Christ proposes what became known as the Lord's Prayer, we find that 'The light of the body is the eye' (Luke 11:34); and in John 8:12: 'Then spake Jesus again unto them, saying, I am the light of the world: he that followeth me shall not walk in darkness, but shall have the light of life.' In II Corinthians 4:6, these ideas are pointedly extended: 'For God, who commanded the light to shine out of darkness, hath shined in our hearts, to [give] the light of the knowledge of the glory of God in the face of Jesus Christ.'

142 Charles de Bouelles, *Agonologiae Iesu Christi libri quatuor* (Paris, 1533), fols 94–95. The preface, dated from Noyon, February 1531, deals with the crucifixion in minute circumstantial detail, for example in its timing.

143 Thomas à Kempis (*c.* 1379–1471), *Of the Imitation of Christ*, trans. from the Latin by William Benham (London, 1905). See Book III (On Inward Consolation), part iv, chapter 38. A prolific theologian, Thomas was born at Kempen near Düsseldorf but spent most of his very long life in a religious community near Zwolle in the Netherlands. Whitford was a Cambridge scholar who wrote many devotional works. He became a monk at Syon monastery, Isleworth, and (with interludes) remained there until its dissolution in 1539.

144 *Theologia Germanica*, trans. from the German by Susanna Winkworth (2nd edn, London, 1893; new edn, London, 1966). It is now usually ascribed to Johannes de Francfordia (*c.* 1380–1440). Cf. *Lexikon für Theologie und Kirche*, 2nd edn, x, col. 62.

145 He goes on to explain how the artist may disguise the result, for example making a head look like a landscape, but Holbein plays no such secondary tricks with his anamorphosis. See Baltrusaitis, *Anamorphic Art*, pp. 30–32.

146 For an idea of the history of this particular art in Basel from the time of the younger Holbein see Adolf Glaser, *Die basler Glasmalerei im 16. Jahrhundert seit Hans Holbein d. J.* (Winterthur, 1937). For his father's work see C. Beutler and G. Thiem, *Hans Holbein der Älter: die spätgotische Altar- und Glasmalerei* (Augsburg, 1960).

147 Albrecht Dürer, *Underweysung der Messung mit dem Zirkel und Richtscheyt* (Nürnberg, 1525), fol. Nii verso. For references to Leonardo and discussion of Holbein's possible uses of the tracing technique, see Parker, *The Drawings*, pp. 29–31.

148 On Alberti's perspective methods using his so-called 'veil' (meant chiefly for representing limited areas of a scene rather than complete paintings), see L. B. Alberti, *Opere volgari*, ed. C. Grayson, iii (Rome/Bari, 1975), p. 54, and *On Painting and Sculpture*, ed. and trans. C. Grayson (London, 1972), pp. 67–69. The veil had coloured threads at intervals making it resemble graph paper to modern eyes. Astronomers had long used similar rulings, just as they had been familiar with perspective techniques for designing instruments from antiquity onwards. On the reference to glass, see the edition cited, pp. 27–28.

149 The illumination at the end of the projected image of the skull is just under a fifth of its value at the top. The fact that a candle is not as small a source as many we can now produce, and that it would not have been easy to use it with a small (pinhole) stop, is in practice of little consequence.

150 Pliny (AD 23–79), *Natural History*, book xxxv, 81-83. Apelles lived in the fourth century BC and there are many stories attached to his name. The historical importance of the friendly contest has been much discussed. See Bätschmann and Griener, *Hans Holbein*, pp. 13–14 and 19–21, for a discussion and several references.

151 See Bätschmann and Griener, *Hans Holbein*, pp. 21–22, for this, the compliment paid to Dürer by Celtis, and the earliest known instance (an inscription for Fra Angelico, d. 1455). For Folly's remarks, see B. Radice's translation, p. 149, or J.-B. Kan's, p. 50.

152 R. B. McKerrow and F. S. Ferguson, *Title-Page Borders Used in England and Scotland, 1485–1640* (London and Oxford, 1932), no. 8; cf. Bätschmann and Griener, *Hans Holbein*, pp. 22–23.

153 Rowlands, *Holbein*, p. 63.

154 The argument in Bätschmann and Griener for Holbein's self-view rests partly on the artist's inscription on his portrait of Melanchthon, which seems to them to contradict Dürer's idea that painters could only treat of the body of the sitter, and not of the soul. Apelles had claimed that the aim of art was complete similitude. See Bätschmann and Griener, *Hans Holbein*, pp. 31, 34. They also reproduce the Leland poems at p. 212 (after S. Foister's transcription of Bodleian Library, Oxford, MS Tanner 464, iv, fols 55r, 64r). Leland pays a similar Apellean compliment to Holbein in a poem that was published in 1542 along with a Holbein woodcut of the aged poet Sir Thomas Wyatt (reproduced in Rowlands, *Holbein*, p. 95).

155 J. W. Norton-Kyshe, *The Law and Customs Relating to Gloves* (London, 1901), and J. Braun, S.J., *Die liturgische Gewandung* (Freiburg im Breisgau, 1907), pp. 359–82.

156 Most of the rules concerning black are rules banning its use, for instance during the display of, or procession with, the eucharist. Cloth of this colour may not carry funereal emblems.

157 Wyld, 'The Restoration History', p. 8. Levey had earlier noted (*The German School*, p. 47) that there were two signs of reworking (known in the trade as *pentimenti*, changes of mind) in de Selve's cheek. The question of the liturgical colours used in different places in Holy Week will be touched upon again briefly in chapter 11 below.

158 Such terms are used very loosely. Just as 'pentacle' (originally meaning a five-pointed figure) is often used confusingly of figures with six points, so 'Solomon's Seal' can be used of a five-pointed star. In medieval use, the endless five-pointed star or 'knot' was often used as a talisman to protect the bearer. It could be taken to represent the five wounds of the crucified Christ. Both five- and six-pointed stars are found on children's cradles. See J. Schouten, *The Pentagram as a Medical Symbol* (Nieuwkoop, 1968), pp. 32–33. 'Magen David' in Jewish liturgy signifies God as the shield of David. The symbol has no biblical or Talmudic authority but it was used by medieval Jewish mystics and later taken by the Jewish community of Prague as an official symbol. There is no reason to think that in Holbein's time the hexagram was widely considered a symbol of Judaism. Its two principal roles in modern history – in Nazi Germany and the state of Israel – are well known.

159 The white line on the turkey rug has a certain width of its own,

leading to some uncertainty in estimating the hidden diameter. Working from the middle of the white, as in the suggested reconstruction in our figure, we find the diameter quoted here. Working from the upper or lower edges of the white will change the implied radius by just under an inch, up or down.

160 While the following data cannot be absolutely exact, especially as we cannot know whether the Moon's position was calculated with or without lunar latitude, all plausible variants of them fit extremely well to the painting. With the Sun at longitude 31.5° (a rounded figure for Good Friday) and an altitude of -14° (that is, with the Sun below the horizon), it will be at azimuth about 49° west of north. Taking the Moon to be on the ecliptic at longitude 244° it will be at altitude about -11° and at azimuth 110° east of north. If the globe was meant to have the Sun and Moon positioned on it according to the evening situation (taking its position to be a true indication of the state of the heavens in the evening), the Moon's azimuth would have been about 112° and the Moon would then have been a couple of degrees lower in altitude. The painting as interpreted here does not allow us to decide between these two situations, but it does allow us to confirm with high probability that the *date* is 11 April 1533, for on no other day would the Sun and Moon positions fit together with such perfect symmetry. The quoted (negative) altitude of the Sun fits well with the main line of sight up to Christ, which crosses the globe at its extreme right-hand edge, where the Sun is, as long as we measure altitudes from the top surface of the horizon ring (as is correct). I suspect that, when drafting the globe, Holbein put his compass point in the *middle* of the bar, and so slightly too low, but it is difficult to make out the centre he chose since so much of the circumference is obscured.

161 On the Armenian symbolism I follow Gantzhorn, *Oriental Carpets*. See especially pp. 36–42 and illustrations 248–90 and associated text. I have here concentrated only on what Holbein or his friends might easily have learned. The irregular octagons on the carpet when opened out (squares with corners snipped off) have a more difficult cosmographical meaning that they might not have known. The swastika-like forms in the trellis squares are common. There is said to be another meaning for the 'S', in which Armenians are said to have seen not only a sign for God but a representation of a dragon symbolising goodness and wisdom. Another shape is representative of the Tree of Jesse.

These are unlikely candidates for reuse in the painting. Already in the first edition of this book I conjectured that there was a cross in the middle of the painting. Confirmation of the idea came from Pico della Mirandola, *Conclusiones nongentae, in omni genere scientiarum: quas olim Io. Picus Mirandula Romæ disputandas proposuit:* [etc.] (Nuremberg: Johann Petreius, 1532). See especially pp. 154–55 and 159 in this edition of the work, which was first published in 1496. Pico's great European influence cannot be doubted. We recall that Thomas More translated some of his works, for example. The letters in the central vertical of Pico's hexagram, reading down, are *aleph-shin-mem* (making *'asham*), while the short horizontal is (right to left) *yod-shin-waw* (reading *Yeshu*). The two together make a cross proclaiming that Jesus is a sacrifice. (There are only verbal descriptions in Pico's book, and no matching diagrams.) Professor Bernard Goldstein points out to me that the word *'asham* usually denotes guilt or guilt offering, and not a lamb or ram (whether or not as a zodiacal sign). The switch of meaning was often used, however, in Christian commentary on the writings of St Paul, so that it might be significant that the beam of the invisible crucifix in the painting goes through the ram's head on the horizon ring of the celestial globe. For much on this question see further our chapter 15. There are many examples in Christian art of a lamb depicted on a crucifix, but at the crossing. For a valuable discussion of Pico's cabalism, see Brian P. Copenhaver, 'Number, shape and meaning in Pico's Christian Cabala', in Anthony Grafton and Nancy Siraisi (eds), *Natural Particulars: Nature and the Disciplines in Renaissance Europe* (Cambridge, Mass., and London, 1999), pp. 25–76. Note the many examples in Pico's book of his interest in trinitarian ciphers and the mystery of the number 27. Note too his interest in the number 40 as the sum of the geometric progression 1+3+9+27 (Copenhaver, p. 56). Could this explain the use of 40 inches as a module for Holbein's painting?

162 Hervey, *Holbein's 'Ambassadors'*, pp. 225–27. William Lethaby noted the resemblance independently of her, a few years later. See Richard Foster, *Patterns of Thought: The Hidden Meaning of the Great Pavement of Westminster Abbey* (London, 1989, 1991), especially pp. 58–60 for the Holbein association. The Cosmati who laid such pavements take their name from that of the leading family responsible for work of this sort in Italy in the middle ages, Cosmatus. Their work nevertheless stands in a tradition of mosaic

design going back to antiquity, and there are many similarities between, for example, the overall placement of medallions in relation to a square in antiquity and in medieval Cosmati work.

163 More often spelt 'Odoric'. A shadowy figure, perhaps better named as Petrus Oderisius or Odericus. On his identity see Foster, *Patterns of Thought*, pp. 21–27.

164 This will be touched on again at p. 253 below. 'Neoplatonism' is a term used to describe the revived and revised philosophy of Plato that was dominant in the Greco-Roman world from the third century to the sixth. It had a profound influence on Jewish, Christian and Islamic thought.

165 Typical passages referring to this prediction are *Opus maius*, ed. J. H. Bridges, 2 vols (Oxford, 1897), i, p. 220; and *Opus tertium*, ed. J. S. Brewer, in *Fr. Rogeri Baconi opera quaedam hactenus inedita* (London, 1859), i, p. 49. Bacon follows the text of Albumasar fairly closely. See North, *Horoscopes and History*, n. 90, with the relevant passage from E. Garin's edition of Albumasar, *De coniunctionibus.*

166 'But he that received seed into the good ground is he that heareth the word, and understandeth it; which also beareth fruit, and bringeth forth, some an hundredfold, some sixty, some thirty' (Matthew 13:23). This was said to have as its hidden meaning that virgins and prelates score 100, as it were, for their chastity and sanctity, while widows and the continent score 60 and the conjugal 30. See V. F. Hopper, *Medieval Number Symbolism* (New York, 1969), p. 104.

167 H. and M. Schmidt, *Die vergessene Bildersprache christlicher Kunst* (München, 1995), pp. 232–33.

168 George Ripley, *The Compound of Alchymy* (London, 1591), at the end.

169 Foster, *Patterns of Thought*, pp. 101–03, citing also William R. Lethaby, *Westminster Abbey and the King's Craftsmen* (London, 1906), p. 311.

170 Foster, *Patterns of Thought*, p. 153.

171 Thus note the passage commenting on Plato's doctrine of creation in the commentary on the *Timaeus* of Plato written by Honorius of Autun: 'Haec eadem a Platone dicitur archetypus mundus: mundus, quia omnia continet quae in mundo sunt; archetypus, id est principalis forma. Archos (*sic*) enim est princeps, typos (*sic*) forma vel figura.' Migne, *Patrologia latina*, clxxii, col. 251.

172 The best edition is now that by Valerie I. J. Flint, 'Honorius

Augustodensis *Imago Mundi*', *Archives d'histoire doctrinale et littéraire du moyen âge*, 49 (1982), pp. 7–153. Some writers have questioned its ascription to this particular Honorius (a Benedictine monk whose working life was around 1098–1140), but they are not convincing.

173 Claussen, 'De doppelte Boden', pp. 182–85. This is the central thesis of his article, which requires him to be somewhat sceptical of Foster's conclusions. He acknowledges the cosmic aspect of the pavement, however, at which he suggests Kratzer might have marvelled. For those interested in the Westminster pavement, Claussen makes a valuable supplement to Foster. Among other things he draws attention to the marked similarity of a section of the pavement in the church of S. Crisogono in Rome to the central part of the Westminster pavement.

174 Foster, *Patterns of Thought*, p. 60.

175 For his designs for the decoration of house façades and for his other monumental work see Paul Ganz, *The Paintings*, pp. 260–75.

176 Rowlands, *Holbein*, cat. no. 60, colour plates 30–31, plates 96–97. Rowlands assigns it to the middle of Holbein's second English period, and sees Cranach's roundel portrait of Luther as a precedent and Dürer's engraving of Melanchthon (1529) as a model, a third portrait perhaps helping with the features. On Melanchthon's astrology see Stefano Caroti's chapter on the subject in Paola Zambelli (ed.), '*Astrologi Hallucinati*': *Stars and the End of the World in Luther's Time* (Berlin and New York, 1986), pp. 109–21.

177 The series was engraved by Hans Lützelburger and first printed at Lyon by Melchior and Gaspar Trechsel in 1538, but it was completed before Holbein left Basel in 1526. It has often been reprinted with other material, for example: A. M. Hind (ed.), *Hans Holbein the Younger: His Old Testament Illustrations, Dance of Death and Other Woodcuts* (London, 1912).

178 John Robyns (or Robins) was one of the leading English astronomers of his time, but was deeply concerned with technical astrological matters too. An Oxford graduate and fellow of All Souls College, he taught for a time at Henry's Oxford foundation. He eventually became canon at Windsor. His treatises on comets are in Trinity College, Cambridge, MS O.1.11, fols 1r–52v, and the Bodleian Library, Oxford, MS Ashmole 186, fols 1–14 (the first signature is misbound).

179 See Bernard Capp, *Astrology and the Popular Press: English Almanacs, 1500–1800* (London, 1979), pp. 27–28. He suggests that the first apparently native English printed work with prognostications was as late as 1539.

180 On the failure of Luther's mother's memory, see Henry Bennet, *A Famous and Godly History* (London, 1561), fol. B2r–v. The problem was one not of the hour or day but of the year, and hence of his legitimacy. Bennet cites Melanchthon.

181 Johannes Engel, *Opus astrolabii plani* (Augsburg, 1488). See my *Horoscopes and History,* Warburg Institute Surveys and Texts, 13 (London, 1986), pp. 153–55.

182 For many of the technicalities of computing these things see my *Horoscopes and History.*

183 In all strictness the data were not correct for London (lat. 51.5°) but neither were they for Augsburg (lat. near 48°). They were for the latitude of 45°, making for easy calculation. When the ascendent is near the head of Libra, however, the results are fortunately very roughly the same at all latitudes.

184 Jerome Cardan (Girolamo Cardano), *In Ptolemaei librorum de judiciis astrorum libri IV commentaria* (Lyon, 1555), p. 370 (for the drawn horoscope). See my *Horoscopes and History*, pp. 163–73 for further examples of Christ's natal horoscope. For Rossigliano, who was writing before 1521, ibid., p. 166.

185 Foister, Roy and Wyld, *Making and Meaning*, p. 83. That painting is now in Dresden.

186 The Matthäus Schwarz portrait, on pine, 61.5 x 74 cm, is now owned by the Fondazione Thyssen-Bornemisza, Lugano. There is a paper with various data, resting on the window sill. See the reproduction in Lorne Campbell, *Renaissance Portraits: European Portrait-Painting in the Fourteenth, Fifteenth and Sixteenth Centuries* (New Haven and London, 1990), p. 24. The models for the portraits were manuscript illustrations in a costume book annotated by the couple's son Konrad (born 30 October 1541), who is also portrayed in it with his own horoscope. For a detailed study of the manuscript see A. Fink, *Die Schwarzischen Trachtenbücher* (Berlin, 1963), pp. 14–15, 182–89. The whereabouts of the portrait of Barbara Schwarz were unknown to Fink. The three horoscopes were cast by Regiomontanus' method (not the standard method of the Augsburg handbook). Amberger has moved both horoscopes to the window pane. Matthäus Schwarz's is for his birth at 6:30 a.m. on a civil date of 20 February 1497. This is the moment

of sunrise. The date is misread as an afternoon date on the previous day by those who do not realise that the astronomer counts the day as commencing at noon. Confusingly the horoscope has 1542 (and only that) within the central square, as though the horoscope was for the moment of painting, and there is a mistake on the painted paper, which gives the time of painting correctly in astronomical time but wrongly in civil time. It is *daybreak*, 4:15 a.m. (before sunrise), on 23 March 1542. Our view of the sitter's character surely changes a little in the light of knowledge of the circumstances under which he chose to be portrayed, even though the fact that the portrayal was done in two stages confuses the issue.

187 For the various options see my *Horoscopes and History*. For the record, here are the house divisions on the Regiomontanus system for this value of the ascendent point at the latitude of London (51° 30′), with values on the standard system added in parentheses: house I begins at the ascendent, 180° 20′ (same); II 209° 29′ (204° 14′); III 231° 04′ (234° 21′); IV 270° 26′ (same); V 309° 43′ (306° 29′). The other six divisions are diametrically opposite these, and are found by adding 180° to each of the quoted angles.

188 This is more or less the same as accepting Good Friday as falling between 10 and 13 April inclusive.

189 I quote all these planetary positions as they would have been calculated by Kratzer (Holbein almost certainly could not have done it) using the best tables of the period, the Alfonsine. They are as follows: Sun 31°08′ (Taurus); Moon 243°57′ (Sagittarius); Mercury 17°06′ (Aries); Venus 2°52′ (Aries); Mars 336°43′ (Pisces); Jupiter 268°03′ (Sagittarius, Jupiter's domicile); Saturn 98°18′ (in Cancer, Jupiter's exaltation).

190 See my *Chaucer's Universe* for a discussion of the meaning of this phrase.

191 *Caput Draconis* and *Cauda Draconis*, the head and tail of the dragon respectively, are the mythical names given to the points in which the apparent paths of the Sun and Moon through the stars appear to cross (they are the so-called ascending and descending nodes of the Moon's orbit, respectively).

192 The Sun and Moon, often with human faces, are very frequently drawn on either side of the cross in medieval and renaissance art, for example to illustrate religious books, church windows and altar retables. There are literally thousands of known examples. The Sun is usually on the left and the Moon on the right,

although this is by no means always the case. They were said to be placed there to symbolise the two natures of Christ: the Sun his divine nature and the Moon his human nature. (St Gregory the Great writes on this theme in his second homily on the Evangelist.) There is naturally no hint of an eclipse in such drawings. For the bare mention of a miraculous eclipse, however, see Sacrobosco's words in Lynn Thorndike, *The Sphere of Sacrobosco and its Commentators* (Chicago, 1948), pp. 116–17 (Latin) and 142. This is elaborated upon in the commentary ascribed to Michael Scot, ibid., pp. 341–42. Cecco d'Ascoli, ibid., pp. 409–11, argued that it was neither natural nor miraculous, and noted other explanations that were circulating (cometary or planetary obscuration, magic stones, etc.).

193 On the form of the medallion in the painting see Foister, Roy and Wyld, *Making and Meaning*, pp. 13, 89, 91; and Wyld, 'The Restoration History', pp. 10–11. The Holbein sketches (black chalk and grey wash on paper) are in the Öffentliche Kunstsammlun (Kupferstichkabinett), Basel. Foister conjectures that the sketches may have been made because Dinteville had not brought his medallion with him, but this is almost certainly wrong, since by the rule of the order he was obliged to wear it daily, in a form appropriate to the occasion. It would also have been an important accessory for ambassadorial display. For much on the rules of the order see Hervey, *Holbein's 'Ambassadors'*, pp. 207–09. For another connection between Holbein and English angels, see p. 19 above. The English kings touched for the king's evil at various times of the church year, including Holy Week. The continental custom was thought to go back to Clovis, and in England it survived with relatively few changes until the eighteenth century.

194 It has pre-Christian precedents and a surprisingly continuous history. Leopold Kretzenbacher, *Die Seelenwaage*, Buchreihe des Landesmuseums für Kärnten, 4 (Klagenfurt, 1958), includes sixty-five illustrations.

195 Kretzenbacher, *Die Seelenwaage*, plate 58, reproduced from W. Speiser, *Sankt Michael in der Kunst* (Basel, 1947).

196 See Euclid II.11 and IV.10 for the basic theorems. The construction of the golden section begins with a square such as that of the painting (without its edging strips). Draw a median line like *UK* in Fig. 26. Let an arc, centre *K* and radius *KA*, meet *KA'* produced at *S*. Draw now an arc centred at *A'* with radius *AS*, meeting *AA'*. The point where they meet divides *AA* in the required ratio.

197 William Tyndale, *The Obedience of a Christen Man* (Marlborow in the Lande of Hesse, 1528); *Collected Works*, i, p. 303.

198 In the Vulgate the text runs: 'et venerunt in locum qui dicitur Golgotha quod est Calvariae locus . . .' Cf. Mark 15:22 and John 19:17.

199 Bätschmann and Griener, *Hans Holbein*, pp. 51–53. The altarpiece (limewood, outer panels 136 x 31 cm and inner 149.5 x 31 cm) is now in the Öffentliche Kunstsammlung, Basel. Von Sandrart had copied it when it was in the Rathaus, to which place it had presumably been moved in 1529 for its protection.

200 The table is in the Hessiches Landesmuseum, Kassel. Each of the arts is represented by a woman seated in bucolic surroundings and engaged in work the significance of which is described in a text at her side. As an example: Geometry sits at a table, holding dividers over a set of geometrical figures. She is said to be correlated with the colour blue, with Thursday and the day's planet Jupiter, and with the metal tin (or pewter). And similarly for the other arts, which follow a slightly odd order: Grammar (with book), Rhetoric (with crucifix), Arithmetic (working, modern style, without abacus), Logic (crowned and with child at breast), Geometry (note the scales on the ground), Music (with zither, lute and song book), and Astronomy (armillary sphere, monstrance and snake). The central region is filled with blue sky from which the planets personified beam down their influences on their subjects. With two figures to each side of the table (which is not quite a square) one space has been left to be filled by a bald scholar, with a dog at his feet, books around him, and a desk on which is not only a lectern but a globe. The simple representation of the arts by women has a long history. One famous example is in the *Hortus deliciarum* (now only available in a nineteenth-century copy) by Herrad of Hohenbourg (often called Landsberg), ed. Rosalie Green and others, Warburg Institute, 2 vols (London, 1979), ii, p. 57.

201 On the technical meanings of 'house' see p. 223 above.

202 The painted numbers are 25 and 29.

203 For a concise collection of numerous examples, extensively annotated, it would be hard to improve on Edgar Wind, *Pagan Mysteries in the Renaissance* (London, 1958), pp. 39–50. And since the name of Petrus Apianus occurs often in a scientific connection in our book, it might be worth mentioning that in 1534 he too went in for the sport, drawing parallels between Ovid's *Fasti* and Trinitarian theology (*Pagan Mysteries*, p. 46 n. 1).

204 Plato, *Timaeus*, 34A–36D, for which see the translation and commentary by F. M. Cornford, *Plato's Cosmology* (London, 1937), pp. 57–93. Compare Aristotle, *De caelo*, 268a.12–14: 'For, as the Pythagoreans say, the world and all that is in it is determined by the number three, since beginning and middle and end give the number of an "all", and the number they give is the triad.' The passage has much more on the number three. There were many ancient texts dealing more with numerology than arithmetic proper. For thirteen such works see F. E. Robbins, in *Nicomachus of Gerasa: Introduction to Arithmetic*, trans. M. L. d'Ooge (New York and London, 1926), pp. 90–91.

205 I single out one writer who takes this line, since he has made such a close study of a key aspect of the painting, anamorphosis, and has been very influential. Jurgis Baltrusaitis, *Anamorphic Art*, pp. 94–103, pursues relentlessly the idea that there is a 'vanity of human knowledge' theme in the painting. He draws a comparison with the marquetry panels by Vincenzo dalle Vacche (1520–23) in the Louvre, which display various instruments, books, a skull, and a lute with broken string, its case upside down in shadow. He relates the Vanity theme, for instance, to the Holbein brothers' drawings in the margins of Erasmus's *Folly*, and I think has his gaze too firmly fixed on the irony of that book. 'Instead of being honoured,' he writes, 'the Arts and Sciences are presented under the symbol of Death. The anxieties of a tormented mind of the North confronted with Italian humanism are similarly manifested . . .', ibid., p. 98. He finds an Agrippa quotation that meshes with all this and conjectures that Holbein and he might have met in Italy.

206 Baltrusaitis, *Anamorphic Art*, pp. 203–05.

207 Joachim Camerarius, *Symbolorum et emblematum ex re herbaria desumtorum* (etc.) (Nürnberg, 1590), i.19.

208 Quoted by Foster, *Patterns of Thought*, p. 58, from Lethaby, *Westminster Abbey*, p. 132, and appendix, pp. 370–71.

209 Foister, *Making and Meaning*, p. 48, following M. Levey (1959) and D. Piper (1961).

210 The penitential confraternities of Spain, especially Seville, are better known for their Holy Week processions and their characteristic dress, with pointed hoods and eyeholes. Members of the Italian group I have mentioned had (and still in principle have) the unglamorous mission to bury and say prayers for the unclaimed dead, which gave them a natural role at the end of the

Holy Week drama. For their history see Francesco Sepe, *Arciconfraternita della Morte ed Orazione di Roma* (Sorrento, 1992). Groups of this sort throughout Christendom had customs (probably including that of the 'skull-and-crossbones' badges) going back to the fourteenth century and earlier, and it is not directly to them but to that common fund of custom that Dinteville's badge probably belongs.

211 R. N. Wornum, *Some Account of the Life and Works of Hans Holbein* (London, 1857), p. 180 (cited by Hervey, p. 203).

212 'In all your works remember your last things and you will not sin against the eternal.' Ecclesiasticus 7:40. More's unfinished work was first published posthumously with his collected English works (1557).

213 There is a Talmudic warrant for this view. The idea was that a three-cornered house is immune from contagion. See R. C. Thompson, *Semitic Magic* (London, 1908), pp. 186–89. On the other hand there is plenty of evidence that some necromancers thought of the circle as a place to which spirits could be summoned in safety.

214 Richard Kieckhefer, *Magic in the Middle Ages* (Cambridge, 1989), p. 161.

215 Augustine, *City of God*, books IX and X.

216 Francis Barrett, *The Magus* (London, 1801), i, p. 88, and ii, pp. 41, 80, 109. Barrett was a believer rather than a scholar, but he had combed the early literature thoroughly.

217 Book of Revelation 12:7–9.

218 H. and M. Schmidt, *Die vergessene Bildersprache*, p. 150.

219 See for instance Jerome (Hieronimus) Cardan, *De subtilitate rerum, lib. xx*, in *Opera* (Lyon, 1663), iii, p. 662.

220 'By Abraham Colorno by order of the duke of Mantua.' In London alone there are copies of the French version in the British Library, MSS Harley 3981, Kings 288, Sloane 3091; and in the Wellcome Institute, MS 4658.

221 The relevant page is reproduced (from the version in the Arsenal Library, Paris, MS 2348) by Grillot de Givry in his *Witchcraft, Magic and Alchemy*, trans. J. C. Locke (New York, 1931), p. 105.

222 The figure of the throne (ascribed to Vassallettus, late thirteenth century) is from Edward Hutton, *The Cosmati: The Roman Marble Workers of the Twelfth and Thirteenth Centuries* (London, 1950), plate 27. The pulpit is illustrated in his plate 36. For the biblical account of Solomon's throne see 2 Chronicles 9:17–19. On

the medieval iconography of the throne and treatment of this text see Francis Wormald, 'The Throne of Solomon and St Edward's Chair', in Millard Meiss, (ed.), *De Artibus Opuscula XL : Essays in Honor of Erwin Panofsky*, 2 vols (New York, 1961), i, pp. 532–39 (with illustrations in ii, pp. 175–77). The Westminster chair dates from *c.* 1299. The painting on the back might have been of Edward the Confessor, since the Scone Stone of Destiny was solemnly offered to his memory by Edward I in 1297, later to be incorporated into the chair. It has recently been returned to Scotland, showing how tenacious is the belief in the occult held by both parties.

223 Petrus Apianus, *Cosmographicus liber*, col. 63. He adapts the principles of the astrolabe to the terrestrial surface in a most unusual way, as mentioned in connection with the image of the Earth on the Greenwich ceiling. The book has many volvelles in it (cut-out paper parts that can be rotated around pivots provided by knotted threads), and there is the pivoted rule with a hexagram carefully drawn at its centre, as illustrated in our Fig. 58. Rotating around the north pole is a volvelle resembling an astrolabe rete, without stars but with a zodiac (ecliptic) ring. This revolves over a 'plate' with a world map in polar projection, and so allows the Sun to be put on the meridian for any identifiable place on the map. It cannot be said to have had many practical uses, but it does allow for the easy evaluation of time differences for different locations. The map shows most of the known world, including east and west coasts of southern America. It was very probably the source of the idea behind an Augsburg instrument dated 1557, thought to be by Christoph Schissler, now in the Österreichisches Museum für angewandte Kunst, Vienna (catalogue no. F. 1357). On this the hexagram is replaced by a flower with six petals. See Gerhart Egger (ed.), *Theatrum Orbis Terrarum: die Erfassung des Weltbildes zur Zeit der Renaissance und des Barocks* (Vienna, 1970), item 27, plates 20–22.

224 See J. Perkins, *The Crowning of the Sovereign of Great Britain and the Dominions Overseas* (London, 1953; 1st edn 1937), pp. 156–57. The area was covered with a cloth at the coronation of Charles I, but presumably not from its first use.

225 For the lesser known of these two critics see Jan R. Veenstra, *Magic and Divination at the Courts of Burgundy and France* (Leiden, 1998).

226 Hervey, *Holbein's 'Ambassadors'*, pp. 130–32. The symbol of a winged globe was put over a dormer window in the building

known as the Maison de l'Aûmonier, dating from 1545. It is likely that both brothers had a hand in the design. She found the same symbol used as a printer's device by Gryphius of Lyon in 1542, where it is accompanied by a motto having the same meaning, 'Fortune the Companion of Merit'.

227 For more details on the three with much relevance here see D. P. Walker, *Spiritual and Demonic Magic from Ficino to Campanella* (London, 1958), pp. 45–53. Since Ficino is such a crucial figure there is an extensive literature on him. A standard work in English remains P. O. Kristeller, *The Philosophy of Marsilio Ficino* (New York, 1943), but the original Italian (Florence, 1953), is fuller. See also André Chastel, *Marcel Ficin et l'art* (Geneva, 1954).

228 Thorndike, *A History of Magic*, vi, pp. 442–43. The writings at issue by Bouelles date from around 1510, while Gesner ('the German Pliny') was commenting in 1545.

229 The sequence of novels in five books, the fifth posthumous and probably not all by Rabelais, begins with *Pantagruel* (1532 or 1533). The passage mentioned is in Book ii, chapters 18–20. There are numerous editions and translations. See for example François Rabelais, *The Histories of Gargantua and Pantagruel*, trans. J. M. Cohen (Harmondsworth, 1955). Rabelais was protected by several powerful liberal French politicians and ecclesiastics, including Cardinal Jean du Bellay. A Franciscan with medical training, Rabelais was much beholden to the ideas and example set by Erasmus and More.

230 For numerous alternatives see Hopper, *Medieval Number Symbolism*, for instance p. 27.

231 By adding God to the scheme, the number 28 results, which is 'perfect' in the sense that it is the sum of its factors (14, 7, 4, 2, 1). There are reasons for thinking that much of Jewish gematria was taken over from earlier Babylonian and Mesopotamian traditions, since the Greek archaic alphabet had the 27 letters needed by it, while most semitic alphabets had only 22. Hebrew gematria therefore depends on the assignment of separate numerical values to the medial and final forms of five letters (*kaph, mem, nun, pe* and *sade*). For further background material see Simo Parpola, 'The Assyrian Tree of Life: Tracing the Origins of Jewish Monotheism and Greek Philosophy', *Journal of Near Eastern Studies*, 52 (1993), pp.161–208.

232 Thorndike, *A History of Magic and Experimental Science*, vi (New York and London, 1941), p. 453.

233 Thorndike, *A History of Magic*, v (1941), p. 128. He visited Paris in an effort to recover his place at court, and when that failed he moved on to the Netherlands. For a time he was at the court of Margaret of Austria, regent of the Netherlands, in Antwerp. His most notorious prognostication concerned Charles, duke of Bourbon, and the success that would reward his attack on Rome in the spring of 1527. He omitted one important detail, namely that the intrepid duke would be killed by a point-blank arquebus shot as he climbed a scaling ladder, leading from the front the first assault on the city.

234 Walker, *Spiritual and Demonic Magic*, p. 90.

235 It is often suggested that his sceptical work indicates a complete change of heart towards the occult arts in general, but this is to overlook the fact that he continued to work on his earlier project. As Vittoria Perrone Compagni has shown, the two works are part of a single plan, and in using the sceptical book to contrast human sciences and divine Revelation, Agrippa's aim was nothing less than the restoration of a specifically Christian magic. See Compagni's '"Dispersa Intentio": Alchemy, Magic and Scepticism in Agrippa', *Early Science and Medicine*, 5 (2000), pp. 160–77. She notes that the most important concepts in the *De vanitate* are by no means restricted to Agrippa, for they are taken from books by Johannes Reuchlin (on the cabalistic art) and Francesco Giorgio (on world harmony).

236 Walker, *Spiritual and Demonic Magic*, p. 95. The gospel quotation is from John 11:9, which Agrippa misrepresents. It is part of the two-sentence parable of the man who walks in light and the man who walks in darkness.

237 Munich, Staatsbibliothek, Codex Germanicus 598. In one image, the body of the crucified Christ is split into a double 'German' eagle.

238 For a brief survey of literature on the relations between alchemy and Christian religion see Robert Halleux, *Les textes alchimiques* (Turnhout, 1979), pp. 140–44. The link was forged early. Eneus of Gaza (sixth century) likened the ennobling of base metals to the transfiguration of resurrected bodies.

239 Prof. Luuk Houwen has reviewed many scores of dove images for me without finding others of the sort, outside this tradition. It is possible to trace the sacred marriage theme back to the ancient Near East and cultures even beyond, and doing so has created a veritable industry, thanks largely to the writings of the psycho-

logist Carl Gustav Jung. He used it (and drew on religion and alchemy in doing so) to bolster his ideas about the collective unconscious. For reference to Jung's writings and a measured critique of them which is as valid as when it was written, see R. C. Zaehner, *Mysticism Sacred and Profane* (Oxford, 1957), pp. 118–22. For a survey of the Sun-Moon imagery in a German context see Joachim Telle, *Sol und Luna: literar- und alchemiegeschichtliche Studien zu einem altdeutschen Bildgedicht* (Hürtgenwald, 1980).

240 Walker, *Spiritual and Demonic Magic*, pp. 79–80. On Ficino's attitude, see p. 275 above.

241 As far as the alchemical text is concerned, there might even be a link with the often-cited dictum that 'the Sun needs the Moon as a cock needs a hen' ('Sol indiget luna ut gallus gallina'). For several references, some pointing back to the classical Arabic author Senior Zadith, see Helmut Birkhan, *Die alchemistische Lehrdichtung des Gratheus filius philosophi in Cod. Vind. 2372* (Vienna, 1992), pp. 228–29.

242 Hervey, *Holbein's 'Ambassadors'*, pp. 152–53. De Selve spoke some German, but the text in question ('Autres remonstrances faictes par ledict De Selve auxdicts Alemans') is in French.

243 Hervey, *Holbein's 'Ambassadors'*, pp. 227–31. She notes that W. F. Dickes had linked Holbein's use of the lute image with Alciati's emblem in 1891, but that he had not noticed the broken string. Oddly enough, she calls it a ten-stringed lute – there are ten strings unbroken. Alciati's *Liber emblematum* was printed in very many editions. The most useful single modern source of such material is Arthur Henkel and Albrecht Schöne, *Emblemata: Handbuch zur Sinnbildkunst des XVI. und XVII. Jahrhunderts* (Stuttgart, 1967; reprinted in compact form 1996), but it has to be used with caution, since it coalesces Alciati's emblems with those from many similar works. There were additions to later editions. See the following note.

244 See F. W. G. Leeman, *Alciatus' Emblemata* (Groningen, 1984), pp. 8, 50 and 117 n. 5. The printer was Reynold Wolfe and the cut is of boys bringing down apples from a tree.

245 Hervey, *Holbein's 'Ambassadors'*, p. 230.

246 Hervey, *Holbein's 'Ambassadors'*, p. 230 n. 2.

247 See Anthony Colantuono, in Cropper, *The Diplomacy of Art*, especially pp. 65–67. The acts of incorporating the conceits of the painting 'into a living diplomatic discourse' are for him what render the artwork 'significant'. The latter part of his chapter has

better examples from later history, and does not return to Holbein at all.

248 M. Rasmussen, 'The Case of the Flutes'. She speaks of the military association as the primary one in Germany in Holbein's time; but, even if this were true, it would say nothing of the use of the symbol in a court painting. Rasmussen does not consider the meaning of the empty tube or tubes, and has nothing to say about the possible tonal ranges of the instruments – a difficult question, since we cannot judge their lengths reliably.

249 See Starkey (ed.), *The Inventory of King Henry VIII*, items 11906–11, 11923, 11940–43. Cases in this list typically held three or four flutes. Lutes (with cases) were more than twice as common. A single item (11905) mentions twenty-three lutes, each with a case.

250 Illustrated in Strong, *Holbein and Henry VIII*, p. 12. On the class difference between instruments see E. Winternitz, *Musical Instruments and their Symbolism in Western Art* (New Haven and London, 1979), pp. 152–53.

251 Christoph Graf zu Waldburg Wolfegg, *Venus und Mars: Die mittelalterliche Hausbuch aus der Sammlung der Fürsten zu Waldburg Wolfegg* (München, 1997), p. 35.

252 Vega would have been at about 278° ecliptic longitude and 62° latitude. This bright star was on every conventional astrolabe, on which it would have been seen to have sunk more or less to the horizon, near where it crosses the meridian line (see Fig. 73). On Chapuys see Rowlands, *Holbein*, p. 88.

253 Conrad Celtes (1459–1508; the surname is Greek for 'Pickel', his German name) gave instructions for the drawings in his publication (1507). See Wind, *Pagan Mysteries*, pp. 48–50. The Pegasus analogy is explained by the fact that the hoof of the horse brought forth the fountain of Helicon, 'the spirit moving over the waters'. As Wind notes, the pedantic way of making explicit divine secrets that were meant to be hidden would not have pleased an ordinary Italian humanist.

254 Printed by J. B. Trapp, in *The Complete Works of St Thomas More*, ix (New Haven and London, 1979), pp. 173–212.

255 Honorius, *Summa xii quaestionum*, printed in Migne's *Patrologia latina*, clxxii. See especially quaestiones 1 and 8.

256 William Harris Stahl and Richard Johnson with E. L. Burge, *Martianus Capella and the Seven Liberal Arts*, ii (New York, 1977), p. 281. The passage is from book 7 of the *Marriage*, on Arithmetic. Book 9, the last book, is entirely devoted to Harmony.

257 See Robin Headlam Wells, 'Number Symbolism in the Renaissance Lute Rose', *Early Music*, 9 (1981), pp. 32–42, especially pp. 35–37, quoting Hawthornden at greater length. Wells draws on the work of Friedmann Hellwig. He notes that African rebabs use the hexagram motif, the instrument being treated as an image of a harmonious universe. The idea expressed earlier (p. 176) that the observer of the painting might have been told to put his eye opposite the lute rose, as though Dinteville's fingers were touching the strings, gets new significance if the lute rose contains a hexagram. I owe the idea in part to Mr Austin Prichard-Levy. He tells me that lute technique of the period was still 'thumb inside the fingers', so that the thumb and fingers could alternate in striking the strings to give a more varied sound and greater emphasis on alternate notes. Dinteville's unbusinesslike hold on his dagger might be explained in this way.

258 Agrippa, *Occult Philosophy*, Book II, ch. 26.

259 Ganz, *The Paintings*, plate 127 (Berlin, Deutsches Museum), cat. no. 84; and Rowlands, *Holbein*, plate 84, cat. no. 49. The man has two music books in front of him, and might have been a court musician. Hervey thought him to be Dinteville, and the resemblance is strong. Ganz disagreed, as do probably most others today, but still he favoured the idea of a French sitter.

260 A slightly different position taken by Stebbins ('The Astronomical Instruments', p. 52) should not be confused with this. He thought that Holbein was indifferent to the *astronomical* function of the instruments and that any symbolism in them was not 'dependent on astronomy for its interpretation'.

261 For an introduction to Colet's thought see Leland Miles, *John Colet and the Platonic Tradition* (Chicago, 1961; London, 1962). For the solar analogies see especially pp. 57, 99–101, 104, 131–32, 136.

262 A. W. Reed's Introduction to Thomas More, *The English Works*, ed. W. E. Campbell (London, 1931), i, p. 18.

263 Erasmus, *Enchiridion*, in *Opera omnia*, v, ch. 8, rule 5.

264 In his *The Babylonian Captivity* (written in Latin) in 1520 Luther said that to be valid a sacrament must have been instituted by Christ, and that therefore only baptism, the mass, and penance (but without the need for a priest) were valid. Ordination, confirmation, marriage and extreme unction were thus dismissed.

265 Trapp, *Works of More*, ix (1979).

266 Garry E. Haupt, *The Complete Works of St Thomas More*, xiii

(New Haven and London, 1976). The theological core is at pp. 137–43. The work was begun before he went into prison.

267 Martin Luther, *Werke*, xxxi, pp. 52–53. The Heidelberg Disputation gained several influential recruits for Luther's views, including Martin Bucer, the later reformer of Strasbourg.

268 Erasmus, *Praise of Folly*, trans. Radice, p. 6.

269 Translated by Bernard McGinn, *Visions of the End: Apocalyptic Traditions in the Middle Ages* (New York, 1979), p. 281, from an edition by A. Crucitti.

270 *Convivio*, IV, xxiii, lines 129ff. Dante holds that Christ died in his thirty-fourth year, before the peak of the arch of life, so that he should not experience decline, and that he died at the sixth hour, before the day had begun to decline.

271 Hours in the Bible are counted from sunrise, which at Passover, a time near the equinox, was close to our six o'clock. The hours used in the Bible are of a length that varies with the season; but again, near the equinox they are more or less of the same length as our hours of the clock. The sixth hour was therefore from eleven o'clock until noon, and so forth.

272 In its Middle English versions the very popular apocryphal Gospel of Nicodemus has the centurion telling of how at Christ's death the Sun 'wex all wan wele thre mile way or more'. The Sun, that is, grew dark for an hour or more. This is obviously a confused version deriving from Matthew's Gospel, but the time interval might have been read as time *after* three o'clock. See W. H. Hulme, *The Middle-English Harrowing of Hell and Gospel of Nicodemus*, Early English Text Society (London, 1907), pp. 66–67 (four versions, the fourth very corrupt). A 'mile way' was a common measure of time, usually the twenty minutes supposedly needed to walk a mile. For the reference to St John's Gospel see Peter Nockolds's review of the first edition of the present book in *Culture and Cosmos*, 6 (2002), pp. 73–5. Note also his remarks on the fact that by gematria the name of Cephas (Simon called Peter) has a value of 729, the square of 27, and that of his brother Andrew 361, the square of 19. It would be intriguing to find a sixteenth-century work mentioning these properties.

273 For many references see Engelbert Kirschenbaum and others, *Lexikon der christlichen Ikonographie* (Freiburg im Breisgau, 1972), iv, art. 'Widder'.

274 Thomas Aquinas, *Summa Theologica*, ii.1 q. 102, art. 5, reply to objection 2 and iii q. 46, art. 9, reply to objection 1. Maimonides

is a possible source, but Prof. B. R. Goldstein has drawn my attention to a very apposite thirteenth-century Jewish text by the Spanish scholar Ramban (Nachmanides). See his *Commentary on the Torah: Exodus*, trans. and annotated by C. B. Chavel (New York, 1973), pp. 118–9.

275 The ecliptic and the equator, which fix the beginning of Aries, seem secure, and a third circle is the horizon circle. The fourth is usually taken to be a so-called colure, in this case a great circle running through the equinoctial points and the north and south poles of the sphere.

276 The Plato reference is *Timaeus*, 36B–D, for which see Cornford, *Plato's Cosmology*, pp. 72–73. On the theology of the correspondence between OT creation and NT redemption see Leo Scheffczyk, *Creation and Providence*, trans. Richard Strachan (London and New York, 1970), especially pp. 22–46.

277 For the Gregory text and the analysis that shows the equivalences of his names (Greater Cross, Lesser Cross or Alfa, and Omega) with ours (Cygnus, Delphinus, and Lyra) see Stephen C. McCluskey, 'Gregory of Tours, Monastic Timekeeping and Early Christian Attitudes to Astronomy', *Isis*, 81 (1990), pp. 9–22.

278 Alessandro Piccolomini, *De la sfera del mondo*, published together with the atlas, namely *De le stelle fisse* (Venice, 1540), in Tuscan dialect. Lyra and Cygnus are discussed at fols 65 verso and 66 recto and drawn at 87 recto and verso. Wilhelm Schickard's book in its rare first edition is *Astroscopium: pro facillima stellarum cognitione noviter excogitatum a Wilhelmo Schickhardo, ad cuius succinctam hanc explicationem et insertas quaestiones astronomicas respondebit Joh. Casparus Wägelin* (Werlin, 1623). There are manuscript and architectural instances from an early period, several collected together in David J. Ross, 'The Bird, the Cross and the Emperor', *Culture and Cosmos*, 4 (2000), pp. 3–28, drawing much from McCluskey, 'Gregory of Tours', and F. Heiland, 'Die astronomische Deutung der Vision Kaiser Konstantins', *Sondervertrag im Zeiss-Planetarium Jena*, 2 Auflage (September 1952). The story of Constantine the Great (272–337) really begins when he has a vision of the Sun-god Apollo with three crosses, believed to signify that Constantine has thirty years left to him. Christian writers tend to overlook this. At the end of his life, after his conversion, he claimed to have seen a *single* cross above the Sun with the now famous words *In hoc signo vinces*, 'In this sign shalt thou conquer'. (Eusebius, *Life of Constantine*, i.28, is the chief but not the only

source.) He sent his soldiers into battle at Saxa Rubra with crosses on their shields and they were victorious although heavily outnumbered. The same motto, as it happens, was put under the title of William Roper's *Life of Sir Thomas More*, but it is often found quoted, for example in our 'alchemical wedding' treatise, where the words are said to have been found inscribed together with a little cross on a seal made of a metal 'heavier than gold'.

279 Johannes Bayer, *Uranometria: omnium asterismorum continens schemata* (Augsburg, 1603). Engravings are by Alexander Mair. There are forty-six Ptolemaic constellations drawn, each on its own map, and twelve southern constellations on a single extra sheet, with two final synoptic maps, one north and one south. (Cygnus is plate IX, Lit. I.) The discussions of them all (on the backs of the sheets) were later reprinted without illustrations. See for instance: *Explicatio characterum aeneis uranometrias imaginum* (etc.) (Augsburg, 1627; Ulm, 1640; Augsburg, 1654, etc.). Cygnus is said to have the astrological character of Venus and Mercury. There is much classical information about the constellations compressed into a small space in this highly important atlas. It was Bayer (modifying a system devised by Alessandro Piccolomini) who gave us our system of assigning Greek letters to the stars in each constellation in order of their brightness.

280 The best edition of Kepler's *De stella nova* (1606) is Max Caspar (ed.), *Johannes Kepler: Gesammelte Werke*, i (München, 1938), pp. 147–390; see pp. 293–312 for *De stella Cygni*, especially p. 297.

281 One famous example is in the twelfth-century *Hortus deliciarum* cited earlier.

282 Henry John Feasey, *Ancient English Holy Week Ceremonial* (London, 1897), p. 26. Lewisham, near Greenwich, had a rood cloth of green silk in the time of Edward VI (ibid., p. 35), and there are several other Kentish examples. For a concise survey of the rituals of this part of the Christian year, see J. G. Davies, *Holy Week: A Short History* (London, 1963).

283 For more detail on the contents of this paragraph see J. W. Tyrer, *Historical Survey of Holy Week, its Services and Ceremonial* (Oxford, 1932), especially pp. 81–84, 128–42. Note that the 'three hour service', still popular in Catholic and Anglican circles, running from noon and ending with the words *crucifixus mortuus* as the clock strikes three, was a seventeenth-century Peruvian invention.

284 Lynn Thorndike, *A History of Magic and Experimental Science*, vi (New York and London, 1941), p. 491.

285 For a general account of this movement see Norman Cohn, *The Pursuit of the Millennium* (revised edn, London, 1970), ch. 13.

286 Anon., *Ein Rechen Büchlin vom End Christ* (Wittenberg, 1532); and *Vom End der Welt* (Wittenberg, 1532). See Viktor Kommerell, 'Michel Stifel: Schwäbische Lebensbilder', *Württemb. Kommission für Landesgeschichte*, 3 (Stuttgart, 1942), pp. 509–24, and Joseph E. Hofmann, 'Michael Stifel, 1487?–1567', *Sudhoffs Archiv*, ix, 1968.

287 Good Friday 1533 was also the feast of Leo I, 'the Great'. 'And I say also unto thee, That thou art Peter, and upon this rock I will build my church; and the gates of hell shall not prevail against it. And I will give unto thee the keys of the kingdom of heaven: and whatsoever thou shalt bind on earth shall be bound in heaven: and whatsoever thou shalt loose on earth shall be loosed in heaven' (Matthew 16:18–19). In the Vulgate: 'Et ego dico tibi, quia tu es Petrus . . . Et tibi dabo claves regni *coelorum*. Et quodcumque solveris super terram, erit solutum et in *coelis*.'

288 *De inventione crucis*, in Migne, *Patrologia latina*, clxxii, cols 941–44.

289 Paul Binski, 'What was the Westminster Retable?', *Journal of the British Archaeological Association*, 140 (1987), pp. 159–65. See Foster, *Patterns of Thought*, pp. 159–61. Binski wishes to supersede the old view of the globe as pointing to Genesis. He sees it as representing the four elements, which of course in a sense it does; but it has living creatures too.

290 See my *Chaucer's Universe* (revised edn, Oxford, 1990).

291 Victoria Rothschild, '*The Parliament of Fowls*: Chaucer's Mirror up to Nature', *Review of English Studies*, new series 35 (1984), pp. 164–84. *The Faerie Queene*, books I-III appeared in 1590, books I-VI in 1596, and books I-VI with the fragment of book VII known as the 'Mutabilitie Cantos' posthumously in 1609.

292 'By that the Maunciple hadde his tale al ended, / The Sonne fro the south lyne was descended / So lowe that he nas nat, to my sighte, / Degrees nyne and twenty as in highte. / Foure of the clokke it was tho, as I gesse, / For ellevene foot, or litel moore or lesse, / My shadwe was at thilke tyme, as there / Of swiche feet as my lengthe parted were / In sixe feet equal of proporcioun. / Therwith the moones exaltacioun[.] / I mene, Libra alwey gan ascende, / As we were entryng at a thropes ende; / For which oure Hoost, as he was wont to gye, / As in this caas, oure joly compaignye, / Seyde in this wise: "Lordynges everichoon, / Now lakketh us no tales mo than oon. / Fulfilled is my sentence and

my decree; / I trowe that we han herd of ech degree; / Almoost fulfild is al myn ordinaunce . . ."' From *The Riverside Chaucer*, 3rd edition (Boston, 1987), ed. L. D. Benson (general editor); based on *The Works of Geoffrey Chaucer*, ed. by F. N. Robinson. Note my suggested change in punctuation. See also Appendix 11 below.

293 When writing my *Chaucer's Universe* I was only able to narrow down the date to one of three different years. For more on the solution offered here, see my 'Chaucer, Holbein, Libra and the Crucifixion', in Menso Folkerts and Richard Lorch (eds), *Sic Itur ad Astra: Studien zur Geschichte der Mathematik und Naturwissenschaften* (Wiesbaden, 2000), pp. 461–73.

294 See p. 233 above. While I believe the date derived to be no longer open to doubt, I have considered a spread of dates here in order to head off criticism that starts from the claim that we cannot read the cylinder dial accurately.

295 Francis Wormald, 'The Crucifix and the Balance', *Journal of the Warburg Institute*, 1 (1937–38), pp. 276–80.

296 The second, closely resembling it, is reproduced at plate 40b of Wormald's article, from Rome, Biblioteca Casanatense, MS 1404.

297 Chauncey Wood, *Chaucer and the Country of the Stars: Poetic Uses of Astrological Imagery* (Princeton, 1970), especially pp. 280–97.

298 Wood, *Chaucer*, figs 27 and 28. See also the work of R. G. Salomon to which Wood refers: *Opicinus de Castris* (London, 1936).

299 For more details see my 'Chaucer, Holbein, Libra and the Crucifixion'. More details of the wider historical context will be found in Wolfgang Hübner, *Zodiacus Christianus* (Königstein, 1983).

300 This altarpiece was painted by Raphael around 1503 for the side chapel of the church of S. Domenico in Città di Castello. It is now in the National Gallery, London. My proposal (which I owe in part to a suggestion made by Mr Peter Nockolds in 1999) is based on the geometry of the cross in relation to the semicircular top of the painting. Briefly, this is divided into six equal arcs of 30 degrees by the central vertical, the upper edge of the cross-beam of the cross, and radii through the centres of the Sun and Moon. (These remarks will be barely intelligible without reference to the painting.) The nail through Christ's feet would have been on the full circle, if drawn, and with the upper edge of the cross-beam it defines an equilateral triangle. If we identify the six arcs with signs of the zodiac, the uppermost pair being taken naturally as Cancer

for the Moon and Leo for the Sun, then the sign of Libra 'hangs' from the extended cross-beam. For reasons set out in Appendix 1, I should feel more confident that this was all deliberate if Raphael's biography were akin to that of Piero della Francesca, a competent mathematician.

301 The design is not especially significant for its contents – a laurelled head above, between two sphinxes, naked boys climbing up the sides, and a procession of naked boys below, one of them carried by six others. This device is copied closely from one used earlier by the printer Froben of Basel for the title page of a work by Erasmus (*Aliquot epistolae*) and for the same author's appendix to Thomas More's *Utopia.* Other variants were used for German books from 1524. The Thynne edition has been twice reprinted in facsimile, most recently with an introduction by D. S. Brewer (Menston, 1973). On the many uses of the title-page woodcut see McKerrow and Ferguson, *Title-Page Borders*, no. 19, and A. F. Johnson, *German Renaissance Title Borders* (Oxford, 1929), no. 63.

302 Much circumstantial detail of this is in G. H. Kingsley, *Chaucer: Animadversions . . . Sett Downe by Francis Thynne*, London, Early English Text Society (London, revised 1875 but dated 1865). The *Animadversions* is an attack on another Chaucer editor, Thomas Speight. This rag-bag of information by Kingsley and others has been superseded in many respects, but it has the great merit that it does not filter out references to scientific material. On Thynne as an editor see J. E. Blodgett in P. G. Ruggiers (ed.), *Editing Chaucer* (Norman, Oklahoma, 1984), pp. 35–52.

303 This and the bare facts known about Thynne are from the *Dictionary of National Biography*, compact edition, entry 'Thynne, William' (Oxford, 1975), pp. 853–54. The main source for him and Tuke is the series *Letters and Papers of Henry* VIII. Thynne's son Francis also scrutinised and edited Chaucer carefully, but needs to be read with caution.

304 The finest portrait is now in Washington. In it Tuke wears an elaborate crucifix. An inscription (in Latin) asks 'Will my days not soon come to an end?' The date of the painting is uncertain (between the limits 1528–1541) and there is nothing to be gained here by considering its imagery. See Rowlands, *Holbein*, cat. no. 64, plate 102, disagreeing with J. O. Hand, 'The Portrait of Sir Brian Tuke by Hans Holbein the Younger', *Studies in the History of Art*, 9 (1980), pp. 33–49, where it is connected with a serious illness of Tuke's in 1528.

305 *Dictionary of National Biography*, compact edition, entry 'Tuke, Sir Bryan' (Oxford, 1975), pp. 122–23. Polydore Vergil's most significant work from an English perspective was his *English History Comprising the Reigns of Henry VI, Edward IV and Richard III* (to take the title of the 1844 edition), which was later to be of great influence on Raphael Holinshed and hence on Shakespeare.

306 Known only through a copy on wood (49 x 38 cm) now in the Bayerische Staatsgemäldesammlung, Munich. See for example Bätschmann and Griener, *Hans Holbein*, plate 238.

307 For the quotation see *Chaucer: Animadversions*, ed. Kingsley, p. 61. Francis Thynne (ibid., p. 6) tells us that Chaucer had several times written the words *examinatur Chaucer*. There is in fact one surviving astronomical manuscript (that which contains what is now called 'Equatorie of the planetis') which was almost certainly Chaucer's and in which the word *examinatur* ('it is (being) checked') occurs repeatedly; and there is another in which a contracted use of what might be *examinatur* is found, so the story rings true. As to the genuineness of the former treatise, which is often denied with no good reason, see my *Chaucer's Universe*, pp. 143, 171–72, 177–81.

308 A view based on the starkly realistic character of that painting, in which we see only the laid-out corpse confined within a low and oppressive horizontal frame. See *Eine italienische Reise* (Leipzig, 1914), pp. 23–24. Fyodor Dostoyevsky in *The Idiot* (1868–69) made many references to the same work, which reputedly led him in real life to doubt the truth of the Resurrection story. Tradition has it that Holbein used a body fished out of the Rhine as his model.

309 Baldassare Castiglione, *Libro del cortegiano* (Venice, 1528), quoted here from the translation by Sir Thomas Hoby, *The Book of the Courtyer* (London, 1561), book I. There were over forty editions of this work published in the sixteenth century in Italy alone (1531, 1533, etc.), and Georges de Selve is almost certain to have read it, in view of his office.

310 Leonardo da Vinci, *Libro di pittura*, I.17. See the edition in Claire J. Farago, *Leonardo da Vinci's 'Paragone'* (Leiden, 1992), pp. 206–07. As Leonardo says (ibid., pp. 254–55), if painters have not described their art and reduced it to a science that is perhaps because they have no need to make a profession of writing to earn a living. He seems to have studied parts of astronomy dealing with gnomonics and projection in the late 1490s. See Carlo Pedretti,

The Literary Works of Leonardo da Vinci, 2 vols (Berkeley and Los Angeles, 1977), i, pp. 151–52. One might say that here he was his own Kratzer.

311 Henry Hallam, *Introduction to the Literature of Europe in the Fifteenth, Sixteenth and Seventeenth Centuries*, 3 vols (London, 1837–39), ch. 7.

312 Wind, *Pagan Mysteries*, pp. 188–89.

313 Marilyn Aronberg Lavin and B. A. R. Carter, *Piero della Francesca's Baptism of Christ*; and Kenneth Clark, *Piero della Francesca: A Complete Edition* (2nd edn, Oxford, 1981), pp. 23–26. See also n. 85 on p. 399 above.

314 See his 'Piero della Francesca et notre temps', *L'amour de l'art* (December 1923), p. 767, discussed by Rosalind E. Krauss, 'The Grid, the True Cross, the Abstract Structure', in Marilyn Aronberg Lavin (ed.), *Piero della Francesca and his Legacy* (Washington, 1995), pp. 303–12.

315 Piero della Francesca, *Trattato d'abaco*, ed. Gino Arrighi (Pisa, 1970), pp. 208–09.

316 See my 'Celestial Influence, the Major Premiss of Astrology', reprinted in *Stars, Minds and Fate*, pp. 243–98.

317 Peter Drinkwater, *The Sundials of Nicholaus Kratzer.*

318 For an important essay on sestina structure, see Alastair Fowler, *Conceitful Thought: The Interpretation of English Renaissance Poems* (Edinburgh, 1975), pp. 38–58.

BIBLIOGRAPHY

Maryan Ainsworth, '"Paternes for Physioneamyes": Holbein's Portraiture Reconsidered', *Burlington Magazine*, 132 (1990), pp. 173–86.

R. H. Allen, *Star Names: Their Lore and Meaning* (New York, 1963); originally *Star-Names and Their Meanings* (1899).

Sydney Anglo, *Spectacle, Pageantry and Early Tudor Policy* (Oxford, 1969).

Petrus Apianus, *Astronomicum Caesareum* (Ingolstadt, 1540).

Petrus Apianus, *Cosmographicus liber . . . studiose collectus* (Landshut, 1524).

Petrus Apianus, *Eyn newe unnd wohlgegründte Underweysung aller Kauffmanns Rechnung* (Ingolstadt, 1527).

Petrus Apianus, *Introductio geographica* (Ingolstadt, 1533).

St Augustine, ed. David Knowles, *City of God* (Harmondsworth, 1972).

Roger Bacon, ed. J. S. Brewer, *Opus tertium*, in *Fr. Rogeri Baconi opera quaedam hactenus inedita*, i (London, 1859).

Roger Bacon, ed. J. H. Bridges, *Opus maius*, 2 vols (Oxford, 1897).

J. Baltrusaitis, trans. W. Strachan, *Anamorphic Art* (Cambridge, 1977).

Francis Barrett, *The Magus*, 2 vols (London, 1801).

Oskar Bätschmann and Pascal Griener, *Hans Holbein* (London, 1997).

Johannes Bayer, *Uranometria, omnium asterismorum continens schemata* (etc.) (Augsburg, 1603). A later publication, his *Explicatio* (etc.) (1627, 1640, 1654, etc.) has the annotations without the plates.

A. David Baynes-Cope, 'The Investigation of a Group of Globes', *Imago mundi*, 33 (1981), pp. 9–20.

C. Beutler and G. Thiem, *Hans Holbein der Älter: die Spätgotische Altar- und Glasmalerei* (Augsburg, 1960).

Paul Binski, 'What was the Westminster Retable?', *Journal of the British Archaeological Association*, 140 (1987), pp. 159–65.

Helmut Birkhan, *Die alchemistische Lehrdichtung des Gratheus filius philosophi in Cod. Vind. 2372* (Vienna, 1992), pp. 228–29.

J. E. Blodgett in P. G. Ruggiers (ed.), *Editing Chaucer* (Norman, Oklahoma, 1984), pp. 35–52.

Maria Luisa Righini Bonelli, *Il Museo di Storia della Scienza a Firenze* (Florence, 1968).

Charles de Bouelles, *Agonologiae Iesu Christi libri quatuor* (Paris, 1533).

Nicolas Bourbon, Παιδαγωγειον: *Carmen de moribus* (Lyons, 1536).

J. Braun, S.J., *Die liturgische Gewandung* (Freiburg im Breisgau, 1907).

J. S. Brewer et al., (eds), *Letters and Papers, Foreign and Domestic of the Reign of Henry VIII* (etc.) (London, 1862–1932), vol. vi, for 1533, arranged and catalogued by James Gairdner (1882).

Elizabeth A. R. Brown, 'Sodomy, Treason, Exile and Intrigue: Four Documents Concerning the Dinteville Affair (1537–38)', *Sociétés et idéologies des temps modernes: hommage à Arlette Jouanna*, 2 vols (Montpellier, 1996), i, pp. 512–32.

Elizabeth A. R. Brown, 'The Dinteville Family and the Allegory of Moses and Aaron before Pharaoh', *Metropolitan Museum Journal*, 34 (1999), pp. 73–100.

Joachim Camerarius, *Symbolorum et emblematum ex re herbaria desumtorum* (etc.) (Nürnberg, 1590).

Jerome Cardan (Hieronimus, or Girolamo Cardano), *In Ptolemaei librorum de judiciis astrorum libri IV commentaria* (Lyon, 1555).

Jerome Cardan, *De subtilitate rerum*, in *Opera*, iii, lib. xx (Lyon, 1663).

Stefano Caroti, 'Melanchthon and Astrology', in Paola Zambelli (ed.), *'Astrologi Hallucinati': Stars and the End of the World in Luther's Time* (Berlin and New York, 1986), pp. 109–21.

B. A. R. Carter, art. 'Perspective', *Oxford Companion to Art*, ed. Harold Osborne (Oxford, 1970).

David Cast, *The Calumny of Apelles: A Study in the Humanist Tradition* (New Haven and London, 1981).

Baldassare Castiglione, *Libro del Cortegiano* (Venice, 1528), trans. Sir Thomas Hoby, *The Book of the Courtyer* (London, 1561).

A. B. Chamberlain, *Hans Holbein the Younger*, 2 vols (London, 1913).

André Chastel, *Marcel Ficin et l'art* (Geneva, 1954).

Marshall Clagett, *Archimedes in the Middle Ages*, iii, part 3, Memoirs of the American Philosophical Society, 125B (Philadelphia, 1978).

Kenneth Clark, *Piero della Francesca: A Complete Edition* (2nd edn, Oxford, 1981).

Peter Cornelius Claussen, 'De doppelte Boden unter Holbeins Gesandten', *Hülle und Fülle: Festschrift für Tilmann Buddensieg*, ed. Andreas Beyer, Vittorio Lampugnani and Gunter Schweikhart (Alfter, 1993), pp. 177–202.

Norman Cohn, *The Pursuit of the Millennium* (revised edn, London, 1970).

Vittoria Perrone Compagni, '"Dispersa Intentio": Alchemy, Magic and Scepticism in Agrippa', *Early Science and Medicine*, 5 (2000), pp. 160–77.

Brian P. Copenhaver, 'Number, shape and meaning in Pico's Christian Cabala', in Anthony Grafton and Nancy Siraisi (eds), *Natural Particulars: Nature and the Disciplines in Renaissance Europe* (Cambridge, Mass., and London, 1999), pp. 25–76.

Francis MacDonald Cornford, *Plato's Cosmology* (London, 1937).

J. Cox-Rearick, 'Sacred to Profane: Diplomatic Gifts of the Medici to Francis I', *Journal of Medieval and Renaissance Studies*, 24 (1994), pp. 239–58.

Elizabeth Cropper (ed.), *The Diplomacy of Art: Artistic Creation and Politics in Seicento Italy*, Papers from a Colloquium Held at the Villa Spelman, Florence, 1998 (Milan, 2000).

J. G. Davies, *Holy Week: A Short History* (London, 1963).

Elly Dekker, entries in G. Bott (ed.), *Focus Behaim Globus*, ii, *Katalog: Germanisches Nationalmuseum Nürnberg, 2 Dez. 1992–28 Feb. 1993* (Nürnberg, 1992), pp. 516–18, 524–25.

Elly Dekker and Kristen Lippincott, 'The Scientific Instruments in Holbein's *Ambassadors*. A Re-Examination', *Journal of the Warburg and Courtauld Institutes*, 62 (1999), pp. 93–125.

William F. Dickes, *Holbein's Celebrated Picture, Now Called 'The Ambassadors', Shown to be a Memorial of the Treaty of Nuremberg, 1532, and to Portray Those Princely Brothers, Counts of Palatine of the Rhine, Otto Henry . . . and Philipp* (etc.) (London, 1903).

Peter I. Drinkwater, *The Sundials of Nicholaus Kratzer* (Shipston-on-Stour, 1993).

Albrecht Dürer, *Underweysung der Messung mit dem Zirkel und Richtscheyt* (Nürnberg, 1525).

Gerhart Egger (ed.), *Theatrum Orbis Terrarum: die Erfassung des Weltbildes zur Zeit der Renaissance und des Barocks* (Vienna, 1970).

Johannes Engel, *Opus astrolabii plani* (Augsburg, 1488).

(Desiderius) Erasmus of Rotterdam, *Enchiridion militis christiani*, in *Opera omnia*, v (Amsterdam, 1969); and separately edited by A.-J. Festugière (Paris, 1971).

Desiderius Erasmus, *Opus epistolarum*, 12 vols, ed. P. S. Allen (Oxford, 1906–58).

Erasmus of Rotterdam, *Praise of Folly* (written 1509), trans. by Betty Radice, intro. by A. H. T. Levi (Harmondsworth, 1971), from the edition of the text by J.-B. Kan (1898).

Claire J. Farago, *Leonardo da Vinci's 'Paragone'* (Leiden, 1992).

Henry John Feasey, *Ancient English Holy Week Ceremonial* (London, 1897).

Jean Louis Ferrier, *Holbein: Ambassadeurs* (Paris, 1977).

A. Fink, *Die Schwarzischen Trachtenbücher* (Berlin, 1963).

Susan Foister, Ashok Roy and Martin Wyld, *Making and Meaning: Holbein's Ambassadors* (London, 1997).

Richard Foster, *Patterns of Thought: The Hidden Meaning of the Great Pavement of Westminster Abbey* (London, 1991).

Richard Foster and Pamela Tudor-Craig, *The Secret Life of Paintings* (Woodbridge, 1986).

Alastair Fowler, *Conceitful Thought: The Interpretation of English Renaissance Poems* (Edinburgh, 1975).

Volkmar Gantzhorn, *Oriental Carpets: Their Iconology and Iconography from Earliest Times to the Eighteenth Century* (Köln, 1998).

Paul Ganz, *The Paintings of Hans Holbein* (London, 1950).

Grillot de Givry, trans. J. C. Locke, *Witchcraft, Magic and Alchemy* (New York, 1931).

Adolf Glaser, *Die basler Glasmalerei im 16. Jahrhundert seit Hans Holbein d. J.* (Winterthur, 1937).

P. Gouk, *The Ivory Sundials of Nuremberg, 1500–1700* (Cambridge, 1988).

Willem Hackmann, 'Nicholas Kratzer: The King's Astronomer and Renaissance Instrument-Maker', in *Henry VIII: A European Court in England (Catalogue of a Greenwich Exhibition to Commemorate the 500th Anniversary of the Birth of Henry VIII)*, ed. D. Starkey (London, 1991).

Henry Hallam, *Introduction to the Literature of Europe in the Fifteenth, Sixteenth and Seventeenth Centuries*, 3 vols (London, 1837–39).

Robert Halleux, *Les textes alchimiques* (Turnhout, 1979).

J. O. Hand, 'The Portrait of Sir Brian Tuke by Hans Holbein the Younger', *Studies in the History of Art* (National Gallery of Art, Washington), 9 (1980), pp. 33–49.

Joseph Harnest, 'Das Problem der konstruierten Perspektive in der altdeutschen Malerei' (unpublished thesis, München, 1971).

Garry E. Haupt (ed.), *The Complete Works of St Thomas More*, xiii (New Haven and London, 1976).

F. Heiland, 'Die astronomische Deutung der Vision Kaiser Konstantins', *Sondervertrag im Zeiss-Planetarium Jena* (2nd edn, Jena, 1952).

Arthur Henkel and Albrecht Schöne, *Emblemata: Handbuch zur Sinnbildkunst des XVI. und XVII. Jahrhunderts* (Stuttgart, 1967; reprinted in compact form 1996).

Herrad of Hohenbourg, *Hortus deliciarum*, ed. Rosalie Green and others, 2 vols (London, 1979).

M. F. S. Hervey, *Holbein's 'Ambassadors': The Picture and the Men* (London, 1900).

A. M. Hind (ed.), *Hans Holbein the Younger: His Old Testament Illustrations, Dance of Death, and Other Woodcuts* (London, 1912).

Eduard His, 'Holbeins Verhältnisse zur basler Reformation', *Repertorium*, 2 (1879), pp. 156–59.

E. Hofmann, 'Michael Stifel, 1487?–1567', *Sudhoffs Archiv*, ix, 1968.

Honorius of Autun, ed. Valerie I. J. Flint, 'Honorius Augustodensis Imago Mundi', *Archives d'histoire doctrinale et littéraire du moyen âge*, 49 (1982), pp. 7–153.

V. F. Hopper, *Medieval Number Symbolism* (New York, 1969).

Wolfgang Hübner, *Zodiacus Christianus* (Konigstein, 1983).

Johann Huttich and Simon Grynaeus, *Novus orbis regionum* (Basel, 1532).

Edward Hutton, *The Cosmati: The Roman Marble Workers of the Twelfth and Thirteenth Centuries* (London, 1950).

Eric Ives, 'A Frenchman at the Court of Anne Boleyn', *History Today*, 1 August 1998.

Markus Jenny (ed.), *Luthers geistliche Lieder und Kirchengesäng*, in *Archiv zur Weimarer Ausgabe der Werke Martin Luthers*, iv (1985).

G. T. Jensma et al. (eds), *Erasmus: De actualiteit van zijn denken* (Zutphen, 1986).

Johannes de Francfordia(?), *Theologia Germanica*, trans. from the German by Susanna Winkworth (2nd edn, London, 1893; new edn, London, 1966).

A. F. Johnson, *German Renaissance Title Borders* (Oxford, 1929).

H. Keller, 'Entstehung und Blütezeit des Freundschaftsbildes', in *Essays in the History of Art Presented to Rudolf Wittkower* (London, 1967), i, pp. 161–73.

Martin Kemp, *The Science of Art* (London and New Haven, 1990).

Thomas à Kempis, *Of the Imitation of Christ*, trans. from the Latin by William Benham (London, 1905 etc.).

H. Keniston, *Francisco de los Cobos, Secretary of the Emperor Charles V* (Pittsburgh, 1960).

Johannes Kepler, *De stella nova* (1606), in Max Caspar (ed.), *Johannes Kepler, Gesammelte Werke*, i (Munich, 1938), pp. 147–390.

Richard Kieckhefer, *Magic in the Middle Ages* (Cambridge, 1989).

G. H. Kingsley, *Chaucer: Animadversions . . . Sett Downe by Francis Thynne*, Early English Text Society (London, revised 1875, dated 1865).

Engelbert Kirschenbaum and others, *Lexikon der christlichen Ikonographie*, 6 vols (Freiburg im Breisgau etc., 1972; reprinted 1994).

Viktor Kommerell, 'Michel Stifel: schwäbische Lebensbilder', *Württembergisches Kommission für Landesgeschichte*, 3 (1942), pp. 509–24.

Leopold Kretzenbacher, *Die Seelenwaage*, Buchreihe des Landesmuseums für Kärnten, iv (Klagenfurt, 1958).

P. O. Kristeller, *The Philosophy of Marsilio Ficino* (New York, 1943).

Marilyn Aronberg Lavin, with an appendix by B. A. R. Carter, *Piero della Francesca's Baptism of Christ* (New Haven and London, 1981).

Marilyn Aronberg Lavin (ed.), *Piero della Francesca and his Legacy* (Washington, DC, 1995).

Michel Le Bris, *D'or, de rêves et de sang: l'épopée de la filibuste, 1494–1588* (Paris, 2001).

Sydney Lee, *Dictionary of National Biography*, entry 'Thynne, William', compact edition (Oxford, 1975), pp. 853–54.

William R. Lethaby, *Westminster Abbey and the King's Craftsmen* (London, 1906).

Michael Levey, *National Gallery Catalogue: The German School* (London, 1959).

Michael Levey, *The Soul of the Eye* (London, 1990).

Lesley Lewis, *The Thomas More Family Group Portraits after Holbein* (Leominster, 1998).

R. P. Lorch, 'The Astronomical Instruments of Jâbir ibn Aflah and the Torquetum', *Centaurus*, 20 (1976).

M. Maas, 'Nikolaus Kratzer, ein münchener Humanist: ein biographischer Versuch', *Beilage zur Münchner Allgemeinen Zeitung* (18 March 1902), pp. 505–08 and 515–18.

Carel van Mander, *Hans Holbein: A Biography. From the Schilderboeck*, trans. Constant van de Wall (New York, 1935).

Carel van Mander, *The Lives of the Illustrious Netherlandish and German Painters from the First Edition of the 'Schilder-Boeck' (1603–1604)*, 2 vols, ed. H. Miedema (Doornspijk, 1994).

Stephen C. McCluskey, 'Gregory of Tours, Monastic Timekeeping and Early Christian Attitudes to Astronomy', *Isis*, 81 (1990), pp. 9–22.

James Kelsey McConica, *English Humanists and Reformation Politics under Henry VIII and Edward VI* (Oxford, 1965).

Bernard McGinn, *Visions of the End: Apocalyptic Traditions in the Middle Ages* (New York, 1979).

R. B. McKerrow and F. S. Ferguson, *Title-Page Borders Used in England and Scotland, 1485–1640* (Oxford, 1932).

Garrett Mattingly, *Renaissance Diplomacy* (London, 1955).

J.-P. Migne, *Patrologiae cursus completus*, series latina, 217 vols (Paris, 1844–55), clxxii.

Leland Miles, *John Colet and the Platonic Tradition* (Chicago, 1961; London, 1962).

Sebastian Münster, *Horologiographia, post priorem aeditionem . . . recognita* (etc.) (Basel, 1533).

J. D. North, 'Chaucer, Holbein, Libra and the Crucifixion', in Menso Folkerts and Richard Lorch (eds), *Sic Itur ad Astra: Studien zur Geschichte der Mathematik und Naturwissenschaften* (Wiesbaden, 2000), pp. 461–73.

J. D. North, *Chaucer's Universe* (2nd edn, Oxford, 1990).

J. D. North, *Horoscopes and History*, Warburg Institute Surveys and Texts, 13 (London, 1986).

J. D. North, 'Nicolaus Kratzer, the King's Astronomer', in *Science and History: Studies in Honor of Edward Rosen* (Ossolineum, 1978), pp. 205–34; reprinted with short addenda in North, *Stars, Minds and Fate* (1989), pp. 373–400.

J. D. North, *Richard of Wallingford: An Edition of his Writings with Introductions, English Translation and Commentary*, 3 vols (Oxford, 1976).

J. D. North, *Stars, Minds and Fate* (London and Ronceverte, West Virginia, 1989).

J. W. Norton-Kyshe, *The Law and Customs Relating to Gloves* (London, 1901).

Günther Oestmann, 'Ein unbekanntes Bildnis der Reformators und Astronomen Nikolaus Prugner (1488–1557), *Bulletin de la Bibliothèque de Strasbourg*, 22 (1996), pp. 65–70.

Otto Pächt, 'Holbein and Kratzer as Collaborators', *Burlington Magazine*, 84 (1944), pp. 134–39.

Tineke Padmos and Geert Verpaemel (eds), *De Geleerde Wereld van Keizer Karel* (Louvain, 2000). (Catalogue of the Exhibition *Wereldwijs: Wetenschappers rond Keizer Karel*, Louvain, 23 September to 3 December 2000.) See also Verpaemel.

K. T Parker, *The Drawings of Hans Holbein in the Collection of His Majesty the King at Windsor Castle* (2nd edn, Oxford and London, 1945; reprinted with appendix by Susan Foister, London and New York, 1983).

Simo Parpola, 'The Assyrian Tree of Life: Tracing the Origins of Jewish Monotheism and Greek Philosophy,' *Journal of Near Eastern Studies*, 52 (1993), pp. 161–208.

J. O. Payne, *St Paul's Cathedral in the Time of Edward VI* (London, 1893).

Carlo Pedretti, *The Literary Works of Leonardo da Vinci*, 2 vols (Berkeley and Los Angeles, 1977).

Pico della Mirandola, *Conclusiones nongentae, in omni genere scientiarum: quas olim Io. Picus Mirandula Romæ disputandas proposuit* [etc.] (Nuremberg, 1532).

Plato, *see* Cornford.

Pliny the Elder, ed. H. Rackham, *Natural History*, book xxxv, in vol. ix (Cambridge, Massachusetts and London, 1952).

Plutarch, *Les vies de huict excellens et renommez personnaiges grecz et romains . . .*, trans. by Georges de Selve (Paris, 1543 and 1548).

A. E Pollard, *Dictionary of National Biography*, entry 'Tuke, Sir Bryan', compact edition (Oxford, 1975), pp. 1222–23.

François Rabelais, *The Histories of Gargantua and Pantagruel*, trans. J. M. Cohen (Harmondsworth, 1955).

M. Rasmussen, 'The Case of the Flutes in Holbein's *The Ambassadors*', *Early Music* (Feb. 1995), pp. 114–23.

A. W. Reed, Introduction to: Thomas More, *The English Works*, ed. W. E. Campbell, i (London, 1931).

Gregor Reisch, *Margarita philosophica* (Freiburg, 1503; Strasbourg, 1504, 1508, 1512, etc.)

George Ripley, *The Compound ofAlchymy* (etc.) (London, 1591).

F. E. Robbins in Nicomachus of Gerasa, *Introduction to Arithmetic*, trans. Martin Luther d'Ooge, University of Michigan Studies, Humanistic Series, 16 (New York and London, 1926).

P. L. Rose, 'Italian Renaissance Methods of Drawing the Ellipse and Related Curves', *Physis*, 12 (1970), pp. 371–404.

Léon Rosenthal, 'Piero della Francesca et notre temps', *L'amour de l'art* (December 1923).

David J. Ross, 'The Bird, the Cross and the Emperor', *Culture and Cosmos*, 4 (2000), pp. 3–28.

Victoria Rothschild, '*The Parliament of Fowls*: Chaucer's Mirror up to Nature', *Review of English Studies*, new series 35 (1984), pp. 164–84.

John Rowlands, *The Age of Dürer and Holbein: Catalogue of an Exhibition Held at the British Museum* (London, 1988).

John Rowlands; with the assistance of Giulia Bartrum, *The Age of Dürer and Holbein: German Drawings, 1400–1550* (Cambridge, 1988).

John Rowlands, *Holbein: The Paintings of Hans Holbein the Younger. Complete Edition* (Oxford, 1985).

Joycelyne G. Russell, *Peacemaking in the Renaissance* (London, 1986).

E. R. Samuel, 'Death in the Glass: A New View of Holbein's *Ambassadors*', *Burlington Magazine*, 115 (1963), pp. 436–41.

Fritz Saxl, 'Holbein and the Reformation', in *A Heritage of Images: A Selection of Lectures by Fritz Saxl*, ed. by Hugh Honour and John Fleming (London, 1957, and Harmondsworth, 1970), pp. 119–29.

Leo Scheffczyk, *Creation and Providence*, trans. Richard Strachan (London and New York, 1970).

Wilhelm Schickard, *Astroscopium: pro facillima stellarum cognitione noviter excogitatum a Wilhelmo Schickhardo, ad cuius succinctam hanc explicationem et insertas quaestiones astronomicas respondebit Joh. Casparus Wägelin* (Werlin, 1623).

H. and M. Schmidt, *Die vergessene Bildersprache christlicher Kunst* (München, 1995).

J. Schouten, *The Pentagram as a Medical Symbol* (Nieuwkoop, 1968).

Francesco Sepe, *Arciconfraternita della Morte ed Orazione di Roma: rapporto sulle aggregazioni nella penisola sorrentina* (Sorrento, 1992).

Rodney Shirley, *The Mapping of the World: Early Printed World Maps, 1472–1700* (London, 1984).

J. C. L. Sismondi, *Histoire des Français*, xi (Paris, 1836).

Marc H. Smith, 'Les diplomates italiens, observateurs et conseillers artistiques à la cour de François Ier', *Histoire de l'art*, 35–36 (1996), pp. 27–37.

W. Speiser, *Sankt Michael in der Kunst* (Basel, 1947).

William Harris Stahl and Richard Johnson with E. L. Burge, *Martianus Capella and the Seven Liberal Arts*, 2 vols (New York, 1971, 1977).

David Starkey (ed.), *The Inventory of King Henry VIII: Society of Antiquaries MS 129 and British Library MS Harley 1419*, transcribed by Philip Ward and indexed by Alasdair Hawkyard (London, 1998).

F. A. Stebbins, 'The Astronomical Instruments in Holbein's *Ambassadors*', *Journal of the Royal Astronomical Society of Canada*, 56 (1962), pp. 45–52.

W. Stechow, *Northern Renaissance Art, 1400–1600: Sources and Documents* (Englewood Cliffs, New Jersey, 1966).

Michael Stifel [anonymous], *Ein Rechen Büchlin vom End Christ* (Wittenberg, 1532).

Michael Stifel, *Vom End der Welt* (Wittenberg, 1532).

Roy Strong, *Holbein and Henry VIII* (London, 1967).

Roy Strong, *National Portrait Gallery: Tudor and Jacobean Portraits*, 2 vols (London, 1969).

Alexander Sturgis, *Telling Time*, book to accompany an exhibition at the National Gallery, London, 18 October 2000–14 January 2001 (London, 2000).

André Suarès, *Eine italienische Reise* (Leipzig, 1914).

Joachim Telle, *Sol und Luna: Literar- und alchemiegeschichtliche Studien zu einem altdeutschen Bildgedicht* (Hürtgenwald, 1980).

Moriz Thausing, *Dürer: Geschichte seines Lebens und seiner Kunst*, 2 vols (Leipzig, 1884).

R. C. Thompson, *Semitic Magic* (London, 1908).

Lynn Thorndike, *A History of Magic and Experimental Science*, vols v and vi (New York and London), 1941.

William Thynne, *The Workes of Geffray Chaucer Newly Printed with Dyvers Workes Whiche Were Neuer in Print Before [etc.]*, reprinted with introduction by D. S. Brewer (Menston, 1973).

J. B. Trapp (ed.), *The Complete Works of St Thomas More*, ix (New Haven and London, 1979).

William Tyndale, *The Obedience of a Christen Man* (Marlborow in the Lande of Hesse, 1528).

J. W. Tyrer, *Historical Survey of Holy Week, its Services and Ceremonial* (Oxford, 1932).

Steven Vanden Broecke, 'The Limits of Influence. Astrology at Louvain University, 1520–1580' (unpublished doctoral thesis, Louvain, 2000).

Giorgio Vasari, *Le vite de' più eccellenti architetti, pittori et scultori italiani* (Florence, 1550; 2nd edn, 1568); ed. L. Bellosi and A. Rossi (Turin, 1986).

Jan R. Veenstra, *Magic and Divination at the Courts of Burgundy and France* (Leiden, 1998).

Polydore Vergil, *English History Comprising the Reigns of Henry VI, Edward IV and Richard III* (London, 1844).

Geert Verpaemel and Tineke Padmos (eds), *Wereldwijs: Wetenschappers rond Keizer Karel* (Louvain, 2000). (See also Padmos. This is the more popular and more lavishly illustrated volume.)

Christoph Graf zu Waldburg Wolfegg, *Venus und Mars: die mittelalterliche Hausbuch aus der Sammlung der Fürsten zu Waldburg Wolfegg* (Munich and New York, 1997).

D. P. Walker, *Spiritual and Demonic Magic from Ficino to Campanella* (London, 1958).

Peter Whitfield, *The Image of the World: Twenty Centuries of World Maps* (London, 1994).

Derek Wilson, *Hans Holbein: Portrait of an Unknown Man* (London, 1996).

Edgar Wind, *Pagan Mysteries in the Renaissance* (London, 1958).

E. Winternitz, *Musical Instruments and their Symbolism in Western Art* (New Haven and London, 1979).

Alfred Woltman, *Holbein and His Time* (London, 1872).

Chauncey Wood, *Chaucer and the Country of the Stars: Poetic Uses of Astrological Imagery* (Princeton, 1970).

Francis Wormald, 'The Crucifix and the Balance', *Journal of the Warburg Institute*, I (1937–38), pp. 276–80.

Francis Wormald, 'The Throne of Solomon and St Edward's Chair', in Millard Meiss (ed.), *De Artibus Opuscula* XL : *Essays in Honor of Erwin Panofsky*, 2 vols (New York, 1961), i, pp. 532–39 (illustrations in ii, pp. 175–77).

R. N. Wornum, *Some Account of the Life and Works of Hans Holbein* (London, 1857).

Martin Wyld, 'The Restoration History of Holbein's *Ambassadors*', *National Gallery Technical Bulletin*, 19 (1998), pp. 4–25.

R. C. Zaehner, *Mysticism Sacred and Profane* (Oxford, 1957).

R. E. Zupko, *British Weights and Measures: A History from Antiquity to the Seventeenth Century* (Madison, Wisconsin, 1977).

INDEX

References in each entry are grouped (where necessary) into pages, notes, figures and plates. The notes are indexed chiefly for writers, many of whom are not mentioned in the main text, but also for a few themes not mentioned there.